THE A'S AND B'S

of Academic Scholarships

20TH EDITION

ANNA LEIDER

Cover Design by Bremmer & Goris Communications, Inc.
Book Design by Edington-Rand

Address correspondence to:
Octameron Associates
PO Box 2748
Alexandria, VA 22301

703/836-5480 (voice)
703. 836. 5650 (fax)
info@octameron.com (e-mail)
www.octameron.com

ISBN 1-57509-033-3
PRINTED IN THE UNITED STATES OF AMERICA

CONTENTS

PART ONE

FOR ALL YOU BRIGHT YOUNG PEOPLE

This book is a directory of collegiate scholarships—awards given by colleges and universities to enrolled (or soon-to-be-enrolled) students. It does not contain information on scholarships given out by private organizations, foundations, high schools, religious groups, unions or employers.

New Era

For many years, colleges could pick and choose from a horde of baby-boom applicants, so they developed elaborate screening mechanisms to filter out those "unworthy" of admission. Today, these screening mechanisms are still with us, but their main purpose is to identify and attract promising students, not to reject applicants.

While many people feel that college admission is becoming more competitive again, the truth is, for all but the country's most selective colleges, there is a scramble to fill classrooms. Good students, especially, are at a premium. Colleges want them and will work hard to get them. After all, bright students attract good faculty, which attracts grant and research money and helps build a college's reputation. Moreover, bright students are likely to succeed after graduation, brag about their alma mater, give it credit for their accomplishments, and make generous alumni contributions Get the picture?

To make themselves more attractive to prospective students, especially bright prospective students, colleges began offering more merit-based scholarships, abandoning their long-held practice of awarding aid based solely on financial need. According to a joint survey by the National Association of Student Financial Aid Administrators (NASFAA) and the College Board, the number of four-year schools offering merit-based aid has remained relatively constant during the 1990s (hovering just over 80%), however, the dollar amount of merit-based aid has skyrocketed. Private four-year colleges award 300% more merit-based aid now than they did in 1988. Public four-year colleges award over 150% more merit-based aid.

Can You Qualify for Academic Scholarships?

The answer is yes if you are any one of these people:

- You have worked very hard in school and it shows. Your GPA is a B or better, you stand in the upper third of your class, and your SAT/ACT scores are above the national average: SAT I—500 Math/500 Verbal (after recentering), ACT Composite-20.7. Or...
- You have a wide range of interests and have been active in school, community, and club activities, taking a leading role in organizing and advancing worthwhile programs. Or...
- You are talented—in music, art, drama, or dance, or writing. Or...
- You are doing well at a two-year community college and now want to transfer to a four-year baccalaureate program. Or...
- You seek financial aid that is not based on financial need.

A Few Words About College Entrance Exams

The SAT debate has raged for years. You read that it's not an intelligence measure. Nor is it a predictor of academic success. It can't measure determination or ambition. And it's biased against women and minorities.

The College Board maintains the SAT is not culturally biased, that every question is painstakingly analyzed and that questions posing difficulties for any one "subgroup" are discarded. The College Board asserts "score differences among groups are not the result of bias on the SAT but reflect the unequal educational opportunities that still exist in our country."

And, in fact, test scores do reflect family income. Prior to recentering, the average score for students from families with incomes under $10,000 was 769, while the average score for students from families with incomes over $70,000 was 1004. Worse yet, since SAT scores weigh into financial aid distribution, they perpetuate the problem of unequal educational opportunity, regardless of the care taken to ensure fairness.

The New SAT I

Despite their insistence that the SAT is a fair test, the College Board has modified the examination. First, they changed the test name from "Scholastic *Aptitude* Test" to "Scholastic *Assessment* Test" to demonstrate that the SAT should not be considered equivalent to an IQ test.

Second, they increased the length of reading passages, and included questions that focus on the comprehension of themes rather than facts.

Third, they replaced 20% of the multiple-choice questions in the math section with open-ended ("grid-in") questions, and began allowing students to use calculators. According to the College Board, the revamped math section emphasizes data interpretation and applied mathematics.

And finally, they decided to "recenter" test scores. When the College Board began administering the SAT in 1941, the average score on both the Math and Verbal sections of the test was set at 500—the midpoint on the possible scoring scale of 200 to 800. Over time, however, average scores slid downward to the point where test-takers only scored an average 424 on the Verbal section of the exam and 478 on the Math section of the exam.

To make scores easier to interpret, the College Board eliminated this difference between average Math and Verbal scores by "recentering" the scale—returning average scores to 500 on both sections of the test. The College Board's new scale is based on a reference group of over one million test takers from 1994 instead of the 10,000 test-takers in 1941. According to College Board officials, this larger, more academically and socially diverse group of 1990s test-takers provides a "more meaningful reference group for today's students." These explanations have not satisfied test critics, however, who charge that by "recentering," the College Board is setting a lower standard as the "norm" rather than attacking the general decline in educational quality that has taken place over the past fifty years.

The College Board provides schools with conversion tables to facilitate comparisons between current scores and the scores of previous-year test-takers. Even so, not all schools using SAT scores to award academic awards have adjusted their score requirements to reflect the new scale. Be sure to ask school officials about this issue if you're applying for any scholarships that list a minimum SAT score among their eligibility criteria.

Increasing Your Eligibility

Even with recentering, the number of students with high SAT scores has declined drastically. If you're one of those high scorers, colleges want you.

Let's suppose you see an award worth $8,000 per year or $32,000 over four years. But the award has an SAT requirement of 1200 and your latest score was only 1140. What should you do now? Turn away and look for other awards with SAT requirements of 1140 or less? Of course not. Take a good SAT preparation course. Evidence shows sound coaching can raise scores. And higher scores can put big money in your pocket. In our example, investing $500 in an SAT course which raises your score 60 or 70 points translates into $32,000 worth of scholarships.

But one word of caution. Beware of courses that promise fast results for little work on your part. SAT preparation is not easy. It requires a proven coaching method, an extended participation period, and effort and diligence on your part. The two best known test prep companies have offices nationwide—The Princeton Review (800/2-REVIEW) and Kaplan (800/KAPTEST). You should also ask your counselor if he or she recommends any local test prep services.

SAT prep software, costing from $30 to $60 is a less expensive route to better test scores. Princeton Review (800/258-2088), Kaplan INteractive (800/KAP-ITEM) and The Learning Company (800/852-2255) all publish CD-Roms that entertain while they drill, test and explain. Internet users can take a free course at WebWare for the SAT (www.testprep.com). If you go the high-tech route, remember, even the best computer-oriented test prep products cannot replace paper and pencil practice.

Gathering Your References

First, find a comprehensive college guide in the library, guidance office, or bookstore. Many of these guides now come packaged with software that allows you to quickly search for schools that meet your personal requirements. Make sure your references are up-to-date. A guide that's more than a year old can seriously mislead you about attendance costs, most of which will continue to increase by approximately 6% per year.

Next, get *Don't Miss Out* from Octameron Associates, P.O. Box 2748, Alexandria, VA 22301, www.octameron.com ($10.00 postpaid). The search for academic scholarships should be only one part of an overall financial aid strategy. Other elements include grants, loans, personal finance techniques, and interaction with financial aid administrators. This reference will help you estimate how much you will be expected to contribute to college costs, and show you how to integrate all of these strategies into one sound master plan.

Finally, get *The Student Bulletin* from the National Merit Scholarship Corporation. One American Plaza, Evanston, IL 60201 (Free). This booklet lists the nearly 200 colleges that participate in the National Merit Scholarship competition.

How Schools Use Academic Scholarships

Even though over 80% of the nation's four-year colleges offer merit-based aid, these academic scholarships are controversial. Don't look in this book for schools like Amherst, Bates and Harvard. They subscribe to a statement issued by the Eastern Group of Admission Directors which reads in part: "We oppose the concept of no-need (merit) scholarships. If we awarded financial aid on the basis of merit, everyone enrolled in our institutions would receive financial assistance. Students are admitted to our institution on merit. Financial aid is given only to those with demonstrated need." (Editor's Note: Even at these schools some students are perceived to be more meritorious than others, and are likely to receive better financial aid packages). Other critics of academic scholarships argue that they are bribes to attract bright students for marketing reasons or that they eat up funds that could be used for needy students. The scholarships' supporters counter that they're rewarding talent and achievement in the American tradition, and say their need-based programs don't suffer.

Academic scholarships fall into two categories:

- Recruiting devices to get students to apply. These awards usually have quantifiable criteria—GPA, class rank, SAT/ACT score—and the number of awards is usually unlimited. Every student who meets the criteria and enrolls receives the stated award.
- Enrollment incentives to get students to accept an admission offer. These schools realize gifted students routinely apply and gain acceptance to several colleges. To tip the student's choice, they sweeten their offer with an academic scholarship. These awards have variable dollar ranges and few quantifiable prerequisites. Take note of this built-in flexibility. It allows for bargaining. A $2,000 offer can easily be increased to $3,000 if the college really wants you and believes you will enroll only if you receive the higher award.

No-Need vs. Need-Based Awards

While this book emphasizes no-need awards, most colleges offer need-based assistance as well. To make sense of them both, you must first understand the difference between "need" and "needy." Need is a number—nothing more, nothing less. This is how to determine the need number:

Visualize two bars, Bar A and Bar B. Bar A will represent your family's contribution to college costs. Bar B will be the cost of college. Bar A—your contribution—remains fairly constant (unless there is a drastic change in your family's situation). It doesn't matter where you plan to buy your education. The amount you must contribute from your own purse will be about the same. Bar B—the cost of attendance—is a variable. It will vary from college to college. It can even vary within one school, depending on your student status, the courses you take, how far away you live, etc. If Bar A is smaller than Bar B, you have financial need.

Let's illustrate this concept of need for a family judged capable of contributing $5,000 per year to college costs—they consider three colleges, College X which costs $20,000; College Y which costs $15,000; and College Z which costs $5,000. At College X, that family's need is $15,000; at College Y it is $10,000; and at College Z the family has no need at all.

Review *Don't Miss Out* for a more detailed explanation of need, as well as information on calculating "family contribution" and "cost of college."

Financial Aid Packaging

Here's a quick explanation of how no-need awards affect family contribution and financial aid packages:

- If you have no-need, and you win a no-need award, the college reduces your bill by the amount of your award.
- If you have financial need, and you win a no-need award, federal regulations require the college to consider your award an additional family resource. Your out-of-pocket expenses remain unchanged.
- If you have financial need, and you win a no-need award that exceeds your financial need, your family contribution will decrease by the amount of the excess. Example: Your first choice school costs $15,000. Your family contribution is assessed at $10,000. Your need is thus $5,000. Your good grades nab you a $7,500 Academic Achievement Award. The $7,500 will wipe out your need, and the extra $2,500 may be applied to your EFC so your family now contributes only $7,500 out-of-pocket.

As we said before, merit scholarships are frequently used as enrollment incentives, which means their value is negotiable. If a school really wants you but knows you are on the fence, it may increase your award by a thousand dollars and use the scholarship to replace a loan or work-study component of the aid package. Other schools will permit students to use academic scholarships to pay for books and personal expenses. Unfortunately, some schools simply apply the scholarship towards a reduction in need-based grants, preferring to shift their limited scholarship funds to other students. Applying the merit award toward a reduction in self-help is obviously financially best for you—ask your schools' financial aid administrators how they package academic scholarships.

What about need-based awards? These go only to students with demonstrated financial need and reduce your need, not your family contribution. This type of award can never be larger than your need. That's why you should enter the competition for non-need dollars knowing in advance what your approximate need will be at each college that interests you. If Pseudonymous U. offers a $3,000 need-based award and you've calculated your need there to be $3,500, it makes sense to compete for that award. But if your Mom has just made a bundle in the stock market, so your need is reduced to just $400, you probably won't be eligible for the award (or benefit from it much anyway).

Note that some awards are hybrids—a fixed scholarship based on merit, with larger awards to students who demonstrate need. It pays to ask.

Your Award's True Value

If you receive an academic scholarship and have remaining need after receiving the award, you are likely to:

1. Get a better financial aid package than less gifted students (e.g., a package with more grants than loans). Seventy-three percent of private four-year colleges and 28% of public four-year colleges say they package need-based aid based on academic desirability.
2. Receive first priority on aid, especially when resources are scarce. Colleges are more likely to meet the full need of their brighter applicants.

Consumer Tips on Academic Scholarships

As usual, informed consumers get the better deal. For example, always check to see if awards are renewable. Some colleges will offer you a generous award for your first year, only to strand you later.

Also, before you accept a full-ride merit scholarship to Podunk U., ask the school if it has special programs for bright students. A student with a 4.0 GPA who accepts a full scholarship to a school where the average GPA is 2.0 will probably get bored in class and develop expert doodling skills rather than his or her mind. To challenge brighter students, some colleges have created special honors programs. Each is different, but look for access to senior faculty, special seminars and colloquia, and the opportunity for independent research. Some universities have gone one step further and turned their honors programs into honors colleges. These feature special classes, faculty, and dormitories for participants.

PART TWO

1200 COLLEGES AND 100,000 AWARDS

Table of Collegiate Academic Awards

Our master table is organized by state, with schools listed alphabetically within each state. The word college is often omitted. If a school is listed as "Kenyon," refer to it as Kenyon College. Universities are listed as such, e.g., Florida State University, or Florida State U. Following the school is the city and zip code. If the school and its location have the same name, only the school name and zip code are used, e.g., Boston University, 02215.

To describe the awards as fully as possible, yet keep down our costs and yours, we've conserved space by using codes and abbreviations. Here's a column-by-column explanation of our codes:

NAME OF PROGRAM. In most cases, we omit "Scholarship," "Award," and "Grant" from the program name. If you inquire about a program identified as "Presidential," refer to the "Presidential Scholarship."

NUMBER OF AWARDS. Self-explanatory.

VALUE RANGE. "Total" or "All Costs" generally means the cost of tuition, fees, room and board, but NOT books, transportation, or miscellaneous expenses. "Tuition" means the award covers tuition only; for a state college or university, it is the charge for in-state students. If the value is expressed as a range, look at the Need-Based column to better estimate the size your award might be. If the award is need-based, its value most likely corresponds to the size of your need. If, however, the award is not need-based, its value most likely corresponds to your academic qualifications. The higher your class standing, GPA and test scores, the larger your award.

CLASS STANDING. This is usually expressed as a percentage or a fraction, such as 10%, meaning the top 10% of the class. It might also be expressed as a numeric standing, such as 1-2 for valedictorian/salutatorian (Val/Sal) scholarships. An "X" means class standing is considered when evaluating students for awards.

GRADE AVERAGE. This may be listed as a grade point average (3.0, 3.5), a percentage average (85, 90), or an letter grade average (B+, A-). Grade averages are usually calculated from "hard" courses such as Math and English. Grades in basket weaving and synchronized swimming are not usually included. An "X" means grades are considered when evaluating students for awards.

SAT/ACT. Three- and four-digit figures refer to combined SAT math/verbal scores while two-digit figures refer to the ACT composite score. A percentage such as 90%ile means students must score higher than 90% of all students taking the test. An "X" means SAT/ACT scores are considered when evaluating students for awards.

NEED-BASED. An "N" means the award is not based on financial need. A "Y" means the award is given only to students with financial need. An "X" means need may be considered.

OTHER CRITERIA. Most colleges use several criteria to evaluate students. The following codes are used in this column:

E — Essay or competitive exam

I — Interview

L — Leadership

R — Recommendation or nomination

T — Talent (portfolio or audition)

O — Other criteria, check with school

STUDY FIELDS. Some awards are given only to students who major in a particular discipline, while others are given to students of all majors the school offers. The following codes are used in this column:

A — All majors

O — Other fields, check with school

RENEWABILITY. Most awards are renewable for up to 4 years of college, as long as you maintain your student status and a certain GPA. If the required GPA is known, it is listed in this column, e.g., "3.2." A "Y" means the award is renewable but the school didn't list a minimum GPA. An "N" means the award is not renewable. An "X" means some awards are renewable and others are not.

RESTRICTIONS. Some awards have restrictions. The following codes are used in this column:

N — No restrictions

S — State or local residents only

D — Denominational members only

M — Minorities only

W — Women only

O — Other restrictions, check with school

APPLY DATE. The following codes are used in this column:

A — All applicants considered

B — Separate application required

C — Verify application date/procedure with school

D — No application date, but the earlier the better

TRANSFER. A "Y" means transfer students are eligible for the award. If the "Y" is followed by a number, that number represents the minimum GPA necessary for transfers to earn the award. An "N" means they are not eligible. Some schools may have transfer-only scholarships not listed here. Write and ask.

Before you study the following scholarship listings, use the worksheets in *Don't Miss Out* to approximate your family contribution to college costs. Also get a copy of a current college handbook so you can estimate college costs (remember to add 5-6% to the costs if the published data is for 1998-99 and you won't start college until 1999-2000). Ultimately, a scholarship and its dollar value are meaningless unless you can relate them to your family contribution and the college's costs.

Other Listings

We also asked schools about several other tuition-reducing opportunities, most of which are not related to financial need. You'll see these listed under the "program" column:

HONORS PROGRAMS AND/OR HONORS COLLEGE means the school has designed a special program for top students.

ADVANCED PLACEMENT (AP) EXAMS means the school awards credit for good scores on AP exams. Policies vary, however, in general, schools require at least a "3." Also, some schools set a maximum on the total number of credits you can earn via AP exams.

FAMILY DISCOUNTS means the school offers discounts when two or more family members enroll at the same time.

ALUMNI DISCOUNTS means the school offers discounts to sons and daughter of alumni.

CO-OP EDUCATION means the school arranges cooperative education opportunities with local businesses.

PAID INTERNSHIPS means the school helps students find internships.

	Program	No. of Awards	Value Range	Award Criteria					Study Fields	Renew-ability	Restric-tions	Apply Date	Transfer
				Class Stndg.	Grade Avg.	SAT/ ACT	Need Based	Other					
ALABAMA													
Alabama A&M U., Normal 35762	Academic	Varies	700-6800		3.0	800/20	N	E-L-R	A	3.0	N	B-5/1	Y-3.4
	Music	Varies	200-3000		2.0		Y	T-R	A	2.0	O	C	Y-2.0
	Alumni	Varies	500-1000		3.0		Y	L-R	A	3.0	O	C	N
	Presidential Leadership	10	6800		3.0		N	T-R	A	3.0	N	B-5/1	Y-3.4
	Honors Program												
Alabama State U., Montgomery 36195	Academic	80	2178-6491		3.0	980/24	N		A	3.0	N	B-2/15	Y
	Athletic	164	200-6271		2.5	16	N	T-I	A	2.5	N	C-2/15	Y-2.5
	Band	75	400-1500		2.5	16	N	T-I	N	2.5	N	C-2/15	Y-2.5
	Deans	30	1728-3456		3.0	870/21	N		A	3.0	N	B-2/15	Y
	Honors	30	1723-3456		3.0	750/18	N		A	3.0	N	B-2/15	Y
	Incentive	Varies	1608-3108		3.0		N		A		N		
	Leadership	20	1000		3.0	680/16	N		A	3.0	N	B-2/15	Y
	Music/Choir	50	750-1500		2.0	16	N	T-I	A	2.5	N	C-2/15	Y-2.5
	Presidential	90	2178-6491		3.0	1090/27	N		A	3.0	N	B-2/15	Y
	President's	45	2900-4900		3.5	840/20	N		A	3.0	N	B-9/1	Y
	University Scholar	152	300-2000		3.0	745/16	N	T-L-R	A	3.0	N	B-9/1	Y
	Honors Program												
Auburn U., Montgomery 36193	Alumni Academic	40	800		3.5	1250/29	N		A	N	N	A-2/1	N
	Blount Presidential	1	5000		3.5	1360/31	N	E-L-R-I	O	3.5	S	A-2/1	N
	Chancellor's	125	1200	X	X	25	N		A	3.5	S	B-3/1	Y
	Dudley Academic	50	1250		3.5	1250/29	N		A	N	N	B-2/1	N
	Dudley Achievement	10	500		3.5	1250/29	N		A	3.5	N	B-2/1	N
	Dudley Opportunity	15	1250		3.5	1250/29	N		A	3.5	N	B-2/1	N
	McWane Foundation	1	6000		3.5	1410/32	N	E-L	A	3.5	N	B-2/1	N
	Presidential Opport.	Varies	1250		3.5	1250/29	N	E-L	A	3.5	N	A-2/1	N
	President's Scholar	25	1250		3.5	1250/29	N		A	3.5	N	B-2/1	N
	Vice Chancellor's	125	1200	X	X	25	N		A	3.5	S	B-3/1	Y
	Vulcan/Presidential	1	6600		3.5	1410/32	N	E-L-I	A	Y	N	A-2/1	N
Birmingham-Southern College, 35254	Church	Varies	500-1500		X	X	Y	R	A	2.0	D	B-D	Y
	Church/College Partnership	Varies	1000-3000	X	X	X	Y	L-R-O	A	2.0	D	B-3/1	Y
	Fine Arts	Varies	1000-5000		X	X	N	T-L-R-I	O	2.0	N	B-C	N
	Gorgas	1	Tuition	X	X	X	N	E-L-R-I-O	O	3.0	N	C	N

	Health Careers	10	To Tuition	10%	X	X	N	E-L-0	0	3.0	N	B-1/2	N
	Hess Computer Science	2	5000	X	X	X	N	E-L-R-I	0	3.0	N	B-1/2	N
	Honors Finalists	60	6000	10%	X	X	N	0	A	3.0	N	B-1/6	N
	Junior College	6	6000	X	X	X	N	L-R	A	2.0	N	B-1/2	Y
	McWane Finalists	4	To 7700	10%	X	X	N	0	A	3.0	N	B-1/6	N
	McWane Honors	1	To Tuition	10%	X	X	N	0	A	3.0	N	B-1/6	N
	Model Senate	2	1000-3000	X	X	X	N	E-L-R-I-0	0	3.0	N	C	N
	Phi Beta Kappa	4	Tuition	10%	X	X	N	E-L-R-I	A	3.0	N	B-1/2	N
	Presidential	75	1000-2500	X	X	X	N	E-L-R	A	2.0	N	C	N
	Trustee	Varies	1000-2500	10%	3.0			L-R-I					
	AP Exams												
	Alumni Discounts												
	Internships												
	Honors Program												
Huntingdon, Montgomery 36106	Academic Competitive	Unlimited	500-Tuition		2.25	920/20	Y	E-I	A	2.0	N	B-C	N
	Performing Arts	Varies	500-1/2 Tuition		2.25	920/20	Y	T-I	0	2.0	N	B-C	Y
	Honors Program												
International Bible, Florence 35630	Academic	Varies	1/2 Tuition	1-2				L	A	N	N	A-7/1	N
	New Student	Varies	1200	X	2.0		N		A	Y	D	B-7/15	Y
	Honors Program												
Jacksonville State U., 36265	David Boozer Scholarship		Full Tuition						A	Y	N	C-3/15	
	Elliott Memorial		Full Tuition						A			B-3/15	
	Faculty Scholars	100	1650			1320/28	N		A	3.3	S-0	B-3/15	N
	Leadership	200	1650				N	L-R	A	N	N	B-3/15	Y
	Martha Fitzpatrick Memorial		3000						A	Y	N		
	AP Exams												
	Distance Learning												
	Co-op, Internships												
	Honors Program												
Judson, Marion 36756	Academic	Varies	1500-4400	10%	3.0	25	N	E-R-I	A	3.0	W	B-4/1	Y
	Garner Webb Honor	5	Tuition	X		1280/30	N	-0	A	3.2	W	A-B-4/1	N
	Lockhart	6	2000-Tuition	X	X	X	N	0	A	Y	W	B-C	N
	Music	3	1500				N	0	0	Y	W	B-C	N
	Honors Program												
Mobile College, 36613	Presidential	Varies	1000		X	26	N	L-R-I	A	3.5	N	B-5/1	N
Oakwood, Huntsville 35896	Academic	Varies	500-1820		3.0	890/20	N	L-0	A	3.5	N	A	Y-3.0
	Val/Sal	Varies	1200	1-2			N		A	Y	N	C	N
	Honors Program, Honors College												

	Program	No. of Awards	Value Range	Award Criteria: Class Stndg.	Grade Avg.	SAT/ ACT	Need Based	Other	Study Fields	Renew-ability	Restric-tions	Apply Date	Transfer
ALABAMA *(Continued)*													
Samford U., Birmingham 35229	Academic	50	500-3000	10%	3.25	1200/27	Y	E-L-R	A	3.0	O	A	Y-3.0
	Honors	25	Varies	20%	3.0		N	E-R	A	3.0	N	B-C	N
	Leadership	30	1000	50%	3.0	1000/22	N	E-L-R	A	2.5	O	A	N
	National Merit	15	5000	5%			N		A		N	C	
	Presidential	15-20	Tuition	5%	4.0	1250/30	N	E-L-R-I	A	3.0	O	B-C	N
	Honors Program												
Selma U., 36701	Fine Arts	Varies						O					
	Davis Memorial	Varies						O	Q		O		
Southeastern Bible C., Birmingham 35243	Honors	8	3000	10%	3.5	1170	N		A	Y	N	B-5/1	Y
	Music	2	1000				N	T-R-I	A	N	N	B-5/1	Y
	Honors Program												
Spring Hill, Mobile 36608	Faculty Merit/Pres. Honors	20	To Tuition/Rm.	X	X	X	N	E-L-R-I	A	3.0	N	A-D	N
	Leadership	Varies	500-1500		2.5	850	N	E-L-R-I	A	2.75	N	A-D	N
	Academic	Varies	3000-7500		2.75	850	N	E-R-I	A	3.0	N	A-D	Y-3.25
	Honors Program												
Stillman College, Tuscaloosa 35403	Academic	Varies	200-5200	X	3.0		Y		A	X	N	A	Y-3.0
	Bellingrath	8	All Costs	5%	3.5	1000/22	N		A	Y	N	B-3/18	Y
	Eckerd Award	20	Tuition	X	3.0	800/18	N		A	Y	N	A	Y-3.0
	Music	Varies	200-8160					T				A-6/15	
	Honors Program												
Talladega College, 35160	Academic	100	1000-5000	25%	3.0	742/16	N		A	3.0	N	A-D	Y
Troy State U., 36082	Chancellor's		1800-3210		3.5	1100/26	N	R	A	Y	S	A-D	N
	Scholar's		Total Costs		3.7	1260/30	N		A	Y	S	A-D	N
	Leadership		1/2-Full Tuition		3.0	800/21	N		A	Y	S	A-D	N
	Honors Program												
Tuskegee University 36088	Academic	Varies	500-1000	X	3.25	1000/20	Y		A	3.5	N	B-3/31	Y-3.25
	Academic	Varies	500-4850	X	2.5		N	T-R	A	3.25	N	X	Y-3.25
	Music	Varies	250-750		2.0		N		A	2.0	N	A	Y-2.0
	Presidential	10	500-3500	5%	3.7	1000/26	N	L-R	A	2.75	N	B-3/31	Y-3.7

U. of Alabama, Birmingham 35294	Academic Excellence	3	4000	5%	3.7	1300/30	N	E-L-R-I	A	3.0	N	B-2/1	N
	Angelo Bruno	5	2500	10%	3.5	29	N	L-R-I	A	3.0	N	B-2/1	N
	Deans	14	1000	20%	3.5	1250/27	N	L-R	A	3.0	0	B-2/1	Y-3.5
	Dottie Monro	1	2500	10%	3.5	24	N	-R-I	A	3.0	N	B-2/1	N
	Dupuis	6	2350	10%	3.5	1250/27	N	0	0	3.0	N	B-2/1	N
	Hanson	1	2500	1%	4.0	1358/31	N	L-R-I-I	A	3.0	S	B-2/1	N
	Hill	8	2000	20%	3.5	1250/27	N	L-R	A	3.0	N	B-2/1	N
	Ireland	1	6000	1%	4.0	1358/31	N	L-R-I-I	A	3.0	N	B-2/1	N
	Minority Presidential	10	3500	15%	3.5	24	N	L-R-I	A	3.0	N	B-2/1	Y
	UAB National Alumni Society	5	1000	20%	3.5	27	N	L-R-I	A	3.0	N	B-2/1	N
	University Scholars	50	Tuition & Fees	10%	3.5	1250/29	N	E-L-R-I	A	3.0	N	B-2/1	N
	Honors Program												
U. of Alabama, Huntsville 35899	Freshman Merit		300-600			970/21	N		A	Y	N	A-D	N
	Academic Excellence	1000-1500	1000-1500			1240/28	N		A	Y	N	A-D	N
	Presidential		1650-2900			1400/32	N		A	Y	N	A-D	N
	Honors Program												
U. of Alabama, Tuscaloosa 35487	Alumni Honors	20	4068	10%	3.5	1240/30	N	L	A	3.0	0	B-10/15	N
	Alumni Leadership	50	2068	20%	3.0	920/22	N	L-R	A	N	N	B-12/1	N
	Blount	1	6000	1%	4.0	1350/32	N	E-L-R-I	A	3.5	S	B-10/15	N
	Computer Based Honor	6	2500	10%	3.5	1300/31	N	I-0	A	3.0	0	B-12/20	N
	Honors Awards	Varies	1500-7000	10%	3.5	1240/30	N	R-I	A	3.0	N	C-2/1	Y-3.5
	National Merit Presidential	Unlimited	Tuition										
	Presidential	100	2068-5166	10%	3.5	1240/30	N	L	A	3.0	0	B-12/1	N
	Vulcan	1	Tuition+7000	1%	4.0	1350/32	N	E-L-R-I	A	3.5	0	B-10/15	N
	Honors Program												
U. of Montevallo, 35115	Alumni Honors	2	2600		3.0	29	N		A	3.25	N	C-12/1	
	Freshman Honors	10	2400		3.0	28	N		A	3.25	N	C-12/1	
	Freshman Leadership	15	2200		3.0	22	N		A	3.25	N	C-2/1	
	Jr. Coll. Dean's Scholarship	20	2000		3.0					3.25	0		Y
	Jr. Coll. Pres. Scholarship	24	2000		3.25					3.25	0		Y
	M.L. King, Jr. Scholarship	12	Tuition & Fees		3.0	22			A	3.0	M-0	C-4/1	
	Presidential Merit	Varies	All Costs				N		A	3.5	N	B-4/1	N
	Honors Program												
U. of N. Alabama, Florence 35632	Academic	250	500-1800		3.0	26	N		A	Y-3.0	N	B-2/15	Y-3.75
	Leadership	90	500-1800		2.75	21	N	E-T-L	A	Y-2.75	N	B-2/15	N
	Endowed	60	200-1800		X		X	0		X	0	B-2/15	N
U. of S. Alabama, Mobile 36688	Presidential	110	1500-5000		3.5	27	N		A	3.0	N	A-4/1	Y

	Program	No. of Awards	Value Range	Award Criteria: Class Stndg.	Grade Avg.	SAT/ ACT	Need Based	Other	Study Fields	Renew-ability	Restric-tions	Apply Date	Transfer
ALABAMA *(Continued)*													
University of West Alabama., 35470	Academic	100	750-2190	1-2	3.0	1010/22	N		A	3.0	N	B-3/15	Y-3.0
	Leadership	100	600-2190		2.0	850/18	N	L	A	3.0	N	B-3/15	Y-2.0
	AP Exams												
	Co-op, Internships												
	Honors Program												
ALASKA													
Alaska Pacific U., Anchorage 99508	Distinguished Scholar	15	Tuition		3.5	1200/27	N		A	3.6	N	B-3/15	N
	University Award	20	1/3 Tuition		3.0	1000/22	N		A	N	N	B-3/15	N
	Trustee Scholarship	35	1/3 Tuition		3.25		N		A	3.25	N	B-3/15	Y-3.25
	Department Awards	6	1000				N	T-L-R	A	N	N	B-C	Y
Sheldon Jackson, Sitka 99835	Honor	30	2000		2.25		N			2.25			
	Alaska Scholarship	Unlimited	3425-6850	10%	2.75		N			2.25			
	Referral	20	2000		2.25		N	R		2.25			
	AP Exams												
	Alumni Discounts, Family Discounts												
U. of Alaska, Anchorage 99508	Academic Tuition Waivers	293	100-3105	X	2.5		N	E-T-L-R	A	2.5	N	B-C	Y
	AHAINA Tuition Waivers	14	414-3105	X	2.5		N	E-T-L-R	A	2.5	N	B-3/31	Y-2.5
	Honors Program												
U. of Alaska, Fairbanks 99775-0700	Talent	4	2100-6250				N	E-T-R		N	N	B-3/15	N
	Chancellor's	12	2100-6250		3.6	1270/28	N	E-R	A	N	N	B-3/15	N
	National Merit	Varies	4266-8750				N		A	3.0	N	C	N
	Honors Program												
U. of Alaska, Juneau 99801	University	50	250-5400		2.0		Y	E-R-R	A	Y	O	C	Y
	Academic	65	250-3000		3.0		N	E-L-R	A	Y	O	C	Y-3.0
	Talent	30	250-1000		2.0		Y	E-T-L-R	A	Y	O	C	Y-2.0
ARIZONA													
Arizona College of the Bible, Phoenix 85021	President's Academic	5	2500		3.9	23	Y	E-I	A	Y-3.9	N	B-3/31	Y-3.9
	Performing Arts	7	200-1500		2.5		Y	T-R-I	A	Y-2.5	N	B-3/15	Y-2.5

	Leadership	Varies	200-500		2.5		Y	E-T-L-R-I	A	Y-2.5	N	B-3/15	Y-2.5
	Dean's Academic	8	1500		3.7	21	Y	E-I	A	Y-3.7	N	B-3/31	Y-3.7
Arizona State U., Tempe 85287	ASU Regents	2100	1362-6846	5%			N		A	3.25	S	C	N
	Leadership	15	Tuition+	X	X		N	E-R-I	A	Y	S	B-C	N
	Medallion Merit	120	1200-1400	10%	X		N	L-R	A	N	N	B-C	N
Grand Canyon, Phoenix 85017	GCU Honors	Varies	1286-1715		3.5		N		A	3.25	N	A-D	Y-3.5
	Scholars 100	10	6432-8576	1 or 2	4.0		N	T-L-R	A	3.8	O	A-3/15	N
	Top 10%	Varies	1734	10%			N		A	3.25	N	A	N
	Top 5%	Varies	3468	5%			N		A	3.5	N	A	N
	Transfer Student	Varies	1286-1715		3.5		N		A	3.25	N	A-D	Y-3.5
	AP Exams												
	Distance Learning												
	Honors Program												
Prescott College, 86301	Prescott College Schp.	Varies	500-3600				Y	E-L-R	A	N	N	B-4/15	Y
	President's	Varies	1000				Y	E-L-R	A	N	O	B-4/15	Y
Southwestern, Phoenix 85032	Presidential	Varies	3/4 Tuition		3.75	25	N		A	N	N	B	
	Dean's	Varies	1/2 Tuition		3.5	23	Y		A	N	N	B	
	Music Scholarship	Limited	1000				N	E-T-L	A	N	N	B-C	Y
	Honors Program												
U. of Arizona, Tucson 85721	President's	Varies	Varies	X			N	L-R	A	3.5	S	B-C	N
	Regents'	1890	All Fees	5%			N	R	A	3.5	S	B-C	N
	Schaefer	25	1000	X	X		N	E-L-R	A	3.5	S	B-C	N
ARKANSAS													
Arkansas State U., Jonesboro 72467	Academic	Varies	900	10%	3.0	24	N		A	3.0	S-O	B-4/1	N
	Academic Distinction	Unlimited	1536-2160	10%	3.0	1010/24	N		A	3.0	S-O	C-4/1	Y-3.0
	President's	Unlimited	1536-2160			1090/26	N	O	A	3.0	S	C-4/1	Y-3.0
	Trustees'	Unlimited	3936-5640			1260/30	N	O	A	3.5	S	C-4/1	N
	Honors Program												
Arkansas Tech U., Russellville 72801	Honor	150	1200-1600		3.0	24	N		A	3.0	S	B-3/15	N
	Music	25	600-1200				N	T-I	A	2.25	S	B-4/15	N
	National Honor	10	2400		3.0		N		A	3.0		B-3/15	
	President's	20	600-1200		3.0	21	N	L-R-I	A	N	S	B-3/15	N
	Valedictorian	10	1200	1%			N		A	3.25	S	B-6/1	N
Central Baptist College, Conway 72032	Dean's	Unlimited	2/3 Tuition	X	3.25	24	N	R	A	3.0	N	Y-8/15	N
	Leadership	Unlimited	1/2 Tuition		3.0	20	N	L	A	3.0	N	B-2/1	N
	Presidential	Unlimited	3/4 Tuition		3.5	27	N		A	3.25	N	B-8/15	N
	Trustees'	10	All Costs		3.8	30	N		A	3.5	N	B-8/15	N

	Program	No. of Awards	Value Range	Award Criteria					Study Fields	Renew-ability	Restric-tions	Apply Date	Transfer
				Class Stndg.	Grade Avg.	SAT/ ACT	Need Based	Other					
ARKANSAS *(Continued)*													
Central Baptist College, Conway 72032 *(Continued)*	AP Exams												
	Distance Learning												
Harding U., Searcy 72149	Academic	Varies	1000-5000		3.0	46	N		A	3.0	N	A-D	Y-3.25
	Trustee	20	Tuition		3.5	43	N		A	3.25	D	A-3/1	N
	National Merit	Varies	Tuition & Fees				N		A				
Henderson State U., Arkadelphia 71923	Presidential Academic	150	Tuition	10%		24	N		A	3.0	S	B-3/15	N
	Board of Trustees	10	1420-3460	10%		31	Y		A	3.5	N	B-3/15	N
Hendrix, Conway 72032	Academic Merit	Varies	1500-15,000		3.5	1140/25	N	L	A	2.0			
	Leadership	Varies	500-2800				N	L	A	2.0			
	Performance	Varies	500-1000				N	T		2.0			
	AP Exams												
	Internships												
John Brown U., Siloam Springs 72761	Academic	Varies	800-2000		3.40	80%ile	Y	R	A	3.2	N	A-5/1	Y-3.4
	Athletic	65	1000-15000		2.5	40%ile	Y	T-L-R-I	A	2.5	N	B-C	Y-2.5
	Divisional	20	3000	10%	3.5	90%ile	N	E-L-R		3.4	N	B-1/1	Y-3.4
	Engineering	20	3000	25%	3.5	90%ile	N	E-L-R-O		3.4	N	B-D	N
	Leadership	Varies	1000	10%	3.8	90%ile	N	E-L-R	A	3.4	N	B-1/1	Y-3.4
	Music	10	1000-2500				N	T-I-I	A	3.4	N	B-4/15	Y
	National Merit	Unlimited	1000	10%	3.5	95%ile	N		A	3.4	N	A-D	N
	Presidential	10	9000	5%	3.9	95%ile	Y	O	A	3.4	N	B-12/1	N
	AP Exams												
	Honors Program												
Lyons College, Batesville 75201	Brown	5	4810		3.75	1250/27	N	E-L-R-I	A	3.25	N	B-3/1	N
	$1800 Endowed	Varies	1800		3.5	1030/22	N		A	2.8	N	B-6/1	Y-3.1
	$1300 Endowed	Varies	1300		3.0	970/20	N		A	2.6	N	B-6/1	Y-3.0
	$900 Endowed	Varies	900		2.5	970/20	N		A	2.4	N	B-6/1	N
	Honors Program												
Ouachita Bapt. U., Arkadelphia 71998	Presidential	7	6000		X	X	N	L	A	3.0	N	A-2/15	N
	Scholastic Excellence	Unlimited	1000-4500			990/24	N		A	2.5	N	A-C	N
	Trustee's	Unlimited	Total Costs				N	-O	A	3.0	O	A-6/1	Y-3.0
	Honors Program												

Southern Arkansas U., Magnolia 71753	Presidential	Unlimited	4252			30	N		A	3.0	N	B-3/15	N
	Alumni	Unlimited	1752			24	N		A	3.0	N	B-3/15	N
	Departmental	20	1752		3.0		N	R	A	3.0	N	B-4/15	N
	African-American Ldrshp.	Unlimited	1752		3.0	20	N	L-R	A	2.5	M	B-3/15	N
U. of Arkansas, Fayetteville 72701	Sturgis	Varies	11,500		3.8	1350/30	N	E-I-L-R	A	Y		B-2/1	
	Bodenhamer	4	11,000		X	1420/32	N	E-I-L-R		Y		B-2/15	
	Chancellor's	Varies	4,000-8,000		3.5	1400/32	N	E-L		3.2		B-2/15	
U. of Arkansas, Pine Bluff 71601	Academic	96	100-700	10%	3.0		N	L	A	3.0	S	A-D	Y
	Band/Choir	120	100-3600		2.0		N	E-T	A	2.0	N	A-D	Y
	Honors College												
U. of Central Arkansas, Conway 72032	Academic	350	Tuition-1500		X	23	N	R	A	3.25	S	B-C	N
	Music, Art, Speech	150	To Tuition				N	T-R-I	0	2.0	N	B-C	Y
U. of the Ozarks, Clarksville 72830	Recognition	Varies	400-2000		3.5	23	N		A	3.0	0	A-C-D	N
CALIFORNIA													
Art Center Coll. of Design, Pasadena 91103	Scholarships	Varies	To Tuition		3.0		Y	T	A	3.0	0	C	Y-3.0
	Entering Grants	30	2500		3.0		Y	T	A	3.0	0	C	Y
	Irvine Minority Grants	10	Tuition		3.0		Y	T	A	3.0	0	C	Y
Azusa Pacific U., Azusa 91702	Dean's	Varies	3000-3500		3.3	1100/24	N		A	3.6	N	A-D	Y
	Presidential	Unlimited	3500-4000		3.7	1200/27	N		A	Y	N	A-D	N
	AP Exams												
	Distance Learning												
	Alumni Discounts												
	Co-op, Internships												
	Honors Program												
Bethany Bible, Santa Cruz 95060	Academic	192	1000-6550		3.2		Y		A	3.2	N	B-8/1	Y-3.2
	Leadership	37	250-1200		2.0		Y	E-L-R	A	2.0	N	B-8/1	Y-2.0
	Athletic	8	100-3250		2.0		Y	E-T-I	A	2.0	N	B-8/1	Y-2.0
Biola U. La Mirada 90639	Academic	78	3000-5000	15%	4.0		N	R-I-I	A	3.3/3.4	D	A	Y-3.4
	Academic	34	5000-6000	5%	4.0		N	R-I-I	A	3.5	D	A	Y-3.5
	Community Service	70	2200		2.75		N	E-L-R-I	A	2.75	D	B-3/15	Y-2.7
	Ethnic	20	2500		3.0		N	E-L	A	3.0	M	B-3/15	Y
	AP Exams												
Brooks Institute of Photography, 93108	Academic	Varies	500-1000		3.2	1100/25	Y		A	Y	0	B-C	
	Academic	Varies	500-1000		3.2	1100/25	N	T	A	Y	0	B-C	Y

School	Program	No. of Awards	Value Range	Award Criteria: Class Stndg.	Grade Avg.	SAT/ ACT	Need Based	Other	Study Fields	Renew-ability	Restric-tions	Apply Date	Transfer
CALIFORNIA *(Continued)*													
California Baptist, Riverside 92504	Academic	Unlimited	1600		3.5	900/21	N		A	3.3	N	B-D	Y-3.3
	Presidential Merit	18	3500-7000		3.7	1100/24	Y	E-T-L-I	A	3.3	N	C	Y-3.5
	Music	Varies	To 1/2 Tuition				Y	T-R-I	O	Y	N	B-D	Y
	Athletic	Varies	500-7000				N		A	Y	O	D	N
	Drama	Varies	500-2000				N		A	Y	O	D	N
	Religion	Varies	500-5000				N		O		O	D	N
CA Christian Coll., Fresno 93703	Academic	Varies	1000-3000	10%	3.0	1100/25	N	R-I	A	3.0	N	B-3/1	N
CA C. of Arts & Crafts, Oakland 94618	Presidents	2	6000		3.0		N	O	A	3.0	N	B-3/1	N
	AICA	Varies	500-7000		3.0		N	E-T-L-R-I	A	N	O	B-2/1	N
	CORE	1	7475		3.0		N	O	A	3.0	N	B-3/1	N
	Creative Achievement	40	500-1500		3.0		N	O	A		N	B-3/1	N
	DORM	1	2500		3.0		N	O	A		N	B-3/1	N
	Faculty Honors	40	1000-5000		3.25		N	O	A		N	3/15	N
	Alumni Honors	25	2000-5000		3.25		N	O	A		N		N
	CCAC Scholarship	varies	1000-9000		2.5		Y	O	A	Y	N		N
	Honors Program												
CA Inst of Tech, Pasadena 91125	Caltech Merit Award	40	5000-Tuition				N	O	A		O	C	N
CA Lutheran U., Thousand Oaks 91360	Merit	Varies	1500-6000		3.25	1000/24	N	E	A	3.0	N	B-1/1	Y-3.25
	Performance Awards	Varies			3.0	1000		T-O			N	C	Y-2.5
CA Poly. St. U., San Luis Obispo 93407	Miscellaneous	Varies	500-12000		3.0		Y		A	X	O	B-3/2	
CA State Polytech., Pomona 91768	Miscellaneous	Varies	300-1500		2.0		Y		A	N	S	B-3/2	Y-2.0
	Kellogg Scholars	35	1500	10%	3.75	1200/21	Y	E-T-L-R					
	Honors Program												
CA State U., Bakersfield 93311	Personalized Honors	45	420		3.25	X			A	N	O	A	N
	Pelletier Presidential	30	750		3.0			E-L-R	A	N		B-C	Y
	Hispanic Excellence	40	1000		3.0			E	A	N	M	B-C	Y
	Dr. Ernst E. Williams	10	1000		2.7			E-L-O	A	N	M	B-C	Y
	A/S Merit Scholar Prog.	10	1000		3.8	1150/26		O	A		O	B-C	N
	GSX Merit Science Sch.	2	1000		3.0			E-L	O	3.0	O	B-C	N
	Honors Program												

CA State U., Carson 90747	Presidential	5	2000	33%	3.4		N	E-L-R	A	3.5	S	B-3/6	Y
	Faculty & Staff Schol.	10	1816		3.0		N	E-L-R	A		S	A-2/4	N
	CSU Future Scholars	30	1000		3.0		N	E-L-R-0	A		S-0	A-2/4	Y
	Loker Scholarship	1	2000		3.0		N	E-L-R-0	A	3.0	S-0	A-2/4	N
	Hy & Deena Goldman	1	1816		3.0		N	E-L-R-0	A		S-0	A-2/4	N
	Senator Kennick	1	1816		3.0		N	E-L-R	A		S	A-2/4	N
	Honors	300	500		3.0		N	E-R	A	3.0	S	B	Y
	AP Exams												
	Distance Learning												
	Co-op, Internships												
	Honors Program												
CA State U., Chico 95929	Academic	250	100-1000	X	X		X	0	A	X	0	A-2/1	Y
	Honors Program												
CA State U., Fresno 93740	Academic	900	100-2000	46%	3.0		X	E-L	A	X	N	B-2/1	Y
CA State U., Fullerton 92634	President's	12	1500		3.75	1150/28	N	E-L-R-I	A	3.5	S	ʼ b-3/1	N
	AP Exams												
	Distance Learning												
	Co-op, Internships												
	Honors Program												
CA State U., Hayward 94542	Academic	Varies	250-1000		3.5		Y	E-R-0	0	3.0	N	B-5/1	Y-3.5
	Academic/NGGD	Varies	200-1000		3.0		Y	R-0	0	3.0	S-M	B-5/1	Y-3.0
CA State U., Long Beach	President's Scholars	60	2000-5300	1			N	0	A	Y	S	B	N
	AP Exams												
	Distance Learning												
	Honors Program												
CA State U., Los Angeles 90032	Freshman Honors	5	500		3.5		N	L-R	A	Y	N	B-4/1	N
	Samuel Freeman	Varies	500		3.0		N	R	A	N	M	C	Y-3.0
	General	Varies	100-2500		3.0		Y	R	A	X	X	B-C	
CA State U., Northridge 91330	CSUN	325	250-1500		3.0		N	E-L-R-0	A	3.0	N	C	Y
	Departmental	250	500-1500		X		N	0	0	X	0	C	N
	Honors Program												
CA State U., San Bernardino 92407	A.F. Moore	8-12	1200		3.5		N	E-R	A	3.0	N	B-3/2	N
	Harris/Meyers	1-2	1200		3.5		N	E-R	A	3.0	S	B-3/2	N
CA State U., Turlock 95380	Rogers	15	3500		3.0		N	R-0	A	Y	0	C	N
	Honors Program												

	Program	No. of Awards	Value Range	Award Criteria					Study Fields	Renew-ability	Restric-tions	Apply Date	Transfer
				Class Stndg.	Grade Avg.	SAT/ ACT	Need Based	Other					
CALIFORNIA *(Continued)*													
Chapman, Orange 92666	Academic	Varies	5200-8700		3.25		N		A	3.0	N	B-3/1	Y-3.25
	Performance	Varies	3500-9600		2.5		N	T	A	2.25	N	B-3/1	Y-2.5
	Honors Program												
Christian Heritage, El Cahon 92021	Academic	Varies	500-Tuition	5%	3.5	1200/36	Y	L-R	A	3.3	O	B-3/1	Y-3.5
	Academic Merit	2	500-4500	10%	4.0	1250/28	Y	L	A	N	N	B-6/15	N
	Christian Service	Unlimited	500-1000				Y	L	A	N	N	B-6/15	Y
	Honor	Unlimited	500-2000	20%	3.5	1100/26	Y	L	A	N	N	B-6/15	Y
	Assistance	Unlimited	500-2000				Y		A	2.0	O	B-6/15	Y
	Honors Program												
Claremont McKenna, Claremont 91711	McKenna	30	2500	10%		1200	N	O	A	B	N	C	Y
	McKenna Achievement Award	25-30	2500-3000	5%	3.8	1400/31	N	E-L-R-I	A	3.5	N	C-1/1	N
Cogswell College, Sunnyvale 94089	Academic	Varies	1000-3160		3.0		Y		A	3.0	N	B-D	N
	Academic	Varies	1000-3160		3.0		Y		A	3.0	N	B-D	Y-3.0
College of Notre Dame, Belmont 94002	Regents'	6	2000		3.5		N	E-T-L	A	3.0	N	A-B-4/1	Y-3.0
	Honors at Entrance	Varies	3000		3.5		N	T-L-R	A	3.0	N	A	N
	President's	10	4000		3.5		N	E-T-L	A	3.0	N	A-B-3/2	
Concordia University, Irvine 92715	Athletics	Varies	Varies				Y	T	A	2.0	O	D	Y
	Christ College Grant	Varies	1000-3000				Y	O	O	2.5	D-O	B-D	Y
	Dean	Varies	2500		3.5	900/21	Y		A	3.2	O	A-D	Y-3.5
	Drama	Varies	Varies				Y	T-R-I	A	2.0	O	B-4/1	Y
	Endowment Grants	Varies	Varies				Y		A	2.5	D-O	A-D	Y
	Lutheran HS Grad.	Varies	1000				Y	O	A	2.5	O	A-D	Y
	Merit	Varies	1500		3.2	900/21	Y		A	3.0	O	A-D	Y-3.2
	Music	Varies	Varies				Y	T-R-I	A	2.0	O	B-4/1	Y
	President's	Varies	Tuition			900/21	Y	-O	A	3.4	O	A-D	Y
	Regent	Varies	4000		3.8	900/21	Y		A	3.4	O	A-D	Y-3.8
	Trustees	Varies	Varies				Y		A	2.5	M-O	D	Y
Dominican, San Rafael 94901	Alana Leadership/Merit	5	6945-10150		3.0		N	E-L-R	A	3.0	N	B-3/1	Y
	Presidential	10	6945-10150		3.5		N	E-L-R	A	3.0	M	B-3/1	Y
	Dean's	10	4630-6766		3.3		N	E-L-R	A	3.0	N	B-3/1	Y
	Dominican Achievement	Varies	2000				N	E-T-L-R-O	A	3.0	N	B-3/1	Y
	Honors Program												

Fresno Pacific, Fresno 93702	President's	102	500-Tuition		3.6	900	Y	E-T-L-R-I	A	3.5	N	B-2/15	N
	Dean's	150	1000-2000		3.6	900	Y		A	3.0	N	A-D	Y-3.6
	Service/Leadership	115	500				Y	T-L-R	A	Y	N	A-D	Y
	Academic	Varies	400-1600		3.4		N		A	3.0	N	A-D	Y-3.4
	Honors Program												
Holy Names, Oakland 94619	Athletic Grant	Varies	500-10,000		2.4		Y	T	A	2.4	N	3/1	Y-2.4
	Honors at Entrance	5	3000		3.5		N	E-L-R	A	3.0	N	B-3/1	N
	Music	Varies	5000+		2.8		N	T	0	2.8	N	3/1	Y-2.8
	President's	10	1/2 Tuition		3.0		Y	E-L-R-0	A	3.0	N	B-3/1	Y-3.0
	Regents'	5	Tuition		3.5		Y	E-L-R-0	A	3.0	N	B-3/1	Y-3.5
	AP Exams												
	Internships												
Humboldt State U., Arcata 95521	University	240	100-1500		3.0		X		A	N	0	B-3/2	Y
	Cornelius Siemens	12	500		3.75	1200	N	L	A	3.0	N	A-4/1	N
Loma Linda U., 92350	Wilson Richards	Varies					Y	0	0	3.0	S-W	C	
	Mabel Warren	Varies	2000-8000				Y	0	0	Y	0	C	
	LLU General Scholarship	Varies					Y	0	0	Y	0	C	
Loyola Marymount U., Los Angeles 90045	CSF	4	500-2000	X		X	Y		A	Y	0	B-3/2	N
	Leadership	20	6000	X	X	X	N	E-L-R	A	3.0	0	A-2/1	N
	Presidential	20	7500	X	3.5	1200	N	E-L-R	A	3.0	N	S-3/2	N
	Jesuit Community	5	4000	X	X	X	Y	E-L-R	A	Y	0	B-2/1	N
	Trustee	10	Tuition	X	3.6	1200/29	N	E-L-I-0	A	3.25	N	A-2/1	N
	Honors Program												
Master's, Newhall 91322	Academic	Unlimited	To Tuition		3.6	1000	N		A	3.6	N	B-6/15	Y-3.6
	Accomplishment		750		3.25	1100/24	N		A	3.25	N	B-3/1	Y-3.25
	National Merit		Half-Full Tuit.				N		A	3.5	N	B-3/1	N
	Servant-Leader		1000		2.5		N	E-L-R	A	2.5	N	B-3/1	Y-2.5
	Distinguished Scholar		3000		3.85	1250/28	N		A	3.9	N	B-3/1	Y-3.85
	Honors		2250		3.65	1200/27	N		A	3.65	N	B-3/1	Y-3.65
	Achievement Award		1500		3.45	1150/25	N		A	Y	N	B-3/1	Y
	Music/Talents	10	300-1800				N	T-I	0	N	N	B-8/15	Y
Menlo, Atherton 94027	Menlo Presidential		3000		3.5	1100/26	N		A	3.5	0	B-4/30	N
	Menlo Leadership		1000				N	L	A	3.0	0	B-4/30	N
	Menlo Transfer		3000		3.0		N			3.0	0	B-4/30	Y-3.0
Mills, Oakland 94613	Carroll Donner Music	1	5000	X	X	X	N	T-R-0	0	3.2	W	A-2/15	Y
	Davis Science	1	2000	X	X	X	N	T-R-0	0	3.0	W	B-2/15	Y
	Regional	10	5000		3.2	1100	N	E-L-R	A	3.2	W	A-2/15	N
	Transfer	2	5000		3.5		N	E-L-R	A	3.2	W	A-4/1	Y

	Program	No. of Awards	Value Range	Award Criteria: Class Stndg.	Grade Avg.	SAT/ ACT	Need Based	Other	Study Fields	Renew-ability	Restric-tions	Apply Date	Transfer
CALIFORNIA *(Continued)*													
Mills, Oakland 94613 *(Continued)*	Trustee	13	2000-10000		3.5	1200	Y	0	A	3.5	W	A-2/15	N
	AP Exams												
	Internships												
Mt. St. Mary's, Los Angeles 90049	Future Teacher	Varies	To 1/2 Tuition		3.2	900	N	E-R-I	0	3.0	N	A-3/1	N
	President's	Varies	To Tuition		3.7	1100/24	N	E-L-R-I	A	3.5	N	A-3/1	N
	Honors Program												
National U., San Diego 92108	Leadership	Unlimited	1000				Y	E-L-R	A	N	0	B	Y
	Collegiate Hon.	Unlimited	1000		3.5		N	E-R	A	N	0	B	Y-3.8
	NU Presidential	75	2500		2.3		Y	0	A	Y	M-0	B	Y-2.4
New College of CA, San Francisco 94102	Academic	Inquire	Varies				Y	R	A	N	0	C	Y
Northrop U., Los Angeles 90045	John K. Northrop	Varies	To 1/2 Tuit.	10%	X	X	N	E-R-0	0	3.0	N	B-D	Y-3.0
	James L. McKinley	3	To Tuition	5%	3.5	X	Y	E-R-I-0	A	3.5	N	B-D	N
Occidental, Los Angeles 90041	Carnation	Varies	3000	10%	3.5	1200/25	N	E-T-L-R	A	3.0	N	A-2/1	N
	Margaret Bundy Scott	Varies	8000-10000	10%	3.5	1200/25	N	E-T-L-R	A	3.0	N	A-2/1	N
Otis/Parsons, Los Angeles 90057	Art & Design	Varies	Varies	25%	3.0		Y	T-R	0	Y	N	B-3/1	Y
	Dean's Scholars	10	1000-2000	10%	3.0	1000/24	N	T	A	3.0	N	A-3/1	Y
Pacific Christian, Fullerton 92631	Honors	10	1/2 Tuition		3.0		N	E-L-R	A	3.0	N	B-3/2	Y
	Music Award	Varies	100-1000				N	T	0		N	B-4/30	Y
	Pres. Sch. for Acad. Ach.	Varies	25-100% Tuition			1100/25			A	2.9-3.5	0	B-7/1	Y
Pacific Oaks College, Pasadena 91103	George Mayer Merit	1	5000	2%			N	T-L-R	A	N	0	B	N
	John Stauffer Merit	2	2500-5000	2%			N	T-L-R	A	N	0	B	N
Pacific Union, Angwin 94508	Honor Award	Unlimited	600-1950	10%	3.8		N		A	N	N	A-D	Y-3.25
	Leadership	Unlimited	825-2100				N	T-L	A	N	N	A-D	N
	Minority Leadership	Varies	Varies				N	0	A		M	C	N
	ACT/SAT	Unlimited	1050-1500			1200/28	N		A	N	N	B-C	N
Patten College, Oakland 94601	Jerry Clark	10	200-2000	30%	3.00		Y	E-L-R-I	A	3.0	N	B-C	Y-3.0
Pepperdine U., Malibu 90265	Dean's	260	10,000		3.85	1330/31	N	E	A	3.25			
	Regents	30	14,000		3.95	1470/34	N	E	A	3.25			
	AP Exams												

	Co-op, Internships												
	Honors Program												
Pitzer, Claremont 91711	Trustee	20	10,000	X	X	X	N	L-T	A	Y	N	A-2/1	N
	Chevron Merit	1	2000	10%	3.5	1100	N	E-L-R	A	3.0	N	B-2/15	N
	AP Exams												
	Co-op												
Point Loma Nazarene, San Diego 92106	President's	207	3300		3.7	1220/31	N		A	Y	N	B-4/10	Y
	Dean's	147	1900		3.5	1150/29	N		A	Y	N	B-4/10	Y
	PLN College	234	1400		3.2	1000/24	N		A	Y	N	B-4/10	Y
	Honor	72	5088-10176		3.8	1025/25	N		A	Y	N	B-4/10	N
Ryokan College, Los Angeles 90066	Academic	Varies	1500-2500				Y	E-L-R	A	Y	N	B-11/1	Y
San Diego State University 92182	Academic						N	E-L-I	A		0	B-2/1	Y-3.5
	Honors Program												
Santa Clara U., 95053	Honor's Program	50	2000-3000	25%	3.5	1350	X	L-0	A	3.0	N	B-2/1	N
	Bruscher Theatre Arts	10-20	2000-4000				X	T-R-I	0	2.0	N	B-2/1	Y
	Music	5-8	200-2500				X	T-R-I	0	2.0	N	B-2/1	Y
	Debate	8-10	200-2500				N	T	0	2.0	N	2/1	Y-2.0
	Athletics	100-150	200-Tuition				N	T-0	A	2.0	N	2/1	Y-2.0
	Dean's Scholars Awards	60	500-3000	10%	3.5	1250	Y	0	0	3.0	0	A	N
	Honors Program												
San Francisco Art Institute 94133	Community College	21	4250		3.0		N	R-I	A		0	B-3/1	Y-3.0
	Sobel	60	3700-5500		3.0		N	R	A		0	A-3/1	Y-3.0
San Jose State U., San Jose 95192	SJSU Scholarship	50	2500		2.0		Y	T-L	A	2.0	N	B-3/1	N
Scripps, Claremont 91711	James E. Scripps	20	7500	5%	3.5	1350	N	E-I-T-L-R	A	3.0	W	B-11/15	N
	Chevron Merit	1	5000	10%	3.5	1200	N	E-T-L-R	0	3.0	W	B-4/15	N
	Dorothy Drake Scholarship	8	3500-5000	10%	3.5	1250	Y	E-T-L-R	A	3.0	W	A-2/1	N
	AP Exams												
Simpson, Redding 96003	Honors at Entrance	Varies	700-2500		3.5	1100/25	N		A	3.5	N	B-3/31	Y-3.5
	Leadership Grant	Varies	400-1000		2.5		N	L-R	A	N	N	N	Y
	Performance Awards	10	Varies		2.5		N	T-R-I-0	A	N	N	B-3/1	Y
Sonoma State, Rohnert Park, 94928	University	150-175	250-2000		3.0		N	E-L-R	A	N	0	B-3/1	Y-3.0
	Presidential Scholar	20	1000		4.0		N		A	4.0	N	B-5/1	N
Southern California, Costa Mesa 92626	Presidential	Unlimited	5000	X	3.75	X	Y	0	A	3.2	N	A-B-3/2	N
	Academic Dean	Unlimited	3240	X	3.5	X	Y	0	A	3.0	N	A-B-3/2	N
	Vanguard Leadership	Unlimited	2500	X	3.2	X	Y	0	A	2.8	N	A-B-3/2	N

	Program	No. of Awards	Value Range	Award Criteria: Class Stndg.	Grade Avg.	SAT/ ACT	Need Based	Other	Study Fields	Renew-ability	Restric-tions	Apply Date	Transfer
CALIFORNIA *(Continued)*													
U. of California, Berkeley 94720	Regents'/Chancellor's	223	500-14000	5%	4.0	1400	Y	O	A	3.0	N	A-11/30	Y-4.0
	Honorary	1200	300-500		3.8		N		A	N	N	B-3/1	Y
U. of California, Davis 95616	Alumni	Varies	500-1000		3.25		N	E-L-R-I	A	N	N	11-30	Y-3.25
	Regents'	Varies	1000-All Need		3.25		N	E	A	3.25	N	11-30	Y-3.25
U. of California, Irvine 92717	Tierney	Varies	1000		3.0		N		O	N	O	B-3/2	N
	Town & Gown	Varies	Varies		3.0		N		A	N	O	B-3/2	Y
	Chancellor's Club	Varies	1000		3.75	1250	N	O	A	3.0	N	B-1/23	Y-3.4
U. of California, Los Angeles 90024	Alumni	150	1000-3500		3.85	1000	N	E-R-I	A	Y	S	B-2/1	Y
	Regents'	100	500-6000	3%	4.0	1350	Y	E-L-R	A	3.0	S	C	Y
	Honors Program												
U. of California, Riverside 92521	Engineering	9	500-1500		3.75	1200/28	N	ER	O	3.0	N	C-11/30	N
	Alumni	30	1000		3.65	1200/28	N	E-T-L-R-I	A	N	S	C-11/30	N
	Academic	250-500	250-500		3.5	800	N		A	3.0	S	C-11/30	Y
	Honors Program												
U. of California, San Diego 92093	Regents	55	1000-13,450	5%	4.0	1400	Y		A	3.0	N	A-11/30	N
	AP Exams												
	Honors Program												
U. of La Verne, 91750	Dean's	Unlimited	1/5 Tuition		3.6		N		A	Y	N	B-3/1	Y
	President's	Unlimited	1/4 Tuition		3.8		N		A	Y	N	A-3/1	Y
	Honors Program												
U. of the Pacific, Stockton 95211	Deans'		25% Tuition		X	X						B-2/15	N
	Pacific Scholarship	3	90% Tuition		3.85	1350/31	N	R	O	3.0	N	B-2/15	N
	President's	150-250	33% Tuition		3.33	1170/26	N	R	A	3.0	N	B-2/15	N
	Regents'	80-100	50% Tuition		3.65	1300/30	N	R	A	3.0	N	B-2/15	N
	Valedictorian Scholarship		75% Tuition	1	3.80	1250/28						B-2/15	N
	AP Exams												
	Co-op, Internships												
	Honors Program												
U. of Redlands, 92373	Achievement Award	Unlimited	1000-5000		3.0	1000/23	N	E-T-L-R-I	A	2.3	N	A-12/15	N
	Award of Merit	10	Full Tuition				N		A	3.0	N	C-12/15	N

	Music Scholarship	Varies	500-4000				N	T	O	Y	N	B-3/1	Y
	Presidential	Unlimited	500-1500		3.5	1000/23	N	E-L	A	3.5	O	A-12/15	N
	Honors Program												
U. of San Diego, 92110	Catholic Leadership	Varies	200-1000		2.8		Y	E-L-R	A	2.5	D	B-C	Y
	Presidential	Varies	7500		3.6	X	N	E-L-R	A	3.25	N	A-C	N
	Trustee	Varies	8500		3.8	X	N	E-L-R	A	3.45	N	A-C	N
	Dean's Scholarship	Varies	6000		3.5	X	N	E-L-R	A	3.25	N	A-C	N
	Honors Program												
U. of San Francisco, 94117	University	20-25	3/4 Tuition		3.8	44	N		A	3.25	O	A-2/1	N
	Honors Program												
U. of Southern California, Los Angeles 90089	Alumnae	Varies	500-5000		3.0		N	E-T-L-I	A	3.0	N	B-2/15	Y-3.0
	Alumnae Achievement	Varies	1000				N	T-L-I	A	N	N	B-2/15	N
	Alumni Club	Varies	500-4000				N	L-I	A	N	O	B-2/15	N
	Asian Pacific American	10-20	1000-2500		3.0		N	E-R	A	N	M	B-C	Y
	Black Alumni	25	Varies				Y	I	A		M	B-1/1	Y
	Caldwell Neighborhood	Varies	3000				N	E-L-R	A		O	B-12/15	N
	Dean's	250	6000		3.6	1360	N	E-T-L	A	3.0	N	B-12/1	N
	Mexican American	250	400-4500				Y		A	A	M	B-6/29	Y
	Norman Topping	25-30	1500-4000				Y	E-L-R	A		N	B-2/15	Y
	Presidential	100	50% Tuition				N	E-T-L	A	3.0	N	B-12/1	N
	Private Donor	Varies	Varies				N	E-L	A	3.0	O	A-2/15	Y
	Scion	Varies	1000-3000		3.6	1250	Y	E-L-I	A	3.0	O	B-2/15	Y
	Trustee	80	Tuition				N	E-T-L	A	Y	N	B-12/1	N
	USC Associates	15	7500		3.6	1250	N	E-L	A	3.0	N	B-4/1	Y
	AP Exams												
	Alumni Discounts												
	Honors Program												
United States Int'l University 92131	Presidential	Varies	30% Tuition		3.6		N	L	A	3.2	N	A-D	Y-3.6
	University	Varies	24%Tuition		3.0		N	L	A	3.0	N	A-D	Y-3.0
	Diversity Scholarship	Varies	50-5400	Varies	3.2	Varies	Y	O	A	3.0	O	A-5/2	Y-3.2
	Honors Program												
West Coast U., Los Angeles 90020	Development	10-25	500		3.0		Y	E-R-I	A	3.0	N	D	Y
Westmont, Santa Barbara 93108	President's Scholarship	350	5000		3.6		N		A	3.25	N	A-5/1	N
	Provost's Scholarship	200	3500		3.3		N		A				
	Westmont Scholarship	100	2000		3.0		N		A				
	Trustee's Scholarship	3	To Tuition				N	T-L-R-I	A	3.5	N	A-1/15	N
	Honors Program												

	Program	No. of Awards	Value Range	Award Criteria: Class Stndg.	Grade Avg.	SAT/ ACT	Need Based	Other	Study Fields	Renew-ability	Restric-tions	Apply Date	Transfer
CALIFORNIA *(Continued)*													
Whittier College, 90608	Talent		7500				N	E-T-I	A	2.0	0	B-2/15	N
	John Greenleaf Whittier		1000-17300	10%	3.5	1150	N	E-L-R	A	3.0	0	C	N
	Alumni		1000				N		A		N	A	Y
Woodbury U., Burbank 91510	Academic Scholarship	50	1500-5000		3.0		Y	0	A	3.0	S	A-3/1	N
	High School Award	20	1000		3.0		N	R	A	2.5	N	A-3/1	N
	Community College Awards	5	1000		3.0		N	R	A	2.5	0	0	Y
COLORADO													
Adams State, Alamosa 81102	Activity	200	100-1500		2.5		N	T-I	A	2.5	N	B-3/15	Y
	Adams	200	400-900		3.25	740/19	N		A	3.25	N	B-3/15	Y
	National	200	2000-2400			850/21	N		A	2.5	0	B-3/15	Y
	President's	570	1920-2000		3.2	970/21	Y		A	3.4	N	B-3/15	Y-3.2
	Woodard	24	3000-4500		2.5	850/21	Y	L-0-R	A	2.5	N	B-3/15	Y
	Honors Program												
Colorado Christian U., Lakewood 80226	Academic Achievement	279	1000-2000		3.2-4.0		N		A	N	N	B	Y-3.2
	Business	31	1000-1800				Y	L-0	0	N	0	B-4/15	Y
	CCU Academic	183	1000-2000		3.5-4.0		N		A	3.5	0	B	N
	Drama	53	200-1500		2.0		N	T-R-0	A	N		B	Y-2.0
	Drama/Music	50	200-1000				N	T-I-0		2.5	N	B-4/1	
	Education	14	500-1000		3.0		N	0	0	N	0		Y-3.0
	Humanities & Science	2	200-500				Y	L-0	0		0		
	Incentive	100	300-500		2.0		N	0		2.0	N	B-4/1	
	Music	161	50-2400		2.5		N	T-R-0	A	N	0	B	Y-2.5
	National Merit	4	Tuition				N	0	A	3.85	N	B	Y
	Presidential	227	500-1000				N	E	A	N		B-3/15	Y
	Stephen's Scholarship	9	500-1000				Y	E-L-0	A	N	0	B	N
	Young Scholars	150	600-1000		3.6		N	0		3.25	N	B-4/1	Y-3.25
Colorado College, Colorado Springs, 80903	Barnes Chemistry	5	Tuition				N	0	0	Y	N	A-2/15	N
	Barnes Natural Science	5	Tuition				N	0	0	Y	N	A-2/15	N
	CC Faculty Minority	5	1000-1500				Y	E	A	Y	M	A-2/15	N
CO School of Mines, Golden 80401	Academic Talent	20	1000-10000	10%	3.7	1200/27	N	L	A	2.5	N	D	N
	Athletic	150	1000-11000				N	T-R-I-0	A	2.0	N	C-6/1	Y

	Band/Chorus Scholarship	20	2200				N	T-R-I-0	A	2.0	N	B-3/1	Y
	Board of Trustees	50	2200	10%	3.7	1200/27	N	L-0	A	2.50	N	C-5/1	N
	Mines Medal	50	1000	10%	3.7	1200/27	N	R	A	N	N	C-3/1	N
	Presidential	20	1500-2500	15%	3.5	1100/24	N	L-0	A	2.5	N	C-5/1	N
	AP Exams												
	Co-op, Internships												
	Honors Program												
Colorado State U., Ft. Collins 80523	Arts	347	100-1000		2.4		N	T	0	2.4	A-H	B-C	Y
	Colorado Scholars	82	1000	X	3.0		N		A	3.0	A-H	B-C	Y
	Distinguished	100	2000	X	X	X	N	0	A	3.5	0	A-C	N
	Dean's	400	500	X	X	X	N	0	A	N	N	A-C	N
	Meritorious	300	300	X	X	X	N	0	A	N	N	A-C	N
	President's	410	1000	1%	3.85		N		A	3.85	0	A-C	Y
Fort Lewis, Durango 81301	Presidential	95	1000-1500	20%	3.5		N	R-0	A	N	S	A-D	N
	Dean's	50	600		3.0	24							
	Performing Arts	Varies	800-1500		3.0		N	T-R-I-0	0	3.0	S	C	Y-3.0
	Honors Program												
Mesa State, Grand Junction 81502	Bookcliff	121	To Tuition	15%	3.0	23	N	L-0	A	3.0	N	A-3/1	Y-3.0
	Monument	17	Tuition & Fees	15%	3.5	23	N	0	A	3.2	N	A-3/1	Y-3.5
	Grand Mesa	12	Tuition & Fees	15%	3.5	23	N	0	A	3.5	N	A-3/1	Y-3.5
	Ambassador	13	Tuition & Fees		2.5		N	L-0	A	2.5	N	A-3/1	N
	Colorado Continuing	70	700		3.0		N		A		N	B-3/1	N
	Colorado School Schp.	85	To 700		3.0		N		A		N	B-3/1	N
	Diversity Grant	103	500-2000		2.0		Y	0	A	2.0	M	B-3/1	N
	Mt. Garfield Non-Resident	250	1/2 Tuition		3.0		N	0	A	3.0	0	B	Y-3.0
	Scholars	9	2933-3668	10%	3.6	1100/25	N	E-I-0	A	3.5		12/1	N
Metropolitan State, Denver 80217	Colorado Scholars	200	250-1000		3.0		N		A	N	A	C	Y
	HS Presidential	50	900-1850	20%	3.0	980/23	N	E-L-0-R	A	3.5	A	B-3/16	N
	Transfer Presidential	25	450-1850		3.25		N	E-L-0-R	A	3.5	A	B-11/18	Y
	Honors	50	250-1000		3.25			0			A	C	Y
	Honors Program												
Naropa Institute, Boulder 80302	Collin Wollcot	1-2	1150-2300				Y	T	0	N	0	C	N
	Friendship House	To 5	1200				Y	T-I	0	N	0	C	N
	Ted Berrigan	1	1000				N	T	0	N	0	C	N
Regis College, Denver 80221	Athletic Grant	Varies	250-Tuition				N	T-0	A	Y	N	C	
	Blue and Gold	Varies	10000		3.6	1200/26	N	E-L-0-R	A	3.0	N	B-3/15	N
	Board of Trustees	Varies	4000-7000		3.2	1130/24	N	E-L-0-R	A	3.0	N	B-3/15	N
	Colorado Scholarship	Varies	500-1500		3.4		N	E-L-0-R	A	N	N	B-3/15	Y
	Endowed Scholarship	Varies	500-8000	X	X	X	N	0	A	Y	N	C	

	Program	No. of Awards	Value Range	Award Criteria: Class Stndg.	Grade Avg.	SAT/ ACT	Need Based	Other	Study Fields	Renew- ability	Restric- tions	Apply Date	Transfer
COLORADO *(Continued)*													
Regis College, Denver 80221 *(Connecticut)*	Forensic Award	Varies	1/2 Tuition				N	O	A	Y	N	C	N
	Natural Science	12	Tuition				N	E	O	3.0	A	B-3/15	Y
	Regis Grant	Varies	To 7000				Y	O	A	Y	N	C	
	Honors Program												
U. of Colorado, Boulder 80309	Dean's Scholars	325	100-1200	X	X		N		A	Y	N	A-C	N
	President's	250	200-1000	X	X		N	L-O	A	Y	N	B-2/1	N
	Regents'	300	500	3%			N		A	N	A-O	A-C	N
U. of Colorado, Colorado Springs 80933	Colorado Scholars	120	400-800		3.0		N	R	A	Y	A-O	B-6/1	N
	Regents'	50	400-800	11%		1050/24	N		A	N	A	B-C	Y
	H. A. Arnold	Varies	600-1200	50%			N	R	A	2.5	M-O	B-4/1	N
	Minority Graduate	Varies	500-1000				Y		A	Y	M-O	B-4/1	Y
U. of Colorado, Denver 80204	Regents'	Varies	800-2000		3.5		N		A	N	A	A-3/1	Y
	Chancellor's		500-1500		3.5		N		A	N	A-O	C-4/1	Y-3.5
	Honors Program												
U. of Denver, 80208	Alumni Scholarships	6	Tuition	5%		1300/28	N	L	A	3.2	N	A-2/15	N
	Johnson	1	All Costs		3.5		Y	I	A	3.0	S	A-2/15	N
	Martin Luther King	6	Tuition	5%		1300/28	N	L	A	Y	N	A-2/15	N
	Merit Awards	490	4000-6000	30%	3.2	1100/24	N		A	Y	N	A-2/15	Y-3.5
	AP Exams												
	Co-op, Internships												
	Honors Program												
U. of Northern Colorado, Greeley 80639	President's Honor	Varies	Varies	10%			N		A	Y	A	C	N
U. of Southern Colorado, Pueblo 81001	President's Academic	Varies	400-800		3.0	22	N	R	A	3.0	N	B-3/1	Y
	President's Talent	Varies	400-800		2.5		N	T-R	A	2.5	N	B-3/1	Y
	Honors Program												
Western State, Gunnison 81230	Academic Excellence	250+	500-1000		3.2	20	N		A	3.2	O	D	N
	Academic/Leadership	50	1500		3.0	21/870	N	O	A	Y	A	B-3/1	N
	Borick Scholars	4	3000		3.6	1000/25	N		O	3.5	A-M	B-C	N
	Bruce Johnson Memorial	Varies	1000		2.5		N	O	A	N	A	B-C	N
	Honors	30	800	15%		22	N		A	Y	A	A-4/15	Y
	Non-Resident Trustees	30	2300	40%	3.0	870/21	N		A	Y	O	A-C	N

	Presidential	30	1000	5%		25	N		A	Y	A	A-4/15	Y
	Reichle Memorial Fund	5	1000		3.25		N	0	A		A-0	B-C	
	Rouse Scholarship	Varies	To 1.5 x Tuit.	X	X	X	Y	R-0	0		A-0	B-C	
	W-H-M Diversity	3	2500		3.25		N		A		A	B-C	
	WSCS	30	600	25%	3.0	20	N		A	3.2	A	A-4/1	Y
CONNECTICUT													
Albertus Magnus, New Haven 06511	New Haven Area	Varies	1/4-3/4 Tuition	50%	Var.	800-1000	N	R-I-0	A	3.0	S-0	A	
	Mohun	Varies	4000	Var.	3.0	900/20	N	R-I-0	A	3.0		A	
	Presidential	Varies	1/3 Tuition	20%	Var.	1000/23	N	R-I-0	A	3.5		A	
	Valedictorian/Salutatorian	Varies	1/2 Tuition	X	Var.	1100/25	N	R-I-0	A	3.7		A	
	Transfer	Varies	1500	Var.	3.0			R-I-0	A	3.0		A	Y-3.0
	Honors Program												
Connecticut, New London 06320	*Sykes Scholars Honors Program*												
Eastern Conn State U., Willimantic 06226	Honors	44	4000	20%	3.3	1100	N	E-R-L	A	3.0	N	B-4	Y-3.3
	Competitive Sch. Program	50	250-2500	20%	2.5	1050	Y	E-L-0-R	A	N	N	B-2	Y
Fairfield U., 06430	Fellows	20	10,000	10%	3.8	1300/30	N	E-I-L		3.0			
	Presidential	30	8500	10%	3.5	1200/27	N	E-I					
	Dean's	75	6000	20%	3.3	46	N	E					
	AP Exams												
	Family Discounts												
	Internships												
	Honors Program												
Quinnipiac, Hamden 06518	Dean's	Varies	3000-6000	15%		1100	N	I-0	A	3.0	N	A-2/15	N
	Quinnipiac	Varies	1000-2000	25%		1000/24	N	I-0	A	3.0	N	A-2/15	
	Diversity Scholarship	Varies	500-6500				Y	L-0-R-0	A	3.0	M	C	Y-3.0
	Honors Program												
Sacred Heart U., Fairfield 06432	Presidential	25	500-2000	10%	3.5	1100/24	N	E-0-I	A	Y	N	B-D	Y
Teikyo Post U., Waterbury 06708	Transfer	Varies	3500-5500	10%	3.5		N	0	A	3.0	N	A-4/15	N
	Presidential	Varies	5450-10900	10%		1100	N	0	A	3.0	N	A-3/15	N
	Institutional	Varies	2500-7500	X	X	X	N	0	A	Varies	0	A-C	
	Donor	Varies	Varies	X	X	X	N	0	A	Varies	0	C	
University of Bridgeport	Acad. Excell. & Leadership	135	13,400-20,210	25%	3.6	1200/29	N	L-R-T-0	A	3.0	N	B-1/15	Y-3.6
	Academic Scholarship	57	8800-13,400	25%	3.4	1150/24	N		A	2.8	N	A-5/1	Y-3.4
	Academic Grant	25	4400-6700	50%	3.2	1000/23	N	R-I-0	A	2.75	N	A-5/1	Y-3.2
	AP Exams												
	Distance Learning												
	Family Discounts												

	Program	No. of Awards	Value Range	Award Criteria: Class Stndg.	Grade Avg.	SAT/ ACT	Need Based	Other	Study Fields	Renew-ability	Restric-tions	Apply Date	Transfer
CONNECTICUT *(Continued)*													
University of Bridgeport *(Continued)*	Co-op, Internships												
	Honors Program												
U. of Connecticut, Storrs 06268	Alumni	25	1000		3.7		N	I	A	Y	N	B-12/29	N
	University	30	All Fees		3.7		N	I	A	Y	N	A-C	N
	Admission Schp.	500	1000-6000		3.0		N	R-O	A	3.0	N	A-3/1	Y
	Honors Program												
U. of Hartford, W. Hartford 06117	Artistic Merit	Varies	1000-12,000				N	T	O	3.0	N	B-2/15	Y-3.0
	Health Professions	Varies	7000-9000		3.0	1140	N		O	3.0	N	B-2/15	N
	Performing Arts	Varies	1000-17,180				N	E-I-T	O	3.0	N	B-2/15	Y-3.0
	President's	Varies	8000	50%	3.0	1140	N		A	3.0	N	A-2/15	N
	Regents'	Varies	9000	10%	3.0	1270	N		A	3.0	N	B-2/15	N
	AP Exams												
	Family Discounts												
	Co-op, Internships												
	Honors Program, Honors College												
U. of New Haven, 06516	Academic	60	500-2000	10%			Y		A	Y	N	A-D	N
	Presidential	Varies	1000	10%	3.0	1000	N		A	3.0	O	A	Y
	University Excellence	5	5000	10%	3.5	1100+	N		A	3.5	N	A	Y-3.5
Wesleyan U., Middletown 06457	*Honors Program*												
DELAWARE													
Goldey-Beacom C., Wilmington, 19808	Academic Excellence	54	7000	40%	3.0	1050	N	R-I-O	A	3.0	N	B-C	N
	George D. Hanby Mem		1500		3.0	1050		L-R	A	2.0	A	B-C	
	J. Wilbur Hirons Schol.		1500						A	2.0		B-C	
	Mark E. Jenkins Mem		1000		3.0	1000		R	A	2.0		B-C	
	Presidential	5	4000	40%	3.0	1000	N	I-O	O	2.0	N	B-C	N
	Stewart B. Jackson Mem		1000		3.0	1000		R	A	2.0		B-C	
	Honors Program												
U. of Delaware, Newark 19716	Eugene duPont	Varies	All Costs	X	X	X	N	I	A	3.0			
	UD Scholar Award	Varies	1000-6000	X	X	X	N		A	3.0			

	AP Exams												
	Distance Learning												
	Family Discounts												
	Co-op, Internships												
	Honors Programs												
Wesley, Dover 19901	Academic	Varies	3000-5000	20%		1000	N	R	A	3.0	N	A	4
	Merit	40-60	3000-5000	20%		1000	N		A	3.0	N	A-1/1	N
	Reynolds duPont Merit	3	4000		3.3		N	E-L-O-R	O	3.3	N	B-3/15	N
	Transfer	Varies	3000		3.5		N		A	N	N	A-3/15	3/15
	Wesley Scholars	10	7500	10%		1100	N	E-L-R-O	A	3.0	N	B-1/1	N
DISTRICT OF COLUMBIA													
American University, 20016	Presidential	Varies	To Tuition	top 10% of applicant pool			N		A	3.3	N	A-3/1	N
	Dean's Scholarship	Varies	6000-8000	next 15% of applicant pool			N		A	3.2			
	Leadership	Varies	3000-6000				N	L	A	2.0			
	Full Tuition	Varies	Tuition			X	N	E-O	A	3.2			
	AP Exams												
	Co-op, Internships												
	Honors Program												
Catholic University, 20064	Archdiocesan	30	Tuition	10%	3.5	1200	N	L-O-R	A	2.5	N	A-2/1	N
	Cardinal Gibbons	20	2000	20%	3.2	1200	N	L-O-R	A	2.5	N	A-2/1	Y
Corcoran School of Art, 20006	Dean's Scholarship	Varies	500-1500	25%	3.0	1000/23	N	T-R	O	N	N	B-3/15	N
Georgetown University, 20057-1051	John Carroll	79	500-2500				Y	R-O	A	Y	O	C-2/1	Y
	Bellarmine/Ignatian	27	500-18300	5%			Y	R-O	A	Y	O	C-2/1	N
	Honors Program												
George Washington U., 20052	Merit	Varies	6000-15,000	10%		1270	N	E-R-O	A	2.7			
	Arts	20	8000				N	E-R-T-O		2.7			
	Special Program		10000	10%			N	E-R-O		Y			
	AP Exams												
	Family Discounts												
	Co-op, Internships												
	Honors Program												
Howard University, 20059	Chapman	6	500-1000		2.75		Y	L	O	2.75	A-O	B-7/1	N
Southeastern U., 20024	Academic Achievement	20-30	300-2640		3.2		N		A	N	O	B-4/15	N
Trinity College, 20017	Patterson	Varies	3000-8000	10%	3.4	1130	Y	E-L-R-O	A	3.0	W	C-2/1	N
	Presidential	Varies	750	50%	3.0		N	R-I	A	3.0	S	C	N
University of DC, 20008	*Honors Program*												

	Program	No. of Awards	Value Range	Award Criteria: Class Stndg.	Grade Avg.	SAT/ACT	Need Based	Other	Study Fields	Renew-ability	Restric-tions	Apply Date	Transfer
FLORIDA													
Barry U., Miami 33161	Trustees	Varies	Tuition		3.5	1100/27	Y	L-R	A	3.3	N	B	N
	Transfer	Varies	1000-3000		3.0	1000	Y	L-R	A	Y	N	B	Y-3.0
	Presidential	Varies	2000-8000		3.25	1000/24	N	L-R	A	3.2	N	B-3/1	N
	Academic Achievement	Varies	4000		3.0	1000/24	Y	E-L-R	A	3.0	N	B	N
	Phi Theta Kappa	1	Tuition		3.5		N	E-L-R-O	A	3.3	N	B-3/15	Y-3.3
	Honors Program												
Bethune-Cookman, Daytona Beach 32115	Presidential	150	1000-4000	25%	2.75	900/24	N	L-O-R	A	2.75	N	B-7/1	Y-2.75
Clearwater Christian, 34619	President's	Varies	3000			1300/28	N		A	3.25		B-5/1	Y
	Academic	Varies	1500-2000		3.25	1300/28	N		A	3.25	N	B-5/1	Y-3.25
	Music	Varies	6500		2.0		Y	T-R-I-O	O	2.0	N	B-5/1	Y-2.0
Eckerd, St. Petersburg 33711	Presidential	25	8000-10,000	10%	3.8	1300/28	N	E-L-R	A	3.0			
	Special Honors	15	16,000-17,500	10%	3.9	1400/30	N	L-R	A	3.2			
	Special Talent	50	5000-8000	33%	3.0	1100/22	N	L-R-T	A	2.0			
	AP Exams												
	Internships												
	Honors Program												
Flagler, St. Augustine 32084	Lewis	5	All Costs	10%	3.5	1200	N	L-O-I	A	Y	N	B-2/1	N
	Presidential	50	200-1000	X	X	X	N	L-O-R-I	A	Y	N	B-3/1	Y
Florida Atlantic U., Boca Raton 33431	FAU Community College	Varies	1550				N	R	A	Y	N	B-7/1	Y
	FAU Presidential	35	2000		3.5	1270/27	N	E-O	A	2.5	N	B-4/1	N
	M. Brenn Green	2	1000				N		O	Y	M-O	B-4/1	N
	Martin Luther King Award	Varies	1550				Y		A	Y	M	B-4/1	N
	Martin Luther King Scholar	Varies	1800		3.0	1000/25	N	E-O	A	2.5	M	B-4/1	N
	Minority Educational	40	1550				N		A	Y	M	B-4/1	Y
	National Merit	Varies	3000-5000				N	O	A	2.8	N	B-4/1	N
	NM Semifinalist	Varies	2000				N	O	A	Y	N	B-4/1	N
	Phi Theta Kappa	Varies	1550				N	R	A	Y	N	B-C	N
	Salutatorian	Varies	1000				N		A	Y	N	B-4/1	N
	Tuition Waivers	Varies	25-2313		3.0		N	R	A	Y	O	B-4/1	N
	Valedictorian	Varies	1500	1-2			N	O	A	Y	N	B-C	N
	Honors Program												

FL Christian, Kissimmee 32743	Music Scholarships	2	1000				N	T	0	Y	0	C	N
	Bible Bowl	Varies	100-4300				N	E-T	A	N	O	C	Y
FL Inst. of Tech., Melbourne 32901	Astronaut	Varies	Varies		3.0		Y		0	3.0	N	B-3/1	
	Barnett Bank	Varies	Varies		3.0		Y		A		A-S	B-3/15	
	Cis Bank	Varies	Varies		3.0		Y		A		A-S	B-3/15	
	Ella J. Horn	Varies	Varies		3.0		Y		A	3.0	A-S	B-3/1	
	FIT Articulation		2500				N		A	3.0	A	B-3/1	Y
	FIT Faculty Merit		3500	10%			N		A	3.0	A-S-O	B-3/1	
	FIT Presidential		5000	5%		1200+	N		A	3.0	O	B-3/1	
	FIT Trustee		10000	1%		1200+	N		A	3.0	O	B-3/1	N
	FITCORP	Varies	1000-2500		3.5		N		A	3.5	A-S	B-2/28	
	FITGAP	110+	600-900			900-1100	N		A	N	N	A-D	Y
	Fl. Engineering Society	Varies	Full Tuition				N		O	3.0	A-O	B-12/16	
	Fl. Science Fair	Varies	Full Tuition				N			3.0	A	B	
	Foster	3-4	To 1000		3.0		Y		A	3.0	A-S	B-3/15	
	L.P. Whitehead	Varies	500-1500		3.0		Y		A	3.0	A-D-W	B-3/1	N
	Nat'l Action Council	Varies	250-2500	X	2.5	X	X		O	2.5	M-O	B-5/1	Y
	Nat'l Soc. Profes'l. Engin.	Varies	Full Tuition				N		O	3.0	N	B-11/15	
	Neese	Varies	Varies		3.0		N		O		O	B-3/15	
	Reliance Bank	Varies	Varies		3.0		Y		A		A-S	B-3/15	
	Selby	Varies	500-1500		3.0		Y		A	3.0	A	B-5/1	Y-3.0
	Sun Bank	2	Varies		3.0		Y		A		A-S	B-3/15	
	Susan Galds Eason	2	Varies		3.0		N		O		W-O	B-4/14	
	Wood	1	Varies		3.0		Y		O	3.0	N	B-3/15	
FL International U., Miami 33199	Academic Opportunity	35-50	600-1200		3.0	850	Y	R	A	2.3	S-M	B-1/30	N
	Faculty Scholars	100	1600	10%	3.5	1270/28	N		A	3.0	N	A-D	N
	Nat'l. Merit/Ach. Hispanic	Varies	3000-6600				N	O	A	3.0	N	A	N
	Phi Theta Kappa	1	2000	3			N	E-L-R-O	A	3.0	N	B-3/15	Y-3.0
	Theater & Music	Varies	500-1000					T			N	B-6/1	Y
	University Scholars	100	500		3.2	1140/25	N		A	3.0	N	A	N
	Val-Sal	Varies	1000-2000	1-2	3.5		N	R	A	N	N	A	N
	Honors Program												
Florida Memorial, Miami 33054	Honors Academic	75	1000	X	X	X	N		A	Y	N	X	N
Florida Southern, Lakeland 33802	Academic Merit	Varies	3000-6000	33%	3.2	1150/24	N		A	3.0	N	A-3/1	N
	Academic Recognition	Varies	1000-4000		3.5		N		A		N	A-3/1	Y-3.5
	Music/Fine Arts	Varies	500-3000				N	T-I-O	O	Y	N	B-D	Y
	AP Exams												
	Alumni Discounts, Family Discounts												

	Program	No. of Awards	Value Range	Award Criteria					Study Fields	Renew-ability	Restric-tions	Apply Date	Transfer
				Class Stndg.	Grade Avg.	SAT/ ACT	Need Based	Other					
FLORIDA *(Continued)*													
Florida State U., Tallahassee 32306	Accounting Excellence	28	500		3.5	1200/28	N		O	3.0	N	B-3/1	Y
	FSU Incentive	50	500-2000		2.6	900/20	Y		A	N	M	A-4/1	Y
	Leeb	20	200-2000		25.0	1200/27	Y		A			5/15	
	New Generation	14	300-600				Y	E-T-O	A	2.0	A	B-C	Y
	School of Music	150	200-1800				N	T	O	3.0	N	B-3/31	Y
	Science Research	4	1000		3.2	1000/23	N	O	A	3.2	A	B-C	N
	Selby	40	2000		3.0	1100/26	Y		A	X	3	A-3/1	Y
	SW Georgia	10	1200		3.5	1100/26	N		A	N	O	A-4/1	Y
	University	180	500-2000		3.9	1200/28	Y	R	A	3.2	A	B-12/15	N
	University Transfer	48	500-1000		3.5		Y	R	A	3.2	A-O	B-3/1	Y
Jacksonville U., 32211	Alumni Discounts												
	AP Exams												
	Fine Arts		Varies					T					
	Internships												
	Presidents	Varies	9000-14000	10%	3.3	1100	N	L-R-I-O	A	3.0	A-S	B-1/15	N
	Trustees	Varies	2000-5000		3.0	1000	N	L-O-R	A	3.0	N	A-2/15	Y-3.0
	University	Varies	5000-9000		3.5	1220							
	Williams	2	18920				N	E-L-O-R-I	A	3.0	N	B-12/31	N
	Honors Program												
Lynn University, Boca Raton 33431	Transfer Scholarship		2000-6000				N	O	A	3.0	N	A-9/1	Y
	Presidential	5	Tuition		3.75	1200/24	N		A	3.5	N	C	
	Florida Resident Award	Unlimited	7000	30%	3.0	1000/22	N		A	3.0	A	C	
	Honors Program												
Nova Southeastern U., Ft. Lauderdale 33314	Nova Honors Award	Varies	2000-7000		3.2		N	E-R-I-O	A	3.0	N	A	Y-3.2
Palm Beach Atlantic College, 33401	Christian Leadership	Unlimited	500-1500				N	R	A	2.0	N	B-D	Y
	Deans	Varies	500-1200		3.25	1000/24	N			3.25	N	A-C	Y-3.25
	Honors	30	1000-Tuition	5%	3.5	1200/29	Y	E-R-I-O	A	3.5	N	A-C	N
	Opportunity	Unlimited	500-1500				Y	O	A	Y	N	B-D	Y
	Phi Theta Kappa	10	3500		3.5		N	E-R-I-O	A	3.5	O	A-C	Y-3.5
	Presidential	Varies	500-1800		3.5	1100/26	Y	E-R-I-O	A	3.5	N	A-C	Y-3.5
Ringling School of Art & Design, Sarasota 34234	Portfolio	Unlimited	500-1000			930/23	N		A	3.0	N	B-D	Y
	Presidential	1	2500				N	T	O	Y	N	C	

Rollins, Winter Park 32789	Donald Cram	Varies	5000				N		0	3.2	N	C-3/15	N
	Ellen Harcourt	4	7500				Y	E-I-0	A	2.0	N	C-2/1	N
	Music Dept.	Varies	2000-5000				N	T	0	3.0	N	C-3/15	Y
	Nelson Music	Varies	7000				N	T	0	2.0	N	C-3/15	Y
	Parker Theater	Varies	6000				N	T	0	2.0	N	C-3/15	Y
	Presidential		1000-10000		3.2		N	E-0	A	3.2	N	C-2/1	N
St. Leo College, 33574	Trustees	3	1000-9900		3.5	1200/27	Y		A	3.5	N	B-3/1	N
	Presidential	12	1000-4950		3.25	1100/24	Y		A	3.25	N	B-3/1	N
	Honors Program												
St. Thomas U., Miami 33054	Presidential	50	375-3960	X	X	X	N	L-R	A	Y	N	A-4/1	Y
	Dean's	20	4000-5000				Y	E-0	A	3.0	N	5/15	N
	University	30	2500-3500				Y	E-0	A	2.5	N	5/15	N
	Achievement	40	1500-2500				Y	E-L	A	2.5	N	5/15	N
	Honors Program												
Stetson U., Deland 32724	Edmunds	4	22,385	10%	3.5	1300/30	N	E-I-L-R	A	3.0			
	Stetson	200	1500-7500		3.0	1000	N	I	A	2.7			
	Presidential	25	8000-10,000	10%	3.5	1300/30	N	I	A	2.7			
	AP Exams												
	Alumni Discounts												
	Internships												
	Honors Program												
U. of Central Florida, Orlando 32816	Presidential	Varies	500-5000	X	X	X	N		A	3.2			
	AP Exams												
	Distance Learning												
	Co-op, Internships												
	Honors Program												
U. of Florida, Gainesville 32611	National Merit	170	4,000	X	X	X							
	Achievement	39	4,000	X	X	X							
	National Hispanic	110	4,000	X	X	X							
U. of Miami, Coral Gables 33124	Bowman-Foster-Ashe	Varies	3/4 Tuition	1%	4.0	1360/31	N	R	A	Y	0	A-3/1	
	Henry K. Stanford	Varies	1/2 Tuition	10%	3.75	1270/28	N	R	A	Y	0	A-3/1	Y
	Isaac B. Singer	Varies	Tuition	1%	4.0	1360/31	N	R	A	Y	0	A-3/1	N
	Jay F.W. Pearson	Varies	5200	20%	3.5	1180/26	N	R	0	3.0	0	A-3/1	N
	Honors Program												
U. of North FL., Jacksonville 32216	Community College	5	1000		3.5		N	E-L-0	A	Y	A-S-0	B-3/31	Y
	Eartha M. M. White	10	1000		3.0	860/20	N		A	Y	M	B-3/3	N
	National Merit Finalist	3	4500-6780	X	X	X	N	0	A	3.2	N	B-3/3	N
	Pajcic	Varies	All Costs				N		A	Y	0	B-3/3	N

	Program	No. of Awards	Value Range	Award Criteria: Class Stndg.	Grade Avg.	SAT/ ACT	Need Based	Other	Study Fields	Renew-ability	Restric-tions	Apply Date	Transfer
FLORIDA *(Continued)*													
U. of North FL., Jacksonville 32216 *(Continued)*	Presidential-Int'l Baccal.	4	1500		3.0		N	E-R-O	O	3.0	N	B-3/3	N
	University	10	1200		3.5	1200/29	N	E-R-I-O	A	3.2	H	B-3/1	N
	Honors Program												
U of South Florida, Tampa 33620	Alumni	20	1000-2000		3.5	1000/23	N	E-L-O-R	A	N	O	B-2/1	Y
	Black Scholar	40	1500		3.0		N		A	3.0	A-M	A-6/1	Y
	Freshman Scholar	Varies	1000-1500		3.5	1200/28	N		A	X	H	B-1/15	N
	President's Endowed	3	800-1000	X	X	X	N	L	A	3.0	S	A-2/1	Y
U. of Tampa, 33606	Dean's	Unlimited	4500-5500		3.0		N		A	2.8			
	Presidential	Unlimited	5000-6500		3.5		N		A	3.0			
	Transfer	Unlimited	3000-6000		2.8		N		A	2.8			
	AP Exams												
	Co-op, Internships												
	Honors Program												
U. of West FL., Pensacola 32514	Achievement	Varies	1200		3.0		Y	R-O	A	3.0	N	B-D	Y
	Foundation	Varies	1000		3.0		Y	R-O	A	3.0	N	B-D	Y
	John C. Pace I	43	4000	10%			N	E-L-R-I-O	A	3.0	A-S	B-3/1	N
	John C. Pace II	8	1000				N		A	3.0		A-3/1	Y-3.0
	Minority Scholarship	21	1000				N	R	A	2.5	M	A	N
	National Achievement	Varies	1500-2500				N	O	A	3.0	N	A	N
	Presidential	5	1000	2%			N	R	A	3.0	N	A	N
	Talent Scholarship	12	1000		3.0		N	T-R-I	O	3.0	N	B-D	N
	Transfer	Varies	1000		3.0		N	O	A	3.0	S	C	Y-3.0
	AP Exams												
	Distance Learning												
	Co-op, Internships												
	Honors Program												
Warner Southern, Lake Wales 33853	Blackford Scholar	Varies	300-1500	X	3.2	X	N	T-L-O	A	N	N	B-4/1	N
Webber, Babson Park 33827	Academic	Varies	750-1300		3.25		N		A	3.25	O	A-8/15	Y-3.25
	Alumni	Varies	10% Tuition				Y	E-O	A	2.0	O	D	Y-2.0
	Florida Freshman	Varies	1000		2.0		Y	E-O	A	N	A	D	N
	Local	Varies	4000		2.0		Y	E-O	A	2.0	S	2/28	N
	Presidential	Varies	100-1000		2.0		Y	E-L-O	A	2.0	O	B-4/15	Y-2.0

	Souhail Sabbagh	Varies	500-2000		2.0		Y	E-L-O	A	2.0	O	A-7/15	Y-2.0
	Sunshine Scholars	Varies	4000		3.0	950/22	N	O	A	3.0	O	A	N
GEORGIA													
Agnes Scott, Decatur 30030	Presidential	3	21055	2%	3.8	1480	N	I	A	3.5			
	Honor	Varies	8500-15000	2%	3.25	1180	N	L-O-I-O	A	3.25			
	Achievement	20	7000	X	X	X	N	L	O	2.75			
Albany State U., 31705	ASU Foundation	Varies	2000		3.0	1000	N	L	A	3.0			
	Porter	5	3000		3.0	1100	N	L	A	3.0			
	Presidential	10	5400		3.5	1200	N	E-I-L-R	A	3.0			
	AP Exams												
	Distance Learning												
	Co-op, Internships												
	Honors Program												
Armstrong State, Savannah 31419	Miscellaneous	80	500-1000	25%	3.0	1000	Y	E-T-L-O-R	A	3.0	N	B-5/31	Y-3.0
	Honors Program												
Atlanta Christian, East Point 30344	Honors Scholarship	Varies	1000			1000/23	Y		A	N	O	A	N
	Spring Spectacular	Varies	1000-1500				N	T-O	A		N	D	Y
	Bible Bowl	Varies	1160-4640				N	E-T	A		N	D	N
Atlanta College of Art 30309	Dean's	Varies	1000			1200/27	N		A	N	N	A	Y
	Presidential	Varies	500-1000		3.5	1200/27	N	R-T	A	3.5	N	A-2/16	Y-3.5
	School of Excellence	Varies	1000				N	R-T	A	N	N	A	Y
	AP Exams												
	Internships												
Augusta College, Augusta 30910	Boyd Music	2	Tuition & Fees		3.0		N	E-T-R-I-O	O	3.0	N	B-3/1	Y-3.0
	Clay Mitchell Skelton	1	500-657		3.0		Y	E-R	A	3.0	N	B-3/1	Y-3.0
	Faculty/Alum. Schol. Fund	6	Tuition & Fees	5%	3.0	1000	N	E-R-O	A	3.5	N	B-3/1	N
	Frank M. Green Memorial	1	500-3309		3.0		Y	E-R	O	3.0	N	B-3/1	Y-3.0
	Free School Scholarship	10	Tuition & Fees		3.0	1000	N	E-R-O	A	3.0	N	B-3/1	N
	J. Clay Flanders	1	500-808		3.0		N	E-L-R	O	3.0	N	B-3/1	Y-3.0
	Jack/Mary Craven Schol.	1	Tuition & Fees		3.0		Y	E-R-O	A	3.0	O	B-3/1	Y-3.0
	Katherine R. Pamplin	3	750-1710		3.0		N	E-R	A	3.0	N	B-3/1	Y-3.0
	LeRoy Memorial	1	500-849		3.0		N	E-R	A	3.0	N	B-3/1	Y-3.0
	Louise Smith McCollum	1	1428		3.0		N	E-L-R	A	3.0	O	B-3/1	Y-3.0
	W. Bruce McCollum	1	1276		3.0		N	E-L-R	A	3.0	O	B-3/1	Y-3.0
	William T. Maxwell Honor	1	500-3000		3.0		N	E-R	O	3.0	N	B-3/1	Y-3.0
	Honors Program												

	Program	No. of Awards	Value Range	Award Criteria: Class Stndg.	Grade Avg.	SAT/ ACT	Need Based	Other	Study Fields	Renew-ability	Restric-tions	Apply Date	Transfer
GEORGIA *(Continued)*													
Berry, Mt. Berry 30149	Academic	Varies	2350-7000		3.0-3.5	Varies	N		A	3.0	N	A-2/1	N
	Phi Theta Kappa	Varies	2850-3200		3.4		N	0	A	3.0	0	A-2/1	Y-3.0
	Presidential	10	Tuition		3.75	1450/33	N		A	3.0	N	A-2/1	N
	Transfer	Varies	1500-3200		3.4		N		A	3.0	N	A-2/1	Y-3.0
	Honors Program												
Brenau, Gainesville 30501	Brenau Scholars	5	1300		3.5	46	N	E-R-I-0	A	3.5	W	B-C	N
	Faculty Excellence	Unlimited	1000-4000		3.0	900	N	R-I-0	A	3.0	W	C	Y-3.0
	Salutatorian	Unlimited	1500	2			N	R-I-0	A	N	W	C	N
	Talent	20	500-5000				N	T-R-I-0	0	Y	N	C	Y
	Trustee	40	2000-8000		3.0	48	N	R	A	3.0	W	B-C	Y-3.0
	Valedictorian	Unlimited	1500	1			N	R-I-0	A	N	W	C	N
	Honors Program												
Columbus College, 31993	Academic	Varies	1600		3.0	1100	N	L	A	3.2	N	B-3/1	Y-3.5
	Fine Arts	Varies	200-2000				N	E-T-I-0	0	Y	N	C	Inq.
	Honors Program												
Emory U., Atlanta 30322	Emory Scholar	100	To All Costs	10%	3.7	1480/32	N	E-I-L-R-T	A	3.25			
	AP Exams												
	Internships												
	Honors Program												
Fort Valley State C., 31030	James H. Porter	Varies	3000-3600		3.0	1000	N	E-L-I	A	3.0	A	B-4/1	Y
	Regents'	Varies	300-750	X	3.0	X	Y		A	3.0	A	B-4/1	Y
GA College, Milledgeville 31061	Outstanding Student	20	Tuition/Fees		3.3	1000	N	T-L-R-I-0	A	3.2	N	B-2/3	Y-3.3
	Presidential	3	2100		3.5	1100	N	R	A	3.2	N	B-2/3	N
	Honors Program												
Georgia Southern, Statesboro 30460	Southern	5	1000-3000	5%	3.5	1270/26	N	E-L-0-R	A	3.2	N	B-12/1	N
	Presidential	16	1000	10%	3.2	1100/26	N	E-L-0-R	A	N	N	B-12/1	N
	General	20	Varies	X	X	X	Varies		A	Varies	VarOMs	A-4/15	Y
Georgia Southwestern, Americus 31709	Wheatley	Varies	2500		3.0	1050/23	N	L	A	3.0	N	B-4/1	N
	Roney	Varies	2000		3.0	1050/23	N	L	A	3.0	N	B-4/1	N
	Transfer	Varies	1000		3.25		N	L	A	3.0	N	B-7/1	Y

Georgia State U., Atlanta 30303	Leadership	Varies	Tuition		3.2	1000	N	R	A	Y	A	B-5/1	N
Georgia Tech., Atlanta, 30332	Merit Award	Varies	1100				N		A	3.0	N	C	Inq.
	Presidential	Varies	6250		3.2	1350	N	E-R-I	A	3.2	N	C	Inq.
	President's	70	1100-7000		3.9	1350	N	O	A	3.2	N	B-11/15	N
	President's Tuition	Varies	1960		3.2	1400	N	E-R-I	A	3.2	N	C	Inq.
	Recognition	Varies	1300		3.2	1400	N	E-R-I	A	3.2	N	C	Inq.
LaGrange College, 30240	Academic Merit	Varies	1000-4500		3.0	1100	N		A	3.0	N	A	N
	Art & Theatre	1-2	1000-2000				N	T	O	Y	N	B-4/1	N
	Candler	Varies	1000-3000		3.25	1100	N		A	3.25	N	C	Y
	Cunningham	10	4500-5500		3.5	1150/27	N	I	A	3.0	N	A-1/31	N
	Emily Fisher Crum	Varies	1000-3000		3.0	1100/26	N	E	A	3.0	N	C	Y
	John & Mary Franklin	Varies	1000-2000		3.0	1100/26	N	E	A	3.0	N	C	Y
	Mary L. Dodd	1	500-1000				N	T	O	Y	N	C	Y
	Presidential	1	9726-10,389		3.5	1150/27	N	I	A	3.0	N	A-1/31	N
	AP Exams												
	Internships												
Mercer U., Atlanta 30341	Outstanding Student	10	1000	25%	3.3	1000	N	L-O-I-O	A	3.3	N	B-5/1	Y
Mercer U., Macon 31207	Academic Merit	100	500-7000		3.0	1000/24	N	O	A	Y	O	C	Y
	Engineering Exam Schp.	69	4500		3.0		N	E-R-O	O	Y	N	C	Y-3.0
Morehouse, Atlanta 30314	Academic	85-100	1500-9800	25%	3.0	1100/26	N	E-L-R-I-O	A	3.0	O	A-2/15	N
	Honors Program												
Morris Brown, Atlanta 30314	Academic	30	5000-7244		3.1	900/20	Y	E-L-R	A	3.0	N	B-4/1	N
	Presidential	30	6500-13133	10%	3.5	1100/25	Y	E-L-R	A	3.2	N	B-4/1	N
North Georgia, Dahlonega 30597	Academic	Varies	1000		3.0	1150	N	T-L	A	3.0	N	B-4/1	N
	Dismukes	1	1050		3.0	900	N	T-R-I-O	O	3.0	N	B-12/1	N
	Gloria Shott	3	1050		3.0	900	N	T-R-I-O	O	3.0	N	B-12/1	N
	Military	Varies	Total Costs		3.0	900	N	L-R-O	A	2.5	A	B-12/31	Y
	NGC	Varies	1000-3000		3.0	1000	N	L-O	A	3.0	N	B-1/31	Y
	Honors Program												
Paine, Augusta 30910	Freshman	20	1200		3.0	700	N	R	A	Y	N	B-7/15	N
	Presidential	Varies	Tuition		4.0	1000	N	R	A	Y	N	B-7/15	N
Piedmont, Demorest 30535	Academic	Varies	To 9260	10%		1000	Y	O	A	3.4	O	B-2/5	N
	Alumni	30	1000				Y	E-L-O	A	Y	O	B-4/1	Y
	Congregational	Varies	1000-6000				Y	L-R-I-O	A	2.5	D-O	B-C	Y-2.5
	International	8	500-2000				Y	I	A	Y	O	B	Y
	Leadership	Varies	2000				N	L-O	A	Y	O	C	Y
	Merit	Varies	500-2000				Y	E-L-R	A	Y			Y

	Program	No. of Awards	Value Range	Award Criteria: Class Stndg.	Grade Avg.	SAT/ ACT	Need Based	Other	Study Fields	Renew-ability	Restric-tions	Apply Date	Transfer
GEORGIA *(Continued)*													
Piedmont, Demorest 30535 *(Continued)*	Music/Art/Theatre	12	1000				N	T-R-I-O	O	Y	O	C	Y
	Presidential	7-12	4000	15%	3.0	1000	N	E-L-R-I-O	A	3.0	O	B-C	N
	Transfer Honor	7-12	1000-2000		3.0		Y	L-R-I-O	A		N	B-C	Y-3.0
	Trustee's	Varies	To Tuition	10%		1000	N	O	A	3.0	O	B-2/5	N
	AP Exams												
	Distance Learning												
	Family Discounts												
	Co-op, Internships												
	Honors Program												
Savannah College of Art and Design Savannah 31401	E. C. Williams	Varies	2000-5000				N	O	A	3.0	O	A	Y
	Friedman	Varies	4000-10000			1400/33	N	O	A	3.0	O	A	Y
	Henderson	Varies	1500			X	N	O	A	3.0	O	A	Y
	International Competition	Varies	2000-5000				N	E-T-R	A	3.0	N	B	Y
	Portfolio Scholarship	Varies	2000-5000				N	E-T-R-I-O	A	3.0	O	A-D	N
	Trustees	Varies	2000-5000	1	4.0		N	O	A	3.0	O	A	Y
	Whelan	Varies	2000-5000			1200/27	N	O	A	3.0	O	A	Y
Shorter, Rome 30161	Academic	Unlimited	1000-3730	15%	3.25	1200/28	N	R-O	A	3.25	N	B-4/1	Y-3.25
	Music	Unlimited	500-3250				N	T-R	O	3.25	N	A-8/1	Y
	Presidential	Unlimited	2550	1	X	X	N	R-I-O	A	3.3	N	A-8/1	N
	Honors Program												
Southern C. of Technology, Marietta 30060	SCT Academic	5-7	500-1500		3.5		N	R	A	N	A-O	B-4/1	N
Spelman, Atlanta 30314	Dean's Full	25	To All Costs	10%	3.8	1400	N		A	3.1			
	Dean's Academic	40	3500	15%	3.5	1350	N		A	3.1			
	Presidential	5	To All Costs	10%	3.0	1300	N	E-L-R-T	A	3.0			
	AP Exams												
	Co-op												
	Honors Program												
Toccoa Falls, 30598	TFC	30	500	1-5	3.5	1100/21	N		A	N	N	A-6/1	Y
	Music	10	500-1000				N	T-I-O	O	N	N	C-6/1	Y
	Honor/Academic	Varies	500-1000	1-5	3.5	1100/21	N		A	N	N	A-6/1	Y
U. of Georgia, Athens 30602	Charter	top 5%	1000-2000		3.5	1300/31	N	L-O	A	Y	N	A	N

	Foundation	20-25	All Costs	1%	3.5-4.0	1450/31	N	E-I-L-R-0	A	Y		B-12/1	N
	Transfer	25	2000		3.0		N		A		N	B	Y
	Vice Presidential	Varies	1000-2000		3.5	1300/31	N	L-0	A	Y		A	N
	AP Exams												
	Co-op, Internships												
	Honors Program												
Valdosta State, 31698	Odums Scholarship	25	1000-2000		3.0	1230/28	N	L-0	A	3.0	N	C	N
	Whitehead	2	1500		3.0	1230/28	N	L-0	A	3.0	N	C	Y
	AP Exams												
	Distance Learning												
	Co-op												
	Honors Program												
Wesleyan, Macon 31297	Academic	Varies	3500-12500		3.3	1100/24	N	E-I-0	A	3.3	W	B-1/15	Y-3.0
	Pierce Leadership	Varies	4000		2.8		N	E-L-R-I-0	A	2.8	W	B-1/15	N
	Pierce Talent	Varies	500-4000				N	T-I-0	0	Y	W	B-D	Y
	Honors Program												
West Georgia, Carrollton 30118	Presidential	15	Tuition		3.5	1100	N	E-T-L-0-I	A	3.2	N	B-3/15	N
	Miscellaneous	100+	300-1422		3.0	1000	N	R-0	A	3.2	0	C-3/15	Y-3.0
	Honors Program												
HAWAII													
Brigham Young U., Laie 96762	Academic	Varies	560-3960	10%	3.5	1200/25	N	E-L-R-I-0	A	3.5	N	B-6/30	Y
	Talent Awards	Varies	675		2.0		N	T	0	2.0	N		
Chaminade U., Honolulu 96816	Academic	Unlimited	3000-5300		2.25-3.5		N	E-L-0-R	A	Y	N	B-4/1	Y
	Hawaii Grant	Varies	3000				N		A	Y	A	B-4/1	
	Chaminade Transfer	Varies	3000		2.5		N		A		0	B-4/1	Y
Hawaii Pacific U., Honolulu 96813	President's	Varies	3350-7100	10%	3.25	1000/27	N	E-L-0-R	A	3.25	A-0	B-3/15	N
	Phi Theta Kappa	Varies	3350		3.5		N	E-R-0	A	3.5	0	B-6/1	Y-3.5
	Honors Program												
U. of Hawaii, Hilo 96720	Talented Students	25	Tuition				N	T	A	Y	H	B-C	Y
U. of Hawaii at Manoa, Honolulu 96822	Pacific Asian	Varies	Tuition		3.7		N		0	3.7	N	B-C	Y
	Presidential	10	4000+		3.7		N	E-T-L-R	A	Y	S	B-2/1	Y
	Regents'	20	4000+	5%	3.5	1200	N	E-T-L-R	A	Y	S	B-2/1	N
	Tuition Waiver	Varies	Tuition	5%	3.5		N		A	3.5	0	C	Y
	Honors Program												
West Oahu, Pearl City 96782	Chancellor's	Varies	Tuition		3.5		N	E-T-L-0	A	3.5	0	B-10/1	Y-3.5
	Pacific Asian	5	To Tuition		3.5		N	E	0	3.5	0	B-C	Y

	Program	No. of Awards	Value Range	Award Criteria: Class Stndg.	Grade Avg.	SAT/ ACT	Need Based	Other	Study Fields	Renew-ability	Restric-tions	Apply Date	Transfer
HAWAII *(Continued)*													
West Oahu, Pearl City 96782 *(Continued)*	Presidential	Varies	Tuition		3.7		N	E-T-L-O-R	A	3.7	A-O	B-1/15	Y-3.7
	Ruth E. Black	1	Varies		3.5		N		A	3.5	O	C	N
IDAHO													
Albertson College of Idaho, Caldwell 83605	ACI Grant	Unlimited	100-3300				N		A	2.0	N	A-D	Y
	Endowed Scholarships	Unlimited	100-5000										
	Honor Student	Unlimited	1500-4000		X	1090/24	N		A	3.0	N	A-D	Y
	McCain Family	1	All Costs		3.0		Y	O	A	3.0	S	C	N
	Moore Cunningham	20	2000		3.0		Y	O	A	3.0	A	C	Y
	Performance	Unlimited	100-14100		X		N	T	A	2.0	N	A-D	Y
Boise State U., 83725	Academic	974	200-1500		3.0		N		A	N	N	B-3/1	Y
	President's/Dean's	100+	800-1876		3.5		N		A	N	N	B-3/1	N
	Honors Program												
Idaho State U., Pocatello 83209	Freshman	200	100-2180		3.0	20	N	L	A	N			
	Kasiska	50	2000-3000		3.0	25	Y		A	3.3			
	Presidential	50	2000-3000		3.7	25	N		A	3.3			
	AP Exams												
	Distance Learning												
	Co-op, Internships												
	Honors Program												
Lewis-Clark State, Lewiston 83501	Alumni	Varies	100-600		2.0		N	R	A	N	O	B-3/1	Y
	Johnson	10-20	1000-1500		3.0		Y	L-O	O	3.0	N	B-3/1	Y-3.0
	Presidential	97	500		3.5		N	R	A	3.25	N	B-3/1	Y
Northwest Nazarene, Nampa 83686	Activity	Varies	500-1000				N	T-L-O-R	A	2.0	N	B-3/1	Y
	Honor	Unlimited	600-1200		3.4	1000/22	N		A	3.2	N	B	Y
	Honor/Academic	Varies	600-2450		3.4	1000/22	N	L-R-O	A	3.2	N	B-3/1	Y
	President's	10	4000		3.7		N	T-L-R	A	3.3	N	B-3/1	N
U. of Idaho, Moscow 83843	Academic	Varies	100-4000				N		A		N	A-3/1	Y
	Activity	Varies	700.00				N	T-L	A		N	A-3/1	Y
	Alumni Assn. Award	Unlimited	100.00				N	O	A	N	N	A-2/15	Y
	Honors	Varies	1620		3.7	1200/28	N		A	Y	N	A-3/8	N

	Presidential	600.00	500-1000		3.7		N		A		N	A-8/1	Y-3.7
	Scholarship of Merit	Unlimited	1000.00				N	0	A	2.5	N	A-8/1	N
	Tuition Waiver	95	6000				N		A		N	A-2/15	Y
	UI Scholars	Varies	3000		3.5	1420/32	N		A	2.5	N	A-2/15	N
	Honors Program												
ILLINOIS													
Augustana College, Rock Island 61202	Honor	Varies	3500				N	0	A	3.2	N	A-D	3.5
	Performance	Varies	300-2000				N	T-0	A	Y	N	C	Y
	Presidential	50	6984-13968				N	0	A	3.25	N	B-C	N
	Honors Program												
Aurora U., 60506	Alumni Legacy	Varies	1000				N	E-T-L-R-0	A	3.0	0	A-5/1	3.0
	Board of Trustees	Varies	1/2-Full Tuition			26	N	E-T-L-R-0	A	3.0	N	A-5/1	3.0
	Crimi Presidential	Varies	To 1/2 Tuition	10%	3.0	24	N	E-T-L-R-0	A	3.0	N	A-5/1	3.0
	Dean's	Varies	To 3500	25%	3.0	22	N	E-T-L-R-0	A	3.0	N	A-5/1	3.0
	Nursing	Varies	3000				N	E-T-L-R-0	0	3.0	N	A-5/1	3.0
	Phi Theta Kappa	Varies	3500		3.5		N	E-T-L-R-0	A	3.0	N	A-5/1	3.0
	Presidential Minority Ach.	Varies	Total Costs	20%			N	E-T-L-R-0	A	3.0	M	A-5/1	3.0
	Science	Varies	1/2 Tuition			24	N	E-T-L-R-0	0	3.0	N	A-5/1	3.0
	Transfer	Varies	3500		3.0		N	E-T-L-R-0	A	3.0	N	A-5/1	3.0
	Honors Program												
Benedictine University, Lisle 60532	IB Scholars	20	To 6500	20%		28	N	E-L-I-0	A	3.2	N		Y-3.2
	Minority	50	500-4000	33%	2.5	17	N	L-R-0	A	2.5	M	A	Y-2.5
	Music	10	500-2500	50%	2.0	21	N	T-0	A	2.5	N		Y-2.0
	St. Benedict	Unlimited	750-6000	50%		21	N	0	A	3.0	N	A-B	Y-3.0
	AP Exams												
	Distance Learning												
	Alumni Discounts, Family Discounts												
	Co-op, Internships												
	Honors Program												
Blackburn, Carlinville 62626	Academic Achievement	Varies	1000		X		N		A	3.5	0	A	Y-3.5
	Honor Award	Varies	3000	10%	3.3	1050/24	N		A	Y	0	A	N
	Presidential	4	5000	10%	3.3	1050/24	N	L-R-I-0	A	Y	0	B	N
	Community Service Award	28	3000				N	L-R	A	Y	0	B	N
Bradley U., Peoria 61625	Transfer	Unlimited	1000-5000		3.0		N	R	A	3.0			Y
	Dean's Merit	Unlimited	3000-1/2 Tuit.	10%		1240/28	N		A	3.0			
	Presidential	50	Tuition				N	0	A	3.0			
	AP Exams												
	Alumni Discounts												

	Program	No. of Awards	Value Range	Award Criteria: Class Stndg.	Grade Avg.	SAT/ ACT	Need Based	Other	Study Fields	Renew-ability	Restric-tions	Apply Date	Transfer
ILLINOIS *(Continued)*													
Bradley U., Peoria 61625 *(Continued)*	Co-op, Internships												
	Honors Program												
Chicago State U., 60628	CSU Scholars	Varies	Tuition	20%	B	23	N	E-R	A	Y	N	C	N
College of St. Francis, Joliet 60435	Community College	25	1000-3000		3.0	1200/27	N	0	A	Y	N	A-5/1	Y-3.0
	Presidential	15	4000-6000	15%		1250/28	N	I-0	A	Y	N	A-3/1	N
	Trustee	30	2000-4000	25%	3.0	1150/25	N	I-0	A	Y	N	A-3/1	N
	Biology Fellows	3	3000	15%	3.25	1200/27	N	R-I-0	0	Y	N	A-3/1	N
Columbia, Chicago 60605	Ferguson	Varies	3270	X	X	X	Y	E-R	A	Y	N	B-4/15	Y
	Fischetti	Varies	3270				Y	E-T-R	0	N	N	B-4/15	Y
Concordia, River Forest 60305	Presidential	Varies	1000-10500		3.0	24	N	R-0	0	2.5	N	A	N
	Music	Varies	Varies				N	T-R-0	0	N	N	B-D	Y
	Merit	Varies	600-2400		3.25		N	R-0	A	2.5	0	A	Y-3.0
	Honors Program												
DePaul U., Chicago 60604	Arthur J. Schmitt	30	9000	10%	3.5	1220/27	N	E-L-R-I-0	0	3.3	0	B-1/15	N
	Associate's Degree Transfer	30	1500-4000		3.3		N	E-R-I-0	A	3.0	S-0	A-B-7/1	Y
	Dean's Art	10-12	1000-8000	50%	2.5	X	N	E-T-R-I-0	0	2.5	0	A-B-1/15	Y-2.0
	Dean's Business	80	2000-8000	10%	3.5	1220/27	N	E-L-R-I-0	0	3.3	0	A-B-1/15	N
	Dean's Business Transfer	40	1500-4000		3.3		N	E-R-I-0	0	3.0	S-0	A-B-7/1	Y
	Dean's Education	30	2000-8000	10%	3.3	1220/27	N	E-R-I-0	0	Y	0	A-B-1/15	Y-3.3
	Dean's Honors	40	2000-8000	10%	3.3	1220/27	N	E-R-I-0	0	2.75	0	B-1/15	N
	Dean's Science	40	2000-8000	10%	3.5	1220/27	N	E-R-I-0	0	Y	0	B-1/15	N
	Dean's Theatre Design	20	1000-8000	50%	2.3		N	T-R-0	0	2.5	0	A-B-3/1	Y-2.0
	Dean's Theatre Studies	20	1000-8000	50%	2.3		N	T-R-0	0	2.5	0	A-B-3/1	Y-2.0
	Debate	5	1000-6000	50%	2.3		N	E-T-R-I-0	A	2.75	0	B-1/15	N
	Fritz A. Bauer	30	9000	10%	3.5	1220/27	N	E-L-R-I-0	0	3.3	0	B-1/15	N
	John Cardinal Newman	40	2000-8000	1	3.5	1220/27	N	E-L-R-I-0	A	3.3	0	B-1/15	N
	Ledger-Quill	1	Tuition	10%	3.5	1220/27	N	E-L-R-I-0	0	3.3	0	B-1/15	N
	Ledger-Quill Minority	1	Tuition	10%	3.5	1220/27	N	E-L-R-I-0	0	3.3	M-0	B-1/15	N
	Ledger-Quill Transfer	2	1/2 to Full Tuit.		3.3		N	E-R-I-0	0	3.0	0	B-7/1	N
	Mayor's Leadership 2000	8	5000				N	E-L-R-I-0	A	2.75	S-0	B-4/1	Y-2.5
	Melvoin/Strobel	3	1/2 Tuition	10%	3.5	1220/27	N	E-L-R-I-0	0	3.3	0	B-1/15	N
	Monsignor John Egan's	2-3	10000				N	E-L-R-I-0	A	2.75	S-M-0	B-4/1	N

	Music Performance	60	1000-8000				N	T-R-0	0	Y	0	D	Y-2.0
	Phi Theta Kappa	10	1500-4000		3.3		N	E-R-I-0	A	3.0	0	B-4/1	Y
	Presidential	250	2000-8000	10%	3.3	1220/27	N	E-L-R-0	A	3.0	0	B-1/15	N
	Theatre Performance	5	3000				N	T-R-I-0	0	2.5	0	A-B-3/1	Y-2.0
	University Transfer	20	1500-4000		3.3		N	E-R-I-0	A	3.0	S-0	A-B-7/1	Y
	Honors Program												
Dominican, River Forest 60305	Honor	Varies	Varies	10%			N	0	A	3.0	N	A	Y
	Study Abroad	5	5000	20%		1000/24	N	E-R	A	3.0	N	B-2/1	N
	Parish Leadership	20	Varies		2.5		N	L-R	A	2.5	N	C	Y-2.5
	Presidential	2	Full Tuition	10%	3.5	1000/26	N	E-L-I	A	3.5	N	A-3/1	N
	Phi Theta Kappa	Varies	2500				N	R-0	A	3.0	N		Y
	AP Exams												
	Alumni Discounts, Family Discounts												
	Internships												
	Honors Program												
Eastern Illinois U., Charleston 61920	Academic Achievement	10	1000	10%	3.25	X	N	T-L-R	A	N	S	B-4/1	Y
	Talented Student	280	100-Tuition				N	T	A	Y	S	C	Y
Elmhurst College, 60126	Academic Achievement	20	1/2 Tuition	20%	3.5	1140/25	N	I	A	3.0			
	AP Exams												
	Distance Learning												
	Family Discounts												
	Co-op, Internships												
	Honors Program												
Eureka College, 61530	Deans	Unlimited	4000-5000	20%	3.5	25	N		A	3.0			
	Fine Arts	Varies	500-5000				N	T-I-0	A	Y	N	B-2/15	Y
	Presidential	Unlimited	5000-6000	10%	3.5	28	N	I	A	3.0			
	Reagan	5	Tuition		3.5	28	N	E-I-L-R	A	3.0			
	AP Exams												
	Alumni Discounts, Family Discounts												
	Internships												
	Honors Program												
Greenville College, 62246	Achievement	Varies	800-1000		3.25		Y	L	A	3.3	N	A-D	Y-3.25
	Honor	Varies	500-1500	10%			Y		A	3.20	N	A-D	N
	Leadership	Varies	500-1000	20%	3.0		Y	T-L-R	A	2.3	N	A-D	Y-3.0
	Presidential	6	2500	10%	3.3	X	N	E-I-0	A	3.25	N	A-D	N
	Honors Program												
Governors State U., University Park 60466	Community College Schp.	Varies	Tuition		3.5		N	L-R-I	A	3.5	S-0	B-C	Y-3.5
	Talent Tuition Waivers	30	Varies		X		N	E-R	A	Y	N	B-C	Y
	Alumni Academic	Varies	200-400		3.75		N		A	3.75	N	B-5/1	Y

	Program	No. of Awards	Value Range	Award Criteria					Study Fields	Renew-ability	Restric-tions	Apply Date	Transfer
				Class Stndg.	Grade Avg.	SAT/ ACT	Need Based	Other					
ILLINOIS *(Continued)*													
Governors State U., University Park 60466 *(Continued)*	GSU Tuition Waivers	Varies	Tuition				N	O	A		O	B-C	Y
	Honors Program												
Illinois College, Jacksonville 62650	Alumni	8	1/2 Tuition	10%		1200/27	N	E-O	A	3.0	N	C	N
	I.C. Honor	Varies	1000-2000	10%	3.0	1010/22	Y	R-O	A	3.0	N	B-4/1	N
	Presidential	48	1600	10%	3.0	1160/26	N	L-R-O	A	3.0	N	B-4/1	Y-3.0
	Talent	20	500				N	T-L-O	A	Y	N	C	
	Trustee	4	Full Tuition	10%		1200/27	N	E-O	A	3.25	N	C	N
Illinois Inst. of Tech., Chicago 60616	Camras	30	12000-22000	10%	3.5	1250	Y	E-L-R-E-O	O	3.25	N	B-C	N
	Gunbaulus	20	7920	10%	3.5	1250	Y	E-L-R-I-O	O	3.0	N	B-C	N
	Heald	58	920	10%	3.5	1250	Y	E-L-R	A	3.0	N	B-C	N
	Presidential	90	3000-5600	25%	3.6	1100	N	R	A	2.5	N	C	N
Illinois State U. Normal 61790	Pres. Scholars Program	45	3000-6000				N	E-L-R-I-O	A	3.3	N	B-2/15	N
	Community Coll. Fndn. Schp.	25	500-2000		3.3		N	E-L-O	A	Y	O	B-12/31	Y-3.3
	Honors Program												
Illinois Wesleyan, Bloomington 61702	Alumni	Unlimited	3000-11000	25%		1240/28	N	I-O	A	3.0	N	A-D	N
	Alumni Talent	Unlimited	3000-16300	25%			N	T-I-O	O		N	A-D	Y
Judson, Elgin 60120	Adoniram Judson	Unlimited	2000	20%	3.25	1120/25	N	E-I-O	A	3.0	N	A-D	Y-3.5
	Benjamin Browne	Unlimited	1600	25%	3.0	1050/23	N	E-I-O	A	3.0	N	A-D	Y-3.3
	Norma Vincent Peale	5	4000	10%	3.5	1200/27	N	E-I-O	A	3.3	O	A-12/1	N
	Honors Program												
Kendall, Evanston 60201	Honor Scholarship	Unlimited	2500	25%		24	N		A	3.0	N	D	N
	Trustee Scholarship	Unlimited	2500		3.0		N		A	3.0	N	D	Y
	Minority Scholarship	Unlimited	3000	50%			Y		A		M	D	N
	VICA Culinary	3	750-1500				N	E-T-O	O	N	N	C	N
Knox, Galesburg 61401	Academic	Varies	3000-5000				N	O	A	3.0	N	A-2/15	N
	Art	Varies	1500-3000				N	T-R-I-O	A	Y	N	C-2/15	N
	Colorado	1	7500	10%			N	E-L-R-I-O	A	3.0	S	C-2/15	N
	Dow Chemical	1	4000				N	E-R	O	3.0	N	A-2/15	N
	Finley	1	7500	10%			N	E-L-R-I-O	A	3.0	S	C-2/15	N
	Lincoln	12	Tuition	5%			N	E-L-R-I-O	A	3.3	N	C-2/15	N
	Muelder	Varies	7500	5%			N	E-L-R-I-O	A	3.0	N	C-2/15	N

	Root	Varies	5000	10%			N	E-L-R-I-O	A	3.0	M	C-2/15	N
	Scripps	Varies	5000	10%			N	E-L-R-I-O	A	3.0	N	C-2/15	N
	Stephens	1	4000				N	E-R	O	3.0	N	A-2/15	N
	Theatre	Varies	1500-3000				N	T-R-I-O	A	Y	N	C-2/15	N
	Transfer	Varies	7500		3.5		N	L-R-O	A	3.0	O	C-4/1	Y
	Writing	Varies	1500-3000				N	T-R-I-O	A	Y	N	C-2/15	N
	*Honors Program												
Lake Forest College, 60045	Presidential	120	6000-19,800	20%	3.5	28	N	E	A	3.0	S	2/1	N
	Founders'	80	6000-19,800	20%	3.5	26	N	E	A	3.0	N	12/1	N
	Deerpath	100	1000-9000	20%	3.5	24	N	I-L-R-T	A	2.75	N		Y-3.5
Lewis U., Romeoville 60446	Academic	Varies	3500-6000	50%	3.0	870	N		A	2.5	N	A	N
	Alumni	Varies	1000				N	O	A	2.25	N		Y
	Talent	Varies	Varies				N	T	O	Y	N		Y
	Transfer	Varies	2500-3500		2.5		N		A	2.5	N	A	Y
	AP Exams												
	Distance Learning												
	Internships												
	Honors Program												
Loyola U., Chicago 60611	Academic	Varies	1000-Tuition	10%		1150/27	Y		A	Y	N	B-5/1	Y
	Condon	2	Tuition				N	O	O	Y	N	B-3/1	N
	First National Bank	Varies	Tuition	10%		1250/28	N	L-I	O	Y	N	A-1/31	N
	Honorary	Varies	1000	10%		1150/27	N		A	Y	N	B-5/1	Y
	Honors	3	Tuition				N	E-I-O	O	Y	N	B-3/15	N
	Plocieniak	Varies	Varies				N	E-O	A	Y	O	B-5/1	N
	Public Accounting	1	2500				N		O	Y	N	B-3/1	N
	Theatre	Varies	Varies				N	T-O	O	Y	N	B-2/15	N
MacMurray, Jacksonville 62650	Fine Arts	Varies	250-1000				N	T-R	O	Y	N	C	Inq.
	Honor	Unlimited	500-5000	40%	3.0	1050/22	N	O	A	3.0	N	C	N
	Music Talent Waiver	Varies	1000-8000				N	E-T-R-I-O	A	2.5	N	C	Y
	AP Exams												
	Alumni Discounts, Family Discounts												
	Co-op, Internships												
	Honors Program												
McKendree, Lebanon 62254	Community Service	Varies	1000-Tuition				N	E-L-R	A	2.0	N	C-5/1	N
	Music	Varies	500-4000				N	T	O	Y	N	A-2/15	Y
	Presidential	Varies	1000-Tuition	20%	3.4	25	N	R-I-O	A	2.8	N	C-3/1	Y-3.0
	AP Exams												
	Distance Learning												
	Internships												
	Honors Program												

	Program	No. of Awards	Value Range	Class Stndg.	Grade Avg.	SAT/ ACT	Need Based	Other	Study Fields	Renew- ability	Restric- tions	Apply Date	Transfer
				Award Criteria									
ILLINOIS *(Continued)*													
Millikin U., Decatur 62522	Art Talent	Unlimited	500-1/2 Tuition				N	T	0	2.0	N	C	Y
	Millikin Scholars	Unlimited	6250	12%	3.5	1200/27	X	L-R-I-O	A	3.2	N	A-D	N
	Music Talent	Unlimited	500-1/2 Tuition				Y	T	A	2.0	N	C	Y
	No Need	Unlimited	6250	10%	3.6	1200/27	N		A	3.0	N	A-D	Y
	Presidential	5	Tuition	10%	3.5	1200/27	N	L-R-I-O	A	3.7	N	A-D	N
	Theater Talent	Unlimited	500-1/2 Tuition				N	T	0	2.0	N	C	Y
	Valedictorian	Unlimited	1/2 Tuition	1	3.9		N		A	3.0	N	A-D	Y
Monmouth, 61462	Bagpipe	2	Tuition				N	T-R-I-O	A	Y	N	D	N
	Bagpipe Drummer	1	Tuition				N	T-R-I-O	A	Y	N	D	N
	Named Endowed	75	1250	15%		25	N	L-R-I-O	A	Y	N	A-4/30	N
	Phi Theta Kappa	5	1250		3.0		N	L-R-O	A	Y	N	A-4/30	Y
	Presidential	5	3/4 -Tuition	10%	3.5	1100/27	N	R-I-O	A	3.5	N	A-B	N
	Senate	10	1/2 -Tuition	20%		1000/24	N	R-I-O	A	3.2	N	A-B	Y-3.2
	Talent	5	1250				N	T-R-I-O	A	Y	N	A-4/30	Y
	Honors Program												
Moody Bible Institute, Chicago 60610	Institute Grants	450	500-2000		2.0		Y		A	2.0	N		N
	Honors	45	300-1500		2.5		Y		0	N	N		N
	Leadership	16	1000-2000		2.25		Y		A	2.25	N		N
	Honors Program												
NAES College, Chicago, 60659	Commonwealth	5	100-1000				Y		A	Y	S	A	Y
Nat'l College of Ed., Evanston 60201	College Scholars	Unlimited	1000-Tuition	25%	3.0	1000/24	N	E-R	A	Y	N	B-D	Y
North Central, Naperville 60566	Academic Merit 1	Varies	1000-2000	50%		990/24	N	R-I-O	A	2.75	N	A	N
	Academic Merit 2	Varies	2000-3000	10%		820	N	R-I-O	A	2.75	N	A	N
	Academic Merit 3	Varies	2000-3000	20%		910	N	R-I-O	A	2.75	N	A	N
	Forensics	8	400-1500				N	T-R-O	A	Y	N		Y
	Music	Varies	400-1500					T	A	Inq.	0	C	Inq.
	National Merit Finalists	Varies	3/4 Tuition				N	O	A		N	C	
	Presidential 1	Varies	3000-11500	10%		990	N	E-L-R-I-O	A	3.0	N	A	N
	Presidential 2	Varies	3000-11500	20%		1070	N	E-L-R-I-O	A	3.0	N	A	N
	Presidential 3	Varies	3000-11500	30%		1200	N	E-L-R-I-O	A	3.0	N	A	N
	Theatre	8	300-900				N	T-R-O	A	Y	N		Y
	Transfer	Unlimited	1000-6000		3.3		N	E-L-R-I-O	A	3.0	N	B-C	Y-3.3

North Park U., Chicago 60625	Art		500-1500				N	T	A	3.0	N	B-3/1	Y
	Dean's	Unlimited	3500	20%	3.3	1170/26	N	I-O	A	3.0	N	A	Y-3.3
	Drama		500-1500				N	T	A	Y	N	B-3/1	Y
	Leadership	Unlimited	3000	25%	3.3	1100/24	N		A	Y	N	A	N
	Music		500-3000				N	T	A	3.0	N	B-3/1	Y
	Nyvall	Unlimited	6000	10%	3.7	1320/30	N	O	A	3.0	N	A	Y-3.7
	Presidential	Unlimited	4000	15%	3.5	1240/28	N		A	3.0	N	A	Y-3.5
	AP Exams												
	Co-op, Internships												
	Honors Program												
Northern Illinois U., DeKalb 60115	Academic Finalist	25	Tuition+300	5%	3.5		N	L-R-I-O	A	3.0	N	B-2/1	Y
	Tuition Waiver	220	Tuition	5%	2.0		N	R-O	A	X	O	B-2/1	Y
	University Scholar	5	Total Costs	5%	3.5		N	L-R-I-O	A	3.3	N	B-2/1	Y
	Alumni	Varies	600-1200	5%	3.0	25	N	L-R-O	A	N	N	B-2/1	Y-3.0
	Honors Program												
Northwestern U., Evanston, 60208	AP Exams												
	Co-op, Internships												
	Honors Program												
Olivet Nazarene, Kankakee 60901	Olivet Scholar	Varies	50% Tuition		4.0	1340/30	N	R-I-O	A	3.6	N	A-8/1	Y
	Honor	Varies	30% Tuition	5%		1260/28	N	R-I-O	A	3.35	N	A-8/1	Y
	President's	Varies	20% Tuition	10%		1180/26	N	R-I-O	A	3.0	N	A-8/1	Y
	Achievement Award	Varies	10% Tuition			1030/22	N	R-I-O	A	3.0	N	A-8/1	Y
Principia College, Elsah 62028	Trustee	Varies	Tuition	2%	3.75	1300/29	N	E-L-R-O	A	3.6	D-O	A-B-1/15	N
	Presidential	2-6	To 2500	X	3.5	1100/24	N	L-R-O	A	3.5	D-O	A-B-2/15	N
	Arthur F. Schulz Jr.	4-9	To 2500	X	3.5		N	E-L-R-O	A	3.5	D-O	A-B-3/1	Y
	Principia Academic	12	1500	15%	3.5	1100/24	N	L-R	A	N	N	C-8/1	N
	Principia Honors	30	1000	20%	3.0	1100/24	N	L-R	A	3.5	D-O	C-8/1	N
Quincy University, Quincy 62301-2699	Music	Varies	500-5000				N	T-R-O	O	Y	N	B-D	Y
	Presidential	6	Tuit., Rm. & Bd.	5%		1300/31	Y	E-L-R-I-O	A	3.25	N	B-12/16	N
	Transfer Presidential	1	Tuit., Rm. & Bd.		3.0		N	E-L-R-I-O	A	3.25	N	B-2/24	N
	Quincy University	Unlimited	2000-5000		2.0	1000/21	N	O	A	3.0	N	A-D	N
	Quincy University Transfer	Unlimited	2000-4000		3.0		N	O	A	3.0	N	A-D	Y-3.0
	Upperclass Scholarship	Varies	500-2000		3.0		Y	L-O	A	Y-3.0	N	D	Y
	Honors Program												
Rockford College, Rockford 61108	Merit Scholarship	300	6100-9000	10%	3.0	25	N	R-O	A	3.0	N	A-6/1	Y-3.0
	Presidential	15	15,500	10%	3.5	27	N'	I-R-O	A	3.25	N	B-2/28	Y-3.25
	AP Exams												
	Alumni Discounts, Family Discounts												
	*Honors Program												

	Program	No. of Awards	Value Range	Award Criteria: Class Stndg.	Grade Avg.	SAT/ ACT	Need Based	Other	Study Fields	Renew-ability	Restric-tions	Apply Date	Transfer
ILLINOIS *(Continued)*													
Roosevelt U., Chicago 60605	Honors	25	Tuition		3.5	1200/23	N	E-I-L-R	A	3.5	N	2/15	Y-3.5
	Presidential	5	Tuition		3.75	1150/25	N	I-0	A	3.2	N	A-2/15	Y-3.75
	Recognition	Unlimited	2000-6000		3.25	1200/23	N		A	Y	N	2/15	Y-3.4
	Scholar	Varies	3500-6000	20%	3.5	1140/25	N	E-R-0	A	3.5	N	B-3/1	Y-3.5
	Transfer	Unlimited	2000-6000		3.3		N		A		N	2/15	Y-3.3
	AP Exams												
	Distance Learning												
	Internships												
	Honors Program												
St. Xavier, Chicago 60655	Transfer	Varies	3500		X		N	E-I-0	A	3.25	N	A-D	Y-3.5
	Leadership	Varies	500-2000	X	X	X	N	0	A	Y	N	A-B-3/15	N
	Presidential	Varies	2000-7000		X	X	N	E-R-I-0	A	Y	N	A-D	N
	Adult Student Scholarships	Varies	1750-3500		X	X	N	E-I-0	A	3.25	N	A-D	Y
Sangamon State U., Springfield 62708	Alumni Association	2	1000	X	X		N	L	A	Y	S	B-C	N
	UIS Scholarship	85	100-1500	X	X								
	Public Leadership	2-10	2000-5800		3.0		N	L-R-I-0	A	3.0	M-0	C-8/1	Y
	Co-op, Internships												
Southern IL U., Carbondale 62901	Chancellor's	Varies	1500+Tuition	2%		X	N		A	3.5	N	B-D	N
	Academic	Varies	4500	X	X	X	N		A	3.25	0	B-D	Y-3.5
	Foundation Merit	Varies	9000				N	0	A	3.25	N	B-D	N
	Grant	Varies	2250	X		X	N		A	3.25	N	B-D	N
	Phi Theta Kappa	5	4000				N	0	A	3.25	N	B-2/1	Y-3.5
	Academic-Transfer		2500				N		A	3.25	N	B-2/1	Y-3.5
	AP Exams												
	Distance Learning												
	Internships												
	Honors Program												
Southern IL U., Edwardsville 62026	Presidential	20	2000-6000	5%	4.75	1200/28	N	E-T-R-I-0	A	4.0	N	B-2/1	N
	Provost	Varies	300-1600	10%	4.5	1150/26	Y	T-L-R	A	N	N	B-8/1	Y
	Honors Program, Honors College												

Trinity, Deerfield 60015	Presidential	60	1250-2000	10%	3.5	39	N		A	3.4	N	A-7/15	Y
	Academic	232	1250—2000	5%	3.5	25	N		A	3.5	N	A	Y-3.5
	Special Ability	100	250-1500		2.5		N	T-L-R-I-O	O	2.5	N	B-4/1	Y-2.5
	Leadership	15	500-1000	50%	2.5	18	N	T-L	A	2.5	O	C-7/15	Y
	Kantzer Honors	2	50% Tuition	1-2	3.8	1100/28	N	E-L-R-I-O	A	3.5	N	A-2/15	Y-3.8
	Honors Program												
Trinity Christian, Palos Heights 60463	Honor	Varies	1500-4000		3.3	910/24	N		A	3.3	N	A-2/15	Y-3.3
U. of Chicago, 60637	College Honor	Varies	Tuition	5%	3.2	1350/28	N	R-I-O	A	Y	N	B-1/15	N
U. of Illinois, Champaign 61820	Academic	Varies	Varies	X	X	X	X	O	A	X	O	C	Y
	AP Exams												
	Co-op, Internships												
	Honors Program												
U. of Illinois, Chicago 60680	Academic	Varies	1000	15%		26	N		A	Y	N	B-C	N
	University Scholar	Varies	Tuition+	X	X	X	N		A	Y	N	B-3/1	N
	Freshman	Unlimited	1000			1220/30	N		A	N	O	A	N
	President's	Varies	500-Tuition+	50%		880/22	Y	R	A	Y	S-M	C	N
	Chancellor's	35	1000	15%		690/18	N	R	A	N	S-M	C	Y-3.25
	FMC Excellence	Varies	1000	X		X	N		A	N	O	A	N
	Honors Program, Honors College												
Western Illinois U., Macomb 61455	A.L. Knoblauch	5	300	1-2	3.5		N	R	A	N	O	B-3/15	N
	Alumni Assoc.	5	500	15%	3.5	25	N		A	N	N	B-3/15	N
	Community College	Varies	Varies		3.5		N		A	N	N	B-2/15	Y
	DuSable	4	500-1000	33%	3.2	23	N	R	A	3.0	M	B-3/15	N
	L.Y. Sherman		800	15%	3.5	26	N		A	N	N	B	N
	Phi Theta Kappa Transfer	1	500		3.5		N	L-R-O	A	3.5	N	B-4/1	N
	Presidential	15	1500	15%	3.5	28	N	R	A	3.5	N	B-12/10	N
	Undergraduate Asst.	Varies	Varies	10%	3.0	25	N	R	A	Y	N	B-C	N
	University Women	2	300	15%	3.5	25	N	R	A	N	W-O	B-3/15	N
	WIU Foundation	4	3000	15%	X	30	N	L-R-O	A	3.5	O	B-12/14	N
	Honors Program												
Wheaton College, Wheaton 60187	Presidents Award	Varies	1000		3.6	1400/32	N		A	3.0	N	A	N
	Burr Scholarship	Varies	800-1500		3.5	25	Y		A	Y	M	C	Y-3.3
	Pres. Honor Award, Music	15	1000				N	T-I-O		Y	N	A-C	Y
	National Merit	40	750-2000				N	O	A	Y	N	A	N
	President's Achievement	Varies	750-2000				N	O	A	Y	M	C	N
	Special Ach. in Music	Varies	1000-2500				N	T	O	N	O	C	Y
	AP Exams												

	Program	No. of Awards	Value Range	Award Criteria: Class Stndg.	Grade Avg.	SAT/ ACT	Need Based	Other	Study Fields	Renew- ability	Restric- tions	Apply Date	Transfer
INDIANA													
Anderson University, Anderson 46012	Academic Honors	Varies	8000	10%		1100/26	N	L-R-I-O	A	3.25	N	A-3/1	Y
	Valedictorian	Varies	1/2 Tuition	1		1000/23	N		A	3.5	N	A-3/1	N
	Presidential Scholarship	30	All Costs	10%		1200/28	N	L-R-I-O	A	3.5	N	A-11/1	Y-3.5
	Distinguished Student	50	3000	10%		1100/26	N	L-R-I-O	A	3.25	N	A-12/1	Y-3.5
	Merit Scholarship	Varies	1000-3700	10%		1000	N		A	3.25	N	A-3/1	Y-3.5
Ball State U., Muncie 47306	Academic	30	N. R. Fees	50%	3.0		N		A	2.0	O	C	Y
	College/Departmental	Varies	Varies				Y	O	O	Varies	O	B-C	N
	Emens	5	In-State Fees				N	E-L-R	A	Y	N	B-3/1	N
	National Merit	Varies	500-2000				Y	O	A	3.0	O	B-3/1	N
	Presidential	440	1524-3912	20%		1290/24	N		A	3.0	N	B-2/15	N
	Whitinger	10	Fees+Rm&Bd	10%		1290/24	N	E-R-I-O	A	3.0	N	B-3/1	N
	Honors Program, Honors College												
Bethel, Mishawaka 46545	Academic	Unlimited	2000	25%		1100/29	N		A	3.0	N	A	Y-3.3
	Bethel Grant	Unlimited	500-2000				N	T-L-I	A	3.0	N	A	Y-2.0
	Faculty	Unlimited	2500	20%		1150/25	N		A	3.0	N	A	Y-3.5
	Matching Church	Unlimited	250-1000		2.0		N	O	A	2.0	N	A-D	Y
	Merit	Unlimited	1000	40%		1000/22	N		A	3.0	N	A	N
	Presidential	Unlimited	3000	15%		1200/26	N		A	3.0	N	A	Y-3.75
	Trustee	Unlimited	4000-10000	5%		1300/30	N	E-L-I-O	A	3.0	N	A-3/1	N
	AP Exams												
	Family Discounts												
	Co-op												
Butler U., Indianapolis 46208	Academic	160	3000-7000	10%		1200/26	N	L	A	3.0	N	2	N
	Audition	Varies	1585-6340		2.0		N	T	O	Y	N	B-D	Y
	Presidential	20	6340	5%		1350	N	L	A	3.5	N	B-12/1	N
Calumet C. of St. Joseph, Whiting 46394	Academic Tuition	Varies	3168-3960	25%	3.25	1000/19	N	I-O	A	3.0	N	B-C	N
	Freshman	10	400-2000	20%	3.0	1100/26	Y		A	3.0	N	C-6/1	N
	GED Scholarship	Varies	792-3960				N	I-O	A	3.0	N	B-C	N
DePauw U., Greencastle 46135	Holton	55	1000-All Costs	10%	3.8	1200/26	N	E-I-L-R-O	A	2.0			
	African-American Leadership	15-20	5500	25%			N	L	A	2.75	M	A-2/15	Y
	Hispanic/Latino Leadership	15-20	5500	25%			N	L	A	2.75	M	A-2/15	Y
	Distinguished Rector	10	7500	10%		1150	N		A	3.25	N	A	Y

	Presidential Rector	6	Full tuition	10%	3.8	1300/28	N	I	A	3.0			
	Rector	50	11,000	10%	3.6	1200/26	N		A	3.0			
	Merit	Unlimited	4000-9000	X	X	X	N			2.0			
	AP Exams												
	Alumni Discount												
	Co-op, Internships												
	Honors Program												
Earlham, Richmond 47374	C. B. Edwards	2	5000			1200/26	N	I-O	O	Y	N	B-1/15	N
	Earlham Honors	60	5000			1200/26	N	E-T-I-O	O	Y	N	B-1/15	N
	Clarence Cunningham	5-10	1500-5000	30%	3.0	1050/21	N	E-L-R-I-O	A	2.0	M	B-1/15	N
	Community Service Award	40	1000-2000				N	L-R	A	N	N	B-1/15	N
Franklin College, 46131	Ben Franklin	5	13860	5%		1100/27	N	E-L-R-I-O	A	3.0	N	B-2/1	Y
	Dean's	Varies	6700	30%		1000/25			A	3.0	N		Y
	Indiana Acad. Honors Prog.	Varies	1000				N	O	A	3.0	S		N
	Outstanding Junior	Varies	7000-13820	10	3.5	1000/25	N	E-T-L-R-I	A	3.0	O	C-2/1	N
	President's	15	9990	10%		1100/27	N	E-L-R-I-O	A	3.0	N	B-2/1	Y
	Honors Program												
Goshen College, 46526	Alumni Grant	Unlimited	1000				N			N	O	A	Y
	Goshen College Merit	Unlimited	750-2000				X	O	A	3.0	N	B-C	N
	Honors	Unlimited	1600	15%	3.5	1100/24	N		A	3.0	N	A-3/1	Y
	Menno Simons	Unlimited	2000	1	3.8	1270/29	N		A	3.0	N	A-3/1	Y
	Multicultural Leadership	Unlimited	1000	0.5	2.5			L-R-O		2.0	M	A	Y-2.0
	President's Leadership	10	1/2 Tuition	X	3.8	1270/29		E-T-L-R-O	A	3.0	N	C-2/1	N
	Honors Program												
Grace, Winona Lake 46590	Talent	60	200-2376				N	T-R-I-O	A	Y	N	C	Y
	Presidential Merit	Unlimited	500-5000	10%	3.85	1300/29	N		A	3.5			
	Leadership Merit	10-15	500-1500		2.7			L	A	2.7			
	AP Exams												
	Distance Learning												
	Family Discounts												
	Internships												
Hanover College, 47243	Admissions	30	100-1000	15%	3.0	1150/25	N	L	A	2.5	N	A-D	N
	Crowe/Long	10	4700	10%	3.5	44	N	E-T-R-I	A	3.0	N	B-1/12	N
	Horner	10	Tuition	5%	4.0	44	N	E-T-R-I	A	3.5	N	B-1/12	N
	Presidential	30	100-1500	10%	3.5	1200/27	N	L	A	3.0	N	A-D	N
	Trustee	3	Tuition/Rm/Bd	5%	4.0	44	N	E-L-R-I-O	A	3.5	N	B-2/1	N
Huntington College, Huntington 46750	Art	Varies	200-1000		2.3		N		O	2.0	O	B-4/1	Y-2.0
	Communication	Varies	200-1000		2.3		N		O	2.0	O	B-4/1	Y-2.0
	Dean's	4	4000	10%	3.6	1250/28	N		A	3.4	N	A-1/15	N

	Program	No. of Awards	Value Range	Award Criteria: Class Stndg.	Grade Avg.	SAT/ ACT	Need Based	Other	Study Fields	Renew-ability	Restric-tions	Apply Date	Transfer
INDIANA *(Continued)*													
Huntington College, Huntington 46750 *(Continued)*	H.C. Honor	Unlimited	500-2000	10%	3.2	1000/21	N		A	3.2	N	B-D	Y-3.2
	Music	Varies	200-1500		2.3		N		0	2.0	0	B-4/1	Y-2.0
	Presidential	4	7500	10%	3.6	1200/28	N	L-R-I-0	A	3.4	N	A-2/1	N
	Theatre	Varies	500-1400		2.3		N	T-R-I-0	A	2.0	0	B-4/1	Y-2.0
	YFC	Varies	2000-3500		2.7	900/19	N		A	2.5	0		Y-2.5
IN Inst. of Tech., Ft. Wayne 46803	William Hess	Varies	To 1000		3.0		Y		A	3.0	N	A-3/1	N
Indiana State U., Terre Haute 47809	ISU Academic	Varies	1500	10%			N	E	A	2.5	N	B-2/15	N
	Dean's	Varies	1100	25%			N	R	A	2.5	N	B-2/15	Y
	Presidential		Tuition	10%			N	E-L-R-I	A	2.5	N	B-2/15	N
	Alumni		Tuition	10%			N	E-L-R-I	A	2.5	N	B-2/15	N
	Warren M. Anderson		1100	25%			N	L-R-I	A	2.5	M	B-2/15	N
	Creative and Perform. Arts		1100				N	T-R-I	A	2.5	N	B-2/15	Y
	Honors Program												
Indiana U., Bloomington 47401	Honors	20	2000	8%		1300	N	L	A	3.3	Y	A-1/15	Y
	Wells	20	Tuition, Room	X	X	X		T-L					
	Honors Program												
Indiana U. Northwest, Gary 46408	Special Academic	Varies	Tuition	10%		1100	N	0	A	3.3	N	A-3/15	N
	Chancellor's	Varies	Tuition+fees	1			N	0	A	Y	N	A-3/15	N
	Misc. Endowed	Varies	To All Costs				X		A	X		C	
	Honors Program												
Indiana U., South Bend 46634	Distinguished	4	1000	10%		1300	N	L-R-I	A	3.75	N	B-3/1	Y-3.75
	Merit	Unlimited	100-200	10%	3.3	1000	N		A	3.3	N	B-3/1	Y-3.3
Indiana U. SE, New Albany 47150	Academic	22	500-1200	10%		1100/26	N	E-L-I-0	A	3.0	N	B-3/1	N
	Distinguished	Varies	2000				N	E-L-R-0	A	Y	N	B-D	N
Indiana U.-Purdue U., Ft. Wayne 46805	Chancellor's	30	1/2 Tuition	10%		1100	N		A	3.5	N	B-3/1	N
	Honors Program												
Indiana U.-Purdue U., Indianapolis 46202	Merit Recognition	70+	1000	15%		1180/26	N		A	3.0			
	IUPUI Outstanding Freshman	6	2500	15%		1180/26	N	E-I-L	A	3.3			
	Val/Sal	10-15	500	1-2			N		A	N			
	IUPUI Distinguished Scholar	5	3000	10%	3.5	1300	N	E-I	A	3.5			

	Summer Research	10+	2000				N	I-R		N			
	Minority Achievement	10	2000	30%	3.0	1010/22	N	E-L-R		3.0			
	Honors Fellows	20	1000	25%	3.2		N	E	A	N			
	Honors Scholarships	20	2000	15%		1180/26	N	E-I-L	A	3.3			
	Minority Research	7+	Tuition +$1000	25%		1000/21	N			X			
	Undergraduate Research	15+	1500				N	0					
	AP Exams												
	Distance Learning												
	Co-op, Internships												
	Honors Program												
Indiana Wesleyan, Marion 46953	Freshman Honor	Varies	1000-4000		3.2	950/21	N	I-0	A	N	N	B-4/1	N
	Music	Varies	200-1000				N	T-I-0	0	Y	N	B-4/1	Y
	Salutatorian	Varies	500	2			N	I-0	A	N	N	B-4/1	N
	Transfer Honor	Varies	1000-4000		3.4	950/21	N	0	A	N	N	B-4/1	Y-3.4
	Valedictorian	Varies	1000	1			N		A	N	N	B-4/1	N
Manchester College, 46962	Alumni	Unlimited	500				N		A	N	N	A-D	Y
	Church of the Brethren	Unlimited	1000				N		A	Y	D	A-D	Y
	Dean's Scholarship	Unlimited	1500-4000	20%		1100/24	N	0	A	3.0	N	A-D	Y-3.0
	Director's Award	Unlimited	1500-2000	20%		1100/24	N		A	2.7	N	A-D	Y
	Honors Fellowship	2	Tuition	10%		1200/31	N		A			3/1	
	Honors Stipend	Unlimited	1000	10%		1200/31	N	E-R-0	A	3.5	0	C	Y-3.5
	Minority Leadership	Unlimited	2000				N	0	A	Y	M	B	Y
	Presidential	Unlimited	3500-5000	5%		1200/27	N	L-R-0	A	3.3	N	A-D	N
	Presidential Leadership	3	50% Tuition	5%		1200/31	N	L	A	3.5		3/1	
	AP Exams												
	Alumni Discounts, Family Discounts												
	Internships												
	Honors Program												
Marian, Indianapolis 46222	Cardinal Newman	Unlimited	1/2 Tuition	5%	3.5	1100/25	N		A	Y	N	B-D	Y
Martin U., Indianapolis 46218	Eldrige Morrison	Varies	Varies				Y	E-R	0	N	0	B	Y
	Mary McLeon Bethune	Varies	Varies				Y	E-R	A	N	0	B	Y
	Revs. Brown & Sanders	Varies	Varies				Y	E-R	0	N	0	B	Y
Oakland City University, 47660	Academic	37	To Tuition	10%	3.2	800/20	N	E-L-R-I-0	A	3.0	N	B-C	Y
	Denominational	Varies	To 1/2 Tuition				N	R	A	Y	D	B-C	Y
	Presidential	10	Tuition		3.5	1000	N	E-R-I	A	Y	N	B-4/1	Y
Purdue U. Calumet, Hammond 46323	Talent Awards	40	500-1500	10%	3.0	1200	N		A	3.0	N	B-3/1	Y-3.0
	Merit	60	500-1500	10%	3.0	1200	N		A	3.0	N	B-3/1	Y-3.0

	Program	No. of Awards	Value Range	Award Criteria: Class Stndg.	Grade Avg.	SAT/ ACT	Need Based	Other	Study Fields	Renew-ability	Restric-tions	Apply Date	Transfer
INDIANA *(Continued)*													
Purdue U., W. Lafayette 47907	Anderson Consulting	Varies	1250	15%	X	1200/28	N	O	O	X-3.0	N	3/1	N
	Cecil & Mabil Hamman	Varies	1500	15%	X	1200/28	N	O	O	X-3.0	N	3/1	N
	CFS Deans Honor Schol.	Varies	1000	5%	X	1300/29	N	O	O	N	N	D	N
	CFS First Year Merit Award	Varies	500	10%	X	1200/27	N	O	O	N	O	4/15	N
	CFS Minority Scholarship	Varies	1000	20%	X	X	N	O	O	Y	O	4/15	N
	Claude M. Gladden	6	500-1000	X	X	X	N	O	O	X	N	D	N
	Deans Engineering	85	1250	5%	X	1300/30	N	O	O	N	N	3/1	N
	Dean's Freshman Scholar	Varies	1000	10%	X	1200/27	N	O	O	N	N	7/1	N
	Dean's Scholar Program	Varies	1000	X	X	1200/27	N	O	O	N	N	D	N
	Departmental	Varies	To 2000	15%	X	X	N	L-O	A	X	O	B-C	Y
	Earth Science Fresh. Minority	Varies	10,000	X	X	X	N	O	O	N	M	D	N
	Fred B. and Mary F. O'Mara	Varies	1000-6000	15%	X	1200/28	N	O	O	X-3.0	N	3/1	N
	Freshman Scholar Program	Varies	1000	X	X	1100/26	N	O	O	N	N	D	N
	Henry Silver Fresh. Minority	Varies	2000	X	X	X	N	O	O	N	M	D	N
	Krannert Alumni Mgmt.	Varies	1500	15%	3.0	1200/28	N	O	O	X-3.0	N	3/1	N
	Leighty Chemistry Schol.	Varies	2200	10%	3.3	X	N	O	O	3.4	N	1/31	N
	Mauri Williamson	1	3000	5%	X	1300/28	N	O	O	Y	N	3/1	N
	Minorities in Engineering	Varies	500-3000	X	X	X	N	L-O	O	X	M	3/1	N
	Minority Merit Scholarship	Varies	750-1000	X	X	X	N	O	O	Y	M	4/30	N
	Mobil Corporation Schol.	Varies	1250	15%	X	1200/28	N	O	O	X-3.0	N	3/1	N
	Nursing Freshman Schol.	Varies	1000	X	X	1200/27	N	O	O	X-3.0	N	2/1	N
	Peterson-Lawrence Schol.	Varies	10,000	15%	X	1200/28	N	O	O	X-3.0	N	3/1	N
	Presidential Honors	5	All Costs	10%	3.9	1450/33	N	L	A	3.5	N	A	N
	Rosenthal Scholarship	Varies	700	X	X	X	N	O	O	Y	O	3/1	N
	Schol. Award of Excellence	1	1500	10%	X	1100/26	N	O	O	N	N	3/1	N
	School of Education Schol.	Varies	750	X	X	1230/28	N	O	O	N	N	D	N
	Science Scholarship	Varies	2500	10%	X	1200/27	N	O	O	Y	N	7/1	N
	Walter Fritsch Memorial	Varies	1000-6000	15%	X	1200/28	N	O	O	X-3.0	N	3/1	N
	Winfield F. Hentschel Mem.	Varies	1000-6000	15%	X	1200/28	N	O	O	X-3.0	N	3/1	N
	Women in Engineering	5	1250-5000	5%	X	1300/30	N	O	O	N	W	2/1	N
	AP Exams												
	Distance Learning												
	Co-op, Internships												
	Honors Program												

Purdue U., Westville 46391	Murdock-Woodard	2	500	10%			N	E-I	0		N	B-2/17	N
Rose-Hulman, Terre Haute 47803	Honors	Varies	500-5000	X	X	X	N	0	A	Y	N	A	Y
U. of St. Francis, Ft. Wayne 46808	Art Schol.	50	750-1500				N	T-R-I-0	0	3.2	N	C-8/15	
	Honors	75	1000-5000	15%	3.2	800/19	N	0	A	3.2	N	A	N
	Science Symposium	25	1000-2000				N	R-I-0	0	3.2	N	C-8/15	
	Honors Program												
St. Joseph's, Rensselaer 47978	Dean's	Unlimited	4500	15%	3.2	1100/24	N	L-R	A	3.25	N	A	Y-3.25
	Honors	Unlimited	6000	10%	3.4	1240/28	N	L-R	A	3.25	N	A	N
	Minority Leadership	10	3500	X	X	X	N	L-R			M	B-3/1	
	Performance		1500					T				B	
	Presidential	3	All Costs	15%	3.0	1100/24	N	E-L-R-I-0	A	3.25	N	B-12/1	N
	SJC	Unlimited	3000	25%	2.85		N	R	A	3.0	N	A	N
	AP Exams												
	Alumni Discounts, Family Discounts												
	Co-op, Internships												
	Honors Program												
St. Mary-of-the-Woods, 47876	Creative Arts	Unlimited	2000				N	T-L-R	0	2.5	W	B-D	Y
	Guerin	Unlimited	500	25%			N	L-R	A	2.5	W	C	N
	Presidential	Unlimited	2000	15%	3.5	1200/25	N	L-R	A	3.5	W	C	Y
	Providence	Unlimited	3000		3.5	1000/23	N	L-0	A	3.4	W	A	Y-3.5
	Sesquicentennial	3	Full Tuition		3.75	1200/27	N	E-T-L-R-I-0	A	3.75	W-0	A-3/1	N
	Woods	Unlimited	1000-2000		3.3	900/20	N	0	A	3.3	W	A	Y-3.3
St. Mary's College, Notre Dame 46556	Presidential Merit	Varies	7500	5%	3.76	1100/25	N	E-L-R-I	A	3.4		A	
	Saint Mary's	Varies	3000	15%	3.12	1000/22	N	E-L-R-I-0	A	3.2			
	Dean's	Varies	5000	10%	3.27	1000/24	N	E-R-I-L	A	3.3		A	
St. Meinrad College, 47577	Presidential Merit	Varies	To Full Tuition	X	3.75	1350/28	N	L-0	A	3.5	D-F	A	N
	Faculty	Unlimited	To 1/3 Tuition	X	3.25	1250/25	N	L-0	A	3.0	D-F	A	N
	Transfer	Unlimited	To 1/3 Tuition	X	3.25		N	L-0	A	3.0	D-F-0		Y-3.25
	Honors Program												
Taylor University, Fort Wayne 46807	Dean's Scholarship	Varies	750-1500	15%	3.5	1150	Y		A	3.2	N	A-3/1	N
	Founders	40	1500-3000	15%	3.2	1150/25	N	E-I-R	A	3.0	N	A-3/1	Y-3.2
	President's Scholarship	Varies	1000-2000	10%	3.8	1250	Y		A	3.2	N	A-3/1	N
	Trustees	60	750-1500	20%	3.2	1050/22	N	E-I-R	A	3.0	N	A-3/1	Y-3.2
	AP Exams												
	Distance Learning												
	Alumni Discounts												
	Co-op, Internships												
	Honors Program												

	Program	No. of Awards	Value Range	Award Criteria: Class Stndg.	Grade Avg.	SAT/ ACT	Need Based	Other	Study Fields	Renew-ability	Restric-tions	Apply Date	Transfer
INDIANA *(Continued)*													
Taylor U., Upland 46989	Dean's	Unlimited	750-1500	15%	3.5	1200/27	Y		A	3.2	N	A-3/1	N
	President's	Unlimited	1500-3000	10%	3.8	1300/29	Y		A	3.2	N	A-3/1	N
	Leadership	30	1000-80% Tuit.		3.0	1100/24	N	E-L-R-I-0	A	Y	N	B-10/1	N
	Honors Program												
Tri-State U., Angola 46703	President's	Limited	8000	10%	3.5	1200/30	N		A	Y-3.0	N	A-3/1	Y-3.0
	Dean's	Limited	2400-6000	30%	3.0	1000	N		A	Y-2.5	N	A-3/1	Y-3.0
U. Of Evansville, 47722	Ensemble Participation	Unlimited	400				N	T-0	0	2.0	N	B-3/1	Y-2.0
	Faculty Scholarship	1	Full Tuition	5%		1300/32	N	0	A	3.25	N	B-12/1	N
	Leadership Activity Award	Unlimited	1000-3000	35%		800/19	N	L-0	A	2.0	N	A-3/1	N
	Legacy Award	Unlimited	4000	50%		900/21	N	0	A	Y	0	C	2.5
	Multicultural Scholars	Unlimited	2000-7000	30%		920/19	N		A	2.0	M	A	N
	UE Acad. Depart.	Unlimited	2000-7000	30%		1100/24	N		A	X	N	3/1	Y-3.0
	UE Methodist	Unlimited	2500				N	R	A	2.0	D	B-3/1	Y
	Honors Program												
University of Indianapolis, 46227	Alumni	40	To 30% Tuition	15%		1100	N	L-R	A	2.7	N	B-2/15	N
	Dean's	Unlimited	To 50% Tuition	7%		1270	N	L	A	3.0	N	A	N
	Presidential	12	To Tuition	5%		1270	N	E-L-I-0	A	3.3	N	B-12/15	N
	Service Award	Unlimited	2500				N	L-R	A	2.0	N	B-5/1	Y
	United Methodist	Unlimited	2500				N	R	A	2.0	D	B-5/1	Y
	AP Exams												
	Co-op, Internships												
	Honors Program												
U. of S. Indiana, Evansville 47712	Bennighoff	Varies	800		3.5		Y		A	3.0	S	B-3/1	N
	Herschel Moore	2	1500		2.75		Y	R	A	2.5	S-M-0		Y-2.75
	Non-Resident	Varies	2400		2.75		N		A	2.5	0	B-C	Y-2.75
	Pott	Varies	1600-3900		3.0	X	N	R	0	2.75	S	B	Y-3.0
	Presidential	Varies	5600-7100	1-2		1000	N		A	3.2	S-0	B-3/1	N
	Various	Varies	400-1000		2.0		X	0	A	X	0	B-3/1	Y
	AP Exams												
	Distance Learning												
	Co-op, Internships												
	Honors College												

Valparaiso U., 46383	Chemistry	8	1000	X		X	N		0	Y	N	A-1/15	N
	Diversity	10	1000-3000				N	L	A	2.0	M	B-2/1	N
	Dow/Chemistry	1	8000	X		X	N	R-I-0	0	Y	0	B-12/31	N
	Foreign Language	Varies	1000	X		X	N	E	0	3.0	N	C	N
	Jove/NASA	6	1000-2500	X		X	N		0	N	S	A-1/15	N
	Music	Varies	500-1800				N	T	0	Y	N	C	N
	Presidential	125	3000-10000	X		X	N		A	3.0	N	A-2/1	N
	University	100	2000	X		X	N		A	3.0	N	A-2/1	N
	Honors Program, Honors College												
Wabash, Crawfordsville 47933	Honor	20	8000-11000				N	E-0	A	3.0	F	C	N
	Lilly	10	16450				N	0	A	Y	F	B-C	N
	President's	Varies	2500-11000	10%	3.0	1100/24	N	0	A	3.0	F	A-C	N
	Fine Arts	5	11000.00				N	0	A	3.0	F	B	N
IOWA													
Briar Cliff, Sioux City 51104	Academic Excellence	Varies	1500-3000		3.2	962/23	N	0	A	3.0	0	A	N
	Board of Trustees	2	13225		3.7	1170/28	N	E-L-I-0	A	3.0	N	B-1/20	N
	Presidential	5	4890		3.5	1087/26	N	E-L-I-0	A	3.0	N	B-1/20	N
Buena Vista, Storm Lake 50588	Art/Drama/Music	Varies	500-2000				N	T	A	2.0	N	C	Y
	Honors	Varies	1000-2500	20%	3.2	25	N		A	Y	N	A-D	Y
	JR Seifer Scholarship	Varies	2000-4500	40%		22	N	0	A	Y	0	A	Y
	Madge White Math/Science	Varies	2000-5000	20%		25	N	E-L-R-I-0	0	3.0	N	C	Y-3.0
	Malone Pre-Law	Varies	2000-5000	20%		24	N	E-L-R-I-0	A	3.2	0	B-1/15	Y-3.2
	Master Teacher	Varies	2000-5000	20%		24	N	E-L-R-I-0	0	3.0	N	C	Y-3.0
	ZZ White Leadership	Varies	2000-5000	30%		22	N	E-L-R-I-0	A	2.5	N	C	Y-3.0
	AP Exams												
	Distance Learning												
	Family Discounts												
	Internships												
	Honors Program												
Central, Pella 50219	Cover/Robertson	3	6000	5%	3.5	1200/27	N	L-R-I-0	0	3.0	N	B-1/1	N
	Hearst	1	6000	5%	3.5	1200/27	N	L-R-I-0	A	3.0	M	B-1/1	N
	Petz	2	6000	5%	3.5	1200/27	N	L-R-I-0	0	3.0	N	B-1/1	N
	Presidential	10	6000	5%	3.5	1200/27	N	L-R-I-0	A	3.0	N	B-1/1	N
	Rolscreen	8	7000- Tuition	5%	3.5	1200/27	N	L-R-I-0	A	3.0	N	B-1/1	N
	Vance	2	6000	5%	3.5	1200/27	N	L-R-I-0	A	3.0	N	B-1/1	N
	Wormhoudt	2	6000	5%	3.5	1200/27	N	L-R-I-0	0	3.0	N	B-1/1	N
	Honors Program												

	Program	No. of Awards	Value Range	Award Criteria: Class Stndg.	Grade Avg.	SAT/ ACT	Need Based	Other	Study Fields	Renew-ability	Restric-tions	Apply Date	Transfer
IOWA *(Continued)*													
Clarke, Dubuque 52001	Presidential	Varies	6500-8500	20%	3.0	1110/24	N		A	3.0	0		N
	Transfer	Varies	3000-8000		3.0		N		A	3.0	0		
	AP Exams												
	Distance Learning												
	Co-op, Internships												
	Honors Program												
Coe, Cedar Rapids 52402	Fine Arts	Unlimited	1500-Tuition	30%	3.0	20	N	E-I-T	0	3.0			
	Academic	Unlimited	4000-9000	25%	3.4	22	N		A	3.0			
	Science	25	1500-Tuition	25%	3.0	20	N	E-I-R	0	3.0			
	Writing	Unlimited	1500-5000	30%	3.0	20	N	T		3.0			
	AP Exams												
	Alumni Discounts												
	Co-op, Internships												
	Honors Program												
Cornell, Mt. Vernon 52314	Acad/Community Enrichment	Unlimited	5000-15,000		3.3		N	L	A	3.0			
	Art	Unlimited	6000-8000				N	T		Y			
	Music	Unlimited	4000-15,000				N	T		Y			
	Theater	Unlimited	8000				N	T					
	AP Exams												
	Co-op, Internships												
Dordt, Sioux Center 51250	Merit	Unlimited	200-1500		3.0		N	E-L	A	3.0	N	B-D	Y-3.0
	Honors	80	1600-2500		3.6		N	E-L	A	3.0	N	B-1/15	Y-3.0
	Major/Program	70	500-1000		3.0		N	E-R	A	3.0	N	B-1/15	N
	Distinguished Scholar	7	5000		3.5	26	N	E-L-R-I	A	3.0	N	B-1/15	N
	Leadership/Activity	100	500-2000		2.5		N	T-L-R-O	A	2.5	0	C-1/15	Y
Drake U., Des Moines 50311	National Alumni	15	14380-19480	5%	3.75	1270/29	N	0	A	3.25	0	B-1/15	N
	Presidential Freshman	Unlimited	4500-5500	15%	3.5	1120/25	N	L-0	A	2.75	0	A-3/1	N
	Cowles Fndn. Multicultural	3	19480	5%	3.75	1270/25	N	0	A	3.25	M	B-3/1	N
	Multicultural Scholarships	Unlimited	4500-5500	15%	3.5	45	N	L-0	A	2.75	M	A-3/1	N
	Drake Achievement	Unlimited	2500-3500	25%	3.0	X	N	0	A	Y	0	A-3/1	N
	Community College	Unlimited	3500-4500		3.25		N	0	A	2.75	0	A-3/1	Y-3.25
	Phi Theta Kappa	6	5500-7000		3.5		N	0	A	3.25	0	B-3/1	Y-3.5
	Honors Program												

Graceland, Lamoni 50140	Academic	175	500-4250		3.0	960/21	N		A	3.0			
	AP Exams												
	Distance Learning												
	Honors Program												
Grand View, Des Moines 50316	Art	20	100-500				N	T-I-O			N	D	Y
	Choral	30	100-500				N	T-I-O			N	D	Y
	Drama	40	100-1000				N	T-I-O			N	D	Y
	Grand View Grant	Unlimited	Up to 6500		2.1	14	N		A	2.0	N	A-D	Y-2.1
	Grand View Scholarship	Unlimited	3500-8000		3.5	24	N		A	3.0	N	A-D	Y-3.51
	Honors Program												
Grinnell College, 50112	Trustee Fund	10	4000	15%	3.5	1000/23	N		A	Y	M	B-3/1	N
	Trustee Honor	40	1900-3000	10%	3.6	1200/28	N		A	Y	N	B-3/1	N
Iowa State U., Ames 50011	Academic Recognition	Varies	500	5%			N	O	A	2.5	N	A	N
	Hixson Opportunity Awards	100	2500				Y	O	A		S	A	N
	ISU Distinguished Scholar	25	2500	5%	X	32	N	O	A	N	N	A	N
	Presidential Scholarship	15	2500	X	X	X			A	3.0	N	A	
	President's Leadership	30	1000			25	N	L	A	N	N	A	N
	AP Exams												
	Distance Learning												
	Co-op, Internships												
	Honors Program												
Iowa Wesleyan, Mt. Pleasant 52641	Academic Achievement	Unlimited	500-3000	20%	3.0		N	O	A	3.0	N	A	Y-3.25
	Goodell Scholarship	Varies	Varies		X		N	T	O	Y	O		Y
	Honors	Unlimited	100-1000				Y	O	A	3.0	N	A	Y-3.0
	Presidential	Varies	4000-9000	15%	3.5	25	N	O	A	3.25	N	B-3/1	N
	Schramm Scholarship	Varies	Varies		X		N	T	O	Y	O		Y
Loras, Dubuque 52001	Academic	Varies	2500-7000		3.3	1140/25	N		A	3.2	N	A-4/15	N
	Loras Grant	Varies	500-8000		2.0	X	Y		A	2.0	N	B-4/1	Y
	Presidential	10	Full Tuition		3.7	1100/24	N	E-I	A	3.2	N	1/1	N
	Regents	2	All Costs		3.7	1100/24	N	E-I	A	3.5	N	1/1	N
	AP Exams												
	Alumni Discounts, Family Discounts												
	Honors Program												
Luther, Decorah 52101	Presidential	Varies	2000-4000	20%	3.0	1140/25	N		A	3.0	N	A-3/1	Y
	Regents'	Varies	6000	10%	3.25	1260/28	N		A	3.25	N	A-3/1	Y
	Weston Noble	Varies	500-1500				N	T	A	N	N	B-3/1	Y
	AP Exams												
	Co-op, Internships												
	Honors Program												

	Program	No. of Awards	Value Range	Award Criteria: Class Stndg.	Grade Avg.	SAT/ ACT	Need Based	Other	Study Fields	Renew-ability	Restric-tions	Apply Date	Transfer
IOWA *(Continued)*													
Marycrest, Davenport 52804	Academic	Varies	1000-3000		3.2	950/22	N	0	A	3.0	N	A-3/1	Y
	Ecumenical Scholar	12	750		3.0	20	N	E-L-R	A	Y	N	B-3/1	N
	International	2	5000				N		A	Y	0	C	N
	Lawler Scholar	5	1000		3.0	20	N		A	Y	N	B-3/1	N
	Newman	2	Full Tuition				N	0	A	3.5	N	B-1/31	Y-3.5
	Performing Fine Arts	15	500				N	T-I-0	0	Y	N	C	N
Morningside, Sioux City 51106	Celebration of Excellence	100	2300-6500	20%		1030/25	N	E-L-R-0	A	3.0	N	B-2/1	N
	Divisional	Varies	200-1000		3.0	910/22	N	E	A	3.0	N	B-3/1	N
	Morningside	Unlimited	2300-5000	20%	3.5	25	N	R-0	A	3.0	N	A	Y-3.0
	Talent Grants	Varies	500-Tuition+				N	T-I-0	0-K-0	2.0	0	B	Y-2.0
	Honors Program												
Mt. Mercy, Cedar Rapids 52402	Academic	150	2500-6800	50%	3.0	880/19	N	E-L-R	A	Y	N	C	Y
	Art	10	200-2500	50%	2.5	800/17	N	E-T-R	A	Y	N	C	Y
	Leadership	85	1500	50%	2.5	800/17	N	E-L-R	A	Y	N	C	Y
	Music	10	200-2500	50%	2.5	800/17	N	T-R-I-0	0	Y	N	C	Y
	Social Work	15	200-2000	50%	2.5	800/17	N	E-L-R	0	Y	N	C	Y
	Speech/Drama	15	200-2500	50%	2.5	800/17	N	E-L-R	A	Y	N	C	Y
Mt. St. Clare, Clinton 52732	Athletic	Varies	500-Tuition	50%	2.0	18	Y	T-L-R-I-0	A	2.5	N	B-3/1	Y-2.0
	Departmental	24	1500				N	E-T-0	A	3.0	N	B-2/1	Y-2/1
	Divisional	18	2000-Full Tuit.		3.2	23	Y	E-T-L-I-0	A	3.5	N	B-3/1	Y-3.5
	Leadership	25	1100				N	L	A	3.0	N	B-3/1	Y-3.0
	Presidential	Unlimited	800-Tuition	20%	3.2	26	N	L	A	3.0	N	A-8/1	Y-3.0
	Honors Program												
Northwestern, Orange City 51041	Academic Achievement	Unlimited	500-2100	25%		23	N	R-0	A	3.0	N	A	N
	Collegiate	Unlimited	1950-3700	10%		26	N	R-0	A	3.0	N	A	Y
	Norman V. Peale	10	6300	15%	3.5	25	N	0	A	3.0	N	B-1/1	N
	Presidential	Unlimited	4300-5200	5%		28	N	R-0	A	3.0	N	A	N
	AP Exams												
	Family Discounts												
	Honors Program												
St. Ambrose, Davenport 52303	Academic	Varies	1000-Tuition		3.25		N		A	3.25	N	A-C	Y
	Performance	Varies	200-Tuition				N	T-L-I-0	0	2.0	N	C	Y

Teikyo-Westmar, Le Mars 51031	Academic	170	1000-6000		3.0	24	N	L-R-O	A	2.5	N	A	Y-3.0
	Talent	340	1000-6000				N	T-L-R-I-O	A	2.0	N	A	Y
	Trustee	Varies	9980		3.0	24	N	E-L-R-O	A	3.0	N	A	N
University of Dubuque, 52001	Honors	Varies	3000-4000	80%ile		80%ile	N		A	3.5	N	A	N
	Presidential	Varies	5000	80%ile		80%ile	N	L-R	A	3.0	N	A	N
	Transfer	Varies	2500-3500		3.25		N		A	3.25	N	A	Y-3.25
	Valedictorian	5	Full Tuition	1	95%ile	95%ile	N	E-I-L-R	A	3.5	N	B-2/8	N
	AP Exams												
	Distance Learning												
	Alumni Discounts, Family Discounts												
	Internships												
U. of Iowa, Iowa City 52242	Presidential	50	7000	5%	3.8	1290/30	N	E	A	3.0		B-C	N
	Dean's	70	1000	5%	3.8	1290/30	N	E	A	3.0	N	A	Y-3.0
	Honors Program												
	Distance Learning												
	Co-op, Internships												
U. of Northern Iowa, Cedar Falls 50614	Achievement	10	500-2000	25%		22	N	E-O	A	Y	M	B-4/1	Y-2.5
	Carver	8	3600		2.8		N	E-R	A	2.8	S	B-C	Y-2.8
	Multicultural Achievement	7	500-1000	25%		22	N	E-O	A	2.75	N	B-2/1	Y
	Presidential	15	6196-10,580	10%		29	N	E-R-I-O	A	3.5	N	B-10/1	N
	Provost	15	2752-7136	10%		29	N	E-R-I-O	A	3.25	N	B-2/1	N
	Scholarship of Distinction	15	2000	10%		27	N	E-O	A	3.0	N	B-2/1	N
	Science Symposium	Varies	5132			X	N	E-L-I-O	O	Y	S	B-C	N
	Social Sciences	10	5132	15%		26	N	O	O	3.1	S	B-C	N
	University Scholar	15	1000	10%		29	N	E-L-I-O	A	3.0	N	B-10/1	N
	AP Exams												
	Distance Learning												
	Co-op												
	Honors Program												
Upper Iowa U., Fayette 52142	Academic	Varies	1300-1800	20%	3.2	25	N		A	3.2	N	A-D	Y-3.2
	President's	Varies	2000	20%	3.8	28	N		A	3.2	N	A-D	Y-3.2
	AP Exams												
	Distance Learning												
	Alumni Discounts, Family Discounts												
	Honors Program												
Vennard, University Park 52595	Academic	Varies	1000-3000		3.5		N		A	3.5	N	B-8/1	Y-3.5
	Leadership	Varies	250		2.0		N	L	A	N	N	B-8/1	Y-2.0
	Presidential	Varies	750	1-2			N		A	N	N	A-8/1	N

Program		No. of Awards	Value Range	Award Criteria: Class Stndg.	Grade Avg.	SAT/ ACT	Need Based	Other	Study Fields	Renew-ability	Restric-tions	Apply Date	Transfer
IOWA *(Continued)*													
Wartburg, Waverly 50677	Meistersinger Music	Varies	380-2500				N	T-O	A	Y	N	B-C	Y
	Regents'	Unlimited	All Costs	10%		1160/28	N	E-L-I-O	A	3.0	N	B-C	N
	Presidential	Unlimited	To 6000	20%		1050/25	N	E-L-I-O	A	2.7	N	B-C	N
	Phi Theta Kappa	4	4000-5000		3.5		N	O	A		O		Y
	AP Exams												
	Alumni Discounts, Family Discounts												
	Internships												
William Penn, Oskaloosa 52577	Ferns Memorial	200	1000-7000	20%	3.5	1050/24	Y		A	3.3	N	A-5/1	Y-3.3
	Community College	Varies	To 6000	X	3.0	X	N		A	3.0	N	A-D	Y-3.0
KANSAS													
Baker U., Baldwin 66006	Baker	Unlimited	1200-2500		2.5		Y		A	2.5	N	C	Y
	Departmental	40	4000		3.0	24	N	L-R-I-O	A	3.0	N	B-2/15	Y-3.0
	Participation	Unlimited	200-1000		2.3		N	T-R-O	O	2.0	N	C	Y
	University	12	5000		3.25	29	N	E-L-R-I-O	A	3.25	N	B-2/15	N
	Honors Program												
Barclay College, Haviland 67059	Academic	Unlimited	900-1950		3.4		N		A	3.4	N	B	Y
	Church Match	Unlimited	To 500		2.0		N		A	2.0	N	B	Y
	Institutional	Unlimited	500-1600		2.5		N		A	2.5	N	B	Y
	AP Exams												
	Distance Learning												
	Alumni Discounts												
Benedictine, Atchison 66002	Academic	Unlimited	1000-6500	50%	2.0	840/18	Y		A	2.0	N	A-4/1	N
	Presidential	5	Tuition	50%	3.0	1200/27	N	E-L-R-I-O	A	3.0	N	B-1/15	N
Bethany, Lindsborg 67456	President's	15	2500-9875	X	X	X	N	E-L-R-I-O	A	3.25	O	B	N
	Bethany	Unlimited	500-2500	50%	3.0	21	N	O	A	2.75	N	A	Y-3.0
	Performance	Unlimited	500-2500	50%	2.5	19	N	T-R-O	A	2.25	N	A	Y-2.5
Bethel, N. Newton 67117	Academic	Unlimited	500-4000		3.0	20	N	I-O	A	3.0	N	A-6/1	Y-3.0
	Performance	Unlimited	500-1500				N	E-T-R-I-O	A	2.0	N	A-6/1	Y-2.0
	Endowed	Unlimited	100-1500				N		A	2.0	N	A-6/1	Y-2.0

Emporia State U., 66801	Endowed	1200	50-3000	15%	3.0	24	N	L	A	3.0	O	B-2/15	Y
	Academic	Varies	50-3000		2.76	24	N		A	3.0	N	B-2/15	Y-3.0
	Honors Program												
Fort Hays State U., Hays 67601	University Gold	30	1000		3.25	29	N		A	3.0	N	B-3/15	Y
	Hays City Silver	160	500			28	N		A	3.0	N	B-3/15	Y
	Fort Hays	220	300			21	N		A	3.0	N	B-3/15	Y
Friends U., Wichita 67213	Dean's	Unlimited	2000		3.7	25	N		A	3.2	N	A-D	Y
	Honors	Unlimited	1500		3.3	23	N		A	3.0	N	A-D	Y
	President's	5	5000		3.7	25	N	O	A	3.4	N	B-2/15	N
	Leadership	50	500		2.5		N	R	A	2.0	N	A-3/15	Y-2.5
	Tower	Unlimited	1000		3.0	20	N		A	2.5	N	B-D	Y-3.0
Kansas City Coll. & Bible School Overland Park 66204	Valedictorian	Unlimited	2500-6500		3.5		N		A	3.0	N	A	Y-3.5
	Salutatorian	Unlimited	1250-3250		3.25		N		A	3.0	N	A	Y-3.5
Kansas Newman, Wichita 67213	Board of Directors	Unlimited	To 1300		3.0	21	Y		A	3.0	N	A	Y-3.0
	Cardinal Newman	4	To 8500	10%	3.8	28	Y	E-L-R-I-O	A	3.4	N	B-3/15	N
	Dean's	Unlimited	To 2500	50%	3.3	23	Y		A	3.2	N	A	Y-3.5
	Presidential	Unlimited	To 4000	10%	3.6	25	Y		A	3.4	N	A	Y-3.9
	Trustee Grants	Unlimited	1000		2.5		N		O	X	S-O	A-D	N
Kansas State U., Manhattan 66506	Activities		500	33%		23	N		A	N	N	B-2/1	N
	Foundation	245	1250	15%	3.8	29	N		A	3.5	N	B-C	N
	Leadership	Varies	1200	33%		26	N	L-R-O	A	N	N	B-2/1	N
	Putnam	105	3000	10%	3.8	32	N	R	A	3.5	S	B-C	N
	AP Exams												
	Distance Learning												
	Co-op, Internships												
	Honors Program												
Kansas Wesleyan, Salina 67401	Activity/Talent	Unlimited	200-4000		2.5		Y	T	A	2.0	N	B-D	Y
	Eisenhower	Unlimited	2500		3.5	1030/22	N		A	3.25	N	D	Y
	Memorial	Unlimited	2000		3.0	950/20	N		A	3.0	N	D	Y
	Presidential	5	4000-4500		3.75	1140/25	N	E-L	A	3.3	N	B-2/1	N
Manhattan Christian College, Manhattan 66502	President's	7	1500	10%			N	O	A	3.0	N	A-B	N
	Trustee's	7	1000			25	N	O	A	3.0	N	A-B	
	Departmental	150	100-1400		3.0		N	R-O	A	3.0	N	B-3/15	Y-3.0
	Music	25	100-850				N	T-I-O	O	2.0	O	B-C	Y-2.0
	Honors Program												
McPherson College, 67460	Academic	Varies	600-1800	25%	3.2	22	N		A	Y	N	A-C	Y

	Program	No. of Awards	Value Range	Award Criteria: Class Stndg.	Grade Avg.	SAT/ACT	Need Based	Other	Study Fields	Renew-ability	Restric-tions	Apply Date	Transfer
KANSAS *(Continued)*													
Mid-America Nazarene, Olathe 66061	Chapman	Unlimited	4500		3.7	1150/28	N	L-O	A	3.7	N	A-C	N
	Dean's	Unlimited	1000		3.0	890/20	N		A	3.0	N	A-C	Y
	Presidential	Unlimited	3200		3.5	1060/26	N		A	3.5	N	A-C	Y
	Superior	Unlimited	1600		3.2	980/24	N		A	3.2	N	A-C	Y
Ottawa U., 66067	Dean's	Unlimited	Varies	10%		800/18	Y		A	3.0	N	A-D	N
	President's	Unlimited	1000	5%		1000/25	N		A	3.0	N	A-D	N
	AP Exams												
	Distance Learning												
	Co-op												
Pittsburg State U., 66762	Academic	100	400	X	X	X	N		A	Y	N	B-3/15	N
	Academic Achievement	Varies	100-1000		3.2	23			A				Y-3.5
	Community Coll. Honors	6	1800		3.75		N	L-R-I-O	A	3.4	N	B-2/15	Y
	Dean's	150	400	15%			N		A	N	N	B-3/15	N
	Presidential	15	6200	5%	3.7	28	N	E-T-L-R-I	A	3.5	N	B-2/15	N
	University	Varies	1800	5%	3.7	28	N	E-T-L-R-I	A	3.5	N	B-2/15	N
	AP Exams												
	Distance Learning												
	Co-op, Internships												
	Honors Program, Honors College												
St. Mary, Leavenworth 66048	Jubilee	3	To 9470	10%	3.5		Y	0	A	3.5	W	12/1	N
	Presidential	Unlimited	2400-3000	10%	3.5	25	N	0	A	3.0	N	A	Y
	Honor	Unlimited	1500-2200	25%	3.0	22	Y	0	A	3.0	N	A	Y
Southwestern, Winfield 67156	Beech Scholar	1	9110		3.75	27	Y	E-L-I-O	O	3.6	O	2/1	N
	Dean's	Unlimited	2300		3.6	26	N	O	A	3.4	N	A-8/1	Y-3.6
	Honor	Unlimited	1750		3.5	22	N	O	A	3.3	N	A-8/1	Y-3.4
	Mastin Scholar	1	9110		3.75	27	Y	E-L-I-O	O	3.6	O	2/1	N
	McNeish Scholar	1	9110		3.75	27	Y	E-L-I-O	O	3.6	O	2/1	N
	Moundbuilder	Unlimited	1200		3.0	20	Y	O	A	3.25	N	A-8/1	Y-3.25
	Presidential	Unlimited	4280		3.75	28	N	L-O	A	3.6	N	A-8/1	N
	Honors Program												
Sterling College, 67579	Academic	228	1000-2200		2.8	790/20	N	O	A	2.5	O	A-4/1	Y-3.3
	Performing Arts	Varies	200-2500		2.5		N	T-O	A	2.5	O	B-4/1	Y-2.5

	Athletic *Honors Program, Honors College*	Varies	Varies	50%	2.0	740/18	N	T-L-O	A	2.0	O	A-4/1	Y-2.0
Tabor, Hillsboro 67063	Collegiate	Varies	2072		X	X	Y	O	A	2.5	N	C	Y-2.5
	Dean's	5	5180		X	X	Y	O	A	3.25	N	C	N
	Honors	Varies	3418		X	X	Y	O	A	3.0	N	C-5/15	Y-3.0
	Merit	Varies	2590		X	X	Y	O	A	2.75	N	C-5/15	Y-2.5
	National Merit	Unlimited	1036				Y	O	A		N	C	
	Participation	Varies	Variable				Y	O	A		O	C	
	Presidential	2	7770		X	X	Y	L-O	A	3.5	N	C	N
	AP Exams Distance Learning Alumni Discounts, Family Discounts Internships *Honors Program*												
U. of Kansas, Lawrence 66045	Departmental	1200	50-2000	X	X		X	O	A	X	N	C	Y
	Endowment Merit	75	500-1000	X	X	X	X	L-R-O	A	Y	M	C	Y
	Honor	600	100-1500	10%		30	N		A	X	O	C	Y
	KU	800	100-2500		X		Y		A	X	O	C	Y
Washburn U., Topeka 66621	Academic	1200	200-1400		3.0		N	T-L-R-O	A	3.0	N	C-3/15	Y
	Garvey Competition	50-60	400-1400		3.0		N	E-L-R-I-O	A	3.0	S	B-2/8	N
	Presidential	18	1000	10%	3.5		N	T-L-R-I-O	A	3.5	S	B-3/15	N
	Departmental	500	100-1400		3.0		N	R-O	A	3.0	N	B-3/15	Y-3.0
	*Honors Program												
Wichita State U., 67208	Distinguished	400	250-10000	10%	3.5	24	N	E-L-I-O	A	3.2	N	A-C	N
	President's	19	500	10%	3.5		N	L/L/ERRL	A	3.2	S	B-C	Y
	University	Varies	400-3000	10%	3.4	18	Y	E-T-R	A	3.2	N	C-3/15	Y
	Honors Program												
KENTUCKY													
Alice Lloyd, Pippa Passes 41844	Tuition Scholarship	Unlimited	6360		2.25		N	E-L	A	2.0	N	A-D	N
Asbury, Wilmore 40390	Honors	7	4000-8000		3.9		N	O	A	N	N	B-5/1	Y
	Presidential	120	800-2400		3.25		X		A	3.5	N	B-5/1	Y
Bellarmine, Louisville 40205	Art	5	1000	50%	2.5	950/21	N	E-T-R-I-O	O	2.5	N	B-2/1	N
	Bellarmine Scholars	8	Full Tuition	5%	3.9	1340/30	N	E-L-R-I-O	A	3.5	N	A1/15	N
	Horrigan	150-250	1000-7000	25%	3.4	1100/24	N	E-L-R-I-O	A	3.0	N	A1/15	N
	McDonough Service	15-30	1000-2000	50%	2.5	950/21	N	E-L-R-I-O	A	3.0	N	A-2/1	N
	Minority	10	1500-Tuition	50%	3.0	950/21	N	E-R-I-O	A	3.0	M	A-2/1	N
	Music	5	1000	50%	2.5	950/21	N	E-T-R-I-O	O	2.5	N	B-2/1	N

	Program	No. of Awards	Value Range	Award Criteria					Study Fields	Renew-ability	Restric-tions	Apply Date	Transfer
				Class Stndg.	Grade Avg.	SAT/ ACT	Need Based	Other					
KENTUCKY *(Continued)*													
Bellarmine, Louisville 40205 *(Continued)*	Wilson Wyatt Leadership	15-25	1000-2000	Top 50	2.5	1000/21	N	E-L-R-I	A	2.0	N	A-2/1	N
	Honors Program												
Berea, 40404	AP Exams												
	Co-op, Internships												
Brescia, Owensboro 42301	Academic	40	To All Costs			X	N	R	A	Y	N	B-3/1	Y
Campbellsville College, 42718	Excellence in Action	33	1000-7200		2.0		N	T-L-R	A	2.0	D	B-4/1	N
	Transfer Scholarship	Unlimited	1000-1500		3.25		N	L-0	A	3.0	0	B-4/1	Y
Centre, Danville 40422	Honor	100	2500	10%	3.5	27	N	L-R-I	A	3.0	N	C-2/1	N
	Trustee	1	Tuit., Rm & Bd	5%	3.5	30	N	L-R-I	A	3.6	N	C-2/1	N
	Heritage	10-15	To 7500	10%	3.5	27	N	L-R-I	A	2.5	N	C-2/1	N
	President's	5-10	12700	5%	3.5	29	N	L-R-I	A	3.2	N	C-2/1	N
	Colonel	10	5000	10%	3.5	27	N	L-R-I-0	A	2.7	0	C-2/1	N
	Faculty	50-100	6000	10%	3.5	28	N	L-R-I	A	2.8	N	C-2/1	N
	Dean's	10-25	9000	10%	3.5	28	N	L-R-I	A	3.0	N	C-2/1	N
Cumberland, Williamsburg 40769	Academic	323	1900-5600		X	X	N		A	3.0	N	A	Y-3.0
	Music/Art	25	200-800				N	L-I-0	0	2.0	N	A	Y-2.0
	Leadership	150	400-2200		2.0	740/18	N	0	A	2.25	N	A	Y
Georgetown College, 40324	Trustee	250	2000-Tuition	5%	3.5	25	N	L	A	3.5	N	A-2/1	N
	Presidential	20	1000-2250	10%	3.5	25	N	L	A	3.5	N	A-3/1	N
	AP Exams												
	Co-op, Internships												
Kentucky Christian, Grayson 41143	Academic Excellence	5	6923		4.0	29-30	N			3.5	N	A	Y-3.5
	Honors	Unlimited	1500	X	X	1020/26	N		A	N	N	A-D	N
	Salutatorian	Unlimited	1000	2	X	820/21	N		A	N	N	A-D	N
	Valedictorian	Unlimited	1500	1	X	910/23	N		A	N	N	A-D	N
Kentucky Wesleyan, Owensboro 42301	Academic	Unlimited	20-50%Tuition	25%		900/22	N	E-I-0	A	2.8	N	B-3/15	Y-3.0
	J.G. Brown	10	Tuition	5%	'3.8	1280/29	N	E-I-0	A	3.25	N	B-3/15	N
	Presidential	Unlimited	20-60% Tuition	25%	3.0	1030/22	N	E-I-0	A	'3.25	N	B-3/15	N
	Special Talent	Unlimited	1000-2000				N	T	0	Y	N	C	Y
	Stanley Reed Leadership	80	2000-5000	50%	2.5	910/19	N	E-L-R	A	Y	N	B-C	N

	Transfer	Unlimited	1000-50% Tuit.				N	E-I-0	A	3.0	0	B-3/15	Y-3.0
	Trustee	Varies	60% Tuition	25%		900/22	N	E-I-0	A	3.0	N	B-3/15	Y-3.0
Midway College, 40347	Keenland Scholarship	1-4	1500		3.0	770/20	Y	E-L	0		W	B-3/1	Y
	Leadership Scholarships	20	1000		3.0	21	N	E-L	A		W	B-3/1	Y
	Presidential	15	3650	X	3.3	25	N	0	A	3.0	W	A-C	Y
	Trustee	15	7300	X	3.6	28	N	0	A	3.3	W	A-C	Y
Morehead State U., 40351	Honors Program Scholars	12	600	15%		26	N	L	A	Y	S-0	C	N
	KY Governor's Scholar	Varies	Tuition				N		A	3.25	S-0	A-4/1	Y
	MSU Award	100	1200		3.5	20	N	L-R-0	A	3.0	0	C-3/15	N
	Presidential	25	3600		3.75	28	N		A	3.25	0	B-3/15	N
	Regents'	50	1800		3.5	25	N		A	3.0	0	B-3/15	N
	Regional Honors I	40	3000	1st	3.5	20	N	R	A	3.25	S-0	D	Y
	Regional Honors II	40	2400	2nd	3.5	20	N	R	A	3.25	S-0	D	Y
	Transfer Award	50	650		3.0		N	R-0	A	3.0	0	C-3/15	Y-3.0
	Tuition Assistance Grant	200	1000-2000		3.0	2	N	0	A	3.0	0	3/15	Y-3.0
	Honors Program												
Murray State U., 42071	Academic	Varies	Costs	15%	3.3	21	Y	E-T-L-R-I-0	A	3.0	0	B-2/1	Y-3.0
	Honors Program												
Northern Kentucky U., Highland Heights 41099	Academic Housing	16	Room			25	N	0	A	N	S	C-2/1	N
	Minority Opportunity	8	Tuition				N	R	A	Y	M	C-2/1	N
	Presidential	60	Tuition	1-10		26	N		A	Y	N	C-2/1	N
	Honors Program												
Pikeville College, 41501	Academic	Varies	1234-3534	10%			Y		A	3.0	N	B-3/15	Y-3.0
	Academic	Varies	4100-6400		3.75	27	Y	0	A	3.5	N	B-3/15	Y-3.75
	Presidential	15	Tuition		3.5	25	N	R	A	Y	N	B-3/1	Y
Spalding, Louisville 40203	Academic Major	1/Major	1/4 Tuition				N	T-I-0	0	Y	N	B-3/1	N
	Artistic Grants	Varies	1000-5000		2.5	880/18	N	E-T	0	2.5	N	C-7/1	Y-2.5
	Caritas Awards	Varies	1/2 Tuition		3.0	1010/22	N	E-L-R-I	A	3.0	N	C-2/15	N
	Evers/Chaney	1	800-2000	33%	3.0	X	Y	R-0	A	Y	M	B-3/15	N
	Honors	Varies	3000-4000		3.0	1010/22	N		0	3.0	N	C-7/1	N
	Living & Learning	10	1340				N	L-R-I-0	A	Y	0	B-7/1	Y-2.5
	Presidential	5	Tuition		3.25	1160/26	N	E-R-I	A	3.4	N	C-2/15	N
	Spalding Honor	60	800-3000	25%	3.0	1010/22	Y	T-R-0	A	3.0	N	A-3/15	Y
	Teacher's Choice Service	Varies	1000				N	L-R-I-0	A	N	N	A-3/1	N
	Transfer Honors	Varies	3000-35000				N		0	3.4	N	C-7/1	Y-3.4
	Val/Sal	Varies	6200	1&2		930/20	N		A	3.4	N	C-7/1	N
	AP Exams												
	Alumni Discounts, Family Discounts												
	Family Discounts												

	Program	No. of Awards	Value Range	Award Criteria: Class Stndg.	Grade Avg.	SAT/ ACT	Need Based	Other	Study Fields	Renew-ability	Restric-tions	Apply Date	Transfer
KENTUCKY *(Continued)*													
Thomas More, Crestview Hills, 41017	Presidential	Varies	1000-5000		3.0	1060/23	N		A	3.0			
	Trustee	Varies	Tuition		3.7	1280/29	N	E-I	A	3.5			
	AP Exams												
	Alumni Discounts												
	Co-op												
	Honors Program												
Transylvania U., Lexington 40508	Dean's Recognition	Varies	3500-8500	50%	3.0	1100/24	N	L-R	A	Y	N	A-3/1	Y-2.75
	James Morrison	30	7500	10%	3.5	1200/27	N	E-I-L-R	A	3.2	N	12/8	N
	Pioneer	40	5000	25%	3.25	1100/24	N	E-I-L-R-T	A	3.0	N	12/8	N
	William T. Young	25	Tuition & Fees	5%	3.75	1300/30	N	E-I-L-R	A	3.5	N	12/8	N
Union, Barbourville 40906	Achievement Scholarship	Unlimited	2000			980/21	N		A	2.9	N	A-B-5/1	N
	Dean's	Unlimited	2500			1100/24	N		A	3.2	N	A-5/1	N
	Trustee	5	3500			1210/27	N	L-R-I-O	A	3.4	N	A-3/15	N
	Union Scholars	3	Tuition	10%	3.5	1320/30	N	E-L-R-I-O	A	3.5	N	A-3/1	N
	AP Exams												
	Alumni Discounts, Family Discounts												
U. of Kentucky, Lexington 40506	Academic Excellence	100	1000		3.3	1240/28	N	E-L	A	N	O	B-1/1	N
	Chancellor	40	1000	X	3.3	1240/28	N	E-L	A	3.3	O	B-1/1	N
	Commonwealth	10	2500	X	3.3	1240/28	N	E-L-O	A	3.3	O	B-1/1	N
	KY Valedictorian	50	500	1	X	X	N	O	A	N	S	B-6/15	N
	National Merit Finalist		Varies				N	O	A	3.3	O		N
	Presidential	10	Tuition	X	3.3	1240/28	N	E-L-O	A	3.3	O	B-1/1	N
	Singletary	20	All Costs	X	3.75	1360/31	N	E-L-I	A	3.3	O	B-1/1	N
	Honors Program												
U. of Louisville, 40292	President's	Varies	Tuition	X	3.0	1070/23	N	R	A	3.0	S		
	McConnell	10	6220		3.0	990/21	N	E-I-L-R-	A	3.0	S		
	Commonwealth	Varies	500-1000		3.0	1070/23	N	R	A	N	S		
	AP Exams												
	Distance Learning												
	Co-op, Internships												
	Honors Program												

W. Kentucky U., Bowling Green 42101	Varies	400	300-5300	5%	3.5	1130/25	N	E-I-L	A	X	0	B-2/1	Y
	AP Exams												
	Distance Learning												
	Alumni Discounts												
	Co-op, Internships												
	Honors Program												
LOUISIANA													
Centenary, Shreveport 71104	Centenary Academic	Unlimited	1000-6000		3.0	1130/25	N	E-L-I-0	A	3.0	N	B-3/15	Y-3.0
	Music	Varies	200-7000				N	T-I-0	0	Y	N	C-2/15	Y
Dillard U., New Orleans 70122	University Scholar	Varies	Tuition		3.5	1070/23	N		A	Y	N	B-4/30	N
	University	Inquire	1000-4000	10%	2.5	17	N		A	Y	N	B-C	N
	Honors Program												
Grambling State U., Grambling 71245	Presidential	Varies	Varies	X	X	X	Y	R		3.5			
	Presidential Merit	20	500-4724			1200/25	N	R-I-E-0	A	3.5	N	A-B-7/15	Y-3.5
	Academic	Varies	1500	X	X	X	N	L		3.0			
	Honors Program, Honors College												
Louisiana, Pineville 71359	Alumni	Varies	600-1200		3.0	980/24	N	E-I-0	A	Y	N	B-11/30	N
	Smith	Varies	1800-3000		3.5	1100/27	N	E-I-0	A	Y	N	B-11/30	N
	Presidential	Varies	Varies				N		A	3.0	N	C	N
	LC Scholars	Varies	Varies				N		A	3.0	N	C	N
	Leadership	Varies	Varies				N	L	A	2.5	N	C	
	Honors Program												
Louisiana State U., Baton Rouge 70803	Alumni Association	100	4067-7267		X	X	N		A	Y	N	B-D	N
	Chancellor's	7-10	5667-8867		A	X	N	E-I-0	A	Y	N	B-D	N
	LSU Merit/Achievement	50	4067-7267				N	0	A	Y	N	B-D	N
	LSU Honor	500	1008-3317		X	X	N		A	Y	S	B-D	N
	Honors Program, Honors College												
Louisiana State U., Shreveport 71115	LSUS	20	2680		3.5	28	N		A	3.2	S	B-12/1	N
	Foundation	25	1000-2000		3.0	25	N		A	3.0	N	B-2/1	N
	Annie Lowe Stiles	10	500-2000		3.0	23	N		A	3.0	N	B-2/1	N
Louisiana Tech. U., Ruston 71272	Board of Trustees	Varies	Varies	X	X	25	N	L	A	Y	S	A-12/1	N
	Out-of-State	Varies	Fee Waiver	10%	3.0	24	N	L-I	A	Y	N	A-2/1	Y
	Presidential	Varies	Full Costs	X	X	32	N	L-R-I-0	A	3.0	0	B-12/1	N
	Outstanding	Varies	1000-1500	X	X	27	N	L-R-I-0	A	3.0	N	B-12/1	N
	Honors Program												

	Program	No. of Awards	Value Range	Award Criteria: Class Stndg.	Grade Avg.	SAT/ ACT	Need Based	Other	Study Fields	Renew-ability	Restric-tions	Apply Date	Transfer
LOUISIANA *(Continued)*													
Loyola U., New Orleans 70118	Business	40	3000-6000		3.2	X	N	E-L-R-I	A	3.0	0	A-1/15	N
	Dean	20	2000-8000		3.5	1300/29	N	E-L-R-I-0	A	3.3	N	A-B-1/15	N
	Drama	Varies	1000-5000				N	T-R	0	2.3	N	B-1/15	Y
	Ignatian	10	Tuition/Room		3.5	1300/29	N	E-L-R-I	A	3.3	N	A-1/15	N
	Loyola	450	2500-8000		3.2	X	N	E-L-R-I	A	3.0	N	A-1/15	Y-3.0
	Music	Varies	2000-8000				N	T-I	0	2.3	N	B-3/15	Y
	Social Justice	10	3000-6000		3.0	X	N	E-L-R-I	A	3.0	0	A-1/15	N
	Transfer	40	2000-4000		3.2		N	E-L-R-I-0	A	3.0	0	A-B-6/1	Y
	Visual Arts	1	1000-5000				N	T	0	2.3	N	B-1/15	N
	Honors Program												
Nicholls State U., Thibodaux 70310	Academic	20	300-1800		3.0		N		A	3.0	S	A-4/1	Y-3.0
	Science		1800		3.0		Y	E	0	Y	0	A	
	Honors Program												
Northeast Louisiana U., Monroe 71209	Presidential	Varies	4600	X	3.5	30	N		A	3.0		C	N
	State Board	Varies	1250	X	3.5	28	N		A	3.0	S	C	N
	NLU - 4 Year	Varies	1200-2000	X	3.5	28	N	L-R	A	3.0		C	N
	Greater NLU Ann. Fund-4 yr.	Varies	1000	X	3.5	26	N		A	3.0		C	N
	Greater NLU Ann. Fund-1 yr.	Varies	1000	X	3.5	25	N	L-R	A	N		C	N
	Out-of-State	Varies	2400	10%	3.0	24	N	L-I	A	3.0		C	N
Northwestern State U., Natchitoches 71457	Academic	100	1400	10%	3.5	28	N	T-L-R-I-0	A	3.0	N	B-12/1	N
	Presidential	100	400-1000	15%	2.8	20	N	T-L-R-I-0	A	2.5	N	B-12/1	N
	Performance	200	400-1100				N	T-L-R-I-0	A	2.0	N	B-3/15	Y-2.0
	AP Exams												
	Distance Learning												
	Co-op												
	Honors Program, Honors College												
Our Lady of Holy Cross, New Orleans 70131	Academic	4	3960		3.0	24	N	L-R	A	3.0	N	B-2/1	N
	Moreau	4	3960		3.0	24	N	E-I-L-R	A	3.0	N	B-2/1	N
	Presidential	4	3960		3.0	24	N	E-I-L-R	A	3.0	N	B-2/1	N
	Honors Program												
SE Louisiana U., Hammond 70402	Board of Trustees	25	1900	X	3.0	24	N	R-I-0	A	3.0	S	B-1/29	N
	Presidential Honors	30	1300	X	3.0	24	N	R-I-0	A	X	N	B-1/29	N

Southern U., New Orleans 70126	SUNO	80-100	700-1400		3.0	20	N	L-R	A	3.0	S	B-6/15	Y
	AP Exams												
	Co-op, Internships												
Tulane U., New Orleans 70118	Deans' Honor Scholarships	100	Tuition	5%	A	1400/32	N	E-T-L-R	A	3.0	N	B-12/1	N
	Founders' Scholarships	100	8000	10%	3.5	1250	Y		A	2.7	N	A-1/15	N
	National Merit/Achievement	30	500-2000				Y	0	A	Y	0	1/15	N
	Honors Program												
U. of New Orleans, 70148	Decennial	50	1524-2160		3.0	25	N		A	3.0	S	B-12/31	N
	Honor Student	15	1524	X	3.0		N	R	A	3.0	N	C	Y
	Founder's		1000		2.5	20							
	Bienville		Inquire		2.5	20							
	Freshman Honor		250		3.0	25							
U. of SW Louisiana, Lafayette 70504	Scholarship Testing	268	600-2000	10%	3.0	25	N	0	A	3.0	S	B-11/1	N
	Distinguished Freshman	100	600-1000	10%	3.0	20	N	L-R	A	N	S	B-2/1	N
	Honors Program												
Xavier U., New Orleans 70126	Academic	Varies	1000-7700		3.2	1010/22	N	R	A	Y	N	A-3/1	N
MAINE													
Bowdoin, Brunswick 04011	AP Exams												
Colby, Waterville 04901	Ralph J. Bunche	12-15	200-4450	10%	3.0		Y	0	A	Y	M	B-1/15	N
Husson, Bangor 04401	Academic	10	1000	10%	3.0	X	N	L-R	A	3.4	N	B-4/1	N
St. Joseph's, N. Windham 04062	Student Leadership	Varies	1000-5000	10%	3.0	1200	Y	L	A	2.75	N	A-3/1	Y-3.0
	Minority Assistance Grant	Varies	500-3500	50%	2.5		Y		A		M	3/1	Y-2.5
Thomas, Waterville 04901	BEAM	3	1000-2500				N	E	A	N	S	A	N
	Entrepreneurial	1	500-3000				Y	E-L-R	A	2.7	N	B-4/1	N
	HS Teachers	10	Tuition	10%	3.0	1000	N	0	A	3.0	S	B-C	N
	Thomas	Many	1000-3000	30%	2.5	1000	Y	L-R-I	A	2.5	N	A-D	Y-3.0
Unity College, 04988	Academic Merit	40-50	750-1200	20%	3.25	1000	N	E-R	A	3.25	N	A-B-C	Y-3.25
	Environmental Action	10	500-750				N	E-L-R-0	A	N	N	A-B-4/1	Y
	Presidential	20	2500	10%	3.5	1100	N	L-0	A	N	N	A-1/15	Y-3.5
U. of Maine, Augusta 04330	*Honors Program*												
U. of Maine, Farmington 04930	Alumni Scholars	10	In-state Tuition	10%	3.5	X	N	E-I-L-R	A	3.0	N	B-2/6	N
	Minority	3	In-state Tuition	10%	3.5	X	N	E-R	A	2.5	S-M	4/15	N
	Presidential	Unlimited	2000	50%	3.5	X	N	E-R	A	2.75	0	A-4/15	N
	AP Exams												
	Honors Program												

	Program	No. of Awards	Value Range	Award Criteria: Class Stndg.	Grade Avg.	SAT/ ACT	Need Based	Other	Study Fields	Renew-ability	Restric-tions	Apply Date	Transfer
MAINE *(Continued)*													
U. of New England, Biddeford 04005	Achievement Award	Varies	1000-3000				N	E-T-L-R-0	A	2.5	N	C	N
	Merit Scholarship	Varies	2000-4000		3.0	1100	N	T-L-E-0	A	2.5	N	A	Y
	Presidents Scholarship	Varies	500		3.0	1100	N	I-0	0	3.0	N	A	N
	UNE Grant	Varies	200-5000				Y	I-0	A	Y	N	A	N
	Univ. Scholars Program	Varies	1000-3000		3.0	1100	N	I-0	0	3.0	N	A	N
MARYLAND													
Baltimore Hebrew U., 21215	Various	Limited					Y	I-0	A	Y	0	B	Y
Bowie State College, Bowie 20715	Alumni Assn. Int'l.	Varies	Tuition & Fees		3.5	1000	N		A	3.25	S	C	Y-3.5
	Joanna Fisher Schp.	Varies	Tuition		2.5		Y	E-R-0	A		S-0	C	
	Out-of State Students	Varies	All Costs		3.3	1050/26	N	I	A		0	C	N
	P.G. Chamber of Commerce	Varies	Tuition & Fees		2.5		Y	0	0	Y	S-0	C	
	Presidential	Varies	Tuition & Fees		3.0	1000	N	E-R-I-0	A		S-0	C	N
	Presidential Transfer	Varies	Tuition & Fees		3.25	1000	N	E-R-I-0	A		S-0	C	Y-3.25
	Thurgood Marshall Schp.	Varies	All Costs		3.0	1000/24	N	T-L	A	3.0	0	C	N
	Tuition Waiver	Varies	Tuition	10%	3.5	1200/29	N	T-L-R-0	A		S	A-D	Y
Capitol College, Laurel 20708	Carl English	1	1250-4000		2.75		N	E-R	A	N	M	B-4/1	Y-2.75
	Corporate/Foundation	15	1250-4000		3.0		N	E	A	3.0	N	B-4/1	N
	Distinguished	20	500-2000		3.0	800	N	E-R	A		N	C	
	President's	Varies	3000-4000		3.25	1050	N		A	3.0	N	A-S	Y-3.4
	Wainwright	28	1250-4000		3.0		N	E	A	3.0	N	B-4/1	Y
College of Notre Dame of MD, Baltimore 21210	Academic Merit	Varies	4000-Tuition		3.0	1050-1280	N	E-L-R-I-0	A	2.5	W	A-2/15	N
	Talent	Varies	2000		2.5	950	N	0	A	2.5	W	A-2/15	Y-2.5
	Marion Burk Knott	Varies	Tuition		3.5	1280	N	E-L-R-I-0	A	3.5	S-D-W	A-2/15	N
	Transfer	Varies	1/2 Tuition		3.25		N	E-R-I-0	A	2.75	W-0	B-2/15	Y-3.25
	Engineering	2	5000		3.0+	1100	N	E-L-R-I-0	0-I-0	Y	S-W-0	B-2/15	N
	Leadership/Service	Varies	4000		3.0	950	N	E-L-R-I-0	A	2.5	W	B-2/15	Y-2.5
	Honors Program												
Columbia Union, Takoma Park 20912	Academic (1)	Varies	1500		3.5		N		A	3.5	0	A-C	Y-3.5
	Academic (2)	Varies	1000		3.0		N		A	3.0	0	A-C	Y-3.0
	Athletic	Varies	500-10500		2.0		N	I-0	A	3.0	N	A	Y
	Leadership	Varies	1500		2.5		N	L	A	3.0	N	A-C	Y

	Music	Varies	10,000				N	T-R-I-O	O	2.0	N	A-C	Y-2.0
	National Acad. Testing	Varies	2625-10,500		3.0	90%ile	N	O	A	3.0	N	A	Y
	National Testing Merit	Varies	2625-10,500		3.0	90%ile	N	O	A	3.0	N	A	Y
Coppin State, Baltimore 21216	4-Year Honors Scholarship	30	2999-6213		3.0	950/22	N	R-O	A	3.0	O	A-B-C	N
	Achievement Scholarship	10	2749-5963		3.0	950/22	N	R-O	A	2.5	O	A-B-C	N
	Honors Program	100	250-3590		3.0	800	N	L-I-O	A	3.0	N	D-4/1	Y-3.0
	Opportunity Scholarship	10	1374-3669		2.0	1100/25	N		A	2.5	O	A-C	N
	Upper Division Honors	5	2999-6213		3.0		N	R-O	A	3.0	O	A-B-C	Y-3.0
	Honors Program												
Frostburg State University, 21532	Daily Award	8	500		3.5	1050		O					
	Meritorious Achiev.	100+	Tuition		3.5	1000	N	T-L	A	X	S	C	Inq.
	Music Department	3	250-350				N	T-R-O	O	N	O	D	Inq.
	Residential	50	1000		3.0	1000	N		A	2.0	O	A-D	Y-3.25
	Honors Program												
Goucher, Towson 21204	Perry	Unlimited	8500-10000		3.0	1100/24	N		A	2.67			
	Dean's	15	Tuition	10%	3.5	1350/28	N	I-L-R	A	3.0			
	Artistic Achievement	13	5000		3.0	1100/24	N	R-T	O	2.67			
	AP Exams												
	Internships												
	Honors Program												
Hood College, Frederick 21701	Academic	Varies	2500-17,000	X	X	X			A				
	Beneficial-Hodson	Up to 20	4500-12000	10%	3.5	1200	N	I	A	Y	O	B-3/31	Y
	Pres. Leadership	Up to 20	3000		3.0		N	L-R-I	A	Y	N	A-3/31	Y
	Trustee	50	7500-10,000	20%	3.3	1100	N		A	3.0	N	A-2/15	Y
	AP Exams												
	Family Discounts												
	Internships												
	Honors Program												
Johns Hopkins U., Baltimore 21218	Beneficial-Hodson	15	17000	5%	4.0	1400	N	L-R	A	3.0			
	National Achiev.	30	500-2000				Y	O		Y			
	AP Exams												
	Distance Learning												
	Internships												
Loyola, Baltimore 21210	Claver	Varies	3000-Tuition				N	L-R-I-O	A	Y	M	A-1/15	N
	Loyola	Varies	Varies		3.5	1300	N	L-R-I-O	A	2.5	N	A-1/15	N
	Marion Burk Knott	1	Tuition	10%	3.75	1400	N	R	A	3.0	S-D	A-1/15	N
	Presidential	150	5000-Tuition		3.7	1300	N	L-R-I-O	A	3.0	N	A-1/15	N
	Honors Program												

	Program	No. of Awards	Value Range	Class Stndg.	Grade Avg.	SAT/ ACT	Need Based	Other	Study Fields	Renew-ability	Restric-tions	Apply Date	Transfer
				Award Criteria									
MARYLAND *(Continued)*													
Morgan State U., Baltimore 21239	Institutional	Varies	To Tuition +	10%	3.0	1000	N		A	3.0	N	B-4/1	N
	Curriculum Base	Varies	12000	10%	3.0	1000/22	N	R-I-O	A	3.0	N	B-4/1	N
	Honors Program												
Mt. St. Mary's, Emmitsburg 21727	Mount Scholarships	Varies	4000-8000	30%		1100	N		A		N		
	Merit Grants	Varies	3000-6000	30%	X	1000	N		A				
	Kuderer	3	Tuition		3.25	1200	N	E-O	A		N		
	Funston Collins	Varies	2000-5000	X	X	X	N		A		M		
	Honors Program												
Peabody Institute, Baltimore 21202	Peabody	Varies	1000-8000		3.0		N	T	O	3.0	N	B-2/15	Y-3.0
	Director's	Varies	1000-8000		3.0		N	T	O	3.0	N	A-2/15	Y-3.0
St. John's, Annapolis 21404	St. John's Grant	Varies	1000-18000				Y		A	Y	N	B-3/1	Y
St. Mary's College,St. Mary's City 20686	Ark and Dove	6	1500-3500		3.0	1000	N	E-L-R	A	3.0	S	B-3/1	Y-3.0
	Brent-Calvert	64	1500-4500		3.5	1200	N	E-L-R-I	A	Y	N	B-2/1	Y-3.0
	D'Sousa	20-30	1000-6400	10%	3.0	1000	N	E-L-R-I	A	Y	N	B-3/1	Y-3.0
	Presidential	11	1000		3.0	1000	N	E-L-R	A	3.0	N	B-3/1	Y-3.0
	Honors Program, Honors College												
Salisbury State, 21801	Fulton	5	1000-2000		3.3	1100		L-R					
	Handicapped	Varies	Tuition		2.5	800	N	E	A	2.5	N	B-D	N
	Henson	3	1000-2000		3.25	1150	N		O	3.3	N	C	N
	Minority Status	25	1000-6000		Var.	800	N		A	Y	S-M	D	N
	Perdue	20	1000-2000		3.25	1100	N		A	3.25	N	A-3/1	N
	President's Merit	50	1000-2000		3.25	1100	N		A	3.25	S	A-3/1	N
	Honors Program												
Towson State U, Towson 21204	Community	10	Tuition+Fees		2.75		N	L-O	A	N	S-M	B-3/1	Y-3.6
	Handicapped Student	Varies	Tuition+Fees		3.0		N	E	A	2.75	S-O	B-1/1	N
	Helen Aletta Linthicum	8	1000	10%			N		A	N	S	B-3/1	N
	Minority	25+	1000		3.0	1000	N	L	A	3.0	S-M	A-3/1	Y
	Presidential	50	3200-4000		3.5	1200	N	L-O	A	3.25	N	A-3/1	Y-3.75
	Provost's	50	500-3000		3.0	1050	N	L-R-O	A	3.0	N	A-3/1	N
	University	50	2500-3500		3.5	1100	N	L-O	A	3.0	N	A-3/1	Y-3.5
	Honors Program, Honors College												

U. of Baltimore, 21201	Foundation	25	800-1600		3.25		N	E	A	3.0	N	B-4/1	Y
	Foundation Fellowship	35	1600		3.25		N	R	A	3.0	0	C-4/1	Y
U. of Maryland, College Park 20742	Banneker-Key	100	All Costs				N	E-I-L-R	A	3.0	N		
	President's	1660	2000-4500				N	E-L-R	A	3.0	N		
	Dean's	250	1500				N	E-L-R	A	N			
	AP Exams												
	Co-op, Internships												
	Honors Program												
U. of MD, B'more County, Baltimore 21228	Talented Students	Varies	250-3500	X	X	X	X		A	X	0	C	Y
U. of MD, E. Shore, Princess Anne 21853	Gen. Honors	25	500-Tuition	20%	3.0	1000	N	E-R-I	A	3.0	N	B-3/1	Y
	Henson	1-2	Tuition+1000	X	3.0	X	N	L-0	A	Y	N	B-3/1	N
	Honors	20	Tuition	15%	3.5	1200	N	E-R-I-0	A	3.0	M	B-3/1	N
	NASA	Varies	1600	X	3.0	X	N	0	0	3.0	M	A-D	N
	President's	Varies		X	3.0	X	N	0	0	3.0	N	A-D	N
	Regents	Varies	Tuition+1000	X	4.0	1400	N	0	A	3.5	N	B-2/1	N
	UMES-UMAB	30	500-Tuition	20%	3.0	1000	N	E-R-I	A	3.5	N	B-3/1	Y
	UMES-VMRCVM	5	500-Tuition	20%	3.0	1000	N	E-R-I	0	3.0	S-M	B-3/1	N
	Departmental	Varies	Varies	X	3.0	X	N	0	0	3.0	N	B-3/1	Y
Washington, Chestertown 21620	Scholars	150	10,000-15,000		3.5	1140	N	L-0	A	3.0	N	A-2/15	N
	Phi Theta Kappa	15	10,000		3.5		N	0	A	3.0	N	A-7/1	Y
	AP Exams												
Western Maryland, Westminster 21157	WMC Academic	Varies	1000-Tuition	20%	3.5	1100	N	E-R-I	A	3.0	N	A-2/1	Y-3.5
MASSACHUSETTS													
American International College, Springfield 01109	Academic	Varies	500-11,800	20%	3.0	800	N	R-I-0	A	2.75	N	A	Y-3.0
	Merit	25	900-2000	0.5	2.5		N	L-R-I-0	A	2.67	N	A-4/1	N
	Honors Program												
Anna Maria College, Paxton 01612	H.S. Alliance	Varies	Varies		X	X	N	E-L-R-I-0	A	3.25	0	A-C	N
	Music	Varies	250-1000				N	T	0	Y	N	B-C	Y
	Presidential	Varies	Partial Tuition	10%	3.5	1100	N	E-L-R-I-0	A	3.25	N	A-C	N
	Multicultural	Varies	Partial Tuition	10%	3.5	1000	N	E-L-R-I-0	A	3.25	M	A-C	N
	Transfer	Varies	Partial Tuition		3.5		N	E-L-R-I-0	A	3.25	N	A-C	Y
Babson, Wellesley 02157	Challenge	Varies	1000-Tuition			X	Y	E-L-R	A	Y	M	B-C	Y
	Sorenson	5	2 Courses	X			N	0	A	N	0	C	Inq.
	Presidential	Varies	5000	X	X	X				3.2			
	Honors Program												

	Program	No. of Awards	Value Range	Award Criteria: Class Stndg.	Grade Avg.	SAT/ ACT	Need Based	Other	Study Fields	Renew- ability	Restric- tions	Apply Date	Transfer
MASSACHUSETTS *(Continued)*													
Bentley, Waltham 02254	Freshman Academic	80	Costs	7%		1050	N		A	X	0	A-D	N
	Academic/Minority	5	Costs	5%		1300	N		A	X	0	A-D	N
	Merit		Tuition	3%	A	1300	N	R-I-0	A	3.5	0	A-2/1	N
	Minority		Tuition				N	R-I-0	A	2.8	M-0	A-2/1	N
	Honors Program												
Boston College, Chestnut Hill 02167	Boston College		500-9900	X			Y		A	3.0	N	B-2/1	Y
	Boston College Grant		500-17,900	X	X	X	Y	0	A	Y	N	B-2/1	Y
	Presidential Scholar	10	9000-17,900+	X	X	X	Y	E-L-R-I-0	A	3.4	N	C-11/1	N
	Honors Program												
Boston U., 02215	Arts	Varies	Varies				N	T	0	2.3	N	1/15	Y
	Trustee	26	Tuition, fees	1%	3.9	1500/33	N	R-0	A	3.5	N	B-12/1	Y-3.9
	Dean's Scholarship	Varies	7500	9%	3.6	1280/28	N	R-0	0	3.0	0		N
	University Scholar	350-400	1/2 Tuition	3%	3.8	1380/30	N		0	3.2	N	12/1	N
	Founder's Grant	Varies	5000	18%	3.3	1220/26	Y		0	2.3		1/15	N
	National Achievement	5	500-2000	8%	3.4	1400/33	N	0	A	2.3	M		N
	National Scholar Award	25	1/2 Tuition	15%	3.5	1300/29	N	0	A	3.2	0	1/15	N
	AP Exams												
	Alumni Discounts, Family Discounts												
	Co-op, Internships												
	Honors Program												
Bradford College, 01835	Bradford Scholars	Unlimited	Tuition	10%	3.0		N	L-R-0	A	3.0	N	A-2/15	Y-3.0
	Top 10% Scholars	Unlimited	1/2 Tuition	10%	3.0				A	Y	N	C-2/15	N
	Presidential Scholars	Unlimited	4000	20%	3.0			T-L-R-L	A	Y	N	C-2/15	N
	Leadership Scholars	Unlimited	4000	40%				T-L-R-L	A	Y	N	C-2/15	N
	Arts Scholars	Unlimited	4000	40%				E-T-R	A	Y	N	C-2/15	N
	Transfer Scholar	Unlimited	1/2 Tuition		3.2		N	E-T-L-R-0	A	3.0	0	C-2/15	Y
	Honors Program												
Brandeis U., Waltham 02254	Justice Brandeis	50	15,000	2%		1500	N	R-I	A	3.1	N	A-2/1	N
	Hiatt Challenger Memorial	1	3/4 Tuition	2%		1500	N	E-R-I	A	3.1	N	2/1	N
	Gilbert Grants	1	15000	2%		1500	N	L-R-I	A	3.1	N	A-2/1	N
	Presidential	125	10000	10%			N	R-I	A	3.1	N	A-2/1	N
[illegible]	Presidential	40	100-950	15%	3.3	1100	Y	E-T-L-R	A	3.3	S	B-3/23	N

Clark U., Worcester 01610	Merit Scholarship	200	6500	20%	3.5	1200	N	L-R	A	3.2	N	A-2/15	Y
	Worcester County Alumni	20	1000-Tuition				Y	T-L-R-O	A	Y	S	B-2/15	N
	Achievement	200	3000-4500	25%	3.0	1100-1200	N	T-L	A	3.0	N	A-2/1	N
Eastern Nazarene, Quincy 02170	Activities	6-12	1/4 Tuition				Y	T-L-R	A	N	N	B-2/28	Y
	Honor	Varies	750-Tuition	10%	X	1100	N		A	Y	O	A-C	Y-3.0
Elms, Chicopee 01085	Presidential	Varies	1500-4500	15%		1100	N		A	3.4	W	A-2/15	N
	Chicopee	Varies	To 4/5 Tuition	50%			N		A	Y	S-O	A-2/15	N
	Diocesan	Varies	To 3/4 Tuition	25%			N		A	Y	S-D	A-2/15	N
Emerson, Boston 02116	Restricted	100	3000-6000		3.3		N	T-L-R	A	3.0	N	A-2/1	N
	Trustees	45	8000	5%	3.6	1300	N	E-L-I-O	A	3.25	N	B-2/1	N
	Deans	40	4000-5000	10%	3.3	1200	N	L-I-O	A	3.0	N	A-2/1	N
	Stage	15	3000-4000		3.0	1000	N	T-I-O	O	3.0	N	C-2/1	N
	AP Exams												
	Honors Program												
Emmanuel, Boston 02115	Presidential	Varies	Tuition	10%	3.5	1100	N	E-L-R-I-O	A	3.0	W	A-1/1	N
	Mayor's	1	Tuition	10%	3.0	1100/25	Y	E-L-R-I-O	A	2.0	S-W-O	B-C	N
	Cardinal Medeiros	1	Tuition	10%	3.0	1100/25	Y	E-L-R-I-O	A	2.0	S-W-O	B-C	N
	St. Vincent De Paul	1	Tuition	15%	3.0	1000	N	E-T-R-I-O	O	3.0	W	C-3/1	Y-3.0
Fitchburg State College, 01420	Martin Luther King Jr. Mem.	Varies	500-2500	50%		1000	Y	R	A	2.0	M	B-3/1	N
	President's Free Tuition	Varies	Full Tuition	25%	3.0	1200	N		A	3.5	S	A-3/1	N
	Honors Program												
Hampshire, Amherst 01002	Harold F. Johnson	10	5000-7500	10%	3.5		N	L-R-T	A	Y			
	Schomburg	Varies	7500				N	L-R-T	A	Y			
Harvard-Radcliffe, Cambridge 02138	AP Exams												
	Honors Program												
Lesley, Cambridge 02138	Cambridge Partnership	2	Tuition		3.3	980	Y	O	A	Y	S	B-2/1	N
	Lesley Scholar	15	1000-2500	20%			N	L-R-I-O	A	2.5	W	B-3/15	Y-2.5
	AHNA Scholar	10	Full Tuition				Y	O	A	2.0	M-W	B-3/15	Y-2.0
	Middle School Math/Science	Varies	1000-2000				N	O	O	2.0	W-O		Y
MA Mar. Academy, Buzzards Bay 02532	Presidential	Varies	500-4200	30%	X		Y	E-T-L	A	Y	N	B-4/1	N
	Exceptional Talent	Varies	Varies	20%	3.0	1000/21	N		A	X	N	A-D	N
Merrimack, N. Andover 01845	Academic	300	500-12000	15%	A	1000	Y	L-R	A	2.5	N	A-3/1	Y
Montserrat College of Art, Beverly 01915	Merit	25	1000				N	E-T-R-I-O	A	N	N	A-4/1	Y
	Presidential	1	6000-9000	25%	3.0	1200/24	Y	E-T-L-R-I-O	O	3.0	M	4/1	Y-3.0
	Dean's	3	1000-2000	25%	3.0	1200/24	Y	E-T-L-R-I-O	O	3.0	N	A-4/1	Y-3.0

	Program	No. of Awards	Value Range	Award Criteria: Class Stndg.	Grade Avg.	SAT/ ACT	Need Based	Other	Study Fields	Renew-ability	Restric-tions	Apply Date	Transfer
MASSACHUSETTS *(Continued)*													
Nichols, Dudley 01570	Merit Grant	Unlimited	1000-6500				N		A	2.0	N	A	Y
	Opportunity Grant	Unlimited	Varies				Y		A		N	A	Y
	AP Exams												
	Family Discounts												
	Co-op, Internships												
Northeastern U., Boston 02115	Ell	40	All Costs		3.75	1300	N		A	3.25			
	Lewis	20	Tuition	20%		1150	N		A	3.0			
	Ralph Bunche	15	All Costs	10%		1150	N		A	3.0			
	AP Exams												
	Co-op, Internships												
	Honors Program												
Pine Manor, Chestnut Hill 02167	Resident	2	Tuition	X	X	X	N	E-L-R-I-O	A	Y	S-W	B-3/1	Y
	Minority Resident	1	Tuition	X	X	X	N	E-L-R-I-O	A	Y	S-W-M	B-3/1	Y
	New England	1	Half Tuition		3.0	1000	N	E-L	A	3.0	S	B-2/1	N
	Presidential	25	1000-5000		3.0	1000	N	L	A	3.0	N	A-D	Y-3.0
	Lowery	1	3/4 Tuition				N	L-R-O	A	3.0	N	A-4/1	N
	Reunion	1	1/2 Tuition		2.5	900	N	L	O	Y	N	A-3/15	N
	Honors Program												
Regis College, Weston 02193-1571	Presidential	20	5000	10%	3.5	1000	N	E-L-R-I-O	A	3.5	W	C-1/15	Y-3.5
	Alumnae Sponsor	20	2000	40%	2.5	900-1000	N	E-L-R-I-O	A	2.5	W	C-1/15	Y-2.5
	Merit Program	100	2000-3000	40%	2.5	900-1000	N	E-L-R-I-O	A	2.5	W	C-1/15	Y-2.5
	Minority Schol.	2-5	5000-10000	30%	3.0	900-1000	Y	L-R-I-O	A	2.5	S-M-W	C-3/1	Y-2.5
	Honors Program												
Salem State College, 01970	Honors	46	Tuition	10%	3.3	1000	N		A	3.0	N	C-3/1	Y
	Presidential Arts	20	Tuition		3.0		N	T-R-I	A	3.0	N	C-3/1	Y
	Honors Program												
Simmons College, Boston 02115	Honors	30	1/2 Tuition				N	E-L-R-I-O	A	Y	W	B-2/1	N
	Ferebee	6	1/2 Tuition				N	E-L-R-I-O	A	Y	M-W	B-2/1	N
	President's	15	4500				N		A	Y	W	A-2/1	N
	AP Exams												
	Co-op, Internships												
	Honors Program												

Simon's Rock of Bard College Great Barrington 01230	W.E.B. DuBois	10	Varies				Y	E-T-L-R-I-O	A	Y	M	B-6/15	N
	Acceleration to Excellence	20	26655		3.5	X	N	E-T-L-R-I-O	A	Y	N	B-2/17	N
Stonehill, North Easton 02357	Academic	Varies	1000-10000	10%			Y	L-O	A	3.0	N	A-2/1	Y
	Honors	Varies	1000-13074	5%			Y	L-O	A	3.2	N	A-2/1	N
	Academic Grant	Varies	1000-6000	15%			Y	L-O	A	2.7	N	A-2/1	N
	Honors Program												
Suffolk U., Boston 02108	Chase	4	3000	20%	3.0	1000	N	E-I	O	3.0	N	B-3/1	N
	Fulham	4	3000	20%	3.0	1000	N	E-I	A	3.0	N	B-3/1	N
	Corcoran	5	3000	20%	3.0	1100	N	E-I	A	3.0	N	B-3/1	N
	Stewart	10	5000	50%	2.5	900	Y	T-I	A	2.5	N	B-3/1	Y
	Deans	25	1000-5000	20%	3.0	1000	N	E	A	3.0	N	A	Y
Tufts, Medford 02155	AP Exams												
U. of Massachusetts, Amherst 01003	Alumni Academic	50	4000	10%	3.5	1200	Y		A	3.0	S-M	A-3/1	Y
	Chancellor's Academic	31	5000	5%		1250	N	E-L-R-O	A	2.5	S	C	Y
	Chancellor's Arts	27	Tuition	5%		1250	N	O	O	2.5	N	C	Y
	Academic Honors	60	5000	10%	3.5	1250	N		A	2.5	N	A	Y
	Talented Minority Schp.	40	5000	25%	3.0	1100	N	T-L	A	2.5	N	A	Y
	Honors Program												
U. of Massachusetts, Boston 02125	Bulger	Varies	Tuition				N	E-L-R	A	3.0	S	C	N
	Chancellor's	Varies	Tuition	5%	3.5		N	E-R-I	A	3.0	S	C	Y
	University Community	Varies	Tuition+				N	E-L-R	A	3.0	N	C	Y
	Foster Furcole	Varies	Tuition+	5%	3.5		N	R-O	A	3.5	S	C-7/1	Y
	Boston Globe	Varies	Tuition+				N	L-R-I-O	A	Y	S-O	C-4/1	N
	Faculty Staff	Varies	500+		3.0		Y	E-R	A	N	O	B-C	Y
	Honors Program												
Wentworth Inst. of Tech., Boston 02115	Arioch	30	9000			1200	N	E-R	A	Y	N	B-2/15	N
	President's	40	7000				N	R	A	Y	N	B-2/15	N
	Merit	10	2000-6000				N		A	Y	N	A	Y
	AP Exams												
	Co-op												
	Honors Program												
Western New Eng., Springfield 01119	Admissions	Varies	1000-8400	X	X	X	Y	O	A	3.3	N	A-4/1	Y
Westfield State, Westfield 01086	Special Talent	30	500-1000		2.5		N	T-L-O	A	N	O	B-4/1	Y-2.5
	Presidential	18	1400-3080	25%	3.5	1100	N	L	A	N	S	A-4/1	N
	Honors Program												
Wheaton, Norton 02766	Balfour	Varies	Computer	5%			N	T-L-R	A	N/A	N	A-2/1	N

	Program	No. of Awards	Value Range	Award Criteria: Class Stndg.	Grade Avg.	SAT/ACT	Need Based	Other	Study Fields	Renew-ability	Restric-tions	Apply Date	Transfer
MASSACHUSETTS *(Continued)*													
Williams College, Williamstown 01267	Tyng Scholarship	6	1000-25000	5%		1350/32	Y	0	A	3.0	N	A-C	N
Worcester Poly Tech, 01609	Trustees	10	Tuition	5%	3.5	1350	N	E-I-L-R		3.0			
	President's	60	10,000	5%	3.5	1350	N	E-I-L-R		3.0			
	Dean	125	5,000	5%	3.5	1350	N	E-I-L-R		3.0			
Worcester State College, 01602	Presidential	10	550-1100		3.3		N	L-R	A	3.3	N	B-4/1	Y-3.3
	Regis	10	550-1100		3.0		N	L-R	A	3.0	N	B-4/1	Y-3.0
	Alumni	5	500-1100		3.0		N	R	A	3.0	0	B-4/1	Y-3.0
MICHIGAN													
Adrian College, 49221	Dean's	Unlimited	2000	20%	3.5	1050/25	N	L-I-0	A	2.75	N	A-B-3/15	3.5
	Presidential	Unlimited	3000-6000	20%	3.6	1050/25	N	E-L-I-0	A	2.75	N	A-B-3/15	3.5
	Trustees	8	6000-11000	20%	3.6	1050/25	N	E-L-I-0	A	3.25	N	A-B-3/15	3.5
	Leadership	Unlimited	1000-3/4 Tuit.		3.6		N	E-L-R-I-0	A	3.0	N	B-3/1	
	Honors Program												
Albion College, 49224	Music	20	500-3000			1220	N	T	A	Y	N	B-3/1	Y
	Pres. Recognition	100	10000	5%	3.9	1200/29	N	L-0	A	3.4	N	B-3/15	Y
	Webster	Varies	5000-8000	10%	3.6	1150/27	N	L-0	A	3.1	N	B-3/15	Y
	Trustee	20	15000				N	L-0	A	3.3+	N	B-3/15	Y
	Albion College Sch.	Varies	3000-4000	15%	3.4	1100/25	N	L-0	A	3.1	N	B-3/15	Y
	Visual Arts	10	1000				N	T-0	A	3.0	N	B-3/15	Y
	Theatre	10	1000				N	T-R-0	A	3.0	N	B-3/15	Y
	Ford Institute	8	1000	10%	3.7	27	N	E-R-I	0	3.0	N	B-4/1	N
	Gerestacker Prof. Mgmt.	10	500-3000	10%	3.7	27	N	E-R-I	0	3.0	N	B-4/1	N
	Honors Program												
Alma College, 48801	Distinguished Scholar	Unlimited	Tuition				N	L-0	A	3.0	N	A-D	N
	Community College	Unlimited	3500		3.25		N	0	A	3.0	N	A-D	Y
	Performance	Unlimited	200-1500				N	T-0	0	Y	N	A-D	Y
	Presidential	Unlimited	5000		3.25	25	N	T-0	A	3.0	N	A-D	N
	Trustee Honor	Unlimited	6500		3.75	28	N	L-0	A	3.0	N	A-D	N
	Transfer	Varies	3000		3.0		N	L-0	A	3.0	N	A-D	Y
	Tartan Award	Unlimited	up to 4000	0.2	3.5	25	Y	L-0	A	Y-3.0	N	A-4/1	N

Andrews U., Berrien Springs 49103	Achievement	Varies	1500-2000			X	N		A	3.2	N	C	Y
	Freshman	Varies	1000-1250	10%	3.5		N	L	A	3.2	N	A-C	Y
Aquinas, Grand Rapids 49506	Academic Leadership	Unlimited	4000-7000		3.5	25	N	L	A	3.0	N	A	
	Presidential	20	1000		3.0		N	L-I	A	3.0	N	B-3/1	N
	St. Thomas Aquinas	5	Tuition		3.5	26	N	E-R-0	A	2.5	N	A-D	N
	Monsignor Bukowski	Unlimited	4000-7000		3.5	25	N		A	3.0	N	A	N
	Transfer	Unlimited	1000-6500		3.0		N		A	Y	N	A	N
	Honors Program												
Calvin, Grand Rapids 49546	Faculty Honors	120-150	2000		3.7	26	N	E-L	A	3.3	N	A-2/1	Y
	Honors	120-150	1200	X	3.5	25	N	E-L	A	3.2	N	A-2/1	Y
	Multicultural	20-30	1200		3.0		N		A	2.6	M	A-3/1	Y-3.0
	Presidential	60-70	3500		3.9	29	N	E-L	A	3.5	N	A-2/1	Y
	Stewardship Award	70-80	600		3.2		N	L-R-0	A	N	N	B-2/1	Y-3.2
	National Merit Scholarship	15-20	5000		3.5		N	E-0	A	Y	N	A-2/1	
	Mosaic Scholarship	10	3500		3.5	25	N	E-L-0	A	3.2	M	B-2/1	Y
	Dean's	60-70	2800		3.8	27	N	E-L	A	3.4	N	A-2/1	Y
	Honors Program												
Center for Creative Studies—College of Art & Design, Detroit 48202	AICA	1	Tuition	X	X	X	N	T	0	X	N	C	Y
	Freshman Merit	35	1400-2800				N	T	0	X	N	C	Y
Central Michigan U., Mt. Pleasant 48859	Cofer	10	31 Credits				N	0	0	Y	S	C	Y
	Honors	Unlimited	12 Credits		3.5		N		A	3.25	N	A-D	Y
	Indian Grant	Unlimited	Tuition				N	0	0	Y	M	C	Y
	Minority Advancement	12	31 Credits				N	0	0	Y	0	C	Y
	Outstanding HS	Unlimited	16 Credits	X	3.5		N	0	A	3.25	N	B-C	N
	Centralis Scholar	20	Costs		3.75	28	N	E-I-0	A	Y	N	B-D	N
	Centralis Gold	20	36 Credits		3.75	28	N	E-I-0	A	Y	N	B-D	N
	Special Talents	Varies	100-1200				N	T-L	A	Y	N	B-D	Y
	Centralis Comm. Clg.	12	36 Credits		3.75		N	E-I-0	A	Y	N	B-D	Y
	Wal-Mart Competitive	1	5000	10%	3.5	27	N	E-L-0	0	3.0	0	B-5/1	N
	Honors Program												
Cleary, Ypsilanti 48197	Cleary Scholarship	10	1500		3.0		N		A			C-5/31	
	Cleary Opportunity	10	1000		2.5		N		A			C-5/31	
	Alumni Scholarship	2	1000				N		A			C-5/31	
	Barker Scholarship	10	1000				Y		A			C-4/30	
	Citizens Insurance	1	1000				N		A			C-5/31	
	Society Bank	1	Varies				N		A			C-5/31	
Concordia, Ann Arbor 48105	Music	20	3500				N	T	0	2.8	N	C-5/15	Y
	Honors	Unlimited	1000		3.5		N	0	A	3.5	0	D	N
	Regents	Unlimited	1000-5000		3.0	24	N		A	2.5	N	C-5/15	Y-3.5

	Program	No. of Awards	Value Range	Award Criteria					Study Fields	Renew-ability	Restric-tions	Apply Date	Transfer
				Class Stndg.	Grade Avg.	SAT/ ACT	Need Based	Other					
MICHIGAN *(Continued)*													
Concordia, Ann Arbor 48105 *(Continued)*	Athletics	60	Varies				N	T-R-I	A	Y	O	C-5/15	Y
	Alumni Discounts												
Eastern Michigan U., Ypsilanti 48197	Departmental	400	750-1200		3.0		N	O	A	N	N	A-D	Y
	Recognition of Excellence	300	1500		3.3	21	N		A	3.3	N	A	Y-3.3
	Presidential	10	7000		3.5	25	N	E-I-O	A	3.5	O	B-11/15	N
	Regents'	200	2100		3.5	25	N		A	3.5	N	A	Y-3.5
	National Scholars	100	4100		3.5	25/1050	N		A	3.5	O	A-2/15	N
	International Students	20	1500		2.75		N	R	A	N	O	B-1/31	N
	Campus Leader	110	500		2.5		N	L-R	A	N	O	B-1/31	N
	Honors Program												
Ferris State, Big Rapids 49307	Founders Scholarship	5	6000		3.7	30	N		A	3.25	N	A-1/10	N
	Presidents	10	Tuition		3.7	30	N		A	3.25	N	A-1/10	N
	Deans	30	2500		3.5	27	N		A	3.25	N	A-1/10	N
	Comm. Coll. Transfer	29	1200		3.5		N	R	A	3.25	S	B-4/1	Y-3.5
	Kelso-Battle Sch.	5	4000		3.5	26	Y		O	3.25	N	A-3/1	N
	Academic Opportunity	10	2000		3.0		N		A	2.75	S-M	A-3/1	N
	Upper Division Academic	7	1000-3600		3.5		Y	R	A	N	S-O	B-5/1	N
	Val-Sal	Unlimited	500	1-2			N		A	3.25	N	A-8/1	N
Grace Bible, Grand Rapids 49509	Honors	Varies	750	85%	3.5		N		A	N	N	A-C	N
	Retention	54	200-1000		2.5		N		A	N	O	A-4/13	N
Grand Rapids Baptist College	President's	Varies	600-4000		3.5	920/23	N	O	A	3.5	N	A/61	Y-3.5
	Leadership	25-30	500-1500				N	E-T-L-R-I-O	A	2.5	N	B-2/15	Y-3.0
	Music	Unlimited	200-3000				N	T-I-O	O	3.0	N	B-D	Y-3.0
	Athletic	Unlimited	200-4000				N	T-I-O	A	2.5	N	D	Y
Grand Valley State, Allendale 49401	Award for Excellence	Unlimited	1000		3.5	26	N		A	3.3	N	A-2/1	Y-3.75
	Presidential	Unlimited	4000-6000		3.8	32	N	E-L-I	A	3.5	S	A-2/1	N
	Price	Unlimited	Tuition		3.1	20	N		A	2.8	M	A-2/1	Y-3.1
	Faculty		2000-4000		3.5	29	N	E-R-I-O	A	3.5	S	A-B-2/1	N
	Non-Michigan	Unlimited	3900		3.5	1150/26	N	O	O	3.25	O	A-2/1	3.75
	AP Exams												
	Distance Learning												
	Co-op. Internships												

Great Lakes Christian College Lansing 48917	Dean's	Unlimited	600-2300	1-2		95%ile	N		0	N	N	A-8/1	N
	Music	2-3	705-1050				N	T	0	N	N	B-5/1	N
	Honors Program												
Hillsdale College, 49242	Distinct Honor	3	Tuition	2%		95%ile	N	L-R-I-0	A	3.0	N	A-1/15	Y
	Presidential	15	1/2 Tuition	5%		92%ile	N	L-R-I-0	A	3.0	N	A-1/15	Y
	Trustee	50	1000-5000	10%		88%ile	N	L-R-0	A	3.0	N	A-1/15	Y
	AP Exams												
	Honors Program												
Hope, Holland 49423	Fine Arts	30	2500				N	T	A	Y	N	B-3/1	Y
	Trustees	6	12,000		4.0	1300/32	N	E-L-R-I-0	A	Y	N	A-2/15	N
	National Merit	Unlimited	12,000				N	0	A	Y	N	C	N
	Presidential Scholarships		8000	X	3.6	1240/28	N	E-L-R	A	Y	N	A-2/15	N
	Endowed Scholarships		6000	X	3.6	1240/28	N	E-R	A	Y	N	A-2/15	N
	Distinguished Scholar		5000	X	X	X	N	E	A	Y	N	A-2/15	N
	Alumni Honors		3000	X	3.5	1140/25	N	E	A	Y	N	A-2/15	N
	Biomedical Scholarship	2	8000	X	X	X	N	E-L-0	0	Y	M	A-3/1	N
Kalamazoo College, 49006	Competitive	25	1500-3000				N	E-T-0	0	Y	N	D	N
	Honors	150	3000-10000	20%	3.5	1140/25	N	E-L-R-0	A	2.3	N	A-2/15	Y-3.5
	AP Exams												
	Alumni Discounts												
	Internships												
Kettering University, Flint 48502	Provost	6	3000	5%	3.8	1250/28	N	E-L-R	A	N	N	A	N
	Trustee	6	1/2 Tuition	5%	3.8	1250/28	N	E-L-R	A	N	N	A	N
	Distance Learning												
	Co-op, Internships												
Lake Superior State, Sault Ste. Marie, 49783	Distinguished	40	3600	10%	3.8	90%ile	N		A	3.0	S	A-3/1	N
	Trustees	75	800-2000	20%	3.4	80%ile	X		A	2.5	S	A-3/1	N
	Community College	25	800-Tuition		3.0		X		A	2.7	S-0	C-3/1	Y
	Phil Hart	3-5	Tuition-4000		3.0		X	E-T-L-R	A	3.0	S	B-4/1	Y
	Non-Resident	Varies	Tuition		3.5	80%ile	N		A	3.0	S	A-4/1	N
Lawrence Technological University Southfield 48075	LTU Academic	40	Tuition+Fees	10%	3.5	1150/26	N	R	A	3.0	0	B-3/1	Y-3.5
	LTU Upperclass	10	500-2000		3.5		N		A	3.5	0	B-5/15	N
	Trustee	150	1000-4000	25%	3.0	1000/24	N		A	2.7	0	B-3/1	Y-3.0
	Buell Scholarship	5	All Costs	5%	3.8	1200/28	N	R	A	3.0	0	B-3/1	N
	Alumni	15	2000-6000	25%	3.0	1100/24	N		A	3.0	0	B-5/15	N
Madonna University, Livonia 48150	Trustees	7-20	1250-5000	10%	3.8	27	Y	E-T-R	A	3.2	N	A-B-2/1	N
	Presidential	7-20	1250-5000	10%	3.8	27	Y	E-T-R	A	3.2	N	A-B-2/1	N
	Deans	7-20	1250-5000	10%	3.8	27	Y	E-T-R	A	3.2	N	A-B-2/1	N

	Program	No. of Awards	Value Range	Award Criteria: Class Stndg.	Grade Avg.	SAT/ACT	Need Based	Other	Study Fields	Renew-ability	Restric-tions	Apply Date	Transfer
MICHIGAN *(Continued)*													
Madonna University, Livonia 48150 *(Continued)*	AP Exams												
	Distance Learning												
	Co-op, Internships												
Marygrove, Detroit 48221	Distinguished Scholar	30	2000-8000		3.0		N	E-L	A	3.0	N	C	Y-3.0
	Scholar Award	Varies	2000-Tuition		2.7		N	E-T	O		N	A-4/1	Y-2.7
	Distinguished Talent	10	2000-8000		2.7		N	E-T-L-R-I-O	O	2.7	N	B	Y-2.7
	Honors Program												
Michigan State U. East Lansing 48824	Academic Excellence	500	300-500	5%	3.85		N		A	N	N	A-D	N
	Honors Program												
	Alumni Distinguished	10	5000-7500	5%	A	1300/30	N	E-L-R-O	A	3.2	N	A-12/23	N
	Creative Arts	20	500				X	T	O	Y	S	B-C	N
	Distinguished Fresh.	15	2000-5000	5%	A	1300/30	N	E-L-R-O	A	3.2	N	A-12/23	N
	Distinguished Minority	15	2000	20%	B+		N	L-R-O	A	Y	M	A-2/1	N
Michigan Technological U., Houghton 49931	Board of Control	120	1000-Tuition	X		X	N		A	2.5	S	A-3/1	N
MI Community College	20	1000-Tuition		X	X		N		A	2.5	S	A-3/1	Y
Northern Michigan U., Marquette 49885	Board of Control	Varies	200-2000		3.25		Y		A	3.0	N	C-2/1	N
	NMU Merit Award	Varies	1500-2000		3.0	30	N		A	3.0	N	C-2/1	Y
	Transfer Scholarship	Varies	200-2000		3.25		Y		A	3.0	N	C-2/1	Y
	NMU Academic Honors	Varies	1000		3.0	24	N		A	3.0	N	A-2/1	N
	Valedictorian	Varies	1000	1			N		A	3.0	N	C-2/1	N
	Leadership	Varies	1500		3.5	24	N	L-R	A	3.0	N	B-2/1	N
	Pres./Harden	10	6000	10%	3.5	24	N	E-R-I-O	A	3.0	N	C-10/1	N
	Freshman Fellowship	40	1000		3.0	24	N	I-O	A	N	N	C-2/1	N
	National Academic	Varies	Partial Tuition		3.0		N		A	3.0	O	C-2/1	Y
	AP Exams												
	Distance Learning												
	Alumni Discounts												
	Internships												
	Honors Program												
Northwood University, Midland 48640	Transfer	Unlimited	3000		2.7		N		O	2.7	N	A-8/1	Y
	DECA/BPA	Varies	1000		2.75		N	R-O	A	2.75	N	A	N
	Private Donor Scholarships	Varies	200-5000		2.5		Y	R-I-O	A	N	N	B-4/1	Y-2.5

	Freedom	Unlimited	5000		3.0	1150/25	N		O	3.0	N	A-8/1	N
	Freedom Enterprise	Unlimited	4000		2.7	950/20	N		O	2.7	N	A-8/1	N
	AP Exams												
	Distance Learning												
	Alumni Discounts, Family Discounts												
	Honors Program												
Oakland University, Rochester 48309	Anibal Excellence	2	2500		3.5				A	3.25	N	12/1	
	Alumni Memorial	1	2000		3.75	27	N		A	3.25	N	12/1	
	OU Foundation	2	5000		3.5		N	O	A	3.25	N	12/1	
	OU Music, Dance Theatre	Varies	Varies					T	O	Y	N	12/1	
	Presidential	2	6000		3.5		N		A	3.30	N	12/1	
	Student Life	Varies	1000		3.3		N		A	2.5	N	12/1	Y
	Academic Success	Varies	Varies		3.0	22	N		A	2.3		12/1	
	Foundation Diversity	5	2500		3.3		N	O	A	3.25	N	B-2/1	Y-3.3
	AP Exams												
	Distance Learning												
	Co-op, Internships												
	Honors College												
Olivet College, 49076	Presidential (1)	Unlimited	1500		3.5		N		A	3.2	S	B-8/1	Y
	Presidential (2)	Unlimited	1200		3.5		N		A	3.2	N	B-8/1	Y
	Trustee	Unlimited	500		3.2		N		A	3.0	N	B-8/1	Y
	Performing Arts	Unlimited	250-1000				N		O	Y	N	C-D	Y
Reformed Bible, Grand Rapids 49505	Academic	Unlimited	800		3.67		N		A	3.67		A	Y-3.67
	Academic	Unlimited	600		3.33		N		A	3.33		A	Y-3.33
	Christian Leadership	4	1500		3.2		N	E-L-I	A	3.2	N	B-4/1	Y-3.2
	Family Discounts												
Saginaw Valley State, University Center 49710	Award for Excellence	12	Tuition+		3.5		N	E-R	A	Y	S	B-3/15	N
	Community College	3	1000		3.5		N	E-R	A	Y	S	B-6/1	Y
	Minority	5	1000		3.5		N	L-R-I-O	A	3.0	M	B-4/1	N
	Presidential	5	Tuition+	1-2			N	E-R-I-O	A	Y	S	B-3/1	N
	Residential	6	1000		3.0		N	E-L-R-I	A	Y	S	B-3/15	N
St. Mary's, Orchard Lake 48033	St. Mary's Scholar	1	6300	10%	3.8	27	Y	E-L-R-I-O	A	3.5	O	C-4/30	N
	Presidential Scholar	2	1000	10%	3.5	24	Y	E-L-R-I-O	A	3.0	O	C-4/30	N
	Transfer Merit	30	500-1000		3.0		Y	R-I-O	A	3.0	N	C	Y-3.0
Siena Heights, Adrian 49221	Academic	Varies	1000-3000		3.2	21	N	E-L-R	A	2.5	N	A-D	Y
	Catholic H.S.	30	1000-3000	50%	3.0	21	N	R	A	2.5	O	C-3/1	N
	Presidential	30	3500-5000	25%	3.7	25	N	E-L-R	A	3.0	N	C-3/1	N
	Transfer	Varies	900-2500		3.0		N	E-O	A	2.5	O	B-C	Y-3.0
	Sr. O'Connor	Varies	900-1600		3.0		N	E-L-R-I	A	2.5	N	B-5/15	Y-3.0

	Program	No. of Awards	Value Range	Award Criteria					Study Fields	Renew-ability	Restric-tions	Apply Date	Transfer
				Class Stndg.	Grade Avg.	SAT/ ACT	Need Based	Other					
MICHIGAN *(Continued)*													
Siena Heights, Adrian 49221 *(Continued)*	Valedictorian	10	5000-9630	1-Jan	3.5	21	Y	R	A	3.0	N	C-3/1	N
	Honors Program												
Spring Arbor College, 49283	President's	Varies	5000	X	X	X	N		A	3.5	N	A	N
	Provost	Varies	3000	X	X	X	N		A	3.3	N	A	Y-3.5
	Faculty	Varies	2000	X	X	X	N		A	3.2	N	A	Y-3.3
	National Merit Finalist	Varies	Tuition				N	O	A	3.5	N	A-D	N
	National Merit Semifinalist	Varies	1/2 Tuition				N	O	A	3.5	N	A-D	N
	Honors Program												
U. of Detroit Mercy, 48221	Insignis	10	Tuition/Room	10%		1200/29	N	O	A	2.0	N	A-2/15	N
	Ins. Semi-Finalists	Unlimited	1/2 Tuition/Rm	10%		1200/29	N	E-L-I-O	A	2.0	N	A-2/15	N
	Slaton Memorial	5	Tuition	10%		950/21	N	L-I-O	A	2.0	M	A-3/15	N
	Founders' Transfer	15	Tuition		3.5		N	L-R-O	A	2.0	O	A-3/15	Y-3.5
	Fndrs.' Trnsfr. Semi-fin.	Unlimited	2500		3.5		N	L-R-O	A	2.0	N	A-3/15	Y-3.5
	Benefactors	Unlimited	1/2 Tuition		3.0	1100/26	N	I-O	A	2.0	N	A-5/1	N
	Honors Program												
U. of Michigan, Ann Arbor 48109	Academic	Varies	Varies	X	X	X	N		A	N	O	A-2/1	N
	Bentley	2	40000	X	X	X	N		O	Y	S	A-2/1	N
	Community College	60	500		X		N		A	N	S,O	A-2/1	Y
	Michigan Achievement	Unlimited	1500	X	X	X	X		A	Y	M,O	A-2/10	N
	MI Annual Giving	235	1500		X	X	N	L-R-I	A	N	N	A-3/1	N
	Rackham Undergrad.	4	1000	X	X	X	N		A	Y	O	B-C	N
	Regents' Alumni	345	1000	X	X	X	N	L-R-I-O	A	N	S,O	A-2/10	N
	Martin Luther King	Varies	500-1000	X	X	X	N		A	N	M,O	A-3/1	N
	Scholar Recognition	Unlimited	Tuition	X	X	X	N		A	Y	S,M	A-3/1	N
U. of Michigan, Dearborn 48128	Chancellor's	10	Tuition		3.7	85%ile	N	L	A	Y	O	B-3/1	N
	Regents' Alumni	20	500	X		X	N	R	A	N	S	C	N
U. of Michigan, Flint 48503	Chancellor's	45	1/2 Tuition		3.7	26	N		A	3.0	S	A-D	N
	Heritage	15	1300	10%	3.5		N		A	2.7	S-M	A-C	N
	Honors	20	600-1200		3.5	26	N	R-I	A	3.0	S	B-C	N
	Honors Program												

Wayne State U., Detroit 48202	Merit	350	1700+		3.5	1260	N		A	3.0	S	B-1/10	N
	Talent	Varies	700		2.0	850/20	N	T	O	2.0	S	B-C	N
	Presidential	350	Varies		3.5	27	N	L-R	A	3.0	S	A-3/1	Y
	Honors Program												
Western Michigan U., Kalamazoo 49008	Medallion	21	4800-8000		3.8	1130/25	N	E-I-L-R	A	3.25			
	Trustees	22	2000-6000		3.8	1130/25	N	E-I-L-R	A	3.25			
	Cultural Diversity	5	2000-8000		3.5		N	E	A	3.25			
	AP Exams												
	Distance Learning												
	Honors Program, Honors College												
MINNESOTA													
Augsburg, Minneapolis 55454	MN Transfer Scholarship	5	5000		3.5		N	E-L-R-I-O	A	3.5	O	B-5/1	Y
	Performing Arts	Varies	1500				N	T-R	O	Y	O	B-2/1	Y
	Phi Theta Kappa	15	5000		3.5		N	E-L-R-O	A	3.5	O	B-5/1	Y
	President's	10	Tuition	15%		X	N	E-T-L-R-O	A	X	O	B-2/15	N
	Regents	Varies	Varies	30%		X	N	O	A	2.7	O	B-5/1	N
	Science Scholarship	Unlimited	5000	20%		25	N	T-L-R-O	O	3.3	N	A-5/1	N
	Transfer Regents	Unlimited	5000		3.0		N	L	O	3.0	N	6/1	Y-3.0
	Honors Program												
Bemidji State U., 56601	Faculty	36	600	15%			N		A	N	N	A-D	N
	Full Tuition	20	2500	10%		28	N	E-T-L	A	3.5	S	B-D	N
	Presidential	6	4500	X		X	N	O	A	N	N	B-C	N
	Talent	6	500				N	T-L	A	N	N	A-D	Y
	Transfer	35	600		3.5		N		A	N	N	A-D	Y
	Troppman	25	600	15%			N		A	N	N	A-D	N
	Honors Program												
Bethel, St. Paul 55112	Academic	Unlimited	1000	15%			N		A	3.2	N	A-D	Y
	Dean's	Unlimited	2000	5%			N		A	3.2	N	A-D	Y
	Music Performance	6	1000		2.5		N	T	A	2.5	O	B-4/1	N
	President's	Unlimited	3000	2%			N		A	3.2	N	A-D	Y
College of St. Benedict, St. Joseph 56374	Finalist Recognition	Unlimited	1000				N	O	A	Y	W	A	N
	Academic Leadership	Unlimited	1000-5000	10%	3.35		N		A	Y	W	C	Y
	Fine Arts	Unlimited	500-1000				N	O	A	N	W	C	Y
	Girl Scout Gold	Unlimited	500-1500				N	O	A	Y	W-O	A	N
	Sister Byce Williams	Unlimited	15000-5000				Y		A	Y	M-W-O	A	Y
College of St. Catherine, St. Paul 55105	Alexandria	Varies	2000-6000	15%		1100/26	N	L	A	Y	W	A-2/15	N
	Girl Scout Gold	10	2500				N	L	A	Y	W	A-2/1	N

				Award Criteria									
	Program	No. of Awards	Value Range	Class Stndg.	Grade Avg.	SAT/ ACT	Need Based	Other	Study Fields	Renew-ability	Restric-tions	Apply Date	Transfer
MINNESOTA *(Continued)*													
College of St. Catherine, St. Paul 55105 *(Continued)*	O'Shaughnessy	4	18,104	15%		1100/26	N	L-I	A	Y	W	A-12/1	N
	St. Caecillia	Varies	980-5980				N	T	0	3.0	W	B-C	N
	St. Catherine	100	2000-6000	15%			N	E-L-I	A	Y	W	A-2/15	N
	Honors Program												
College of St. Scholastica, Duluth 55811	Benedictine	Unlimited	1000-6000	Varies		Varies	N	T-L	A	3.0	N	B-3/1	Y
	Sharon Labovitz	5	3000	15%		25	Y	E-T-L-R-0	A	3.0	S	B-2/1	N
	AP Exams												
	Distance Learning												
	Family Discounts												
	Honors Program												
Concordia, Moorhead 56560	Faculty	70	5500	10%	3.8	90%ile	N	E-T-L-I-0	A	3.5	N	B-2/1	N
	Forensics	4	2000	25%			N	T-I-0	A	Y	N	B-12/15	N
	Music	30	2000	25%			N	T-I-0	A	3.0	N	B-12/15	N
	Theatre	2	2000	25%			N	T-I-0	A	3.0	N	B-12/15	N
	Honors Program									3.0			
Concordia, St. Paul 55104	Pres. Academic	5	1/2 Tuition	X	X	X	N		A	3.5	N	B-1/15	N
	Pres. Leadership	5	1/2 Tuition				N	L	A	Y	N	B-1/15	N
	President's Combined	5	1/2 Tuition	10%	3.5	25	N	L	A	3.25	N	B-1/15	N
	Music	1	1000				N	T	0	3.0	N	B-2/15	N
	Transfer	4	1000		3.25		N	L	A	3.25	0	B-11/15	Y-3.25
Crown College, St. Boniface 55375	President's	20	2000	10%	3.5	27	N	E-R-0	A	3.5	N	A	N
	Leadership	Varies	1000-2000	10%	2.5		N	T-L-R-0	A	Y	N	A	Y
	Dean's	20	1500	15%	3.5	24	N	R-0	A	3.3	N	A	Y
Gustavus Adolphus, St. Peter 56082	Alumni	25	2500		3.75	25	N	0	A	3.25	N	B-3/1	N
	Jussi Bjorling Music Schp.	8	2500				N	T-0	A		0	B-3/1	N
	Partners	40	7500	5%		95%ile	N	E-L-I-0	A	3.25	N	B-3/1	N
	Presidential	15	7500	1%		99%ile	N	0	A	3.25	N	D	N
	AP Exams												
Hamline U., St. Paul 55104	Biology Award	6	2500	10%			N	E-R-0	0	3.25	N	B-1/20	Y
	MacCorkle	4	4000	20%			N	R-0	0	Y	N	B-1/20	N
	National Merit	Unlimited	2000				N	0	A	X	N	A	N

	Student Leader	40	5000	15%	3.25	X	N	E-L-R-I-O	A	X	N	B-1/20	N
	Transfer Award	10-15	5000-Tuition		3.5		N	E-R-O	A	3.25	N	B-4/1	Y-3.5
	Writing Award	1	3000	10%			N	E-T-R-O	A	X	N	B-1/20	N
	Honors Program												
Macalester, St. Paul 55105	Catherine Laeltad	Unlimited	10000	25%			Y	O	A	Y	M	A-D	Y
	Dewitt Wallace	Unlimited	10000	15%			Y	O	A	Y	N	A-D	Y
Mankato State U., 56001	Presidential	12	2500	10%		26	N	E-L-R-I	A	3.0	N	B-1/1	Y-3.5
	Talent	Varies	600	50%			N	E-T-I	A	N	O	C	N
	Honors Program												
Martin Luther, New Ulm 56073	Presidential	28	1000	1			N		A	3.75			
	GPA	113	400		3.75	27	N		A	3.75			
	AP Exams												
	Distance Learning												
	Honors Program												
Metropolitan State U. St. Paul 55101	ALLISS Foundation	40	375-900				Y	R	A	Y	N	C	Y
	Academic	25	375-1125				Y	R	A	Y	O	C-6/1	Y
	Reatha King	5	1000-2500				Y	E-L-R	A	Y	N	C	
	S.E.C. Sihol	10	750		3.0		N	E-L	A	Y	N	C	
Mpls College of Art and Design, 55404	Merit	27	1000		2.5		N	T	A	N	O	B-2/26	Y-2.5
	Abby Weed Grey	1	6000				N	T	O	Y	O	B-3/15	Y
	Portfolio	1	6000				N	T	O	Y	O	B-3/15	Y
	Admissions	1-20	2000				N	T	O	Y	O	B-3/15	Y
Minnesota Bible, Rochester 55902	Academic	Unlimited	900	10%	3.3	25	N		A	N	N	A-8/15	N
	Valedictorian	Unlimited	1550	1			N		A	Y	N	A-8/15	Y
Moorhead State U., Moorhead 56563	Honor Apprenticeship	10	2000	5%		28	N	E-L-R	A	3.25			
	Presidential	50	500	25%		24	N	E-L-R	A	3.0			
	AP Exams												
	Distance Learning												
	Honors Program												
North Central Bible, Minneapolis 55404	Dean's	Varies	1500	10%	3.5	26/1070	N		A	3.5	N	B-8/1	Y
	Fine Arts	Varies	300-1000				N	T	A	N	N	B-9/1	Y
	Honors	Varies	1000		3.5	24/990	N		A	3.5	N	B-8/1	Y
	President's	Varies	2000	10%	3.5	29/1200	N		A	3.5	N	B-8/1	Y
	Valedictorian	Varies	500	1			N		A	N	N	B-8/1	N
Northwestern, St. Paul 55113	Honors	180	500-1250		3.0		N	L	A	3.0	O	B-3/17	N
	Presidential	Varies	500-2400	15	3.5		N		A	3.6	N	C	Y-3.5
	STEP	Varies	600	30%	3.0	1030/23	N	E-O	A	N	N	C	N
	ALLISS	40	500	40%			Y	E-O	A	2.5	S	A-D	Y-2.5

	Program	No. of Awards	Value Range	Award Criteria: Class Stndg.	Grade Avg.	SAT/ ACT	Need Based	Other	Study Fields	Renew- ability	Restric- tions	Apply Date	Transfer
MINNESOTA *(Continued)*													
Pillsbury Bible College, Owatonna 55060	ACT Scholarship	Varies	250-500			26	N		A	3.5	O	B-C	N
	Val/Sal Scholarships	Varies	250-500	1-2		20	N		A	3.5	N	B-C	Y-3.5
St. Cloud State U., 56301	Foundation	Varies	2000-4000	10%	3.5		N	E-L-O	A	3.0	N	B-4/1	N
	Merit	Varies	5500			X	N	E-L-O	A	3.0	N	B-4/1	N
	Non-Resident Tuition	Varies	2100	15%		25	N	O	A	3.0	O	C-5/1	N
	Presidential	Varies	500-1000	15%	3.5		N	E-L-O	A	3.0	N	B-4/1	N
	Richard Green	Varies	500-Tuition		2.5		N	E-L-O	A	2.5	M	B-4/1	Y-2.5
	Honors	10	1200	5%	3.5	1200/27	N	E-L-R-O	A	3.0	O	B-4/1	N
	AP Exams												
	Co-op, Internships												
	Honors Program												
St. John's U., Collegeville 56321	Academic Leadership	Unlimited	1000-5000	10%	3.35		N		A	Y	O	C	Y
	Finalist Recognition	Unlimited	1000				N	O	A	Y	O	C	Y
	Fine Arts	Unlimited	500-1000				N	O	A	Y	O	C	Y
	Merrill Lynch	Unlimited	2000				N	L	A	N	O	C	N
	Morton Katz	Unlimited	1500-5000				Y		O	Y	M-O	C	Y
	Regent's	20	6500	5%	3.0	1400/30	N	E-L-R-I-O	A	Y	O	B-2/1	N
	Honors Program												
St. Mary's, Winona 55987	Dorothy Magnus	10	500-2000		2.5		N	T-I	O	2.5	N	B-3/1	Y
	High School Challenge	Varies	500-1000				N	R	A	3.0	N	C	N
	Presidential	100-120	1000-2500	25%	3.0	22	N		A	2.8	N	A	N
	San Miguel Talent	10-20	1000-2500	10%	3.2	1100/24	N	E-T-L-R	A	3.0	N	B-3/1	N
	Thomas More	40-50	3000-4000	10%	3.4	25	N		A	3.2	N	A	N
	Tomorrow's Leaders	1	6000	10%			N	E-L-R-I	A	3.0	O	B-3/1	N
	Honors Program												
St. Olaf, Northfield 55057	Buntrock Academic	450	1500-5000	5%	3.6	1300/28	N	E	A	3.5	N	B-2/1	Y-3.6
	Community Service	38	1500				N	E-L-R	O	3.5	N	B-2/1	Y
	Leadership	38	1500				N	E-L-R	A	Y	D	B-2/1	Y
Southwest State U., Marshall 56258	Academic Scholars	Varies	1250	10%		1200/29	N		A	3.0	N	A-C	N
	ALLISS	40	300-900		3.0		Y		A	Y	S	A	N
	Distinguished Student	20	1000	50%		21	N	T-L-R-O	A	N	N	A-C	N
	Foundation	Varies	300-1000				Y	T-L-R-O	A	Y	O	A	Y

	Gala Ball	23	250-500				N	T-I-O	O	N	N	C	N
	Leadership	Varies	250-500	50%			N	E-T-L-R-O	A	N	N	A-3/1	Y
	Mentoring Award	50	2000	50%		21	N	L-R-O	A	N	N	A-C	N
	Minority	Varies	200-1800				N	T-R-O	A	Y	M	A-3/1	Y
	Presidential	Varies	200-1500	10%		25	N	T-L-R	A	3.0	S-S	A-C	Y
	Schwan's Academic	Varies	500-1500		3.0	25	N	R-O	A	3.0	N	C	N
	Theatre	5	200-500				N	T-O	O	N	N	C	N
	Transfer	Varies	500				N	E-T-L-R-O	A	N	N	A-3/1	Y-3.5
	*Honors Program												
U. of Minnesota, Duluth 55812	Presidential	40	1000	5%			N	L-R	A	Y	S	B-2/1	N
	Academic	Varies	500-1000	20%			Y		A	N	N	A	N
	Pres. Outstanding Minority	Varies	1000-3000	50%			Y	E-L-R	A	3.0	M	B-3/1	N
	Best of Class	Varies	1/2 Res. Tuit.	1-2			N	L-R-T	A	3.0	S	B-2/15	N
	AP Exams												
	Distance Learning												
	Alumni Discounts												
	Co-op, Internships												
	Honors Program												
U. of Minnesota, Minneapolis 55455	Gopher State Scholarship	50	2000	5%	X	28	N	E-L-R	A	N	S	B-1/15	N
	Iron Range	150	1000	Top 5		1300/29	N	E-L	A	3.0	S	B-1/15	N
	Pres. Outstanding Minor.	95	1000-3000	15%			Y	E-L-R	A	Y	M	B-1/15	N
	Presidential Scholar	200	1000-2000	5%	X	X	N	E-L-R	A	Y	S	B-1/15	N
	Honors Program												
U. of Minnesota, Morris 56267	Academic	Unlimited	1000-2000	10%			N		A	N	N	A-3/15	N
	Freshman Academic	Unlimited	1000-2000	10%			N		A	N	N	A-3/15	N
	Merit	Unlimited	Tuition				N	O	A	2.0	N	A-3/15	N
	Presidential	50	8000	5%			N	E-L-R	A	Y	S	A-2/15	N
	AP Exams												
	Distance Learning												
	Co-op, Internships												
	Honors Program												
University of St. Thomas, St. Paul 55105	Achievement	Unlimited	550-2050	10%	3.5	1100/26	N		A	2.8	N	A-5/1	N
	Dean's	Unlimited	1000	X	X	X	N		A	2.75	N	A-5/1	N
	Distinguished	Unlimited	3500-6200	10%	3.5	1100/26	N		A	3.2	N	A-5/1	N
	Recognition	12	2000		3.2		N	E-R	O	3.0	O	B-5/24	Y-3.2
	Science	3	Tuition				N	E-R-I-O	O	Y	N	B-11/15	N
	University	Unlimited	2100-3450	10%	3.5	1100/26	N		A	3.0	N	A-5/1	N
	Honors Program												

	Program	No. of Awards	Value Range	Award Criteria: Class Stndg.	Grade Avg.	SAT/ ACT	Need Based	Other	Study Fields	Renew-ability	Restric-tions	Apply Date	Transfer
MINNESOTA *(Continued)*													
Winona State U., 55987	Presidential Honor	200	750-2500	15%		26	N	E-I-O	A	3.5	N	A-3/1	N
	Academic	200	300-500	20%		24	N	O	A	N	S	A-3/1	N
	Fine Arts	20	300-500				N	T-R-I-O	O	N	N	B-3/1	Y
	Honors Program												
MISSISSIPPI													
Alcorn State U., Lorman 39096	Academic	Unlimited	2376-4824		3.0	910/22	N	I-O	A	3.5	N	C-5/31	Y
	Partial Academic	Unlimited	2376			820/20	N	I-O	A	3.0	N	C-5/31	N
Belhaven, Jackson 39202	Academic	Varies	2800-8000			23	N	L-R	A	Y	O	B-4/1	Y
	Art	Varies	2500		3.4	950/23	N	T	O	Y	N	B-4/1	Y
	Music	Varies	500-8000				N	T	A	Y	O	C	Y
	Honors Program												
Blue Mountain College, 38610	Presidential	10	600	20%	2.5		Y	L-R	A	N	W-O	B-7/1	Y
	Trustee	10	500-1000	10%	3.0		N	L-R-O	A	3.25	W	B-7/1	N
	AP Exams												
	Family Discounts												
Delta State U., Cleveland 38733	Val/Sal	Unlimited	300-500	1-2	3.0		N	L-R-I-O	A	3.0	S	B-D	N
	Academic	Unlimited	550-1600		3.0	26	N	L-I-O	A	3.0	N	A	Y
	Merit	Unlimited	300-500		3.0		N	O	A	3.0	N	B-D	N
	Honors Program												
Jackson State U., 39217	Academic	150	1072-3100	X	3.0	810/18	Y	L-R-O	A	3.0	N	C	Y
	Academic	Varies	610-1000		3.0	700/14	Y		A	3.0	N	C-4/1	Y-2.0
	Costs	Varies	3824	10%	3.25	21	Y		A	3.25	N	B-4/1	Y-3.25
	1/2 Costs	Varies	1913	10%	3.0	18-20	Y		A	3.0	N	B-4/1	Y-3.0
	AP Exams												
	Distance Learning												
	Co-op, Internships												
	Honors College, Honors Program												
Millsaps, Jackson 39210	Millsaps Merit	50	250-4000	25%	X	1100/27	N	I-O	A	Y	N	B-4/1	Y
Mississippi College, Clinton 39058	Presidential	25	2500-5250	15%	3.0	29	N	L-R-O	A	3.25	N	B-1/1	N
	Honors	50	500-2500	15%	3.0	830/20	N	L-R-O	A	2.75	O	B-3/1	N

	Junior College *Honors Program*	40	700-3000	15%	3.0	830/20	N	L-R-O	A	2.75	O	B-3/1	Y-3.0
Mississippi State U., 39762	Academic	Unlimited	Varies	X		28	N	L	A	Y	H	B-4/1	N
	Academic Excellence	Varies	1000-8000	10%	3.0	1100/27	N		A	3.0	N	B-4/1	N
	Schillig Leadership	Varies	4500	10%	3.0	1150/28	N	E-T-L-O	A	3.0	N	B-2/1	N
Mississippi U. for Women Columbus 39701	Academic	Unlimited	350-4300	X	X	21	N		A	3.0	W	A-4/1	Y
	Centennial	Varies	Tuition			28	N	R-I-O	A	3.0	W	A-2/1	N
	Cultural Heritage	Varies	750-1500			21	N	T-L	A	3.0	M	B-3/1	Y-3.0
	McDevitt	3	All Costs	10%	3.5		N	R-I-O	A	3.3	N	1/31	Y-3.5
	Reneau	Unlimited	1150-7000			24	N	I-R	A	3.0	N	B-12/1	N
	University	Unlimited	1200-6500	20%	3.0	1030/24	N	R-I-O	A	3.0	N	11/21	N
	AP Exams												
	Distance Learning												
	Alumni Discounts												
	Internships												
	Honors College												
MS Valley State U., Itta Bena 38941	Academic	Unlimited	750-2200		3.0	760/16	N	R	A	Y	H	B-C	Y
Rust College, Holly Springs 38635	Honor Track	15	6800	10%	3.5	1000	N	E-R	A	3.5	N	B-5/1	N
	Presidential	15	2000	10%	3.25	900	N	R	A	3.25	N	B-5/1	Y-3.25
	Academic Fellowship	15	1500	10%	3.0	700	N	R	A	3.0	N	B-5/1	Y-3.25
	Honors Program												
Tougaloo College, 39174	Academic	Varies	500-5300		3.5	1450/24	N	E-T-R-I	A	3.5	N	4/15	Y-3.5
	Dean's I	Varies	2200		3.25	1000/20	N		A	3.15	N	4/15	N
	Dean's II	Varies	1200		3.0	800/18	N		A	3.0	N	4/15	N
	Presidential	Varies	9000	10%	3.75	1600/27	N		A	3.5	O	4/15	N
	Provost	Varies	3500		3.4	1200/23	N		A	3.3	O	4/15	N
U. of Mississippi, University 38677	Barnard	50	4460-6460		3.0			O	A	3.0			
	Bledsoe	50	2500-4500		3.0				A	3.0			
	Croft	10	7000					E-R	A	3.2			
	AP Exams												
	Distance Learning												
	Alumni Discounts												
	Honors Program												
U. of Southern Mississippi Hattiesburg 39402	Academic Excellence I	100	750-4800		3.0	1230/28	N		A	3.0			
	Leadership	150	2200				N	I-L-R	A	3.0			
	Presidential	10	5000-8500		3.0	1310/30	N	I	A	3.25			
	AP Exams												
	Distance Learning												

	Program	No. of Awards	Value Range	Award Criteria: Class Stndg.	Grade Avg.	SAT/ ACT	Need Based	Other	Study Fields	Renew-ability	Restric-tions	Apply Date	Transfer
MISSISSIPPI *(Continued)*													
U. of Southern Mississippi Hattiesburg 39402 *(Continued)*	Alumni Discounts												
	Co-op												
	Honors Program												
William Carey, Hattiesburg 39401	Honors	Varies	200-600	5%		90%ile	Y		A	Y	N	C	Y
	Honors Program												
MISSOURI													
Avila, Kansas City 64145	Presidential	Varies	1000-Tuition		3.2	1100/21	N	0	A	3.0	N	A-5/1	Y-3.2
	Performance Grants	Varies	1200-9000		2.0		Y	T	0	2.0	N	B-4/1	Y
	St. Theresa of Avila Award	Varies	1500		2.5	19	N	0	A	2.0	0	A-5/1	N
	Focus Grant	20	1500		2.5	22	N	E-T-R-I-0	0	2.5	0	A-B-3/15	N
Calvary Bible C., Kansas City 64147	Academic	Varies	500-1000		3.5	1140/25	N		A	3.5	0	B-C	N
	Departmental	Varies	350-700				N	E-R	A	2.0	N	B-3/31	Y
Central Bible College, Springfield 65803	Academic	Varies	100-2000	X	2.5		N		A	2.5	D	B-7/1	N
	Decade of Harvest	130+	1000				N	R-0	A	N	D-0	A-B-D	N
	Music	6-12	500-1000		2.0		N	E-T-I-0	0	2.0	0	A-B-C	N
	Academic (Freshmen)	8-12	1000-1700	5%			N	0	A	N	0	A-B-C	N
	Honors Program												
Central Methodist, Fayette 65248	Academic	Varies	250-2000	85%	3.0	25	N	L-0	A	3.0	N	A-D	Y
	Hall of Sponsors	Varies	2500				N	T-L-R-0	A	Y	N	A-D	Y-3.0
	Talent	Varies	500-1500	50%	2.0	18	N	T	A	2.0	N	A-D	Y
	Honors Program												
Central Missouri State U. Warrensburg 64093	Distinguished	25	Total Costs	5%	3.75	28	N	E-L-I-0	A	3.75	N	B-2/15	N
	H.S. Recognition	Unlimited	500	25%			N		A	3.25	N	D	N
	Regents'	Unlimited	1200	10%		25	N		A	3.25	N	D	Y
	Presidents	Unlimited	1000	25%		22	N		A	3.25	N	D	N
	National Merit Finalists	Unlimited	Total Costs				N	0	A	2.5	N	B-D	N
	Achievement Awards	Unlimited	200-600				N	E-T	A	N	N	B-2/15	Y
C. of the Ozarks, Pt. Lookout 65726	General	2065	9000-11400			X	Y	L-R-I	A	Y	N	C	Y-2.0

Columbia College, 65216	ACE	Varies			3.3	24	N	O	A	3.4	O	A-B-C	N
	CC Scholar	7			3.6	27	N	L-R	A	Y-3.7	O	A-B-1/31	N
	Honors Program												
Culver-Stockton, Canton 63435	Pillars	8	8800	10%	3.6	1170/26	N	E-I-O	A	3.2	N	B-1/20	N
	Founders	Varies	5000	10%	3.2	1010/22	N		A	3.0	N	A-D	N
	Honors Program												
Drury, Springfield 65802	Academic	Varies	1500-3500	X	3.0	980/22	N		A	3.0	N	B-2/15	Y
	Presidential	4	6000			1300/29	N		A	3.0	N	B-2/15	Y
	Trustees	7	Tuition			1300/29	N		A	3.0	N	B-2/15	Y
	Campus	Varies	1000			900/20	N		A	3.0	N	C-2/15	N
Evangel, Springfield 65802	Academic Achievement	Varies	1500		3.0	1100/27	N		A	3.4	N	A	Y
	Evangel Honor	Varies	1000		3.0	1020/25	N		A	3.2	N	A	Y
	Presidential	Varies	2000		3.0	1260/30	N		A	3.6	N	A	Y
Fontbonne, St. Louis 63105	Alumni	Varies	1000-4000	X	X	X	N	L-R-I-O	A	Y	N	B-3/1	Y
	Campus Service	Varies	500-3000				N	T-L	A	Y	N	A	Y-2.5
	Dean's Competitive	Varies	1000-5000	10%	95%	1200/26	N	L-R-I-O	A	3.4	N	B-3/1	N
	Presidential	3	Tuition	5%	97%	1250/29	N	L-R-I-O	A	3.6	N	B-3/1	N
	Talent	Varies	500-2000				N	E-T	O	Y	N	B-3/1	Y
	Valedictorian	5	5000	1			N	L-R-I-O	A	3.5	N	B-3/1	N
Hannibal-LaGrange C., Hannibal 63401	Academic	Unlimited	10-50% Costs			18	N		A	Y	O	B-C	Y-3.0
	Performance	Unlimited	600-All Costs			18	N	T-I-O	A	Y	O	B-C	Y-2.0
	Denominational	Unlimited	175-800			18	N	T-I-O	A	Y	O	B-C	Y-2.0
	Honors Program												
Harris-Stowe State, St. Louis 63103	Regents'	Varies	550-1200		2.5		Y	E-T-L-R	A	2.5	N	B-4/1	N
Kansas City Art Institute, 64111	Freshman Competitive	20	8000-10000		3.0	950/20	N	T	O	3.0	N	C-12/15	N
	Transfer Competitive	Varies	5000-8000		3.0		N	T	O	3.0	N	B-3/15	Y-3.0
Lincoln U., Jefferson City 65102	Curators	Varies	2366-5094	10%		22	N	O	A	3.25	S-O	B-D	N
	Institutional	Varies	2266-3366	20%		20	N	O	A	3.0	O	B-D	Y-3.0
	Presidential	Varies	2316-3816	15%		21	N	O	A	3.1	O	B-D	N
	Dean's	Varies	Varies	25%	3.0	18	N		A	N	O	B-C	N
	Honors Program												
Lindewood, St. Charles 63301	Honors	Varies	Varies	25%	3.0	946/22	Y	L-R	A	Y	N	A-3/1	Y
	Presidential	Varies	500-Tuition	10%	3.5	1051/24	Y	L-R	A	Y	N	A-3/1	Y
Maryville, St. Louis 63141	Academic Promise	Varies	3000		3.0	22	N		A	3.2	N	A-D	N
	Art & Design	5	2000-5000		3.0	880/21	Y	T-R-I-O	O	3.0	O	B-3/1	Y-3.0
	Jr. Achvmnt. Boys/Girls State	Varies	1200-2400		2.5	21	Y	R	A	3.0	O	C-4/1	N

	Program	No. of Awards	Value Range	Award Criteria: Class Stndg.	Grade Avg.	SAT/ ACT	Need Based	Other	Study Fields	Renew-ability	Restric-tions	Apply Date	Transfer
MISSOURI *(Continued)*													
Maryville, St. Louis 63141 *(Continued)*	Leadership Activity	Varies	1200-2400		2.5	21	N	L	A	3.0	N	C	Y-3.0
	Maryville University	20+	Varies		3.5	24	N	0	A	3.3	0	C	Y-3.2
	Minority University Scholar	Varies	5140-15180		3.3	1050/25	Y	E-L-R-I-0	A	3.3	0	B-2/17	N
	Outstanding Transfer	Varies	2000-4500		3.3		N	0	A	3.3	0	C	Y-3.2
	University Scholar	Varies	5140-15180		3.5	1170/28	Y	E-L-R-I-0	A	3.4	0	B-2/17	N
	Honors Program, Honors College												
Missouri Baptist, St. Louis 63141	Alumni Grant	Varies	4290	50%		950/18	Y	I-0	A	2.0	0	C	N
	Church Matching	Varies	1000	50%		950/18	Y	I-0	A	Y	0	C	Y-2.0
	Dean's	Varies	2570	15%		1100/24	Y	I-0	A	3.0	N	C	Y-3.4
	Denominational	Varies	1000	50%		950/18	Y	I-0	A	2.0	0	C	Y-2.0
	Faculty	Varies	1720	20%		950/20	Y	I-0	A	3.0	N	C	Y-3.0
	Freshman Excellence	4	12,810			1400/30	Y	I-0	A	A	N	C	N
	Full Trustee	6	8580	3%		1280/29	Y	I-0	A	3.5	N	C	Y-3.8
	Ministerial	Varies	3000	50%		950/18	Y	I-0	0	2.0	0	B-C	Y-2.0
	Partial Trustee	27	5150	5%		1240/28	Y	I-0	A	3.5	N	C	Y-3.6
	Performance	Varies	12,810	50%		950/18	Y	T-I-0	A	Y	0	C	Y-2.0
	President's	Varies	3430	10%		1210/27	Y	I-0	A	3.0	N	C	Y-3.5
	Alumni Discount												
	Family Discount												
Missouri Southern State Joplin 64801	President's	Varies	1200-1450	1 or 2		21	N		A	Y	S	B-C	Y
	Regents'	140	800			26	N		A	Y	S	B-C	Y
	Dean's	80	610-860	30%		23	N		A	3.0	N	B-D	Y
	Honors	120	1000-3000		3.5	27	N		A	3.5	N	B-D	Y
	Patron's	250	200-1100		3.0		N		A	3.0	0	B-4/1	Y
	Honors Program												
Missouri Valley, Marshall 65340	Academic	Varies	500-7000				Y	L-R-I-0	A	2.0	N	C	Y-2.0
	Board of Trustees	Varies	5000	50%	2.0	18	N	I-L-R	A	2.5	N	A	Y-2.5
	Talent/Athletic	Varies	1000-10,000	50%	2.0	18	N	I-L-R-T	A	2.5	N	A	Y-2.5
	Presidential	Varies	10,250	10%	3.8	1200/28	N	I-L	A	2.5	N	A	N
	AP Exams												
	Alumni Discount												

	Family Discount												
	Internships												
Missouri Western State St. Joseph 64507	President's	40	Tuition/fees	10%		26	N		A	3.5	0	B-1/1	
	Regents'	Unlimited	1/2 Tuition	20%			N		A	3.0	0	C	N
	Community College (1)	Varies	Tuition/fees		3.5		N		A	3.5	0	B-6/10	Y-3.5
	Community College (2)	Varies	1/2 Tuition		3.0		N		A	3.0	0	B-6/10	Y-3.0
	G.E.D. Awards	Varies	1/2 Tuition				N		A	3.0	0	C	N
	Honors Program												
NW Missouri State U., Maryville 64468	Junior College	25	500		3.0		N		A	3.5	0	B-4/1	Y
	Math/Science Teaching	30	490-1320	5%		16	N		0	3.0	S-0	B-4/1	N
	Minority Achievement	25	1250	50%		21	N		A	2.7	M-0	B-8/1	N
	Minority Transfer	25	1250		3.25		N	0	A	2.7	M-0	B-8/1	Y-3.25
	Presidential Merit	10	Total Costs	5%		29	N		A	3.5	N	B-1/15	N
	Regents' Level I	Unlimited	500	25%		21	N		A	3.3	N	A-D	N
	Regents' Level II	Unlimited	750	25%		23	N		A	3.3	N	A-D	N
	Regents' Level III	Unlimited	1000	15%		28	N		A	3.3	N	A-D	N
	Transfer	4	Tuition		3.5		N	0	A	3.5	N	B-5/1	Y-3.5
Ozark Christian, Joplin 64801	President's	15	4305-5565		3.0		N	T-L-R	A	3.0	N	B-3/10	Y
	Dean's	15	4305-5565		3.0		N	T-L-R	A	3.0	N	B-3/10	Y
	Trustee's	Unlimited	175-275	50%	2.5	18	N		A	2.5	N	A	Y
Park, Parkville 64152	Presidential	Varies	1150	25%	3.25	1100/24	N	L-R	A	3.25	N	B-1/15	N
	Trustee	8	4590	25%	3.25	1100/24	N	E-I-L-R	A	3.5	N	B-1/15	N
	Park/McAfee	4	9190	25%	3.25	1100/24	N	E-I-L-R	A	3.8	N	B-1/15	N
	Transfer	16	1150-2295		3.5		N		A	3.5	N		Y
	AP Exams												
	Distance Learning												
	Family Discount												
	Internships												
	Honors Program												
Rockhurst, Kansas City 64110	Academic	Varies	3000	30%	3.5	1090/24	N		A				
	Chancellor's	Varies	4500	20%	3.7	1260/28	N		A				
	Dean's	Varies	3500	25%	3.6	1160/26	N		A				
	President's	Varies	3/4 Tuition	X	X	X	N	I	A			1/15	
	Service	Varies	2000				N	O	A				
	Transfer	Varies	2000-5000		3.2		N		A				Y-3.2
	Leadership	Varies	1500				N	L	A				
	Trustees	Varies	Tuition	X	X	X	N	I	A				
	AP Exams												
	Distance Learning												

	Program	No. of Awards	Value Range	Award Criteria: Class Stndg.	Award Criteria: Grade Avg.	Award Criteria: SAT/ ACT	Award Criteria: Need Based	Award Criteria: Other	Study Fields	Renew- ability	Restric- tions	Apply Date	Transfer
MISSOURI *(Continued)*													
Rockhurst, Kansas City 64110 *(Continued)*	Alumni Discount, Family Discount												
	Co-op, Internships												
	Honors Program												
St. Louis U., 63103	Academic	300	4150-20,000	X	X	X	N	E-L-R-O	A	Y	N	B-C	N
	Presidential	10	14500-20,000	5%	3.85	1320/30	N	E-L-R-I	A	3.4	N	B-12/1	N
	Dean's	100	5580-7580	10%	3.7	1240/28	N	E-L-R	A	3.2	N	B-12/1	N
	University	200	4150-5650	20%	3.5	1170/26	N	E-L-R	A	3.0	N	B-12/1	N
	Honors Program												
SE Missouri State, Cape Girardeau 63701	Governor's	Varies	Varies	3%		31	N	O	A	3.5	N	B-1/31	N
	Leadership	Varies	500-1000				N	L-R-O	A	N	N	B-1/31	N
	National Merit/Achievement	Varies	All Costs				N	O	A	3.5	N	B-1/31	N
	President's	Varies	1/2 Tuition	20%		24	N	R	A	3.5	N	C	N
	Regents'	Varies	Tuition	10%		90%ile	N	R	A	3.5	N	C	N
	Renaissance Scholarship	Varies	500-1000				N	R-O	A	Y	O	C-1/31	N
	Honors Program												
SW Baptist U., Bolivar 65613	Chancellor's	25	Tuition	5%		90%ile	N	O	A	N	N	B-4/15	N
	Dean's	Unlimited	300	10%		65%ile	N	I-O	A	Y	N	A-D	Y
	President's	Unlimited	500	10%		87%ile	N	R-I	A	Y	N	A-D	Y
	Trustees	Unlimited	400	10%		75%ile	N	I-O	A	Y	N	A-D	Y
	Young American	40	1000	10%		1050/23	N	L-R	A	Y	N	B-5/1	Y
SW Missouri State, Springfield 65804	Academic	Unlimited	2000	20%	3.6	26	N		A	3.25	N	3/1	N
	Achievement	Unlimited	1000	10%	3.8	24	N		A	3.25		3/1	
	Governor's	Unlimited	Fees (in-state)	10%	3.8	28	N		A	3.4	N	3/1	N
	Minority Leadership	Varies	Fees	50%			N	L-R	A	2.0	O	3/1	Y
	Presidential	40	Total Costs	10%		1320/30	N	O	A	3.25	N	1/13	N
	AP Exams												
	Distance Learning												
	Co-op, Internships												
	Honors College												
Stephens, Columbia 65215	Academic	Unlimited	1000-9000		3.0	1140/21	X		A	Y			
	Leadership	Unlimited	1000-3000				N	E-L-R-T		Y			
	Transfer	Unlimited	3000-9000		3.0		X			Y			

	AP Exams												
	Family Discount												
	Internships												
	Honors Program												
Truman State U., Kirksville 63501	Alumni	Varies	Varies	X	X	X	N	E-L-O	A	3.25	N	A-2/1	N
	Fine Arts	Varies	Varies				N	E-T-O	O	2.0	N	B-2/28	Y
	Foreign Language	Varies	Varies	X	X	X	N	E-O	A	3.25	N	A-2/1	Y
	Pershing	12	Total Costs	10%	X	X	N	E-L-R-I-O	A	3.25	N	A-2/1	N
	President's Honorary	Varies	750-1500	X	X	X	N	E	A	3.25	N	A-D	N
	Truman Leadership	Varies	Total Costs	10%		27	N	E-L	A	3.25	S	A-D	N
	AP Exams												
	Internships												
	Honors Program												
U. of Missouri, Columbia 65211	Curators	Unlimited	3500	5%		28	N		A	3.25	S	A-5/15	N
	Excellence Award	Unlimited	1000	15%		27	N		A	3.25	S	A	N
	George Brooks	50	7000	20%			N	E-L-R-I-O	A	2.5	M	B-3/1	N
	MU	Varies	1750	10%		27	N		A	3.25	S	B-12/1	N
	Non-Resident Scholars	Unlimited	2000-4000	25%		27	N		A	2.5	O	A	N
	University	Unlimited	To 1/3 Fees		3.5		N		A	3.5	S	A-D	Y
	Honors Program, Honors College												
U. of Missouri, Kansas City 64110	Clay	Varies	Varies				N		A	Y	N	B-D	N
	University	Varies	Varies		3.5		N		A	N	N	C	
	Scholar	10	2500	10%		26	N	E-L-R-I	O	3.25	S	B-2/1	N
	Chancellor Freshman	53	1000	25%		25	N	E-T-L-R	O	3.0	N	B-2/1	N
	Chancellor Transfer	20	1000		3.25		N	E-L-R-O	O	3.0	N	B-3/15	Y-3.25
	Honors Program												
U. of Missouri, Rolla 64501	Bright Flight		2000			1420/30			A		S	B	
	Chancellor's Scholarships	15	3000	5%		87%ile	N	E-L-R-O	A	3.2	S	B-11/1	N
	Curator's		24 credit hrs.	5%	87%ile	90%ile		R	A	3.25	S	B	
	Distinguished Scholars		750-4000	25%		1090/27			A	2.5		B-11/1	Y-3.0
	Transfer Scholarships	Varies	500				N	R-O	A	N	N	B-11/1	Y-3.0
	University Scholarships	Varies	500-2000	10%		87%ile	N	O	A	3.2	N	B-11/1	N
	AP Exams												
	Alumni Discounts												
	Co-op, Internships												
	Honors Program												
U. of Missouri, St.Louis	Curators	Unlimited	Fee Waiver	3%		90%ile	N	R	A	Y	S	C	N
	University Scholars	Unlimited	Varies		3.5		N		A	Y	S	B-4/1	Y

	Program	No. of Awards	Value Range	Award Criteria: Class Stndg.	Grade Avg.	SAT/ ACT	Need Based	Other	Study Fields	Renew- ability	Restric- tions	Apply Date	Transfer
MISSOURI *(Continued)*													
U. of Missouri, St.Louis *(Continued)*	Talent	75	Total Costs			3%	N	0	A	Y-3.3	S	A-4/1	N
	Chancellor's	Varies	Total Costs	25%		20%	N	0	A	N	N	A-4/1	N
Washington U., St. Louis 63130	Compton	6	Tuition+	10%	3.5	X	N	E-R-I-0	0	Y	N	B-1/15	N
	Conway/Proetz	1	Tuition	10%	X	X	N	T-0	0	Y	N	B-1/15	N
	Dean's Business Schp.	2	1/2 Tuition	10%	X	X	N	0	0	Y	N	A-1/14	N
	Fitzgibbon	1	Tuition+ 1000				N	E-T-L-R-I-0	C	Y	N	B-1/15	N
	John B. Ervin	10	Tuition+ 2500				N	E-L-R-I-0	A	Y	M	B-1/15	N
	Langsdorf	4	Tuition+ 2500	5%			N	E-L-R-I-0	0	Y	N	B-1/15	N
	Lien	3	Tuition+	10%	3.5	X	N	E-R-I-0	0	Y	N	B-1/15	N
	Mylonas	3	Tuition+	10%	3.5	X	N	E-R-I-0	0	Y	N	B-1/15	N
	Woodward	20	1/2 Tuition	5%	X	X	N	E-L-R-I-0	0	Y	N	B-1/15	N
	Honors Program												
Webster U., St. Louis 63119	Academic	Varies	1000-6000	33%	3.0	900/22	N	E-R-I-0	A	3.0	N	C-4/1	Y-3.3
	Monsanto	2-4	All Costs	10%	3.5	25	N	E-L-R-I-0	0	3.5	M	B-3/1	N
Westminster, Fulton 65251	Churchill	10	Tuition		3.8	1280/29	N	E-I	A	3.3	N	A-C	N
	Dean's	Varies	1500-3000	2.75	2.75	1010/22	N	0	A	2.5	N	A-D	N
	President's	Varies	3000-4000	%	2.75	1130/25	N	0	A	3.0	N	A-D	N
	Trustees	Varies	4500-6000		2.75	1240/28	N	0	A	3.3	N	A-D	N
	Leadership	Varies	1000-2000				N	E-L-R-0	A	2.5	N	A-D	N
William Jewell, Liberty 64068	Distinguished Scholars	4	Tuition	5%	3.5	90%ile	N	0	A	3.5	Y	B-1/31	N
	Marian Greene	2	1/2 Tuition	10%	3.5	85%ile	N	0	0	3.0	Y	B-3/1	N
	Academic Excellence	Limited	2000-4000	25%	3.5	75%ile	N	0	A	3.0	N	D	N
	Academic Excellence Transfer	Limited	500-3000		3.0		N		A	3.0	N	D	Y
William Woods, Fulton 65251	Academic	Varies	1500-3000		2.8	840/21	N		A	3.2	W	B-6/1	Y-2.8
	TOP	25	500-2000		2.5		N	L-R-I-0	A	2.5	W	B-2/12	Y-2.5
	McNutt	1	12000		3.5	1020/26	N	E-L-I-0	A	3.25	W	B-2/12	Y-3.5
MONTANA													
Carroll, Helena 59625	Presidential	Varies	1000-5000		3.0	1000/21	N		A	3.0	N	3/1	N
	Transfer	Varies	500-2000		3.0		N	E	A	3.0	N	4/1	Y-3.0

	AP Exams Alumni Discounts, Family Discounts Co-op, Internships *Honors Program*												
College of Great Falls, 59405	Honor	20	2000		3.0		N	E-L-R	A	3.0	N	B-4/1	N
	Merit	Varies	100-1500				N	L-R	A	Y	N	B-4/1	Y
Montana State U., Billings	Chancellor	30	1000	10%	3.5	1060/24	N	E-L-R-T-0	A	N	S	B-3/1	N
	Academic	Varies	50-4000		3.0		N	E-L-R-T-0	A	X	N	B-3/1	Y
	AP Exams Distance Learning Co-op, Internships *Honors Program*												
Montana State U., Bozeman 59717	High School Days	145	100-2000				N	E-T	A	N	S-H-0	C	N
Montana Tech., Butte 59701	Freshman Academic	16	500-1000	X	X	X	N		A				N
	Chancellor's	60	1000-2000	33%	3.2	1140/25	N		A				Y
	Davis Memorial	8	2500	X	X	X	Y		A	3.0			N
	AP Exams Distance Learning Co-op, Internships												
Northern Montana, Havre 59501	President's	20	500	10%	3.2	1000/24	N	L	A	3.0	S	A-3/1	N
	Academic	60	Varies	X	X		Y	R-0	A	X	0	B-2/1	Y
	Talent	40	Varies	X	X		N	E-T-I	A	X	0	B-2/1	Y
Rocky Mountain, Billings 59102	Winston L. Cox	4	1000		3.5		N	E-L-R-0	0	3.5	N	C-4/1	Y-3.5
	Honors	Varies	1500-5000		3.5	24/1100	N	E-L-I-0	0	3.5	0	C-2/15	N
	Academic	Varies	500-1250		3.0	21	N	0	A	3.0	N	C	Y-3.0
U. of Montana, Missoula 59801	Freshman	455	600-1200	25%	3.4	1100/24	Y	E-L-R	A	N	0	B-2/1	N
	General	Varies	600-1200		3.4		Y	E-L-R	A	N	0	B-2/1	Y
	Presidential	30	5000-9600	10%	3.8	1200/28	N	E-I-L-R	A	3.2	N	B-2/1	Y
	AP Exams Distance Learning Co-op, Internships *Honors College, Honors Program*												
Western Montana, Dillon 59725	Academic	65	250-1500	20%	3.2	900/22	N	L-0	A	3.2	N	B-3/1	Y
	Art	30	1000				N	T	A	Y	N	B-3/1	Y
	Band	20	250-500				N	T	A	Y	N	B-3/1	Y

	Program	No. of Awards	Value Range	Award Criteria: Class Stndg.	Grade Avg.	SAT/ ACT	Need Based	Other	Study Fields	Renew-ability	Restric-tions	Apply Date	Transfer
NEBRASKA													
Bellevue University, 68005	Academic	Varies	300-1500	25%	3.0	23	N	L-R-0	A	3.0	N	B-5/1	Y-3.0
	Divisional	Varies	445-1500	25%	3.0	23	N	T-E-0	A	3.0	N	B-6/1	Y-3.0
	Honors Program												
Chadron State, 69337	Board of Trustees	25	1260-1680	25%		1100/25	N	R	A	Y	A	B-1/15	N
	Presidential	40-60	1260-1680	33%	3.0	20	N	L	A	N	N	B-1/15	Y
	CARE	10-15	1000				N		A	Y	N	B-1/15	Y-3.0
	Quivey Bay	20-30	1000		3.0		N		A	N	N	B-1/15	Y
	Honors Program												
Clarkson, Omaha 68131	Presidential	49	3000-7500	25%	3.0	20	N	0		Y			
	AP Exams												
	Distance Learning												
	Co-op, Internships												
College of St. Mary, Omaha 68124	Honor	Unlimited	500-6000		2.8	21	N	0	A	2.5	0	A-D	N
	Dean's	12	1/2 Tuition		3.5	26	N	E-R-I-0	A	2.8	0	B-2/15	N
	Board	3	Tuition		3.7	2.8	N	E-R-I-0	A	3.0	0	B-2/15	N
Concordia, Seward 68434	Regents	Varies	1000-10150		3.0	1070/24	N		A	3.0	N	A-D	N
	Presidential	Varies	750		2.75	950/20	N	E-L-R	A	2.75	N	B-D	Y-2.75
	Talent	Varies	200-2000				N	T-R-I	0	Y	N	B-D	Y-2.75
	Tower Transfer	Varies	1000-10150		3.0	1070/24	N	0	A	3.0	N	A-D	Y-3.0
	Honors Program												
Creighton U., Omaha 68178	Linn	Varies	2500				N	L	A	2.5	N	A-2/1	N
	Presidential	20	3/4 Tuition				N	L	A	3.3	N	A-2/1	N
	Reinert	Varies	5000				N	L	A	3.0	N	A-2/1	N
	Scott	4	Tuition				N	L	0	3.4	N	A-2/1	N
	AP Exams												
	Distance Learning												
	Family Discounts												
	Internships												
	Honors Program												
Dana, Blair 68006	Dana Honor	Unlimited	1000-7000		3.0	970/21	N	E-I-0	A	3.0	N	A-D	Y-3.25
	Presidential	Unlimited	1000-Tuition		3.25	1130/25	N	E-I-0	A	3.0	N	A-1/30	N

	Val/Sal AP Exams Alumni Discounts, Family Discounts Internships *Honors Program*	Unlimited	1/3-1/2 Tuition	1 or 2			N		A	3.0	N	A-D	N
Doane, Crete 68333	Academic Talent *Honors Program*	Varies Varies	500-Tuition 100-2500	40%	2.5	20	N N	 T-R-I	A A	2.5 Y	N N	A-3/15 B-3/15	Y Y
Hastings College, 68901	Academic Special Skills	Varies Varies	500-Tuition Varies	35%		950/23	N N	I-0 I-0	A 0	2.5 2.5	N N	C C	Y Y
Midland Lutheran, Fremont 68025	Academic Talent	276 158	100-All Costs 100-2500	30%	2.5	20	N N	0 T-R-I-0	A A	2.5 N	N N	A-3/15 B-3/15	Y Y
Nebraska Christian, Norfolk 68701	Trustee's Scholarship President's Dean's AP Exams Internships	Unlimited Unlimited Unlimited	2500 1900 1250	2% 5% 15%		29-36 26-28 23-25	N N N	0 0 0	A A A	3.5 3.25 3.0	0 0 0	A-C A-C A-C	Y Y Y
Nebraska Wesleyan U., Lincoln 68504	Board of Governors Wesleyan Scholar Trustees Scholarship President's	10 10-15 30 140	Tuition 4000 2500 1500			 1300/31 1200/29 1070/26	N N N N	0	A A A A	Y Y Y Y	S N N N	A-C B-4/1 B-4/1 B-4/1	N Y Y Y
Peru State College, 68421	President's Trustees	Unlimited 15	Tuition Tuition	25% 25%		24 24	N N	R-0 R-0	A A	Y Y	0 A	B-4/15 B-1/15	N N
Union, Lincoln 68506	NM Standing	Unlimited	500-Tuition				N	0	A	Y	N	B-D	N
U. of Nebraska, Kearney 68849	Board of Regents Chancellors *Honors Program*	45 150	Tuition 1000	25% 25%		24 24	N N	R R	A A	3.2 3.6	N N	B-12/15 B-12/15	N N
U. of Nebraska, Lincoln 68588	David Davis Distinguished Scholar Honors Program Schp. Regents Schp. for New Nebraskans *Honors Program*	135 27 200 200 310 Varies	1000 1000 1000 Varies Tuition Res. Tuition	X X X X X X	X X X X X X	X X X X X X	N Y N N N N	0 T-L-0 0 E-0 0 0	A A A A A A	3.5 N Y Y 3.5 Y	M M 0 N M 0	B-12/15 B-12/15 B-1/15 B-D B-12/15 B-D	N N N Y N Y
U. of Nebraska, Omaha 68182	Miscellaneous *Honors Program*	Varies	100-6500	X	X	X	X	0	A	X	0	C	Y

	Program	No. of Awards	Value Range	Award Criteria					Study Fields	Renew-ability	Restric-tions	Apply Date	Transfer
				Class Stndg.	Grade Avg.	SAT/ ACT	Need Based	Other					
NEBRASKA *(Continued)*													
Wayne State College, 68787	Neihardt	10	2285	25%	3.3	25	N	E-R	A	3.2			
	Leadership Award	12	1450				N	E-L-R-T	A	Y			
	Board of Trustees	30	1785			25	N	R	A	3.25	A	B-1/15	N
	AP Exams												
	Distance Learning												
	Co-op												
	Honors Program												
NEVADA													
Sierra Nevada, Incline Village 89450	Scholarship	Varies	Varies	10%	3.5		N	L-R	A	N	N	B-7/31	Y-3.5
U. of Nevada, Las Vegas 89154	Freshman Academic	270-300	250-2500	10%	3.4	1050/24	Y	O	A	3.0	A-S-M-O	B-2/1	N
	Continuing Students	300-800	150-2500	10%	3.0		Y	O	A	3.0	M-O	B-2/1	Y-3.6
U. of Nevada, Reno 89557	Freshman & Cont'g Students	Varies	Varies	X	X	X	X		A	X	O	B-3/1	N
	Honors Program												
NEW HAMPSHIRE													
Colby-Sawyer, New London 03257	Nichols	4	500-3000				N	T-R	A	N	O	B-4/15	Y
	Presidential	10	7500		3.0	1100/24	N		A	3.0	N	A-2/1	N
	Leadership Award	10	5000		2.5	950/20	N	L	A	2.5	N	A-2/1	N
	Talent	10	5000		2.5	950/20	N	T	A	2.5	N	A-2/1	N
	Community Service	10	5000		2.5	950/20	N	L	A	2.5	N	A-2/1	N
	Honors Program												
Daniel Webster, Nashua 03003	Ex. In Leadership	1			3.0	1000	N	E-I-L-O	A	2.75			
	Presidential	33	7500		3.5	1100	N		A	2.5			
	Merit	100	500-6500		2.5	850	N		A	2.5			
	AP Exams												
	Alumni Discounts, Family Discounts												
Franklin Pierce, Rindge 03461	Presidential	Varies	1000-7000	20%	3.4	1100/24	N		A	3.2	N	A	Y-3.4
	Success Grant	Varies	1000-6000	X	X	X	N		A	2.0	N	A	Y
	Performing Arts	2	2000				N	T	O	2.0	N	A-3/15	Y

	AP Exams												
	Family Discounts												
	Honors Program												
Keene State College, 03431	President's	Varies	All Costs	10%	4.0	1100	N	E-L-R-I	A	3.75	A	B-2/28	N
	Talent	Varies	1000		3.0		N	T	O	3.0	N	C	N
New England College, Henniker 03242	Leadership Award	35	1500				N	L	A	Y	N	A	Y
	Presidential	25	3000		3.0		N	L	A	3.0	N		Y-3.0
	Cox	5	5000		3.5		N	E-L-R	A	3.5	N	B-3/15	N
	Honors Program												
	AP Exams												
	Family Discounts												
	Internships												
New Hampshire, Manchester 03106	Academic	100	1000-6000		3.0		N		A	3.0	N	A	Y-3.0
	Leadership	40	1000		2.5			L	A	2.0	N		N
	AP Exams												
	Distance Learning												
	Alumni Discounts, Family Discounts												
	Co-op, Internships												
	Honors Program												
Notre Dame, Manchester 03104	Presidential Honors	40	2500	25%	3.0	1050	N		A	3.0	O	A-3/15	N
	Moreau Achievement	3	1000		3.5		N	E-R	A	3.5	N	B-4/15	N
	Commuter Honors	40	1000	25%	3.0	1000	N		A	3.0	N	A-3/15	N
	Catholic H.S.	20	1000	25%	3.0		N	L-R-O	A	3.0	D-O	A	N
Plymouth State College, 03264	Plymouth Scholar	To 40	1000	20%	3.0	900	N	T-L-R	A	N	N	A-D	Y-3.0
	Presidential	10	1000	10%	3.5	1000	N	T-L-R	A	3.5	N	B-3/1	N
	Music & Theater Talent	8	2000				N	T-R-I-O	A	X	O	C	Y
	Honors Program												
Rivier College, Nashua 03060	High School Honors	6	1000-4000	20%	3.0		Y	E-L-R-I	A	N		C-3/1	Y-3.0
	Science Scholarship	8	2500	20%			N	E-L-R-I	O	3.0		C-3/1	Y-3.0
	Presidential	6	5000	20%	3.0	1100	N	E-L-R-I	A	3.0		C-3.1	Y-3.0
Saint Anselm, Manchester 03102	Benedictine	Varies	Varies	X	X	X	X		A	Y	O	C	N
	Presidential	80	5000-10,000	20%	3.0	1200	N	L-R-I-O	A	Y	N	A-D	N
	AP Exams												
	Family Discounts												
	Honors Program												
U. of New Hampshire, Durham 03824	Granite State Honor	Varies	7500	X	X	X	N	I-O	A	3.2	S	A	N
	Honors	Varies	1500	X	X	X	N	L-O	A	3.2	O	B	N
	Dean's	Varies	5000	X	X	X	N	L-O	A	3.0	O	A	N

	Program	No. of Awards	Value Range	Award Criteria: Class Stndg.	Grade Avg.	SAT/ ACT	Need Based	Other	Study Fields	Renew-ability	Restric-tions	Apply Date	Transfer
NEW HAMPSHIRE *(Continued)*													
U. of New Hampshire, Durham 03824 *(Continued)*	Presidential	Varies	2600-7000	10%	X	1350	N	I	A	3.2		A	N
	AP Exams												
	Honors Program												
NEW JERSEY													
Bloomfield College, 07003	Academic Grant	Varies	3000-Tuition	33%		900	N	R-I	A	3.0	N	C-4/1	Y-3.5
	Academic Scholarship	Varies	4000-Tuition	20%		1000	N	R-I	A	3.0	N	C-4/1	Y-3.5
	Challenge	Varies	1000-Tuition	50%		800	N	R-I	A	2.5	N	C-4/1	Y-3.5
	Presidential	Varies	2000-3500	33%		970	Y	R-I-O	A	2.75	N	C	N
	Transfer Scholars	Varies	3000-Tuition		3.0		Y	R-I-O	A	3.0	N	5/1	Y-3.0
	Trustees	Varies	3500-Tuition	25%		1050	Y	R-I-O	A	3.0	N	C	N
	Honors Program												
Caldwell College, 07006	Competitive	Varies	1500-Tuition	20%	3.5	1000/24	N	T-R-I-O	A	3.0	N	A-2/15	Y-3.5
	Honors Program												
Centenary, Hackettstown 07840	Leadership	Varies	Varies		2.0		Y	E-I-L	A	Y	N	C	Y-2.0
	Merit	Varies	5200		3.0	940/18	N	E-I	A	2.7	N	A	Y-3.0
	Achievement	Varies	4200		2.7	940/18	N	E-I	A	2.7	N	A	
	AP Exams												
	Alumni Discounts, Family Discounts												
	Internships												
	Honors Program												
College of St. Elizabeth, Morristown, 07960	Presidential	30	Tuition	20%	3.0	1200	N	L-R	A	3.0	O	B-2/15	N
	Elizabethan	20	1/2 Tuition	20%	3.0	1100	Y		A	3.0	O	B-3/1	N
	Seton	20	Varies	20%	3.0	950	N		A		N	C	N
Drew U., Madison 07940	Drew Scholars (1)	Varies	Full Tuition	1%		1450/34	N	T-L	A	3.2	N	A-1/2	N
	Drew Scholars (2)	Varies	3/4 Tuition	5%		1400/33	N	T-L	A	3.2	N	A-1/2	N
	Drew Recognition	Varies	6000-10000	X	X	X	N	T-L	A	Y	N	A-2/15	N
	Presidential	Varies	10000				N	E-T-O	A	2.0	N	C-2/15	N
Fairleigh Dickinson U., All Campuses	Presidential	200	400-3000		B+	1050	N		A	2.0	N	A-3/15	Y
Felician College, Lodi 07644	President's	4	Tuition	10%	B+	1150	N	L-R-I	A	3.5	O	A	N

	Felician College	4-5	1/2 Tuition	10%	B+	1100	N	L-R-I	A	3.3	O	A	N
	Academic	Varies	500-3000	25%	B	Varies	N	L-R-I	A	3.0	N	A	Y-3.0
	NJ Food Council	1	Tuition				N	E-R-I-O	A	Y	N	B-6/10	Y
	Honors Program												
Georgian Court, Lakewood 08701	Academic Excellence	Varies	To 10,500	10%	3.0	1000-22	N	R	A	Y	N	C-4/1	Y-3.0
	Art	2	1000-2000		3.5	1000	N	T-L-R-I	A	3.0	N	C-8/1	Y
	AP Exams												
	Alumni Discounts, Family Discounts												
Jersey City State College, 07305	Presidential	50	1000-4000	25%	3.0	1050	N		A	3.33	N	A-5/1	Y-3.5
	AP Exams												
	Co-op, Internships												
	Honors Program												
Monmouth, W. Long Branch 07764	Monmouth Scholarship	Varies	2000-8500		3.0	1000	N	I-O	A	3.0	N	A	Y-3.0
	Monmouth Grant	Varies	2000-6500		2.25	800	N	I-O	A	3.0	N	A	Y-2.0
	Honors Program												
Montclair State, Upper Montclair 07043	Alumni Association	20	1000		X		N	E-L	A	N	O	B-3/1	Y
	Dortch/Dickson	Varies	1000		X		Y	E-L	A	N	M	B-3/1	Y
	Garden State	600	200-500	10%		X	Y		A	2.0	A-O	A-10/1	Y
	NJ Bell Telephone	2	875		3.5		Y	E-L	A	N	A-O	B-C	Y
	NJ Disting. Scholars	20	1000	5%	X	X	N	R	A	Y	A-O	C	Y
Rider, Lawrenceville 08648	Dean's	Varies	6000	20%	3.0	1050	N	I-O	A	3.0	N	A-3/1	N
	Distinguished Scholar	Varies	12,000	20%		X	N	R-I-O	A	3.0	A	A-C	N
	Diversity	Varies	12,000	25%	3.5	1150	N	I-O	A	2.75	N	3/1	N
	Fine Arts	2	Tuition				N	T-R-I-O	O	3.0	N	C	N
	Minority Transfer	Varies	5000		3.5		N	I-O	A	3.0	M	4/1	Y
	Presidential	Varies	12,000		3.5	1250	N	I-O	A	3.0	N	A-3/1	N
	Transfer	Varies	5000		3.0		N	I-O	A	3.0	N	4/1	Y
	Urban Scholar	Varies	2500	10%		X	N	I-O	A	2.5	A	A-C	N
	AP Exams												
	Internships												
	Honors Program												N
Rowan College, Glassboro, 08028	Trust Fund	40	600-1500		3.5		Y	E-T-L-R	A	N	A	B-3/15	N
Rutgers U., New Brunswick 08903	Camden College of A&S	up to 25	500-1000	14%	3.2	1100	N	O	A	3.0	A	A-5/1	Y
	County College		1750-3500	14%	3.2	1100	N	L-R	A	3.0	A	A-3/1	Y-3.0
	Douglass College	6	1000	14%	3.2	1100	N	L-R-O	A	3.0	O	A-12/1	Y
	Engineering	3	1000	14%	3.2	1100	N	L-R-O	O	3.0	A	A	Y
	James Dickson Carr	up to 75	5000	14%	3.2	1100	N	L-R-O	A	3.0	A	A-3/1	Y-3.0

	Program	No. of Awards	Value Range	Award Criteria: Class Stndg.	Grade Avg.	SAT/ ACT	Need Based	Other	Study Fields	Renew-ability	Restric-tions	Apply Date	Transfer
NEW JERSEY *(Continued)*													
Rutgers U., New Brunswick 08903 *(Continued)*	Livingston College	20	250-1000	14%	3.2	1100	N	O	A	3.0	A	A-5/1	Y
	Mason Gross	4	500-6000	14%	3.2	1100+	N	E-T-R-I	O	3.0	N	A	Y
	Minority	71	1000	14%	3.2	1100	N	L-R-I-O	A	3.0	M	A-3/1	Y-3.0
	National Achievement	14	1000-2000	14%	3.2	1100	N		A	3.0	M	C	Y
	Newark College of A&S	up to 28	500-1000	14%	3.2	1100	N	R-O	A	3.0	N	A-2/1	Y
	Nursing	6	250-1000	14%	3.2	1100	N	R-I-O	O	3.0	N	A-2/1	Y
	Presidential Scholar	15	5000	14%	3.2	1100	N	O	A	3.0	A	A-3/1	Y
	Rutgers College	16	500-2000	14%	3.2	1100	N	O	A	3.0	N	A-5/1	Y
	Honors Program												
St. Peter's, Jersey City 07306	Academic	100	1/2-Full Tuition	20%	3.3	1100	N	I-O	A	3.0	N	A-D	Y-3.0
	Whelan	75	500-2500				N	L-O	A	Y	N	A-D	Y
	Incentive	100	500-4000	25%	3.0	1000	N		A	3.0	N	A-D	Y
	Bastek	1	Full Tuition	10%	3.5	1000	N	E-I	A	3.5	N	B-3/1	N
	AP Exams												
	Co-op, Internships												
	Honors Program												
Seton Hall U., S. Orange 07079	Academic	380	3000-8500	20%	3.2	1050	N		A	3.0	N	A-2/15	Y-3.5
	Chancellor	10	Tuition				N	R	A	3.2	N	B-2/1	N
	Clare Boothe Luce	2	To All Costs			1200	N	E-R	O	3.3	O	B-3/1	N
	Martin Luther King, Jr.	40	Tuition	25%	3.0		N	L-O	A	3.0	O	B-C	N
	Honors Program												
Stevens Inst. of Tech., Hoboken 07030	Scholar of Excellence	Varies	2000-4000				N		A	Y	N	A	N
	Women in Engineering	Varies	1000-4000				N		A	Y	W	Y	N
	Neupauer	Varies	Tuition			1400	N	R	A	Y	N	A	N
	Edwin A Stevens Scholar	Varies	Tuition				N		A	3.0	M		N
	Dickinson-Howe Scholar	Varies	Tuition				N		A	3.0	N	A	N
	AP Exams												
	Co-op, Internships												
	Honors Program												
Stockton State College, Pomona	Academic #1	35	1000	20%	3.4	1050	N	T-L-R-I-O	A	N	N	A	N
	Academic #2	20	1500-Costs	15%	3.6	1100	N	T-L-R-I-O	A	3.2	N	A	N
	Academic #3	25	Tuition, fees	10%	3.7	1200	N	T-L-R-I-O	A	3.2	N	A	N

Trenton State College, 08240	Alumni	150	1500	10%	3.5	1200	N		A	Y	N	A-D	N
	Distinguished Scholar	600	Varies	10%	3.5	1260	N		A	3.0	A	A-D	N
	Trenton State	400	1000-4500	10%	3.5	1260	N		A	3.0	N	A-3/1	N
	Honors Program												
Westminster Choir, Princeton 07540	Achievement	26	250-2500	20%	3.0		N	T-R	O	N	N	A-4/1	Y
	J.F. Williamson	20	500-4000		3.0	1000	N	T-R	O	Y	N	A-4/15	Y
William Paterson, Wayne 07470	Academic Excellence	17	750-1000	15%	90	1100	N	E-L-R	A	3.0	N	A	Y-3.0
	Minority	30	1000	30%	90	950	N	E-R	A	3.0	M	A	N
	Presidential	100	Tuition	15%	90	1200	N	E-L-R	A	3.0	N	A	Y-3.5
	Trustee	50	Tuition	20%	90.0	1000	N	R	A	3.0	N	A	N
	AP Exams												
	Distance Learning												
	Internships												
	Honors Program												
NEW MEXICO													
College of Santa Fe, 87505	Dean's	Varies	3000		3.0	1100/22	N	L-R	A	3.0	N	A	N
	Presidential	Varies	5000		3.5	1100/24	N		A	3.0	N	A-3/1	N
	Presidential Transfer	Varies	2000		3.0		N		A	3.0	N	A-3/1	Y-3.0
College of the Southwest, Hobbs 88240	Academic Excellence	Varies	1250		3.50		N		A	3.5	N	B-6/1	Y-3.2
	Accounting	1-2	1000		3.25		N		L	3.2	N	A-B-6/1	Y-3.2
	Kenneth J. Fadke Honorary	Varies	1150-1300		3.25		N	O	A	3.5	O	A-B-6/1	Y-3.25
	Presidential	Varies	1500		3.20	22	N		A	3.0	N	A-B-6/1	N
	Scholar	Varies	2000-3000	10%	3.50	23	N	L-I	A	3.2	O	A-B-6/1	N
	Thelma A. Webber Merit	Varies	350-700		2.75		N		A	3.0	O	A-B-6/1	Y-2.75
	Trustee	Varies	1025			730/18	N		A	3.0	N	B-6/1	Y-3.0
Eastern NM U., Portales 88130	Presidential	Varies	Varies		3.5	28	N		A	3.25	N	A-8/1	N
	Zia	Varies	Varies		3.25	25	N		A	3.25	N	A-8/1	N
	Silver	Varies	Varies		3.0	22	N		A	3.25	N	A-8/1	N
	Honors Program												
NM Highlands U., Las Vegas 87701	Academic	Varies	To Tuition		3.0	X	Y	R	A	Y	N	B-3/1	Y
NM Inst. of Mining & Tech. Socorro 87801	Presidential	Varies	2000	X	3.0	27	N		A	2.75	N	B-3/1	N
	Regents'	Varies	1500	X	2.5	25	N	R	A	2.75	N	B-3/1	Y
	Competitive	Varies	700-3663	X	2.75	27	N	O	A	2.5	O	B-3/1	Y-3.5
	Counselor's Choice	Varies	1000	X	2.5	21	N	R	A	2.0	O	B-3/1	N
	Silver	Varies	3000		3.5		N		A	3.0	N	A-3/1	N
	AP Exams												

	Program	No. of Awards	Value Range	Award Criteria: Class Stndg.	Grade Avg.	SAT/ ACT	Need Based	Other	Study Fields	Renew-ability	Restric-tions	Apply Date	Transfer
NEW MEXICO *(Continued)*													
NM Inst. of Mining & Tech. Socorro 87801 *(Continued)*	Distance Learning												
	Internships												
New Mexico State U., Las Cruces 88003	President Associates Honors	5	5296		3.5	1100/26	N	E	A	3.5	A	B-3/1	N
	President Associates	10	2500		3.5	1100/26	N	E	A	3.5	A	B-3/1	N
	Regents'	350	2296	10%	X	X	N		A	3.5	N	B-3/1	Y-3.25
	Out-of-State Alumni	100	200-4956		3.5	980/23	N		A	3.25	S-0	B-3/1	Y-3.25
St. John's College, Santa Fe 87501	Southwest Scholar	Varies	2500-5000				Y	E-L-0	A	Y	A-S	B-3/1	N
U. of New Mexico, Albuquerque 87131	Activity/Zia	200	500	30%	3.0	20	N	E-L-R-0	A	Y-3.0	A	B-2/1	N
	Amigo Scholarship	300	Tuition		X	X	N	0	A	Y-3.0	0	B-2/1	Y
	Presidential Scholarship	200	Tuition/Books	15%	3.5	24	N	E-L-R-0	A	Y-3.0	N	B-12/1	N
	Regents' Scholars	15	6500	5%	3.9	30	N	E-L-R-0	A	Y-3.5	N	B-12/1	N
	UNM Scholars	300	Tuition	20%	3.2	22	N	E-L-R-0	A	Y-3.0	A	B-2/1	N
	Honors Program												
Western NM U., Silver City 88061	Regents'	150	400		X	X	X		A	Y	A	B-D	N
	Competitive	Varies	3400		3.0	23	Y		A	3.0	A-S	B-4/1	Y-3.25
	Scholars	Varies	1400	5%	X	25	Y		A	3.0	A	B-4/1	N
	Endowed	Varies	1200		3.0	26	Y		A	3.0	A	B-4/1	N
NEW YORK													
Adelphi U., Garden City 11530	Academic Merit	200	4000-13,500	25%	3.0	1000	N	E-I-R	A	3.0			
	Transfer Scholarship	155	3000-7000		3.0		N	E-I	A	3.0			
	Talent	50	2000-5000				N	E-L-R-T	0	2.0			
	AP Exams												
	Distance Learning												
	Alumni Discounts												
	Honors Program, Honors College												
Alfred U., 14802	Art Portfolio	6	1500				N	T	0	2.0	N	A-2/1	N
	Competition	10	1000				N	E-T	0	3.0	N	C	N
	Junior Achievement	Varies	4000				N	R	0	2.0	N	C	N
	Presidential	Varies	1000-10000	10%	90	1116	N	E-L-R-I-0	A	3.0	N	A-2/1	Y-3.3
	Southern Tier	Varies	1000-10000	10%	90	1116	N	E-L-R-I-0	A	3.0	A-S	A-2/1	N

Bard, Annandale-on-Hudson 12504	Bard	400	500-6500	X	X		Y	E-L-R	A	2.5	N	A-1/31	Y
	Excellence & Equal Cost	40	Varies	10			N	E-T-L-R	A	3.0	N	1/31	N
	Distinguish Science	20	Tuition				N	0	0	3.0	N	B-1/31	N
Baruch, New York 10010	Scholar	20	2600		87	1100		E-R-I-0	A	Y-3.25	N	B-3/1	N
	Excellence	2	1300-3000		90	1200		E-R-I-0	A	Y-3.25	N	B-3/1	N
Binghamton University (SUNY), 13901	Giflitz	4	4000	5%		1300	N	I-0	0	3.25	N	A-C	N
	Presidential	10	3400	5%		1250	N	I-0	A	3.25	N	A-C	N
	Honors Program												
Brooklyn College, Brooklyn 11210	Presidential	25	3200		3.0	1100	N	E-I-R	A	3.5	N	B-2/15	N
	Foundation Honors	25	1000-3200		3.5	1200	N	E-I-L-R-T	A	3.0	N	B-2/15	N
	Freshman	11	500-1600		3.0		N	E-I-R	A	3.0	N	B-2/15	N
	Performing Arts	3-5	1000		2.0		N	T-L-R-I-0	0	2.0	N	B-1/15	Y-3.0
	AP Exams												
	Distance Learning												
	Co-op, Internships												
	*Honors College, Honors Program												
Canisius, Buffalo 14208	Presidential	10	Tuition+Fees	3%	96	1300/30	N		A	3.25	N	A-3/1	N
	Alumni	30-50	Varies	15%	90	1050/24	Y		A	2.75	0	A-3/1	N
	Dean's	100	Varies	15%	90	1000/26	Y		A	2.75	N	A-3/1	N
	Transfer	Varies	Varies	15%	3.0	1000/24	Y		A	2.75	N	A-D	Y
CUNY-Baruch College, NYC 10010	Baruch Scholars	60	3000	10%	87.0	1100	N	E-L-R-I-0	A	3.25	0	B-2/15	N
	Rosenberg Scholars	10	4000		90.0	1300	N	E-L-R-I-0	A	3.25	0	B-2/15	N
	Honors Program												
CUNY-City College, 10031	CC Scholars	36	1000		85		N	E-R-I	A	3.0	S	B-2/1	N
CUNY-Hunter College, NYC 10021	Scholars	14	2450		90	1200	N	E-R-I	A	3.2	N	B-2/15	N
	Scholars w/ Dormitory	6	3650		90	1200	N	E-R-I	A	3.2	N	B-2/15	N
CUNY-Lehman, Bronx 10468	Presidential	Varies	500-1500	10%	3.0	900	N	T-R-I	A	3.3	N	B-C	Y-3.3
	Foundation	80	500-1000		3.5		N	E-L	A	3.7	N	B-5/31	N
CUNY-Queens, Flushing 11367	QC Scholars	40	500-1000	10%	90	1200	N	E-R-I-0	A	Y	N	B-2/1	N
Clarkson, Potsdam 13676	Trustee	1750	500-6000	X	X	X	Y		A	2.7	N	A-2/15	Y
	Merit	Varies	500-1500	10%	3.00	1100/25	N	R-I-0	A	2.7	N	A-2/15	Y-2.7
	Honorary	300	500-1500	X	X	X	N		A	2.7	N	A-2/15	Y-2.7
	Special Departmental	200	500-1000	X	X	X	N		A	N	N	A-2/15	N
	Academic Need	Varies	500-6000	20%	3.0	1000/24	Y	R-I-0	A	2.7	N	C-2/15	Y-2.7
Colgate U., Hamilton 13346	AP Exams												
	*Honors Program												

	Program	No. of Awards	Value Range	Award Criteria					Study Fields	Renew-ability	Restric-tions	Apply Date	Transfer
				Class Stndg.	Grade Avg.	SAT/ ACT	Need Based	Other					
NEW YORK *(Continued)*													
College of Mt. St. Vincent, Riverdale 10471	Alumni Chapter	Varies	5500-Tuition	10%	90	1100	N	L-R-I-O	A	3.0	N	A-2/1	N
	Academic Honors & Pres.	Varies	5500-Tuition	10%	88	1000	N	R	A	3.0	N	A-2/1	Y-3.0
	Corazon J. Aquino	4	Tuition	10%	88	1000	N	L-R	A	3.0	O	A-2/1	N
	WNYW-TV Scholarship	2	Tuition, Rm/Bd		88	1000	Y	E-R-I-O	A	3.0	N	A-2/1	N
	Citizenship Award	Varies	5000		85	900	N	L-R-I-O	A	2.5	N	A-2/1	N
	AP Exams												
	Family Discounts												
	Honors Program												
College of New Rochelle, 10801	Academic	9	5000	20%	90.0	1050	N		A	2.7	N	A-D	N
	Departmental Scholarship	Varies	2000	40%	80		N	R-I-O	A	2.5	N	A-D	N
	Honor	8	7500	10%	91.0	1150	N		A	2.7	N	A-D	N
	Nursing Leadership	3	3000				Y	L	O	Y	O	C	N
	Presidential	6	Tuition	5%	92.0	1200	N		A	3.0	N	A-D	N
	Service Learning Scholarship	Varies	2500-11,300	33%	85	800	N	L-R-I-O	A	2.7	O	A-D	N
	Transfer	Varies	5000		3.0		N		A	2.7	N	A-D	Y
	Women's Leadership	3	1000				N	L	A	2.7	O	A-D	N
	AP Exams												
	Family Discounts												
	Co-op, Internships												
	Honors Program												
College of St. Rose, Albany 12203	Academic	Varies	1000-Tuition	10%	90	1200	N		A	3.0	N	A-2/1	Y
	Talent	10	1000-4000				N	T-R-I-O	O	3.0	N	A-2/1	Y
	Minority	Varies	2000				Y	E-L-R	A	Y	M	B-3/1	Y
Concordia College, Bronxville 10708	Academic	Varies	500-6000	25%	3.0	1000/22	Y	R-I	A	3.0	N	C	Y-3.2
	President's	Varies	700-3500		2.0		N	L-R	A	2.0	D	B-C	Y-2.0
	Music	Varies	700-3500		2.0		N	T-I	A	2.0	N	B-C	Y-2.0
	Honors	Varies	6000	10%	3.5	1200/27	N	E-R-I	A	3.5	N	B-3/15	Y-3.5
	Honors Program												
Cornell U., Ithaca 14853	AP Exams												
	Distance Learning												
	Honors Program												

D'Youville, Buffalo 14201	Presidential	10	6000	10%	90	1100	N	R	A	2.75	N	B-3/1	N
	Resident	15	2560	25%	87	1000	N		A	2.5	N	A-D	N
	Division	60	1000-3000	20%	87	1000	N		A	2.5	N	A-D	Y-2.5
	AP Exams												
	Distance Learning												
	Family Discounts												
	Honors Program												
Daemen, Amherst 14226	Art Portfolio	Varies	250-1000				Y	T-I-0	0	N	N	C	Y
	Babbidge Nursing	Varies	1000	X	X	X	Y	R-I-0	0	Y	N	C	Y
	Dean's	Varies	3000	X	X	X	N	R-I-0	A	3.3	N	A-D	N
	Departmental	Varies	1800	X	X	X	Y	R	A	3.0	N	B-2/15	Y
	Full Tuition	Varies	Tuition & Fees	1%	3.8	1250	N		A	3.5	N	A	Y-3.5
	Legacy		1000				N	0	A	Y	0		Y
	Medical Technology	Varies	2000				N		0	Y	0	A	Y
	Presidential	Varies	1000		85		N	L-I-0	A	N	0	B-2/15	N
	Visual Art	Varies	5000	X	X	X	N	T-I-0	0	Y	N	C	N
	AP Exams												
	Alumni Discounts, Family Discounts												
	Co-op												
Dominican, Orangeburg 10962	Academic	30	500-Tuition	20%	3.5	1000	N	0	A	3.0	N	B-3/15	Y
Dowling, Oakdale 11769	Academic Honor	Varies	1000	33%	B+	1000	N		A	3.0	N	B-D	N
	SAT/ACT Freshman	Varies	2500			1200/21	N	0	A	Y	0	B-D	N
	Academic Honor	Varies	2200		3.8		N	R-I-0	A	3.5	N	A-D	Y-3.8
	Presidential	Varies	800		3.8		N	R-I-0	A	3.0	N	A-D	Y-3.0
Elmira College, 14901	Elmira Key	Varies	1000	10%	3.0		N	L-R	A	Y	N	B-5/1	N
	Presidential	Varies	7500	15%	3.0	1150	N	E-R-I-0	A	3.2	N	B-3/1	N
	Valedictorian	Varies	Tuition	1			N	E-R-I-0	A	3.4	N	B-3/1	N
	Salutatorian	Varies	75% Tuition	X			N	E-R-I-0	A	3.4	N	B-3/1	N
	Founders	Varies	5000	20%	3.0	1100	N	E-R-I-0	A	3.0	N	B-3/1	N
	Iris Leadership	Varies	2500		2.0		N	E-L-R-I-0	A	2.5	N	B-3/1	N
Fashion Inst. of Tech., New York 10001	Academic	Varies	500-2000	10%	3.25	1000/25	Y		A	3.0	N	B-3/15	Y-3.2
Fordham U., Bronx 10458	Dean's	600	7500	10%	B+	1250/28		E-L-R	A	Y	N	A-2/1	N
	National Merit	Varies	Tuition	10%		X	N	E-L-R	A	Y	N	A-2/1	N
	Presidential	15	Tuition+	1-2-3	A	1300	N	E-L-R	A	Y	N	A-2/1	N
	AP Exams												
	Internships												
	Honors Program												

	Program	No. of Awards	Value Range	Award Criteria: Class Stndg.	Grade Avg.	SAT/ ACT	Need Based	Other	Study Fields	Renew- ability	Restric- tions	Apply Date	Transfer
NEW YORK *(Continued)*													
Hamilton, Clinton NY 13323	Bristol	10	5000-10,000	5%		1400	N	L	A	2.0			
	AP Exams												
Hartwick, Oneonta 13820	Academic	20	300-2000	5%	3.5	1200	Y	R-I-O	A	Y	N	A-3/1	Y
	Hartwick	20	300-2000	15%	3.0	1200	Y	R-I-O	A	Y	N	A-3/1	Y
	Music Performance	6	300-3000	X	X		Y	T-R-I-O	O	Y	N	B-4/1	Y
Hobart & Wm. Smith, Geneva 14456	Presidential		5000-7500	15%	3.2	1200	N	L	A		N		Y-3.5
	Trustee	30	13,000	10%	3.5	1250	N	E-I	A	Y	N	B-1/1	Y
	Arts	15	5,000				N	T		Y	N	B-1/1	N
	AP Exams												
	Family Discounts												
	Honors Program												
Hofstra U., Hempstead 11550	Competitive Scholarship	100	2000					E					
	Distinguished Scholar	Varies	Tuition			1300	N		A	3.0	N	C-2/15	N
	Freshman Recognition	Unlimited	2000	10%		1070/23	N		A	3.0	N	A-2/15	N
	Honors Transfer	Unlimited	1000-2000		3.0		N		A	3.2	N	A-2/15	Y-3.0
	Memorial Honors	Unlimited	3000	30%		1380/31	N		A	3.0	N	A-2/15	N
	Phi Beta Kappa	Unlimited	3500	1			N		A	3.0	N	C-2/15	N
	Presidential	Unlimited	Varies	20%		1270/27	N		A	Y	N	C	N
	Honors Program												
Houghton College, 14744	Houghton Heritage	3	8000-11000	5%	3.5	1300/29	N	E-T-L-R-I-O	A	3.0	N	A-B-3/1	N
	Music Performance	20	500-2500				N	T	O	Y	N	C-3/1	Y
	Art	10	500-1500				N	T	O	Y	N	C-3/1	Y
	Excellence	125	1000-5000	15%	3.3	1200/26	N	T-L-R-I-O	A	2.75	N	A-B-3/1	Y-3.25
	Music Presidential	1	2500-5000				N	T-R-I-O	A	2.5	N	A-B-2/1	Y-2.75
Iona, New Rochelle 10801	Academic	Varies	1000-6000	15%	88%		X	L-R-I	A	3.0	N	B-4/15	Y-3.4
	Honors Program												
Ithaca College, 14850	Presidential	20	500-1000	10%	3.5	1200/21	N	I-O	A	3.2			
	Leadership	15	6000	30%		1100	N	E-L-R	A	2.75			
	Talent	1	10,000				N	T	A	2.0			
	Phi Theta Kappa	Unlimited	5000-9000		3.5		N		A	3.0			
	AP Exams												

	Alumni Discounts, Family Discounts												
	Internships												
	Honors Program												
Keuka, Keuka Park 14478	Presidential	6	4990-9980	5%	3.0	1100/25	N	R-I-O	A	3.3	O	A	N
	Academic Achievement	Varies	2000		3.0	920/21	N	R-I-O	A	2.8	N	A-1/15	N
	Leaders	3	3500		2.8	950/24	N	L-R-I-O	A	2.8	N	A-3/1	N
	Honors	25	1000-2000		3.0		Y	L-I-O	A	3.0	O	A-4/1	Y
	Honors Program												
King's, Briarcliff Manor 10510	Academic	Varies	1000-4000	X	X	1200/29	N	O	A	3.0	N	A-D	Y-3.0
	Founders	4	5000	X	X	1100/27	N	L-R-I-O	A	3.0	N	B-2/15	N
	Presidential	Varies	300-1500	X	X	X	X	L-R	A	2.5	N	B-2/15	Y-2.5
	TKC Grant	Varies	Varies		X	800/18	Y		A	1.8	N	A-D	Y
LeMoyne, Syracuse 13214	Presidential	10	7500	10%	A	1300/31	N	E-T-L-R-O	A	3.5	N	B-1/1	N
	Leader	125	2000	25%	B	1000	N	T-L-R-O	A	2.0	N	A-3/15	N
	Honors Program												
LIU-Brooklyn Ctr., 11201	Full Academic	Unlimited	To Tuition	10%	90	1200	N		A	3.0	N	A-5/15	N
	Partial Academic	Unlimited	1/2 Tuition	15%	86	1050	N		A	3.0	N	A-5/15	N
	Transfer Academic	Unlimited	1/2 Tuition		3.3		N		A	3.0	N	A-5/15	Y
LIU-CW Post Campus, Greenvale 11548	Academic Excellence	Varies	6000		88.0	1200	N	R-I-O	A	Y	O	C	N
	Academic Incentive	Varies	3000		85	1100	N	R-I-O	A	Y	O	C	N
	Transfer Excellence	Varies	6000		3.75		N	I-O	A	Y	O	C	Y
	Advanced Study	Varies	3000		3.25		N	I-O	A	Y	O	C	Y
	Univ. Scholarship	Varies	10,000		92	1300	N	R-I-O	A	Y	O	C	N
	Transfer Scholar	Varies	10,000		4		N	R-I-O	A	3.75	O	A-7/1	Y-3.9
	AP Exams												
	Alumni Discounts												
	Honors Program												
LIU-Southampton, 11968	Academic Excellence	43	2500		87	1060/26	N	I-O	A	3.0	N	A	Y-3.5
	Art	30	1000-6000				N	T-I-O	O	3.0	N	A	Y-3.0
	Honors Scholarship	46	1000-3000		87	1150	N	I-O	A	3.3	N	A	Y-3.25
	Merit	200	2500-10,000		87	1060	N	I-O	A	3.0	N	A	Y-3.0
	University Scholar	20	10000		92	1300/30	N	I-O	A	3.0	N	A	N
	Writing	15	750-2500			X	N	T-I-O	O	3.0	N	A-C	Y-3.0
	Honors Program												
Manhattan School of Music, NYC 10027	MSM	300	1000-Tuition				Y	T	O	2.0	N	B-C	Y
Manhattanville, Purchase 10577	Honors	25	3000	10%		1100	N	L-I-O	A	3.0	N	A-3/1	Y
	Leadership	10-15	2000	25%		1000	N	L-I-O	A	3.0	N	A-3/1	Y
	Presidential	1	1/2 Tuition	10%		1100	N	E-L-I-O	A	3.0	N	A-3/1	N

	Program	No. of Awards	Value Range	Award Criteria: Class Stndg.	Grade Avg.	SAT/ ACT	Need Based	Other	Study Fields	Renew-ability	Restric-tions	Apply Date	Transfer
NEW YORK *(Continued)*													
Marist, Poughkeepsie 12601	Presidential	300	1000-5000	10%	3.4	1100/21	N	0	A	2.85	N	A	Y-3.3
	Hudson Valley	50	5000	10%	3.4	1100/21	N	0	A	2.85	S	A	Y-3.3
	AP Exams												
	Co-op, Internships												
	Honors Program												
Marymount, Tarrytown 10591	Academic Distinction	5	2500	10%	3.5	1000	N	E-R	A	3.5	0	B-2/1	Y
	Achievement	45	350-1000		3.0	900	N	E-T-L-R	A	N	0	B-3/1	Y
	Presidential Leadership		2000-4000	20%	3.0	800	N	T-L-R-I-O	0	3.0	0	A-D	Y-2.5
	Mother Butler		7000		3.2		N	T-L-R-I-O	0	3.0	0	A-D	Y-3.2
	Marymount College		8000		3.2	1000	N	T-L-R-I-O	0	3.0	0	A-D	Y-3.2
	Honors Program												
Marymount Manhattan New York 10021	Presidential	13	To 3/4 Tuition	10%	3.5	1250/28	Y	E-R-O	A	3.4	N	A-2/1	N
	Board of Trustees	20	To Tuition	5%	3.5	1300/29	Y	E-R-O	A	3.5	N	A-2/1	N
	Dean's	38	To 4500	12%	3.3	1200/27	Y	R	A	3.3	N	A-2/1	N
	Honorary	15	To 3000	15%	3.2	1000/24	N	R	A	3.0	N	A-2/1	N
	Student Leadership	14	2000	20%	80	1100/24	N	L-R-I-O	A	3.0	N	A-2/1	Y
Medaille, Buffalo 14214	Presidential	Varies	1000-2000		90.0		N	I-O	A	3.0	N	A-D	N
	Trustees	Varies	1250-2500		92.0		N	I-O	A	3.25	N	A-D	N
	Dean's	Varies	750-1500		88.0		N	I-O	A	2.8	N	A-D	N
Mercy, Dobbs Ferry 10522	Trustee	20	1000-7200		3.5		Y	E-L-R-I	A	3.0	N	A-B-8/1	Y-3.2
	Music/Fine Arts	5	1000-5000		2.5		X	T	0	2.0	N	C-3/1	Y
	Transfer Academic	50	100-7200		3.2		Y	E-L-R-I	0	3.0	N	A-B-8/1	Y-3.2
	Freshman Academic	50	100-7200		3.2		Y	E-L-R-I	0	3.0	N	A-B-8/1	N
	Honors Program												
Molloy, Rockville Centre 11570	Dominican	Varies	1000-8500		88	1070/23	N	0	A	3.0	N	B-3/1	N
	Fine/Performing Arts	Varies	2500-Tuition				N	T	0	3.0	N	B-3/1	Y
	Molloy Scholar	10-15	Tuition		93	1180/26	N	0	A	3.5	N	B-12/15	N
	Transfer	Varies	1500-3000		X		N	0	0	3.0	N	A	Y-3.0
	Board of Trustees	Varies	2000		3.0	1070/23	N	0	A	3.0	N	B-3/1	N
	AP Exams												
Moravian, Bethlehem 18018	Comenius	30	3000-11,000	10%	3.0	1250	X	R-O	A	3.0	N	3/15	N
	Thursby	10	500-3000				Y	T-I-O	0	Y	N	3/15	Y

	Banach	2	1000				N	R-I-O	0	3.3	0	3/15	N
	Founders	30	1000-2000	20%		1150	Y	0	A	2.5	N	3/15	Y
	AP Exams												
	Alumni Discounts												
	Co-op												
	Honors Program												
Mt. St. Mary, Newburgh 12550	Presidential	30	4600	20%		1200	N	R	A	3.0	N	A-D	N
	Merit Grant	30	2000-4000	20%	3.3	1100/23	N	T-L-I-O	A	2.5	N	A-D	N
	MSMC Scholar	113	400-2000	X	X	X	Y	T-L-I-O	A	Y	N	A-D	Y
	Honors Program												
Nazareth, Rochester 14618-3790	Alumni Regional	35	500-750	10%	90.0	1180	N	I-O	A	3.0	0	2/15	N
	Art/Music	17	500-2500				N	T-I-O	0	2.5	N	2/15	Y-3.0
	Dean's Scholars	10	2/3 Tuition	2%	98.0	1300	N	I-O	A	3.4	N	A-2/15	N
	Founders	60	1/3 Tuition	10%	90.0	1180	N	I-O	A	3.0	N	A-2/15	N
	Nazareth Scholars	30	1/2 Tuition	5%	95.0	1260	N	I-O	A	3.0	N	A-2/15	N
	Presidential	5	Tuition	1%	99.0	1360	N	I-O	A	3.4	N	A-2/15	N
	Transfer Scholarship	20	500-4500		3.5		N	R-I-O	A	3.0	N	A-4/15	Y-3.5
	Honors Program												
New School for Social Research NYC 10011	Lang College	5	500-1000	X	X	X	N	0	A	Y	N	A-2/15	Y
	Parsons Sch. of Design						Y	T-0	A	2.0	N	B-3/1	Y
	Parsons-Music						Y	T-0	0	2.0	N	B-3/1	Y
NY Institute of Technology, Old Westbury 11568	Steele Memorial Program	Varies	2600		3.0	1180/27	N		A	2.7	N		N
	Transfer	Varies	1650-2500		2.5		N	0	A	2.7	N		Y
	AP Exams												
	Distance Learning												
	Co-op, Internships												
	Honors Program												
New York U., 10012	Assorted Merit Awards	Varies	5000-Tuition	X	X	X	X	0	0	X	X	X	X
	AP Exams												
	Internships												
	Honors Program												
Niagara U., 14109	Honors	Varies	Tuition+		95	1270/29	N	R-0	A	3.25	0	A-2/15	N
	Presidential	Unlimited	3000-9000	20%	85		Y		A	2.75	N	A-2/15	Y-3.0
	Niagara Trustees	Unlimited	3000-9000		X	X	Y		A	3.0	N	A-2/15	N
	Honors Program												
Pace U., NYC 10038 and Pleasantville 10570	University	Unlimited	500-Tuition	10%	85	1200	N		A	3.0	N	B-3/15	Y
	Trustee	Unlimited	To Tuition	25%	3.5	1000	Y		A	Y	N	B-2/15	Y
	President's	Varies	1000-10,000	10%	3.0	1200/27	N	I	A	3.0	N	A-1/15	Y-3.25

	Program	No. of Awards	Value Range	Award Criteria: Class Stndg.	Grade Avg.	SAT/ ACT	Need Based	Other	Study Fields	Renew-ability	Restric-tions	Apply Date	Transfer
NEW YORK *(Continued)*													
Pace U., NYC 10038 and Pleasantville 10570 *(Continued)*	Dean's	500	1000-Tuition		85	1000	N	R-I	A	3.0	N	B-2/1	N
	Transfer	200	2000-Tuition		3.5		N	R-I	A	3.0	N	B-2/1	Y-3.5
	AP Exams												
	Co-op, Internships												
	Honors Program												
Polytechnic Inst. of NY Brooklyn 11201	High School Principal	Varies	8000	10%		1100	N	R-I-0	A	2.5	N	B-2/1	N
	Board of Trustees	Varies	Tuition	5%		1200	N	I-0	A	3.0	N	A	N
	Gieger-Fialkov	Varies	Tuition	5%		1200	N	I-0	0	3.0	N	A	N
	Dean of Engineering	Varies	8000	10%		1100	N	R-I-0	0	2.5	N	B-2/1	N
	Promise Scholarship	Varies	5000				N	I-0	A	2.5	N	A	Y-2.5
	Outstanding Transfer	Varies	6000		3.0		N	I-0	A	2.5	N	A	Y-3.0
Pratt Institute, Brooklyn 11205	Talent Search	Varies	6000-14000		3.0		N	T-0	A	3.0	N	B-1/11	Y-3.0
	Presidential Scholarship	Varies	1500		3.5		N	T	A	3.5	N	B-2/1	Y
	Restricted/Endowed	Varies	200-Tuition				N	T	A	3.5	N	B-2/1	Y
	Presidential Award	Varies	1000		3.0		N	T	A	3.0	N	B-2/1	Y-3.0
Roberts Wesleyan, Rochester 14624	Art	Unlimited	250-1500				N	T-R-I-0	0	Y	N	C	Y
	Athletic	Unlimited	Varies				N	T-L-R-I-0	A	Y	N	C	Y
	Honors Scholarship	Unlimited	3000	25%		1100/24	N	L-R-0	A	3.2	N	A	Y-3.2
	Presidential	Unlimited	4000	15%		1200/27	N	L-R-0	A	3.3	N	A	Y-3.6
	Benjamin Titus Roberts	3	10,000	10%		1200/27	N	E-L-R-I-0	A	3.4	N	A-2/28	Y
	Music	Unlimited	250-2500				N	T-R-I-0	0	Y	N	C	Y
	Dollars for Scholars Match	Unlimited	750				N	0	A	N	N	A	N
	Honors Program												
Rochester Inst. of Technology, 14623	Presidential Scholarship	700	1000-7000	10%		1200/27	N		A	3.0		A-2/15	
	AP Exams												
	Distance Learning												
	Co-op, Internships												
Russell Sage, Troy 12180	Student Sage	Varies	5000	10%	3.5	1000/25	N	E-L-R	A	3.25	0	B-3/15	N
	Dean's Excellence	Varies	3000-4000	50%	3.0	1060	N	R-I	0	3.0	0	A-D	N
	Rehabilitation Science	Varies	3000-4000	50%	3.3	1190/26	N	R-I	0	3.0	0	A-D	N
	International Study	Varies	1000	50%	3.0	1060	N	R-I	0	N	0	A-D	N
	Honors Program												

St. Bonaventure U., 14778	Presidential	20	3500-10,456	10%	3.5	1200/28	N	E-L-R	A	3.0	N	A-3/1	N
	Friars	Varies	1000-5000	20%	90	1000/24	N	E-R	A	3.0	N	C-3/1	Y-3.25
	St. Bona Merit	Varies	1000-3000		3.0	1000	N	R	A	2.75	N	A-2/1	Y-3.0
	Athletics	Varies	1000-15,000				N	T-R-I-0	A	Y	N	C	Y
	Honors Program												
St. Francis, Brooklyn 11201	Presidential	17	Tuition+	10%	3.0	1000	N	0	A	Y	N	A-D	N
St. John Fisher C., Rochester 14618	President's	Varies	1000-5880	10%		1100/24	Y	R-I-0	A	3.0	N	A-4/1	Y-3.5
	Trustees	45	5880-11,760	5%		1280/29	Y	R-I-0	A	3.30	N	A-4/1	N
	Cultural Diversity	20	5880-11,760	5%		1360-32	Y	R-I-0	A	3.33	M	A-4/1	N
	Merit	2	11760	5%		1360/32	N	L-R-I-0	A	Y	N	A-4/1	N
	Honors Program												
St. John's U., Jamaica 11439, Staten Island 10301	Catholic HS	Unlimited	2500-Tuition		87	1100	N	R	A	3.0	0	A-D	N
	Competitive	100	2500		85		N	E	A	3.0	N	B-C	N
	Scholastic Excellence	Unlimited	1/2 Tuition		92	1100	Y		A	3.0	N	A-D	N
	Transfer Grant	Unlimited	1000-1500		3.25		Y	0	A	Y	N	A-D	Y
	Presidential	6	Tuition		95	1200	N	R-I	A	3.0	0	B-C	N
St. Joseph's, Brooklyn 11205 Patchogue 11772	Board of Trustees	Varies	Tuition	X	X	X	N		A	Y	N	A-C	N
	Presidential	Varies	Tuition	X	X		N		A	Y	N	A-C	N
	Achievement	Varies	1000-2800		X	X	N		A	Y	N	A-3/5	Y
	St. Joseph's Scholar	Varies	1000-5200				N		A	Y	N	A-3/15	N
St. Lawrence U., Canton 13617	University Scholar	Varies	500-20,000	10%	3.4	1200/28	Y	E-L-R-I-0	A	3.0	N	b-2/15	N
St. Thomas Aquinas, Sparkhill 10976	Academic	15	1000-2000	10%			N	R-0	A	3.2	N	A-D	Y-3.2
	Presidential	15	2000-1/2 Tuit.				N	L-R	A	3.2	N	A-D	N
	Honors Program												
Sarah Lawrence, Bronxville 10708	Presidential	Varies	500 bk stipend	10%	3.8	1300/28	N			Y			
	AP Exams												
	Internships												
School of Visual Arts, New York 10010	Competitive	160	2000-5000	20%	3.0		N	T-L-R-I	A	3.0	N	A-C	N
	Faculty	2	750		3.0		Y	T-R-I	A	N	N	C	N
	Staff	2	750		3.67		Y	T	A	N	N	C	N
	Alumni	10-20	500-1000		3.0		Y	T	A	N	N	C	N
Skidmore, Saratoga Springs 12866	Skidmore Grant	Varies	400-22000				Y		A	Y	N	B-2/1	N
	Filene Music	4	6000				N	T	A	Y	N	B-2/1	N
Siena, Loudonville 12211	Presidential	25	3000	10%	3.2	1150/25	N	L-R-I-0	A	3.1	A-0	A-1/15	N
SUNY-Brockport, 14420	Academic	Varies	100-Tuition				N	L-0	A	Y	0	A-3/1	Y
	Honors	7	500				N	L-0	A	N	N	A-3/1	N

	Program	No. of Awards	Value Range	Award Criteria: Class Stndg.	Grade Avg.	SAT/ACT	Need Based	Other	Study Fields	Renew-ability	Restric-tions	Apply Date	Transfer
NEW YORK *(Continued)*													
SUNY-Buffalo, 14214	Presidential	80	1000	5%	93	1300	N		A	Y	N	A-1/15	N
	Performing Arts	10	2000	X	90	1150	N	T-I-O	O	Y	N	C	N
SUNY-Cortland, 13045	Alumni	6	1000		3.5	1100/25	N	E	A	2.5	N	A-3/14	Y
	Minority Honors	4	1000		3.0	1100/25	N	E	A	2.75	M	A-3/14	N
	Presidents	8	3400		3.5	1100/25	N	E	A	3.2	N	A-3/14	Y
	Leadership	19	2500		3.5	1100/25	N	E-L	A	2.75	N	A-3/14	Y-3.2
	AP Exams												
	Distance Learning												
	Co-op, Internships												
	Honors Program												
SUNY-Fredonia, 14063	Foundation	Varies	300-2000	10%	3.0	1100/25	X	T-O	A	Y	A-O	A	N
	Academic	Varies	100-1000	X	3.0	1100/25	X	R	A	N	A-O	C	Y-3.0
	President's	Varies	1000	10%	3.0	1100/25	N	R	A	3.25	N	A-2/1	Y-3.25
	Foundation 2	Varies	500-1000	10%	3.0	1100/25	N	R	A	3.25	N	A-2/1	Y-3.5
	Honors Program												
SUNY-Geneseo, 14454	Alumni Fellows	3-5	1350	10%	92	1200-27	N	E	A	N	N	A-D	N
	Honors Program	12	500-1350	5%	94	1250/28	N	E	A	3.2	N	A-D	N
	Kodak Scholars	2	1350	25%	B+	900/21	N	L-R	O	3.0	M	A-D	N
	Music	3-5	500				N	T-I	O	N	N	A-D	N
	Upperclass Scholars	60	300-1350		3.0		N	E-L-R	A	N	N	B-12/1	N
	Honors Program												
SUNY-New Paltz, 12561	New Paltz Honors	20	500	10%	90	1150	N	E-L-R-I-O	A	3.3	N	C	Y
SUNY-Oneonta, 13820	Alumni	Varies	1000	X	X	X	N		A	3.0			
	Presidential	10	1000	X	X	X	X	X	A	2.75	N		
	Bugbee	1-5	1000-5000	X	X	X	Y			2.75			
	Foundation	10	900-1000	X	X	X	Y			2.75			
	Posthill	8	500-1000		2.5		Y	L-R	A	2.5	W		Y-2.5
	Scott-Jenkins	Varies	Varies	X	X	X	Y	T-O	A	2.0	M		
	AP Exams												
	Internships												
	Honors Program												

SUNY-Oswego, 13126	Presidential	180	1000-2500	10%	3.5	1140/25	N		A	3.0	N	A-2/15	N
	Merit	150	1000	15%	3.2	1100/23	N		A	N	N	A-2/15	Y-3.2
	AP Exams												
	Distance Learning												
	Co-op, Internships												
	Honors Program												
SUNY-Plattsburgh, 12901	Foundation	50	500	25%	85	1050/21	Y	I-O	A	N	N	C	Y-3.0
	Presidential	10	3400	5%	92	1150/26	N	E-L-R-I-O	A	3.0	O	C	N
	Louise Heisler	Varies	500-750				N	T-O	O	X	N	A	Y
	Minority Honors	Varies	500-2500	20%	90.0	1100	N	I-O	A	3.0	M	A	Y-3.2
	Academic Excellence	25	1000	10%	92.0	1150/26	N		A	N	N	A-D	N
	Honors Program												
SUNY-Potsdam, 13676	Crane Music	Varies	250-1500				N	T-I	O	3.0	N	A	Y
	Honors Award	125	200-1000	20%	87	1100/23	N		A	3.25	N	A	Y
	AP Exams												
	Honors Program												
SUNY-Purchase, 10577	Annual Fund	6	100-1000		3.0		Y	E-R	A	3.0	N	B-3/16	Y-3.0
	In Praise of Merit	2	100-1000		3.0		N	L-R	A	3.0	N	B-3/16	Y-3.0
	Minority Honor	Varies	1000-3000	10%	3.0	1100	Y	T-R	A	3.0	A-M	C	Y-3.0
	Talent Awards	Varies	500-1500		3.0		X	T-R	O	3.0	O	B-3/15	N
	AP Exams												
	Distance Learning												
	Internships												
SUNY-Stony Brook, 11794	University Scholar	25	500	X	X	X	N		A	Y	O	A-1/1	N
	Presidential	20-30	500-1500		90	1200	X	E	A	3.0	N	B-C	Y
	Honors College	20	500-1500		90	1200	N	E	A	3.0	N	B-C	Y-3.0
SUNY-Utica/Rome 13504	Endowed Scholarships	12	500-Tuition		3.5		N		A	3.25	N	A-D	Y-3.5
	Annual Scholarships	9	333-Tuition		3.5		N		A	3.25	N	A-D	Y-3.5
	Minority Honors	Varies	Tuition		3.5		N		A	3.25	N	A-D	Y-3.0
	Alumni Scholars	5	Tuition		3.5		N		A	3.25	N	A-D	Y-3.5
SUNY Environ. Science, Syracuse 13210	Minority Honor	Varies	1000-3000	33%			N	R	A	2.5	A-M	A-3/15	Y
Syracuse U., 13244	Achiever	Varies	3000	X	X	X	N	O	A	2.5			Y
	Chancellor's	Varies	6000	X	X	X	N	O	A	2.5	N	A	N
	Dean's	Varies	4000	X	X	X	N	O	A	2.5	N	A	N
	Excellence	Varies	5000	X	X	X	N	O	A	2.5	O	A-C	Y
	Performing Arts	Varies	Varies	X	X	X	N	T-I-O	O	2.5	N	C	N
	AP Exams												

	Program	No. of Awards	Value Range	Award Criteria: Class Stndg.	Grade Avg.	SAT/ ACT	Need Based	Other	Study Fields	Renew- ability	Restric- tions	Apply Date	Transfer
NEW YORK *(Continued)*													
Syracuse U., 13244 *(Continued)*	Distance Learning												
	Co-op, Internships												
	Honors Program												
Union, Schenectady 12308	Mosher Citizenship	10	1000	10%		1100	N	L-I-0	A	Y	N	A-2/1	N
	Wright	1	2500	10%		1100	Y	I-0	0	Y	A	A-2/1	N
	Garnet	20	Need	10%		1400/32	Y	I-0	A	2.0	N	A-2/1	N
U. of Rochester, 14627	Xerox	Varies	6000-18,000	X	X	X	N	0-R	A	Y	N	C	N
	Bausch & Lomb	Varies	6000-18,000	X	X	X	N	0-R	A	Y	N	C	N
	Urban League	Varies	6000-18,000	X	X	X	N	0-R	A	Y	N	C	N
	Kodak Young Leader Pgm.	Varies	6000-18,000	X	X	X	N	L-R-0	A	2.0	N	C	N
	Rush Rhees	Unlimited	5000-10,000	X	X	1350/29	N	0	A	2.0	N	A-1/15	N
	Honors Program												
Utica College, 13502	Dean's	Varies	5000	10%	3.2	1110	N	E-R-I-0	A	3.0	N	A	N
	Presidential	Varies	6500-9000	5%	3.5	1200	N	E-R-I-0	A	3.0	N	A	N
	Transfer Merit	Varies	Varies		3.5		N	E-R-I-0	A	3.0	N	A	Y-3.5
	Honors Program												
Wagner, Staten Island 10301	Music/Theatre	Varies	300-600	50%	80	850	Y	T	0	Y	N	B-D	Y
	WC Academic	125	300-2500	33%	85	1000/24	Y	E	A	Y	N	A-D	N
Webb Institute, Glen Cove 11542	Academic	20-25	Tuition	10%	3.2	1300	N	R-I-0	A	Y	0	B-2/15	Y-3.2
	Internships												
	*Honors College, Honors Program												
Wells College, Aurora 13026	Henry Wells College	7	Tuition	10%	90	X	N	E-I-L-R-0	A	Y	W	B-11/5	N
	Merit	10	10,000	10%	90	X	N	E-I-L-R-0	A	Y	W	B-11/5	N
	Leadership	Varies	2000-5000		86		N	E-I-L-R-0	A	Y	W		N
	AP Exams												
	Alumni Discounts												
	Internships												
Yeshiva U., NYC 10033	Dr. S. Belkin	Varies	3000	5%	90	1360	N	L-I-0	A	Y	N	A-D	N
	Academic	Varies	5000	5%	95	1400	N	E-L-R-I-0	A	Y	N	B-C	N
	Distinguished Scholars	Varies	10,000	5%	95.0	1400	N		A	Y	N	C	N

NORTH CAROLINA

Appalachian State U., Boone 28608	Chancellor	Varies	4000	5%	4.0	1335	N	E-L-I	A	3.4	N	B-12/15	Y-3.5
	Academic	Varies	500-1000	10%	3.7	1200	Y	L	A	3.25	N	B-12/15	Y-3.5
	Honors Program												
Belmont Abbey, Belmont 28012	Anne Horne Little	3-6	Tuition	15%	3.5	1050	N	0	A	3.0	N	B-2/1	N
	Presidential	4-7	2000	20%	3.2	1000	N	L-R-I-0	A	3.0	N	B-3/1	N
	Special Merit	4-7	1500	20%	3.2	1000	N	L-R-I-0	A	3.0	N	B-3/1	N
	Merit	30	1000				N		A	3.0	N	C-2/15	N
	Academic	50	1000-8500	30%	3.0	900	N	E-L-R-I-0	A	3.0	N	B-2/14	Y-3.0
	Honors Program												
Bennett, Greensboro 27401	College	Varies	1000-6265	10%	3.0	1000/23	N	T-L-R	A	3.0	0	B-3/1	Y-3.0
Campbell U., Buies Creek 27506	President	100	2200-7000	10%	3.0	1000/23	N	E-L-R-I-0	A	Y	N	A-D	Y-3.0
	Campbell	120	500-2000	20%	2.75	830-19	N	E-L-R-I-0	A	Y	N	A-D	Y-3.0
	Scott-Ellis	Varies	500-2000	20%	2.75	830-19	N	E-L-R-I-0	A	Y	N	A-D	Y-3.0
	Honors Program												
Catawba, Salisbury 28144	Distinguished Scholars	Varies	To Tuition	10%	3.5	1150	N	E-L-R-I-0	A	3.0	N	A-B	N
	Catawba Grant	Varies	1500-5000	50%	2.5	950	N	L-0	A	2.5	N	A-D	Y-2.5
	Honors Program												
Davidson College, 28036	Thompson S. Baker	2	All Costs	1%	4.0	1250	N	E-I-L-R	A	3.0			
	William Holt Terry	2	20,000	10%	3.5		N	I-L-R	A	3.0			
	Cornwell	2-3	10,000					E-I-T		3.0			
	AP Exams												
Duke U., Durham 27706	AB Duke	20	Tuition+	10%	3.7	1300/32	N	E-L-R-I-0	A	Y	N	A-1/15	N
	Alumni	3	8000	10%	3.7	1400/32	N	L-R-0	A	Y	0	A-1/15	N
	Howard Memorial	7	6000	X	X	X	N		A	Y	M	A-1/15	N
East Carolina U., Greenville 27834	Alumni Honor	15	1500	5%	3.5	1150/26	N	E-L-I	A	3.0	N	A-12/15	N
	University Scholars	15	3000	5%	3.5	1200/27	N	E-L-I	A	3.0	N	A-12/15	N
	Chancellor's	1	5000	5%	3.5	1200/28	N	E-L-R-I-0	A	3.0	N	B-12/15	N
East Coast Bible, Charlotte 28208	Academic	Varies	183-4392		3.7	1180/26	N	R	A	3.5	0	A-B-7/1	Y-3.7
	Teen Talent Scholarship	Varies	500-4392				N	T	A	2.0	D-0	A-B-7/1	Y
	Pastoral Discount	Varies	549-2196				N		A	2.0	0	A-B-7/1	Y
Elon College, 27244	Elon Scholars	Varies	1500-2000	X	X	X	N	R	A	Y	N	A-2/10	N
	Honors	Varies	2500-8000	X	X	X	N	E-L-R-I-0	A	3.2	N	A-2/10	N
	Leadership Fellows	Varies	To 1500		3.0	1000	N	L-R-I-0	A	3.0	N	A	N
	N.C. Teaching Fellows	15	5000-Total				N	I-0	0		A	B-C	N
	Presidential	Varies	1000-1500	X	X	X	N	T-L-E	A	3.0	N	A-2/10	N

	Program	No. of Awards	Value Range	Award Criteria: Class Stndg.	Grade Avg.	SAT/ ACT	Need Based	Other	Study Fields	Renew-ability	Restric-tions	Apply Date	Transfer
NORTH CAROLINA *(Continued)*													
Elon College, 27244 *(Continued)*	Science Fellows	Varies	2000	X	X	X	N	E-R-I-O	O	3.2	N	A	N
	Honors Program												
Gardner-Webb, Boiling Springs 28017	Presidential	10	300-5000	10%			N	E-T-L-R-I-O	A	Y	N	A-D	N
	Academic Fellow	3	8000	10%			N	E-T-L-R-I-O	A	Y	N	A-D	N
	University Scholar	Varies	500-3000	25%			N	R	A	Y	N	A-D	N
	Honors Program												
Greensboro College, 27401	Presidential	150+	1500-All Costs		2.5	900	N	E-I	A	2.5			
	Fine Arts	25	500-5000				N	I-R-T	O	2.5			
	AP Exams												
	Family Discounts												
	Internships												
	Honors Program												
Guilford, Greensboro 27410	Honors	20	1/2 Tuition	10%	3.5	1250/29	N	I	A	3.0	N	B-2/15	N
	Guilford Honors	Varies	1000-1/2Tuit.	5%	3.25	1250	N	E-R-I-O	A	3.0	N	B-2/15	Y
	Reynolds	2	Tuition	10%	3.5	1200/28	N	E-L-I-O	A	3.0	M	A-2/15	N
	Honors Program												
High Point University, 27262	Presidential	50	5000		X	X	N	E-L-I	A	3.0	N	A-B-2/1	N
	Presidential/Honors	2	Tuition		X	X	N	E-L-I	A	3.25	N	A-B-2/1	N
	Phi Theta Kappa	2	4500-Tuition		3.0		N	L-R	A	3.0	O	A-C	Y-3/1
	AP Exams												
	Internships												
	Honors Program												
John Wesley, High Point 27265	Academic Honor	Unlimited	10% Tuition		3.3		N		A	N	N	C	N
Johnson C. Smith U., Charlotte 28216	Duke	61	1000-5018	10%	3.0	1000	N	I-O	A	3.0	N	A-5/15	N
	Academic	Varies	1000-6800		3.0	900/23	Y	R-I-O	A	3.0	N	B-8/1	N
	Academic #2	100	500-7500	10%	3.0	700	N	O		3.0	N	A	Y-3.0
	Honors Program, Honors College												
Lenoir-Rhyne, Hickory 28603	Honors	50	5000	10%	3.5	1200	N	L	A	3.0	N	D	N
	Honors Program												

Mars Hill College, 28754	Grayson	37	3000-Tuition	10%	3.2	1000	N	E-L-R-I-0	A	3.2	0	B-2/20	N
	Marshbanks/Anderson	10	3600	10%	3.2	1000	N	E-L-R-I-0	A	3.2	A	B-2/25	N
	Church Leadership	3	3/4 Tuition	10%	3.0	1000	N	E-L-R-I-0	A	3.0	0	B-11/20	N
	Stamey	1	Tuition	10%	3.5	1100	N	E-I-L-R	A	3.2	S-D	A-1/31	N
	Bryan	1	Tuition	10%	3.0		N	E-I-R	A	Y	S	A	N
	AP Exams												
	Honors Program												
	Honors Program												
Meredith, Raleigh 27607	AJ Fletcher	1	7500	X			N	T-I-0	0	3.0	0	B-2/15	N
	Julia Hamlet Harris	12	1500-2000	15%	3.2	1100	Y	E-L-R-I	A	3.0	0	B-2/15	N
	Music Talent	3	500	X			N	T-0	0	3.0	0	B-2/15	N
	Meredith Academic	6	3000	10%	3.2	1200	N		A	3.0	0	A-2/15	N
	Sandra Graham Shelton	1	1275	X	X	X	N	E-T-R-I-0	0	3.0	0	B-2/15	N
	Robert H. Lewis	1	2000	X	X	X	N	T-I-0	0	3.0	0	B-2/15	N
	Eleanor Layfield Davis	1	1500	X	X	X	N	T-I-0	0	3.0	0	B-2/15	N
	R.C & E.P. McSwain	1	850	X	X	X	N	T-I-0	0	3.0	0	B-2/15	N
	AP Exams												
	Co-op, Internships												
	Honors Program												
Methodist, Fayetteville 28311	Incentive	Varies	3000-7500	20%		1000/22	N		A	3.0	N	A-D	Y-3.0
	Talent	Varies	Varies				Y	T-R-I-0	A	2.0	N	C-5/1	Y
	Transfer	Varies	3000-4000		3.2		N		A	3.0	0	A-D	Y-3.0
	AP Exams												
	Co-op, Internships												
	Honors Program												
Mount Olive College, Mount Olive 28365	Scholars	25	2000-3000	10%	3.2	900/20	N	L-R-I-0	0	3.0	0	B	Y-3.2
	Honors	Varies	1000-4000	25%	3.2	1040/22	N	E-L-R-I-0	A	Y	N	A-2/1	Y
	Leaders	25	2000		2.8	940/19	N	L-I-0	0	2.5	0	A-2/1	Y-2.8
	Music/Art	Varies	Varies				N	T			N		Y-3.2
	Honors Program												
NC A&T State U., Greensboro 27411	Chancellor Incentive	Varies		X	X	X	Y	L-0	A		A	C-4/30	N
	National Alumni	Varies	1/2-All Costs		3.0	1000	N	R-0	A	3.0	N	B-2/1	N
	Named Awards	Varies	Varies	X	X	X	X	0	A	X	0	C	
NC School of the Arts, Winston-Salem 27117	Sanford	5	1000				N	T-R-I	A	N	A	A-D	Y
	Nancy Reynolds	22	500-1000				N	E-T-R	A	Y	N	A-D	Y
	Tuition Reduction	80	350-900				N	T-R-I	A	Y	0	A-D	Y
NC State U., Raleigh 27609	Foundation/Freshman	6	1000	5%	3.7		N	E-L-R-I-0	A	3.0	N	B-11/1	N
	Foundation/Recog.	6	1000	5%	3.7		N	E-L-R-I-0	A	3.0	N	B-11/1	N

	Program	No. of Awards	Value Range	Award Criteria: Class Stndg.	Grade Avg.	SAT/ ACT	Need Based	Other	Study Fields	Renew-ability	Restric-tions	Apply Date	Transfer
NORTH CAROLINA *(Continued)*													
NC State U., Raleigh 27609 *(Continued)*	Freshman Honors	35	2000	5%	3.7		N	E-L-R-I-0	A	N	N	B-11/1	N
	John T. Caldwell	20	4000-7500	5%	3.7		N	E-L-R-I-0	A	3.0	N	B-11/1	N
	Merit Awards Program	80	1000-6500	5%	3.7	1200	N	E-L-R-I-0	A	3.0	N	B-11/1	N
	Honors Program												
NC Wesleyan, Rocky Mount 27801	Presidential	25	2500		3.1	1100	N		A	3.0	N	C	N
	Honors	17	1000		3.3	1100/580V	N	E-R	A	3.0	N	B-C	N
	Honors Program												
Pembroke State U., 28372	Chancellor's/Incentive	Varies	700-3000	X	X	X	N		A	3.0	N	B-C	N
	Academic	50	200-2000	10%	3.0	1000	Y	R-0	A	Y	0	B-C	Y-3.0
Pfeiffer, Misenheimer 28109	Honor	10	Tuition	10%	3.5	1050	N	I	A	Y	N	A-D	N
	Presidential	Varies	1000-4000	20%	3.0	1000	N	I-0	A	3.0	N	A	N
	Trustee	Varies	1000-3500		3.0		N	I-0	A	3.0	N	A	Y-3.0
	Music	Varies	500-5000				N	T-R-I-0	0	2.0	N	C	Y
	Honors Program												
Queens, Charlotte 28274	Belk Scholars	Varies	2000-6000			800	N	L	A	Y	N	A-C	N
	Mecklenburg Scholar	Varies	Varies	10%	3.0	1000/24	N	L-R-I-0	A	Y	S	C	N
	Outstanding Minority	5	Varies	10%	3.0	1000/24	N	L-R-I-0	A	Y	M	C	N
	Presidential	10	Tuition	10%	3.5	1200	N	E-L-R-I	A	Y	N	B-1/15	N
	Queens Scholars	Varies	5000-8000	X	X	1000	N		A	Y	N	A-C	N
	Redd Scholars	Varies	1000-5000	X	X	X	N	T	A	Y	N	A-C	N
Roanoke Bible, Elizabeth City 27907	Talent	Varies	150-1080				N	T	A	N	0	C	N
	Academic	6	1760-3520	10%	3.5	1250	N	0	A	3.0	N	B-5/1	N
	RBC Foundation	15	100-250		2.0		N	L-R	A	2.0	0	B-5/1	Y-2.0
	Grant	Unlimited	400-1000				N		A	2.0	N	B-5/1	Y-2.0
	Honors Program												
St. Andrews Presby., Laurinburg 28352	Scholarship	Unlimited	4500-8000		3.0	1000	N		A	3.0	N	A	Y-3.0
	Grant	Unlimited	1000-6000		2.0	700	N		A	2.0	N	A	Y-2.0
	AP Exams												
	Co-op, Internships												
	Honors Program												

St.Augustine's Coll., Raleigh 27610	Academic	Varies	200-11,500	10%	3.0	800	N		A	3.0	N	B-4/15	N
	AP Exams												
	Co-op, Internships												
	Honors Program												
Salem, Winston-Salem 27108	Chatham	2	10000	10%	3.5	1150/26	N	E-L-R-I-O	A	3.0	O	A-1/10	N
	Presidential	5	7000	10%	3.5	1150/26	N	O	A	3.0	O	A-1/10	N
	Dunford Music	Varies	2500				N	T	O	3.0	O	A-1/10	N
	Fletcher Music	1	7500				N	T-R-O	O	3.0	O	A-1/10	N
	Salem Scholar	Varies	6000	X	X	X	N		A	3.0	O	A-1/10	N
	Governor's School	4	8000	X	X	X	N	E-L-R-I-O	A	3.0	O	A-1/10	N
	Heritage	Varies	7000	X	X	X	N	E-L-R-I-O	A	Y	M-O	A-1/10	N
	Gramley Leadership	Varies	6000					L		Y		A-1/10	
	Christian Gregor Music	Varies	2500-5000					T		Y		A-1/10	
	Honors Program												
U. of NC, Asheville 28804	Academic	292	500-5000	10%	3.2	1000	X	E-T-R-I	A	X	O	C	Y-3.2
	Honors Program												
U. of NC, Chapel Hill 27514	Johnston	75	500-13000	5%			Y	L	A	3.0	N	C-3/1	N
	Morehead	50	Full Costs				N	R-I	A	Y	N	C	N
	Pogue	20	6750	10%			N	L-I-O	A	2.5	A-M	B-1/15	N
	College Fellows	10	2500-5000	5%			N	L-R	O	3.0	A	A	N
	H.W. Jackson	5	2500	5%			N	L-R	A	3.0	A	A	N
	W.R. Davie	15	2500-10000	5%			N	L-R	A	3.0	N	A	N
	Julian Robertson	1	All Costs	10%			N	L-R	A	3.0	N	A	N
	Carolina Scholars	1	5000	5%			N	L-R	A	3.0	N	A	N
	AP Exams												
	Honors Program												
U. of NC, Charlotte 28223	Cone/Colvard	7	3000	10%			N	L-R-I-O	A	3.0	O	B-1/15	Y
	C.C.Cameron	2	3500	10%			N	L-R-I-O	A	3.0	A	B-1/15	N
	Special 4-Year	4	3000	10%			N	L-R-I-O	A	3.0	N	B-1/15	N
	Holt-Tate	3	2500	10%			N	L-R-I-O	A	2.5	M	B-1/15	N
	University Merit Award	20	3000-4000	10%			N	E-L-R-I-O	A	3.0	N	B-1/15	N
	Honors Program												
U. of NC, Pembroke	Chancellor's	25	4000	10%	3.5	1000/21	N	R	A	3.0	S	B-3/1	Y-3.5
	Incentive	25	3000	50%	3.0	900	N	R	A	2.0	S	B	Y-3.0
	Academic	Varies	500-1000	X	X	X			A	Y	O	A	Y
	AP Exams												
	Distance Learning												
	Co-op, Internships												
	Honors Program												

	Program	No. of Awards	Value Range	Award Criteria: Class Stndg.	Grade Avg.	SAT/ ACT	Need Based	Other	Study Fields	Renew- ability	Restric- tions	Apply Date	Transfer
NORTH CAROLINA *(Continued)*													
U. of NC, Greensboro 27412	Minority Presence	6	1500	20%	2.75		N	E-L-R	A	3.0	A-M	B-3/1	N
	Merit	65	1000-12000	10%	3.5		N	E-L-R	A	3.0	N	B-1/15	Y-3.5
	Century	50	1000	10%	3.5		N		A	N	N	A-C	Y-3.5
	Honors Program												
U. of NC, Wilmington 28403	CM & MO Suther	1	950	25%	3.0		Y			Y	A	A-3/15	N
	Godwin III Memorial	1	1000				Y		A	Y	S	A-3/15	N
	Incentive Scholarship	Varies	3000				N		A	Y	A-M	C	Y
	James E. L. Wade	8	2000		3.0	80%ile	Y	R	O	Y	O	B-3/15	Y
	Minority Achievement	25	1000-2000		3.0	X	Y		A	Y	M	C	N
	National Science Scholars	2	5000				N	O	O	Y	A-O	C	N
	R & E Electronics	1	1000				Y		O		A-M-O	C	N
	Honors Program												
Wake Forest U., Winston-Salem 27109	Carswell	20	8000-26,450	1%	4.0	1450	N	E-I	A	Y	N	B-1/1	N
	Hankins	35	500-26,450	5%	3.8	1300	Y	E-I	A	Y	O	B-1/1	N
	Minority	7	Tuition	10%	3.5	1250	N	O	A	Y	M	B-1/1	N
	Reynolds	5	Total Costs	1%	4.0	1500	N	E-I	A	Y	N	B-12/1	N
	Pres. Sch. for Dist. Achm't.	20	8000	X	X	X	X	T-L-R-I-O	A	2.0	N	B-12/15	N
	Honors	20	5000	2%	4.0	1400	N	E-I	A	Y	N	B-1/1	N
	AP Exams												
	Internships												
	Honors Program												
Warren Wilson, Swannanoa 28778	Honor	Varies	1000-4000	X	X	X	N	E-L-R	A	3.0	N	B-3/15	N
Western Carolina U., Cullowhee 28723	Patrons of Quality	6	1500-2000	2%	3.8	1200	N	E-L-R-O	A	3.5	N	B-2/1	Y-3.5
	Western	120	1000	10%	3.5	1000	N	E-L-R-O	A	3.5	N	A	Y-3.5
	Chancellor's	20	2000	2%	3.8	1200	N	E-L-R-O	A	3.5	N	A	Y-3.5
	Western Alumni	15	500-1500	10%	3.5	1000	N	E-L-R-O	A	3.5	N	B-2/1	Y-3.5
	Honors Program												
Wingate College, 28174	Centennial	110	2000-2500	25%	3.0	1050/23	N	L-R-I-O	A	2.8	N	B-4/15	N
	Irwin Belk	25	7000-Tuition	5%	3.75	1300/30	N	E-L-R-I-O	A	3.2	N	B-4/15	N
	Music	50	500-2500				N	E-T-R-I-O	O	Y	N	B-4/15	N
	Presidential	90	4000	20%	3.25	1150/26	N	E-L-R-I-O	A	3.0	N	B-4/15	N
	Transfer	50	500-2000		2.5		N	O	A	3.0	N	B-4/15	Y-2.5

	Trustee	50	5000	15%	3.5	1100/28	N	E-L-R-I-O	A	3.0	N	B-4/15	N
	Honors Program												
Winston-Salem State U., 27110	Hanes Group	Varies	1000-3064		3.0	900/15	N	R	A	3.0	N	B-6/1	N
	RJ Reynolds	6	500-1000	25%		900/15	N	R	A	3.0	0	B-D	N
	General	19	200-9000	50%	2.0	700/18	Y	T-L-R-O	A	2.0	A-M	B-3/15	Y-2.5
	Honors Program												
NORTH DAKOTA													
Jamestown College, 58401	Wilson Scholarship	5	Tuition	X	X	X	N	E-I-L	A	Y	N	2/15	N
	Leadership Scholarship	50	3000	X	X	X	N	T-L	A	Y	N		N
	Honor Scholarship	25	4000	X	X	X	N	T-L	A	Y	N		N
	Presidential Scholarship	10	5000	X	X	X	N	E-I-L	A	Y	N	2/15	N
	AP Exams												
	Alumni Discounts, Family Discounts												
	Co-op, Internships												
	Honors Program												
Minot State College, 58701	Regents'	1000	1000	10%			N	E-T-L-R	A	Y	S	C-10/1	N
	Presidential	25	500	10%	3.5		Y		A	3.5	N	A-B-3/1	N
	Cultural Diversity	40	Tuition		2.0		Y	O	A	2.0	M	A-B-3/1	Y-2.0
	STAR	50	500-1000	10%	3.0	28	Y		A	N	N	A-B-3/1	N
	Honors Program, Honors College												
North Dakota State U., Fargo 58105	Foundation Honor	50	500	10%		28	N		A	Y	N	A-2/1	N
	Presidential	15	1500	10%	3.5	31	N	E	A	3.0	A	B-12/15	N
	National Merit	10	2000				Y	O	A	Y	N	B-2/1	N
	Honors Program												
Trinity Bible, Ellendale 58436	Academic Val/Sal	Varies	250-300	1-2	3.0		N		A	Y	O	D	Y
	Dean's Scholarship	Varies	1/2 Tuition	X	X	X	N	E-I-R	A	3.0	O	B-3/1	Y
	President's	3	Tuition	X	X	X	N	E-I-R	A	3.0	O	B-3/1	Y
	Family Discounts												
	Co-op												
University of Mary, Bismarck 58501	Academic	Unlimited	1000-7000	50%	3.0	19	N	R-O	A	Y	N	A-D	Y-3.0
	Athletic	Varies	2500-7900				N		A	Y	O	A-D	Y
	Drama	15	500-2500				N		A	2.5	N	A-D	Y
	Music	Unlimited	1000-6500	50%	2.5		N	T-R	O	Y	N	A-D	Y
	Presidential Merit	Unlimited	1000-7000		3.0	19	N	L-R-I-O	A	2.5	N	A-D	Y
	Speech	15	500-2500				N		A	2.5	N	A-D	Y
	AP Exams												
	Distance Learning												

	Program	No. of Awards	Value Range	Award Criteria: Class Stndg.	Grade Avg.	SAT/ ACT	Need Based	Other	Study Fields	Renew-ability	Restric-tions	Apply Date	Transfer
NORTH DAKOTA *(Continued)*													
University of Mary, Bismarck 58501 *(Continued)*	Family Discounts												
	Co-op, Internships												
	Honors Program												
U. of ND, Grand Forks 58202	Freshman Honor	250-3250	250-3000	10%		X	N	E-R	A	X	O	B-3/15	N
	General Academic	Varies	250	10%			N		A		N	B-3/15	Y-3.56
	AP Exams												
	Distance Learning												
	Co-op, Internships												
	Honors Program												
Valley City State, 58072	Academic	Varies	200-2000	20%	3.0	18	N	T-L-R	A	3.0	N	A-4/15	Y
	Presidents	4	1500	10%	3.5	1260/28	N	O	A	3.5	N	A-C	N
	V-500	75	800-1000		2.75	870/18	N	O	A	N	N	A-C	Y-2.75
	Alumni	10	800-1000		2.75	870/18	N	O	A	N	N	A-C	Y-2.75
	Co-op, Internships												
OHIO													
Antioch, Yellow Springs 45387	A. Hampton Memorial Schol.	1-2	to 5000	X	X	X	N	E-R-I-O	A	Y	M-O	B-2/1	Y
	A. Morgan Pub. Service Sch.	1	to 5000	X	X	X	N	E-R-I-O	A	Y	O	B-2/1	Y
	Antioch Regional Scholarship	16	to 3000	X	X	X	N	E-R-I-O	A	Y	O	B-2/1	Y
	Austin Patterson Chemistry	1-2	400-2000				N		O	N	O	B-C	N
	Basil Pillard	1	6000				N		O	N	O	B-C	N
	Beatrice Kotas	1	1000				N	E-R-O	O	Y	N	B-C	
	Dean Philip Nash Scholarship	1	to 1250	X	X	X	Y	E-R-I-O	A	Y	N	B-2/1	Y
	Dean's Scholarship	1-4	to 3000	X	X	X	N	E-R-I-O	A	Y	N	B-2/1	Y
	Don Todd	1-2	10000				N		A	Y	M-O	A	Y
	Dorothy E. Mooney Schol.	1	to 2500	X	X	X	Y	E-R-I-O	A	N	N	B-2/1	Y
	Gateway	2	2000				Y		A	N	M-O	B-C	N
	Hickson	1	5000				N		A	N	M-O	B-C	N
	Horace Mann Pres. Sch.	1	to 5000	X	X	X	N	E-R-I-O	A	Y	O	B-2/1	Y
	Hughes Science Scholarship	1-2	to 8000	X	X	X	Y	E-R-I-O	O	Y	N	B-2/1	Y
	J.D. Dawson	1	5000				N	E-R-O	O	Y	N	B-C	Y
	Jessie Treichler	2	6000				N		A	N	M-O	B-C	N
	Leonard Evelyn Alschuler	1	6000				N		A	N	O	C	N

	Mari Michener	3	10000				N		A	N	0	C	N
	Nelson Urban	1-2	1000-5000				N	L-R-0	A	N	0	B-C	Y
	Paula Carlson	1	2000				N	E-R-0	A	Y	W	B-C	Y
	Prudence Windsor	1-2	1000				N		0	N	W-0	B-C	N
	Spalt	1	2000				N	E-R-0	0	Y	N	B-C	Y
	Upward Bound	1-2	to 3000				N	E-R-I-0	A	Y	0	B-2/1	Y
	Yip Harburg	1	1500				N		A	Y	M-0	A	Y
	AP Exams												
	Family Discounts												
	Co-op, Internships												
Art Academy of Cincinnati, 45202	Entrance	25	500-3240				N	T-I	0	Y	N	A-3/31	Y
Ashland University, Ashland 44805	Presidential	Unlimited	2000-6000		3.0	970/21	N	R-I-0	A	3.0			
	Scholar Test	44	1000-12,000					E	A	3.0			
	AP Exams												
	Alumni Discount, Family Discount												
	Internships												
	Honors Program												
Baldwin-Wallace, Berea 44017	Griffiths Music	Varies	500-3000				N	T	0	3.0	N	A-D	Y
	Ministerial Grant	Varies	1/2 Tuition				N			Y	D-0	A	Y
	Minority	20	1000-2000	15%		850/20	N		A	2.0	M	A	N
	Presidential	Unlimited	1000-4000	15%		X	N		A	3.0	N	A-D	Y
	Scholar's	100	1000-5000	20%		1040/25	Y	E-L	A	3.5	N	4/1	N
	Trustees	Unlimited	1000-3000	25%		X	N		A	3.2	N	A-D	Y
	Honors Program												
Bluffton College, 45817	Entrance Honor	Unlimited	1500-7000	10%	3.5	1050/25	Y	L-R	A	3.0	N	A-8/15	Y
	Leadership/Service	20	1500-2000	50%	2.5		Y	E-L-R	A	2.5	N	B-8/15	Y
	Tuition Equalization	Varies	6506	25%	3.0	940/23	N		A	2.5	0	A	N
Bowling Green State U., 43403	21st Century Hazel Swanson	45	Varies		3.45	1300/29	N		A	N	N	A-C	N
	Academic	Varies	600-2000	5%	3.5	1300/29	N		A	Y	N	B-1/15	N
	Diversity Achievement	10	2000		3.25		N		A	Y	M	C	N
	Merit Supplemental	Varies	Tuition/Board		3.3		N	0	A	3.25	N	A-2/1	N
	Minority Achievement	10	2000		3.0		N	E-L-R-I-0	A	Y	M-S	B-1/30	N
	President Achievement	Varies	1000-2000		3.5	1280/29	N		A	N	N	A-C	N
	University Professors	15	All Fees		3.8	1300/30	N		A	Y	N	A-D	N
	Honors Program												
Capital U., Columbus 43209	Battelle Leadership	4-Feb	1/2 Tuition		2.9	20/840	N	E-L-I-0	A	2.5	S	B-3/1	N
	Capital Scholars	4	1500-3500		3.0	20/840	N	E-L-I-0	A	2.5	M	A-2/21	N
	Challenge Grant	Varies	500-4500	25%	2.5	17	N	0	A	2.0	N	A	Y-2.0

	Program	No. of Awards	Value Range	Award Criteria: Class Stndg.	Grade Avg.	SAT/ ACT	Need Based	Other	Study Fields	Renew-ability	Restric-tions	Apply Date	Transfer
OHIO *(Continued)*													
Capital U., Columbus 43209 *(Continued)*	Collegiate Fellow	15	Tuition	10%	3.5	24	N	E-I	A	3.0	N	A-B-2/1	N
	Music	Varies	500-10000				N	T-I-O	O	2.0	O	B-3/1	Y-2.5
	Partners in Education	Varies	100-1000				N	O	A	2.0	D	A-6/1	Y-2.0
	University Schol.	Varies	5000-6500	15%	3.0	26	N	O	A	3.0	N	A	Y-3.75
Case Western Reserve U. Cleveland 44106	Academic	Varies	1000-Tuition	10%	X	1300/29	N	E-R-I-O	A	3.5	N	2/1	N
	Creative Achievement	5	1500-6000	X	X	X	N	T-R	A	3.5	N	B-2/1	N
	Ohio Leadership	Varies	2000-5000	X	X	X	N	L-R-I	A	Y	S	B-1/18	N
	President	70	12600	10%		1450/33	N		A	3.4	N	A-2/1	N
	Provost	70	8000	15%		1350/31	N		A	3.2	N	A-2/1	N
	Provost Special	30	10300	15%		1200/28	N		A	Y	N	A-2/1	N
Cedarville College, 45314	Academic	Varies	1500-2100		3.25		Y		A	3.25	O	B-4/1	N
	Academic Achievement	50	600-1400		3.0	1120/25	N	T-L	A	N	N	A-4/1	Y
	Cedarville Scholar	8	1/2 Tuition	5%	3.75	1350/31	N	E-I-L-R	A	3.5	N	B-3/1	Y-3.5
	Chancellor's Scholarship	60	600-1000		3.2	1090/24	N	E-L-R	A	N	N	B-3/15	Y
	Greg-Paxson	1-2	Tuition		3.5	1310/30	N	E-I-R-O	O	3.5	O	B-3/1	Y-3.5
	Jack Wyrtzen	12	600-1800		3.25		N	R	A	N	O	A-4/1	Y
	Leadership	200	500-1800		3.2	1000/21	N	L	A	N	M	A-3/1	Y
	National Merit	Varies	3500				N	O	A	3.5	O	A	Y
	President's	Varies	2000			1310/30	N		A	N	N	A-D	Y
	AP Exams												
	Internships												
	Honors Program												
Central State U., Wilberforce 45384	CSU Academic	100	1000		3.0		N	T-L-R	A	Y	N	A-6/1	Y
Cincinnati Bible, 45204	Presidential	Limited	1000		2.5		Y	O	A	N	N	B-5/1	Y
	Contests	Varies	Varies					O	A				
	Leadership	Varies	1000		2.5	950/20	Y	L-O	A	2.67	N	B-5/1	
	Foster	Varies	Tuition		3.8	1340/30	N	E-I-L-O	A	3.67	N	B-5/1	
	Deans	Varies	2000		3.5	1260/28	N	L-O	A	3.0	N	B-5/1	
	Val/Sal	Varies	2000		3.5	1260/28	N	L-O	A	3.0		B-5/1	
	Honors Program												
Cleveland Institute of Art, 44106	Portfolio Excellence	15-20	1000-8000		3.0		Y	E-T-L-R-I-O	O	3.0	N	A-3/1	N
	[illegible]	[illegible]	[illegible]		[illegible]		Y	[illegible]	O	N	N	A-5/1	Y-3.0

Cleveland State U., 44115	Teacher Recruitment	6	Tuition	25%		22	N	E-R-I-O	O	3.0	N	B-4/1	N
	Presidential	15	Tuition	25%		1000/24	N		A	N	N	B-3/1	N
	Ambrose Engineering	3	Tuition	10%	3.5		N	E-R-I	O	Y	N	B-3/15	N
College of Mt. St. Joseph, 45051	Elizabeth Seton	90	1/2 Tuition	20%	3.0	1050/25	N	L-R	A	3.2	N	A-D	Y
	Presidential	4	Seton + 1000	X	X	X	N		A	3.0	N	B-1/31	Y
	Honors	100	4500	X	X	X	N		A	3.0	N	C	Y
	St. Joseph Award	100	2000	X	X	X	N		A	3.0	N	C	Y
	Leadership	20	500	X	X	X	N	L	A	3.0	N	B-2/15	Y
	Sisters of Charity	11	1000	X	X	X	Y		A	3.0	N	B-1/31	Y
	Sister Mary Lea	1	1500-2500	X	X	X	N		A	3.0	N	B-1/31	Y
	Honors Program												
College of Wooster, 44691	Academic/Achievement	Varies	5000-10,000	X	X	X	N		A	Y	N	A-D	N
	Byron Morris Comm. Service	Varies	1000-5000	20%	3.0			L	A	Y		B-2/15	
	Clarence Allen	10	9000-16,000	20%	3.0	X	N	E-I	A	Y	M	B-2/15	
	College Scholar	35-40	9000-10,000	10%	3.0	1280	N	E-I	A	Y	N	A-2/15	N
	Compton	40	7000-14,000	20%	3.0		N	I	A	Y	S	A-2/15	Y-3.0
	Music	Varies	6000				N	T	A	Y	N	B-C	N
	Science and Math	Varies	6000				N	O	A	Y	O	A-2/15	
	Theatre	Varies	6000				N	T	A	Y	N	B-D	N
	AP Exams												
	Internships												
Columbus College of Arts, 43215	Scholarship	Varies	200-1200		2.0		N	R	A		O	C	
Defiance College, 43512	Defiance	3	Tuition	10%		1200/28	N	E-L-I-O	A	3.5	N	B-3/1	N
	Academic	Unlimited	2500-7500	25%		900/20	N	E-L-R-O	A	2.5	N	A-D	Y-3.0
	Presidential Svc. Fellowship	20	5000-7000	50%	2.5	970/21	N	E-L-R-O	A	2.5	O	B-C	N
	Honors Program												
Denison U., Granville 43023	Batelle Mem. Inst.	1-2	1/2 Tuition	X	X	X	N	L-I-O	A	Y	S	B-C	
	Dunbar Humanities	1	Tuition	X	X	X	N	E-R-I-O	O	Y	N	C-1/10	
	Faculty Achievement	30	Tuition	1-2	X	X	N	E-L-R-I-O	A	Y	O	A	N
	Fisher & Meredith	15-20	6000	25%	3.5	X	N	I-O	A	2.8	M	C	N
	Heritage	Unlimited	1/2 Tuition	X	X	X	N	E-L-R-I-O	A	Y	N	A	N
	Marimac	2	500-2000				Y	T-I-O	O	Y	N	C	N
	Nat'l. Achievement Scholar.	Unlimited	8000				N	O	A	3.2	N	C-1/10	
	National Merit/Founders	Unlimited	1/2 Tuition	X	X	X	N	O	A	Y	N	C-1/10	
	Other Named	Varies	To 8000+	X	X	X	X	O	A	X	O	C	
	Thomas Ewart Scholarship	15	500-2000	X	X	X	Y		A	3.0	N	C-1/10	
	Tyree	30	1/2 Tuition	X	X	X	N	E-L-R-O	A	Y	M	C	N
	Wells Science	1	Tuition	X	X	X	N	I-O	O	Y	N	B-C	N
	Honors Program												

	Program	No. of Awards	Value Range	Award Criteria: Class Stndg.	Grade Avg.	SAT/ ACT	Need Based	Other	Study Fields	Renew-ability	Restric-tions	Apply Date	Transfer
OHIO *(Continued)*													
Dyke, Cleveland 44114	President's Scholar	Varies	1/2 Tuition	X	3.0	X	N	R	O	Y	N	C	N
	Tuition Equalization	Varies	300-3000		3.0		N	R	A	3.0	O	C-D	Y-3.0
	Scholarship-in-Escrow	Varies	100-4000				N	R	A	Y	S-O	C-D	N
Franciscan U. of Steubenville Steubenville 43952	University Scholar	70	1000-3500	40%	3.2	1140/25	N	E-L-I-O	A	3.3	N	B-1/15	Y-3.2
	Presidential	8	5000	1-2	3.8	1470/31	N	E-L-I-O	A	3.5	N	B-1/15	Y-3.5
	Honors Program												
Franklin U., Columbus 43215	Academic & Leadership	10	500-1000	50%	3.0		N	E-I-L-R	A	2.75			
	Frasch Memorial	1	1000	10%			N	E-I-L-R	A	3.0			
	Battelle	1	To Tuition	25%			N	E-I-L-R		3.0			
	AP Exams												
	Distance Learning												
	Internships												
	Honors Program												
Hiram College, Hiram 44234	President's	Varies	7000	10%	3.5	1100/26	N	E-L-R-I-O	A	3.25	N	C-2/1	N
	Trustees	10	12000	10%	3.5	1100/26	N	E-L-R-I-O	A	3.25	N	C-2/1	N
	James A. Garfield	Varies	5000	10%	3.5	1100/26	N	E-L-R-I-O	A	3.0	N	C-2/1	N
Heidelberg College, Tiffin 44883	Dean's	Varies	2000	20%	3.2	1000/24	N		A	3.0	N	A-D	Y
	Presidential	Varies	4000	5%	3.6	1200/28	N		A	3.0	N	A-D	Y
	Music	Varies	2000				Y	T-R	O	2.0	O	C-D	Y
	Honors	10	7500	5%	3.6	1200/28	N	E-T-L-R-I-O	A	3.3	N	A	N
	Leadership	Unlimited	1000		2.5		N	L-R-I-O	A	2.5	S	B-12/15	N
	Honors Program												
John Carroll U., Univ. Heights 44118	American Values	280	1000-3000	X	3.5	X	N	E	A	3.0	O	B-4/1	N
	President's Honor	500	1000-5000	X	3.5	X	N		A	3.0	O	B-3/1	N
	Mastin	4	10000			27	N	E-R-O	O	Y-3.0	N	B-4/1	N
	Volunteer Scholarship	10	3000				N	E-L-R	A	Y	O	B-4/1	N
	Honors Program												
Kent State U., 44242	President's	50	1500	20%	3.0	1050/25	N	E-R-O	A	3.0	N	B-12/31	N
	University	520	500	25%	3.0	900/22	Y		A	Y	S	B-5/1	N
	Sch. for Excellence	Varies	1000	1			N		A	3.0	N	B-5/1	N
	African-Amer. Excellence	Varies	100-250		2.0		N	E	A	N	M	B-4/1	N

	Minority Incentive	Varies	2000-3500		3.0		N	E	A	Y	M	B-5/1	Y-2.75
	Bowman	1	3500		3.2		N	E	A	N	N	B-4/1	Y
	Honors Program, Honors College												
Kenyon, Gambier 43022	Honor Scholar	12	10000-20000	1%	3.5	1350/30	N	E-L-R-I-O	A	3.0	N	B-1/5	N
	African-American/Latino	12	10000-20000	1%	3.5	1350/30	N	E-L-R-I-O	A	3.0	M	B-1/5	N
	Distinguished Achievement	Varies	6000	5%	3.5	1200/28	N	E-L-R-I-O	A	3.0	N	B-1/5	N
Lake Erie, Painesville 44077	Presidential	20	3500		3.25		N		A	3.0	N	B-3/1	N
	Trustee	10	1/2 Tuition		3.5		N		A	3.5	N	B-3/1	N
	Founder's	2	Tuition		3.75		N						
	Community College	Varies	1500		3.25		N		A	3.25	N	B-3/1	Y-3.25
	Equestrian	5	2000		2.75		N	0	0	2.75	N	B-3/1	N
	Mastin	Varies	10000		3.0	27	N		0	3.0	N	B-3/1	N
	Twins	Varies	Tuition		2.75		N		A	2.0	N	B-3/1	N
	AP Exams												
	Alumni Discounts, Family Discounts												
	Internships												
Malone, Canton 44709	President's J.W. Malone	8-10	8000	5%	3.9	30	N	E-L-R-I-O	A	3.5	N	B-1/31	N
	Pioneer	Varies	1000-3000	15%		100/20	N	0	A	Y	N	B-1/31	N
	J. Walter Malone	Varies	3000-5000	10%	3.35	1100/22	N	L-R-I-O	A	3.0	N	B-1/21	N
Marietta College, 45750	Dean's	Unlimited	3500		3.25	1150/25	N	E-R-I	A	3.0	N	A-C	N
	Fine Arts	Varies	3500				N	T-R-I	A	Y	N	A-3/1	Y
	Minority	Varies	3500	10%	2.8	1200/21	Y	E-L-R-I-O	A	Y	M	A-3/1	Y-2.8
	President's	Unlimited	7000		3.5	1200/27	N	E-R-I	A	3.0	N	A-C	N
	Trustee's	Unlimited	12000		3.75	1350/30	N	E-R-I	A	3.25	N	C-3/1	N
	Honors Program												
Miami U., Oxford 45056	Fine Arts	12	1000	25%		24	N	T-O	O	N	N	B-C-2/1	N
	McGuffey Scholars	30	1500	25%		28	N	E-L-R	O	3.0	N	B-2/1	Y-3.0
	Miami Achievement	Varies	200-7600			21	Y	O	A	X	M-O-S	B-2/1	Y
	Minority Scholars	150	1000-4000	25%		28	N		A	2.5	M	B-C-2/1	N
	National Achievement	Varies	750-2000				Y	O	A	X	M-O	B-C-2/1	
	Paper Sci. Engineering	125+	1250-3000	X		25	N		O	Y	N	A-C-2/1	Y
	Peabody	10-15	750-1500		3.0		Y	E-L-R	A	N	O	B-2/1	N
	Presidential	15	2500-6000	3%		30	N	E-O	A	3.5	N	B-C-2/1	
	Scholar Leader	42	1000		3.0		N	L-R-I	A	N	N	B-2/1	N
	University Alumni	1500	500-1500	10%	3.5	30	N	E-L-R	A	3.0	N	B-2/1	N
	Honors Program												
Mount Union, Alliance 44601	Presidential	5	To Tuition	10%		1150/28	N	E-T-L-I-O	A	3.0	N	A-3/1	N
	Minority Student	5	To Tuition	25%			N	E-L	A	3.0	M	B-4/1	N
	Academic Merit Award	Varies	3000-5000	20%	3.5	1050/25	N	O	A	3.0	N	A-D	N
	Legacy Award	Varies	3000				N	O	A	Y	O	A-D	Y

	Program	No. of Awards	Value Range	Award Criteria: Class Stndg.	Award Criteria: Grade Avg.	Award Criteria: SAT/ ACT	Award Criteria: Need Based	Award Criteria: Other	Study Fields	Renew-ability	Restric-tions	Apply Date	Transfer
OHIO *(Continued)*													
Mt. Vernon Nazarene College, 43050	Benner	Unlimited	2500			28	N		A	3.5	N	A-D	Y
	Benner Merit	Unlimited	3250			30	N		A	3.5	N	A-D	Y
	Departmental	Limited	Varies				N	R	A	N	N	C	N
	Distinction	Unlimited	2000			26	N		A	3.3	N	A-D	Y
	Honor	Unlimited	1500			24	N		A	3.1	N	A-D	Y
	Rank	Unlimited	1250	10%		20	N		A	3.1	N	A-D	Y
	Salutatorian	Unlimited	500	2			N		A	Y	N	A-D	Y
	Valedictorian	Unlimited	500	1			N		A	Y	N	A-D	Y
	Honors Program												
Muskingum, New Concord 43762	Academic	Varies	500-Tuition	10%	3.3		N	E-L-I	A	3.0	N	A-3/1	Y-3.0
	Faculty	100	500-4000	15%	3.3	1050/23	N	I-O	A	3.0	N	A-C	Y-2.5
	John Glenn	10-20	Tuition	3%	3.8	1250/28	N	E-I-O	A	3.0	N	C-3/1	N
	Performance	Varies	300-1800				N	T	O	3.0	N	C-3/1	Y
	Presidential	50-70	5000-6000	5%	3.7	1200/27	N	I-O	A	3.0	N	A-C	N
Notre Dame C. of Ohio South Euclid 44121	Academic Excellence	Varies	Tuition	5%	3.85	1200/28	N	E-L-R	A	3.0	N	B-4/15	Y
	Academic Scholar	Varies	750-4000	15%	3.4	1100/24	N	E-L-R	A	3.0	N	B-4/15	Y
	Community Service	10	1000				N	E-L-R	A	N	N	B-3/15	N
	Presidential	Varies	1500		2.5		N	E-R-O	A	2.8	O	B	
	Alumnae	1	1000				Y	E	A		O	B-3/15	
Oberlin College, Oberlin 44074	*Honors Program*												
Ohio Dominican, Columbus 43219	Dominican	20	500-2000	25%	3.0	1000/20	N	R-I-O	A	3.0	O	A-D	N
	General	70	200-2000	25%	3.0	1000/20	N	I-O	A	3.0	N	A-D	Y
	ODC	Varies	500-2500	25%	3.0		N	I-O	A	3.0	N	A-D	Y-3.0
	Honors Program												
Ohio North U., Ada 45810	Academic Honor	6	16,000	10%	3.4	1180/26	N	E-I	A	3.0		B-1/1	
	AP Exams												
	Co-op, Internships												
	Distinguished Achievement	10	12,500		3.0	1070/22	N	E-I-L	A	3.0		B-1/15	
	Family Discounts												
	Presidential	4	20,000	5%	3.6	1250/28	N	E-I	A	3.3		B-2/1	

Ohio State U., Columbus 43210	General University	Varies	300-2000	10%		26	X		A	Y	N	B-3/1	Y-3.7
	OSU	Varies	300-2000	3%		28	X		A	Y	N	B-3/1	N
	Honors Program												
Ohio State U., Newark 43055	Academic	Varies	100-1000	X	X	X	N	R	A	Inq.	0	B-3/1	Inq.
Ohio U., Athens 45701	Distinguished Scholar	Unlimited	Tuition & Fees	10%		1460/33	N		A	3.3			
	Third Century	15	Tuition & Fees	10%		1310/30	N	R	A	3.3			
	President's	10	2500	10%		1310/30	N	R	A	3.3			
	AP Exams												
	Co-op, Internships												
	Honors Program, Honors College												
Ohio Wesleyan U., Delaware 43015	Faculty	60	10,020	5%		1270/28	N		A	3.35	N	A-3/1	Y-3.5
	Presidential	20	20,040	2%		1400/32	N		A	3.5	N	A-3/1	Y-3.5
	Trustee	40	15,030	5%	3.5	1330/29	N		A	3.5	N	A	Y-3.5
	Dean's	100	5000-7500	20%	3.5	1140/24	N		A	2.75	N	A-3/1	Y-4/1
	Honors Program												
Otterbein, Westerville 43081	Endowed	75	600-3700	25%		900/20	N	E-L-R	A	2.5	N	B-D	N
	Otterbein	Unlimited	1500	10%	3.5	1050/23	N		A	3.0	N	A-D	N
	Presidential	Varies	600	25%			N	E-L-R	A	2.5	N	B-D	N
	Academic Merit	Varies	300-4134	10%	3.5	23	N	E-R-I-O	A	Y	N	B-4/1	N
	Talent	Varies	200-1500				N	T-L-R-I-O	A	Y	N	C-4/1	Y
	Honors Program, Honors College												
Tiffin U., 44883	Hankey	7	1000	50%	2.5		N	L-R-O	A	2.5	S	B-3/1	N
	Presidential	Unlimited	1500		3.5		N	L-R	A	3.0	N	A-D	N
	Colvin Accounting	4	1000				N	E	A	N	N	C	N
	University	5	To Tuition				N	E-O	A	3.0	N		N
	Valedictorian	Unlimited	2000	1-2	3.75		N		A	3.0	N	A-D	N
	Merit	Unlimited	650	20%	3.0	22	N	T-L-R-O	A	2.5	N	B	N
	Zahn Scholarship	5	Tuition				N	E-O	A	Y	N	C	N
U. of Akron, 44325	Academic	Varies	500-1000	10%	X	X	N		A	Y	N	B-4/1	Y
	Buckingham Scholarships	Varies	To All Costs	X	X	X	N	O	A	Y	N		
	Honors	Varies	1000-2000	X	X	X	N	E	A	Y	N	B-1/15	Y
	National Merit Finalist	Varies	Tuition+				N	O	A	Y	N	A	N
	Presidential	Varies	2400	5%	X	X	N		A	Y	N	B-2/1	N
	Purnell-Fort	Varies	1500-4000				N	R	A	Y	M	B-2/1	
	Scholarship for Excellence	Varies	Tuition+	X	X	X	N	O	A	Y	N	C	Y
	AP Exams												

	Program	No. of Awards	Value Range	Award Criteria: Class Stndg.	Grade Avg.	SAT/ ACT	Need Based	Other	Study Fields	Renew- ability	Restric- tions	Apply Date	Transfer
OHIO *(Continued)*													
U. of Akron, 44325 *(Continued)*	Distance Learning												
	Co-op, Internships												
	Honors Program												
U. of Cincinnati, 45221	General University	700	1000	5%		1200/27	Y		A	N	N	B-2/1	Y-3.5
	Presidential	1	Tuition	5%		1300/30	N	E-L-R-I	A	3.0	N	B-2/1	N
	Voorheis	400	Tuition	5%		1300/30	N	E	A	3.2	N	B-2/1	N
	Honors Program												
U. of Dayton, 45409	Black Scholars	15	1000-3000	25%		1000/25	N	L-I-0	A	2.5	M	B-1/15	N
	Presidential	300	1000-4500	10%		1200/29	N	L-I-0	A	3.0	N	B-1/15	N
U. of Findlay, 45840	Academic	Varies	Varies		3.2	1000/23	Y		A	3.0	N	A-8/15	Y
	Scholastic	Varies	900-1700		3.2	1000/23	N		A	3.0	N	A-8/15	Y
	Presidential	Varies	1/2 Tuition	10%	3.7	1050/24	N	E-L-R-I-0	A	3.5	N	C	N
	Honors Program												
U. of Rio Grande, 45674	Atwood	15	3000-6000		3.5	25	N	L-R-I-0	A	3.0	S-S	B-3/31	N
	Honors	13	1000-2000		3.5	25	N	L-R-I-0	A	3.0	S-S	B-3/31	N
	Trustee	25	500-1500		3.0	22	N	L-R-I-0	A	3.0	S-S	B-3/31	N
	Honors Program												
U. of Steubenville, 43952	Academic	Varies	500-2500	40%	3.0	1000/23	N	E	A	3.25	N	A-D	Y-3.0
U. of Toledo, 43606	Beyer	71	1000	10%	3.5	25	N	L-R-I-0	A	N	N	B-3/1	N
	Block	6	1000	10%	3.5	25	N	0	0	3.0	N	B-3/1	N
	DeArce-Koch	58	1000	5%	3.7	28	N	L-R	0	3.0	N	B-3/1	N
	Freshman Honor	50	2000	10%	3.5	25	N	L-R-0	A	Y	N	B-3/1	N
	General	15	500	10%	3.5	25	N	L-R	A	N	N	B-3/1	N
	Lempert	17	2000	1%	3.9	30	N	L-R	A	Y	N	B-3/1	N
	Levis	7	2000	1%	3.9	30	N	L-R	A	Y	N	B-3/1	N
	National Merit	up to 60	All costs	10%	3.5	top 1%	N	L-R-I-0	A	3.0	N	B-1/29	N
	One Year Tillotson	70	1000	10%	3.5	25	N	L-R	A	N	N	B-3/1	N
	Presidential	4	All costs	5%	3.7	top 5%	N	E-L-R-I-0	A	3.0	N	B-1/29	N
	Tillotson Renewal	50	1000	5%	3.7	28	N	L-R	A	3.0	N	B-3/1	N
	University of Toledo	58	1000	10%	3.5	25	N	L-R	A	Y	N	B-3/1	N
	Honors Program												

Urbana U., 43078	Dean's	3	7500		3.0	1200/21	Y	E-L-I-O	A	3.0	N	B-2/21	N
	Presidential	2	10000		3.0	1200/21	Y	E-L-I-O	A	3.2	N	B-2/21	N
	Honors	5	5000		3.0	1200/21	Y	E-L-I-O	A	3.0	N	B-2/21	N
	National Merit	Unlimited	All Costs				N	R-I-O	A	3.2	N	A-B-4/1	Y
	Regional	Unlimited	1500	50%	2.2	19	N	R-I-O	A	2.5	N	A-B-6/1	Y-2.0
	Associates	Unlimited	1500				N	O	A	2.5	O	A-B-6/1	Y-2.0
	Alumnus	Unlimited	900-1400				N		A	2.5	O	B-6/1	Y
	NHS Room Grant	Unlimited	1000				N	O	A	2.5	S-O	B-6/1	Y
	Honors Program												
Ursuline, Pepper Pike 44124	Academic	Varies	500-6500	20%	3.0	1000/20	N	E-L-R	A	3.0	N	C-5/1	
	Art	1	1000				N	T-R	O	N	N	C-5/1	
	Besse Scholarship	1	1000		3.0	20	N		A	3.0	S-O	A-3/1	
	Departmental	11	400-1000	X	X	X	N	O	O	X	N	C	Y
	President's Honor	Varies	Tuition	5%	3.85	1200/28	N	E-L-R	A	3.0	N	C	Y-3.85
	St. Angela Schol.	Varies	3000	20%	3.0	1000/20	N	E-L-R-O	A	3.0	O	C-5/1	
Walsh College, North Canton 44720	Academic	Varies	900-1650	33%	3.0	860/22	N	R-O	A	3.0	S	A-B-3/1	Y-3.0
	Honors	Varies	1700-3300	10%	3.5	970/25	N	R-O	A	3.0	S	A-B-3/1	Y-3.5
	Presidential	1	6000	1%	4.0	1230/31	N	O	A	X	S	A-B-3/1	N
	AP Exams												
	Alumni Discounts, Family Discounts												
	Internships												
	Honors Program												
Wilberforce U., 45384	Academic Scholarship		2000-4000	15%	3.1		N	R	A	3.0	N	B-5/30	N
	Honors Program												
	Leader Honor Scholarship	25	6000	20%	3.0	25	N		A	3.3	O	A-3/1	N
Wilmington College, 45177	Presidential Scholarship	Unlimited	6500	20%	3.0	25	N		A	3.3			
	Theatre Talent	5	1000-2000		2.8		N	T-O	O	Y			
	Trustee	Unlimited	5000	20%	3.0	25	N		A	3.3			
	AP Exams												
	Alumni Discounts, Family Discounts												
	Internships												
	Honors Program												
Wittenberg U., Springfield 45501	Achievement	Varies	1000-3000	25%	3.0		N	O	A	3.0	M	A-C	Y-3.0
	Alumni	Varies	1500	10%	3.2	1100/25	Y	L	A	3.0	N	A-D	Y
	Lutheran	Varies	2000	10%	3.2		N		A	3.0	D	A-D	Y
	Music	50	1000-3000				N	T-R-O	A	2.4	O	C	Y
	Teacher Education	Varies	1000-3000	25%	3.0		N	O	O	3.0	M	A-C	Y-3.0
	University	30	1/2 Tuition	5%	3.5	1200/28	N	E	A	3.3	N	C	N
	Honors Program												

	Program	No. of Awards	Value Range	Award Criteria: Class Stndg.	Grade Avg.	SAT/ ACT	Need Based	Other	Study Fields	Renew-ability	Restric-tions	Apply Date	Transfer
OHIO *(Continued)*													
Wright State U., Dayton 45435	Dunbar	30	2500	20%	3.0	870/20	N	O	A	3.0	M	B-3/1	N
	Hewitt	200	1500	10%	3.4	1100/27	N	O	A	3.0	N	B-3/1	
	McLin	20	1750		2.7		N	E-L-R-O	A	2.5	S-M	B-3/1	N
	Rike Transfer	20	2000		3.5		N	E-R-O	A	3.0	N	B-3/1	Y-3.5
	Val/Sal	85	In-state Tuition	1 or 2			N	O	A	3.0	N	B-3/1	N
	WSU Commended Scholar	30	In-state Tuition				N	O	A	3.0	N	B-3/1	N
	WSU National Scholar	4	7500				N	O	A	3.0	N	B-3/1	N
	WSU Semi-finalist	4	In-state Tuition		3.4		N	O	A	3.0	N	B-3/1	N
	AP Exams												
	Co-op												
	Honors Program												
Xavier U., Cincinnati 45207	Service Fellowship	5	Tuit., Rm & Bd	10%		1280/29	N	I-E-L-O	A	3.25	N	B-12/15	N
	St. Francis Xavier	10	Tuition	10%		1280/29	N	I-E-L-O	A	3.25	N	B-12/15	N
	Trustee	100	1/2 Tuition	10%		1280/29	N	I-E-L-O	A	3.25	N	B-12/15	N
	Presidential	100	1/3 Tuition	20%		1200/27	N		A	3.0	N	A-1/15	N
	Honor	100	1/4 Tuition	25%		1130/25	N		A	3.0	N	A-1/15	N
	Academic	Varies	2500-5000	25%		100/22	N		A	2.0	M	A-1/15	N
	Weninger	Varies	2500-Tution	25%		1130/25	N	E-I-L	A	Y	M	A-1/15	N
	AP Exams												
	Family Discounts												
	Co-op, Internships												
	Honors Program												
Youngstown State U., 44555	Dean's	Varies	2000	15%		1140/25	N		A	3.5	N	B-3/1	N
	University Scholars	152	8000	15%		1340/30	N	E-L-R	A	3.5	N	B-3/1	N
	Trustees	Varies	3000	1%	4.0		N		A	3.5	N	B-3/1	N
	President's	Varies	2500	10%		1220/27	N		A	3.5	N	B-3/1	N
	Leadership	Varies	1000	15%	3.0	1070/23	N		A	N	N	B-3/1	N
	Community College Scholars	Varies	1500		3.5		N		A	3.5	N	B-6/1	Y
	Departmental	Varies	1500		3.5		N		A	3.5	N	B-3/1	N
	Martin Luther King	Varies	Varies		2.5		Y	O	A	Y	O	B-3/1	N
	Co-op, Internships												
	Honors Program												

OKLAHOMA

Bartlesville Wesleyan, 74006	Scholar Award	Varies	1100-3500		3.3	1000/22	N		A	3.3	0	B-C	Y-3.3
	Eagle Scholar	3	5600		3.5	1100/24	N	E-R	A	3.75	N	A-B-3/15	N
Cameron U., Lawton 73505	PLUS	40	1500-3000	10%	3.2	20	N	L-I	A	3.0	0	B-3/1	N
	Honors Program												
Central State U., Edmond 73034	Regents'	500	500-600	15%	3.2	23	Y	T-L	A	3.2	S	C-4/1	Y
East Central U., Ada 74820	Academic	300	200-500	33%	3.25	20	N		A	Y	S	B-3/1	Y
	AP Exams												
	Distance Learning												
	Honors Program												
Mid-America Bible C. OK City 73170	President's Academic	Unlimited	3600-4800		3.75	28	N		A	3.75	0	B-D	Y-3.75
	Honor Academic	20	1000	10%	3.5	25	N		A	3.5	0	B-D	Y-3.5
Northeastern State, Tahlequah 74464	Collegiate Scholar	50-75	1250		3.5	26	N		A	3.0	N	B-6/1	N
	Comm. Coll. Connections	10	1250		3.5		N	E-T-L-R-O	A	3.0	N	B-3/1	Y-3.5
	Phi Theta Kappa	10	1000		3.5		N	T-R-O	A	N	N	B-3/1	Y-3.5
	President's Leadership	20-25	2350		3.0	24	N	E-L-R-I-O	A	3.25	N	B-2/15	N
	Regents'	Varies	Varies	X	X	X	N	T-L	A	Y	S	B-3/1	Y
	Sequoia Scholar	10-20	1000	1			N		A	N	N	B-6/1	N
	Honors Program												
Northwestern OK State, Alva 73717	Foundation	Varies	50-3000		3.0		X	L-R	A		N	B-3/1	Y-3.5
	Academic	Varies	200-1200		3.0	21	N	L-R	A	3.5	N	B-3/15	Y-3.5
	Participation	Varies	100-800		2.5		N	T-R	0	2.5	N	B-3/15	Y-2.5
Oklahoma Baptist U., Shawnee 74801	Academic	Unlimited	500-Tuition	50%	2.5	940/23	N		A	Y	N	B-3/15	Y
	Talent	Varies	200-1000	50%			N	T	0	3.0	N	B-3/15	Y-3.0
	Church Vocation	Unlimited	1000		2.5		N	E-L-R	A	2.5	M	B-8/1	Y-2.5
	Music	Varies	200-1000		2.5	720/19	N	T	0	Y	N	B-4/15	Y
	Transfer	Unlimited	500		2.5		N		A	3.5	N	A-C	Y
Oklahoma Christian, Oklahoma City 73111	Presidential	50	1250-2500		3.65	1060/25	N	L-R	A	3.5	N	B-2/15	N
	Academic	Unlimited	250-1000			910/22	N		A	3.0	N	A-D	Y
	Performance	Varies	200-Tuition				N	E-T-R-I-O	0	2.5	N	B-5/1	Y
Oklahoma City U., 73106	Academic	Varies	300-8610		2.5	26	N	T-L-R-I-O	A	2.5	N	B-C	Y-2.5
	Music/Dance	Varies	400-8005	10%	3.0	26	N	R	A	3.0	S-0	C	N
	Nat'l. Acad. Achievement	Varies	200-7050	10%	3.0	26	N	R	A	3.0	0	C	N
	Honors Program												

	Program	No. of Awards	Value Range	Award Criteria: Class Stndg.	Grade Avg.	SAT/ ACT	Need Based	Other	Study Fields	Renew-ability	Restric-tions	Apply Date	Transfer
OKLAHOMA *(Continued)*													
Oklahoma State U., Stillwater 74078	Academic Achiever	100	1000	X	X	X	N		A	N	S-M	B-2/1	N
	Fee/Freshman	Varies	500-Tuit/Fees		3.5	25	N		A	Y	N	B-3/1	Y-3.4
	Freshman	700	500-600	X	X	X	N	L-R	A	X	O	B-1/28	N
	Freshman Excellence	100	1200		3.25	28	N		A	3.0	S	B-2/1	N
	Freshman University	150	1000		3.5	26	N		A	N	S	B-2/1	N
	Non-Resident Incentive	Varies	3000-4000		3.0	24	N		A	3.0	N	B-2/1	Y-3.25
	President's Distinguished	20-30	2000		3.75	27	N	L-R	A	3.0	N	B-2/1	N
	President's Leadership	100	1500				N	L-R	A	N	S	B-2/1	N
	Regents Disting. Transfer	50	1500		3.75		N		A	3.0	S	B-2/1	Y-3.75
	Regents Distinguished	150	1500		3.0	30	N		A	3.0	S	B-2/1	N
	Transfer	Varies	450-500		3.4		N		A	X	O	B-4/1	Y
	Transfer University	100	1200		3.25		N		A		S	B-2/1	Y-3.25
	Honors Program												
Oral Roberts U., Tulsa 74136	Academic	Unlimited	2500-5000	40%	2.6	1000/21	N		A	Y	N	A	Y-3.45
	Scholars	Varies	7112-10,160	40%	2.6	1280/29	N	E-L-R	A	Y	N	B-3/16	N
	Talent	Varies	Varies				N	T	O	Y	O		Y
	AP Exams												
	Distance Learning												
	Alumni Discounts, Family Discounts												
Panhandle State U., Goodwell 73939	Foundation	Varies	Varies	25%	2.5		X		A	3.0	N	C	
	Presidential	16	500	1		1020/26	N	O	A	3.0	N	A-C	Y-3.0
Phillips U., Enid 73702	University	50	400-1500		3.0	20	N	L	A	2.75	N	A-D	N
	Fine Arts	30	400-1000		2.0		N	T-R	O	2.0	N	C	Y
SE Oklahoma State U., Durant 74701	Academic	Varies	100-900	15%	3.0	20	Y	L-R	A	3.0	N	A-B-3/1	Y-3.0
	Presidential Honors	25	1000-1250		3.5	25	N	E-R-I-O	A	3.0	S	B-3/1	C
	Parsons/Honors	4	4500		3.5	25	N	E-R-I-O	A	3.0	S-O	B-3/1	N
	Honors Program												
SW Oklahoma State, Weatherford 73096	Academic Scholar	Varies	4000 + Tuition & Rm.			31	N	O	A	Y	S	B-3/1	N
	Baccalaureate	10	3000 + Tuition & Rm.			30	N	E-T-L-R-O	A	3.25	S	B-3/1	N
	Dist. Freshman	Varies	Tuition				N		A	N	S	B-3/1	N
	Non-resident Fee Waiver	Varies	Non-resident fees		3.5	25	N		A	2.9	N	A-D	Y-2.5
	Non-res. Legacy Fee Waiver	Varies	Non-resident fees				N	O	A	2.9	O	B-D	N

	Residence Hall	Varies	800			28	N		A	3.25	N	B-3/1	N
	Southwestern Scholar	Varies	3/4 Tuition				N		A	N	S	B-3/1	N
	University Scholar	Varies	Tuition & Rm.				N		A	3.25	S	B-3/1	N
	Upperclassman Fee Waiver	Varies	3/4 Tuition				N		A	N	S	B-5/1	Y
	AP Exams												
	Distance Learning												
	Alumni Discounts												
Southern Nazarene U., Bethany 73008	Dean's	Unlimited	550-1100	5%	3.5	980/25	N		A	Y	N	A	Y-3.5
	President's	Unlimited	1100-2200		3.8	1150/29	N		A	Y	N	A	Y-3.8
	Freshman Honors	Unlimited	2200-4400		3.85	1310/32	N		A	Y	N	A	N
	Freshman Honors II	Unlimited	All Costs		3.85	1420	N	O	A	Y	N	A	N
U. of Oklahoma, Norman 73019	Alumni Scholar	40	1000		3.75		N	O	A	3.25	O	B-5/1	N
	American Indian	75	3200				N	O	A	Y	M-O	B-6/1	Y
	Award of Excellence	75	1500				N	O	A	2.8	N	B-2/15	N
	Gunning	10	2000	X	X	X	N	O	A	3.25	S-O	B-5/1	N
	Honors	75	1000				N	O	A	2.8	N	B-2/15	N
	Junior College Merit Council	40	1000				N	L	A	N	N	B-3/1	Y
	Lt. William J. Scott	125	1000				Y	O	A	Y	M-O	B-6/1	Y
	National Merit	245	7600-9200				N	O	A	Y-3.25	N	B-4/1	N
	O.U. Achievement	80	1000				N	L	A	N	M	B-2/15	N
	Passages to Progress	40	1000				N	L	A	N	O	B-3/1	Y
	Pres. Leadership	80	1000				N	L	A	N	N	B-2/15	N
	Transfer Academic Excellence	40	1000				N	L	A	N	N	B-3/1	Y
	University	150	1000				N	O	A	N	N	B-2/15	N
	Valedictorian	25	1000	1			N		A	2.8	S-O	C	N
	Honors Program												
U. of Tulsa, 74104	Arts	5	2500				N	T	A	Y	N	D-4/1	Y
	Honors	Varies	1100	8%	3.9	1250/20	N	E-R-I	A	3.0	N	B-3/1	Y-3.5
	Music	40	1000-Tuition				N	T	A	Y	N	B-4/1	Y
	National Merit Honors	Varies	Tuition				N	O	A	3.0	N	A-4/1	N
	Theatre	5	500-2500				N	T	A	Y	N	D-4/1	Y
	Twyman	2	Tuition, rm.,brd.	1%	3.9	1350/34	N	E-L-I-O	A	3.0	N	B-2/15	N
	University	Varies	3000-5000	15%	3.5	1250/26	N	R	A	3.0	N	A-3/1	N
	Honors Program												
OREGON													
Bassist, Portland 97201	Academic/Talent	Varies	750-1000				N	E-T-L-R	A	N	N	B-3/1	N
Concordia College, Portland 97007	Presidential	Unlimited	500-Tuition		3.5	1000	N		A	3.5	N	B-C	Y-3.5
	Fine Arts	Varies	100-1000		2.0		N	T-I	A	2.0	N	B-C	Y-2.0

	Program	No. of Awards	Value Range	Award Criteria					Study Fields	Renew-ability	Restric-tions	Apply Date	Transfer
				Class Stndg.	Grade Avg.	SAT/ ACT	Need Based	Other					
OREGON *(Continued)*													
E. Oregon State C., La Granda 97850	Presidential	Varies	1000		3.0		Y	T	A	3.0	S	B-3/1	Y-3.0
	Underrepresented Minority	10	Tuition & Fees				N	E-T-L-R-O	A	2.0	M	B-3/1	Y-2.0
	Laurels	55	Tuition		3.5		N	E-T-L-R-O	A	3.0	N	B-3/1	Y-3.0
	Honors Program												
Eugene Bible, 97405	Academic/Need	24	300-4017		2.5		X	E-L-R-O	O	N	O	B-3/1	Y-2.5
	Honors	1	750		3.7				O	B		B-3/1	N
	Focus Competition	2	450				N	T-O	A	N	N	C	N
	Honors Program												
George Fox, Newberg 97132	African American	10	2500		2.5		N	L-R-I-O	A	Y	M	C-D	Y
	Art	6	1000-3000				N	T	O	Y	N	B-2/1	Y
	Benson	Varies	8000	10%	3.75	1300	N	L-R-I-O	A	3.75	N		Y
	Drama	10	500-2500				N	T	O	Y	N	B-2/1	Y
	Duke	Varies	6000		3.75	1200	N						Y
	GFU Science Scholarship	10	3250		3.5	1100	N	R-I-O	O	3.5	N	B-3/15	N
	Hispanic American	10	2500		2.5		N	L-R-I-O	A	Y	M	C-D	Y
	Honors	Varies	4000		3.5	1100	N	R	A	3.5	N		Y-3.5
	Music	30	500-2500				N	T	O	Y	N	B-2/1	Y
	Presidential	Varies	10,000	10%	3.75	1400	N	L-R-I-O	A	3.6	N		N
	AP Exams												
	Distance Learning												
	Family Discounts												
	Honors Program												
Lewis & Clark, Portland 97219	Dean's	60	2500-7000						A	3.0	N	A-2/1	Y
	Forensics	Varies	500-3000				Y	T-R	A	3.0	N	B-2/1	Y
	Music	Varies	500-5000					T	A	Y	N	B-2/1	Y
	National Merit	Varies	750-2500					O	A	Y	N	B-2/1	N
	Neely	10	Tuition					R	A	3.3	N	B-2/1	N
	Sanders	3	Up to 5000					E-R	A	Y	M	B-2/15	Y
	Trustee	15	1/2 Tuition					R	A	3.3	N	B-2/1	N
	AP Exams												
	Family Discounts												
	Honors College												

Linfield, McMinnville 97218	Presidential	3	Tuition				N	E-R	A	3.35			
	Faculty	200	20% Tuition	20%	3.25	1100/26	N		A	Y	N	B-2/15	N
	Trustee	15	8400-12600		3.75	1200	N		A	3.25			
	Faculty	200	3500-8400		3.4	1100	N		A	3.0			
	Presidential Passport	Varies	1500-2500	1			N	E-T-R	A	N	N	B	N
	Trustee Scholar	15	50% Tuition		3.75	1300/31	N		A	3.0	N	A-D	
	Music	12	1500-2500				N	T	O	Y			
	Honors Program												
Marylhurst, 97036	Marylhurst	50	150-3000		X		Y	L-R	A	N	N	B-D	Y
	Mayer	10	300-1500				N	T-L-R-I-O	O	N	N	B-6/30	Y
	Distance Learning												
	Internships												
Northwest Christian, Eugene 97401	Presidential	Varies	3500	15%	3.6	1150/26	Y	E-L-R-O	A	3.2	N	A-3/1	N
	Dean's	Varies	2500	33%	3.4	1070/23	Y	E-L-R-O	A	3.0	N	A-3/1	N
	Achievement	Varies	1500	50%	3.0	970/20	Y	L-R-O	A	2.0	N	A-3/1	Y-3.0
Oregon Inst. of Technology Klamath Falls 97601-8801	Presidential	10-15	1000		3.5	X	N	T-L-R	A	3.2	N	B-3/1	N
	Nonresident Honors	40	1000		3.0	1000/23	N		A	2.5	N	C	Y
Oregon State U., Corvallis 97331	Presidential	50	2500-3000		3.75	1100	N	E-L-R	A	3.25	N	B-2/24	N
	Oregon Laurels	70	2500-3000		3.75	1100	N	E-L-R	A	3.25	S-O	B-2/24	N
	Minority Achievement	72	Tuition		3.0		N	E-R	A	3.0	S-M-O	B-3/1	N
	Honors College												
Pacific NW C. of Art, Portland 97205	Leta Kennedy Freshman	3	2000		3.25		N	E-T-R	A	N	O	B-4/1	N
Pacific U., Forest Grove 97116	Activity Grants	Varies	100-2500		X	X	Y	T-R	A	2.0	N	C-5/1	Y-3.2
	Alumni	Varies	3000		X	X	N		A	Y	N	C	
	Black and Hispanic	Varies	1500		3.0	X	N	L	A	Y	M	C	
	Challenge Grants	Varies	Varies		X	X	Y		A	Y	N	C	
	Presidential	Varies	5000		X	X	N		A	Y	N	C	
	Talent Awards	Varies	Varies		X	X	Y	T		Y			
	Trustee	Varies	4000		X	X	N		A	Y	N	C	
	Honors Program											C-5/1	Y-2.0
Portland State U., 97207	Laurels	25	800-2300		3.5		N	E-L-R	A	3.0	S	B-3/15	N
	Minority Achievement	64	Tuition & Fees		2.75		N	E-L-R	A	2.5	S-M	B-3/1	Y-2.5
	Presidential	10-20	1000		3.5	1100	N	L-R	A	3.5	S-O	B-3/15	N
	Honors Program												
Southern Oregon State, Ashland 97520	Junior Minority Achievement	5-10	Tuition				N	E-L-R-O	A	2.0	S-M-O	B-5/1	A-2.25
	Minority Achievement	10	Tuition		3.0	1010/21	N	E-R	A	4.0	S-M-O	B-3/1	N
	Music	Varies	Varies		2.75	1010	N	T-O	A	N	O	A-B-C	Y-2.25
	Oregon Laurels	60	1000		3.5	1100/24	N	E-R	A	3.0	O		N

	Program	No. of Awards	Value Range	Award Criteria					Study Fields	Renew-ability	Restric-tions	Apply Date	Transfer
				Class Stndg.	Grade Avg.	SAT/ ACT	Need Based	Other					
OREGON *(Continued)*													
Southern Oregon State, Ashland 97520 *(Continued)*	Presidential	10	2000		3.75	1180/26	N	E-R	A	3.0	S-0	B-3/1	N
	Smallins	6	1000				N	T-L-R-0	A	N	S-0	B-3/1	Y-2.5
	Honors Program												
U. of Oregon, Eugene 97403	U of O	100	100-2500		3.5		N	R	A	Y	0	B-3/1	Y
	Presidential	50	1000-2000		3.75	1100	N	E-L-R	A	3.25	N	B-2/1	N
	General University	Varies	600-1000				Y	E-L-R	A	N	N	B-2/1	Y
U. of Portland, 97203	Activity	Varies	100-Tuition		X	X	X	T	0	X	N	C	Y
	President's	Unlimited	2000-7000		3.5	1140	N	L	A	2.0	N	A-3/1	N
	Holy Cross	Unlimited	600-4000		3.35	950	N	L	A	2.0	N	A-3/1	N
	Honors Program												
Warner Pacific, Portland 97215	Academic Merit	Varies	3000		3.0		N	N	A	3.0	N	A-6/1	Y-3.0
	Garlington	Varies	1000		2.75						M	B	
	President's	Varies	5000		3.5	1050/23	N	N	A	3.5	N	A-6/1	Y
	Regents'	Varies	Tuition		3.75		N	N	A	3.75	N	A-6/1	N
	Warner Leadership	Varies	2000		2.75		N	L-R-0	A	Y			
	AP Exams												
	Alumni Discounts												
Western Baptist, Salem 97301	Academic Scholarships	120	500-1000		3.5	800	N		A	3.5	N	A	Y-3.5
	Chancellor Grants	80	300-1000				Y		A	2.0	N	C	Y-3.0
	Departmental	66	300-1400				Y	L-I-0	A	Y	N	B-3/1	Y
	Endowed Scholarships	14	500-1000		3.25		Y	L-R-0	A	N	0	B-3/1	Y-3.25
	Valedictorian	Varies	1000	1%	3.8	1100	N	0	A	N	N		N
	Western Scholarship	180	400-2000				Y	E-T-R-I-0	A	X	N	B-3/1	Y
	Honors Program												
Western Oregon State, Monmouth 97361	Alumni	30	500		3.5	1000/26	N	E-L-R	A	N	N	B-3/1	Y
	Creative Arts	6	200-1500		3.0	1000	Y	T-L-R	0	N	N	B-3/15	Y-3.0
	Honors	8	1000-2450		3.5		N	E-L	A	Y	N	B-D	Y-2.75
	Laurel's	50-70	600-2000				N	E-L-R	A	Y	N	B-3/1	Y-3.5
	Presidential	Varies	1000-2000		3.75	1100	N	E-L-R	A	Y	S	B-3/1	N
	Western	60	300-1500		3.6	1100/26	N	E-L-R	A	N	N	B-3/1	Y
Willamette U., Salem 97301	G. Herbert Smith	10	2500-Tuition		3.7	1200/27	X	L	A	Y	N	B-3/1	N

PENNSYLVANIA

Albright, Reading 19603	Jacob Albright	30	10000	10%	3.5	1050	N	E-L-R-I-O	A	3.0	N	A-2/15	Y-3.5
	Presidential	75	5000-7500	25%	3.0	1000	N	E-L-R-I-O	A	2.67	N	A-2/15	Y-3.0
	Coleman	25	2000-3000	33%	3.0	950	N	E-L-R-I-O	A	2.67	N	A-2/15	Y-3.0
	Talent	10	500-1500				N	T-R-I-O	A	Y	N	A-2/15	Y
	Shirk	25	10000				N	E-L-R-I-O	A	Y	S	B-12/15	N
	Honors Program												
Allegheny, Meadville 16335	Presidential Scholar Award	100	2500-7500	20%	X	X	N	E-R-I-O	A	3.0	N	A-2/15	Y-3.0
	Provost's Merit Award	100	2000-5000	20%	X	X	N	E-T-L-R-I-O	A	2.5	N	A-2/15	Y
	Research/Minority Scholars	up to 8	5000	X	X	X	N	E-R-I-O	O	Y	M	A-2/15	N
	Disting. African-Amer. Sch.	1	10000-22570	X	X	X	Y	E-R-I-O	A	Y	M	B-2/15	N
Allentown C. of St. Francis de Sales, Center Valey 18034	Departmental	Varies	Varies		3.0		N	E-T-I-O	A	Y	N	C-12/1	N
	DeSales	Varies	3500-5000				N		A	A	N	A-2/15	N
	Presidential	Varies	Tuition	5%	4.0	1300/30	N		A	Y	N	A-2/15	N
	Trustee	Varies	5000-1/2 Tuit.				N		A	Y	N	A-2/15	N
	AP Exams												
	Distance Learning												
	Family Discounts												
	Honors Program												
Alvernia, Reading 19607	Franciscan	20	4000-7000	X	X	X	N		A	Y	N	C	N
	Berks Community	30	1500-2500		X		N	O	A	2.0	O	A-5/1	N
	Allentown Diocese	30	1750-3000		X		N	O	A	2.0	O	A-5/1	N
Baptist Bible, Clarks Summit 18411	Academic Merit Grant	Varies	1200-2000			26	N		A	N	N	A-B-4/1	N
	Academic Honors Schol.	Varies	400-1500		3.6		N	O	A	3.6	O	B-4/1	N
	Academic Achievement Sch.	Varies	500		X		N	O	A	N	O	B-4/1	N
	AP Exams												
	Distance Learning												
	Family Discounts												
Beaver, Glenside 19038	Achievement	Unlimited	1000-6000				N	E-L-T	A	2.0		A-8/1	Y
	Distinguished Scholar	Unlimited	1000-16,240	20%	3.0	1030	N	L	A	2.0		A-8/1	Y-3.0
	Grant	Varies	500-9000	40%		X	Y	O	A	2.0	N	A-2/15	Y
	Philadelphia Scholars	5	2000	X	X	X	N	L-R	A	2.0	S	B-2/15	N
	AP Exams												
	Co-op												
	Honors Program												
Bryn Mawr, 19010	Bryn Mawr Grant	650	1000-25,000				Y						
	AP Exams												
	Internships												

	Program	No. of Awards	Value Range	Award Criteria: Class Stndg.	Award Criteria: Grade Avg.	Award Criteria: SAT/ ACT	Award Criteria: Need Based	Award Criteria: Other	Study Fields	Renew-ability	Restric-tions	Apply Date	Transfer
PENNSYLVANIA *(Continued)*													
Bucknell U., Lewisburg 17837	Preferential Awards	100	200-25000				Y	E-T-L-R	A	Y	N	1/1	N
Cabrini, Radnor 19087	Acad. Ach. Transfer	Unlimited	1000-6000		3.0		N		A	2.75	N	B-C	Y
	Achievement	Unlimited	2000-8000		2.8	1000	N		A	2.75	N	B-C	N
	Alumni/Presidential	1	Tuition	10%	3.5	1200	N	E-L-R-I-O	A	3.0	N	B-12/31	N
	Bergen	1	1000-3000	20%	3.0	1100	A		O	N	N	C-3/1	N
	International	Unlimited	1000-3000	20%	3.0		N		A	2.75	O	C-5/1	Y-3.0
	Vice-Presidential	2	1/2 Tuition		2.5	1000	Y		A	2.5	N	B-5/31	N
	Honors Program												
California U. of PA, 15419	Faculty	4	750-1500	20%	3.5	1200	N	O	A	3.5	N	A-C	N
	Minority	15	500-2678		2.5	725	N		A	2.0	M	A-C	Y
	Honors Program												
Carlow, Pittsburgh 15213	Catherine McAuley	Varies	4000		3.25	900/19	N	E-R-I	A	3.0	S-D-W	A-C	N
	Community College	1	3000		3.75		Y	E-O	A	3.0	N	B-6/1	Y-3.75
	Dean's Recognition	Varies	3000				N	O	A	3.0	N	A-C	N
	Divisional	6	4500	X	3.25	950/20	N		A	3.0	N	B-3/24	N
	Elizabeth Carroll	3	2500				N	E-L-R-I-O	A	3.0	O	B-D	Y
	Full-Tuition	2	Tuition		3.75	1200/27	N		A	3.0	N	B-C	N
	Half-Tuition	3	1/2 Tuition		3.5	1100/24	N		A	3.0	N	B-C	N
	Hugh O'Brian	1	4000	X	3.25	900/19	N		A	3.0	S	B-D	N
	PA Gov. Sch. Excel. Alumni	2	4000		3.25		N		A	3.0	S-O	A-B-C	N
	Parish	Unlimited	2500	X	3.0	800/17	N	E-L-R	A	3.0	D	B-D	N
	Presidential	5	4000		3.25	900/19	N		A	3.0	N	B-D	N
	Service	Unlimited	2500		3.0	800/17	N	L-R	A	3.0	N	A	C
	Transfer	Unlimited	2500		3.5		Y	O	A	3.0	N	C-D	Y-3.5
	Transfer Writing	10	1000		2.6		N	E	A	Y	O	C	Y-2.6
	Trustee	1	5000		3.25	1000/21	N	L	A	3.0	N	B-D	N
	Writing	1	4500		3.0		N	E	A	3.0	N	B-C	N
	AP Exams												
	Distance Learning												
	Alumni Discounts, Family Discounts												
	Co-op, Internships												
	Honors Program												

Cedar Crest, Allentown 18104	Allen	3	To 3500	10%		1000	Y	I-0	A	3.0	W	B-2/1	N
	Merit	Varies	500-5000	10%	3.0	1000	Y	I	A	3.0	N	B-2/15	Inq.
	Onyx	Varies	To 2500	25%		1000	Y		A	3.0	W	B-2/1	N
	Presidential	Varies	5000	10%		1200	N	0	A	3.0	N	A	N
	Transfer	Varies	To 2500		3.25		Y		A	3.0	N	B-2/1	N
	Cors	Varies	1000	10%		1000	N	0	A	Y	D	A	
	Honors Program												
Chatham, Pittsburgh 15232	Braun	Varies	2000-5000	X	X	X	N	0	A	3.0	W	A-C	N
	Dean's	Varies	7500	X	X	X	N	E-I-0	A	3.25	W	C	N
	Divisional	Varies	7500	X	X	X	N	E-I-0	A	3.25	W	A-C	N
	Leadership	Varies	1000-3000	X	X	X	N	L-0	A	2.5	W	A	N
	Presidential	Varies	to 10000	X	X	X	N	E-L-I-0	A	3.25	W	C	N
	Ruud	Varies	2000-4000				N	T-0	0	Y	W	C	N
	Theatre	Varies	500-2500				N	T-0	0	N	W	C	N
	Transfer	Varies	1000-5000	X	X	X	N	0	A	3.0	W	C	Y
Chestnut Hill, Philadelphia 19118	Achievement	Unlimited	3000-10,000		2.5		N			2.5	W	A	Y
	Merit	Unlimited	3000-10,000			1000/27	N			3.0	W	A	Y
	Partial CHC	Varies	2000-8000	25%	3.0	1050	N	E-L-R-I-0	A	3.0	W-0	B-3/15	N
	Presidential	1-5	Tuition	10%	3.5	1200/26	N	E-L-R-I-0	A	3.0	W-0	A-1/15	N
	Redmond	1	All Costs	20%	3.0	1100/22	Y	E-L-R-I-0	A	3.0	W-0	A-5/1	N
	AP Exams												
	Honors Program												
Clarion U. of PA, 16214	Presidential	5	1000	X	X	X	N	E-L-R-0	A	Y	0	B-4/1	N
	Edith Davis Eve Foundation	Varies	1000	X	X	X	Y	0	A	Y-2.0	S	C-D	N
	Foundation Honors	Varies	100-700	X	X	X	N	L-0	A	Y	0	C-D	N
	Foundation Leadership	Varies	To 1500	X	X	X	N	0	A	N	N	A-D	N
	Mary Martha Colegrove	2	1000	X	X	X	N	0	A	3.0	W-S	A-D	N
	Minnie D. Croyle	Varies	Tuition & Fees				N	0	A	Y	S	A-C	N
	Eberly Family	Varies	Varies	X	X	X	N	0	A	N	S	A-C	Y
	Dr. & Mrs. Arthur Phillips	Varies	Varies	X	X	X	N	R-0	A	2.75	S	4/15	N
	Presidential	4	1000	X	X	X	N	L	A	Y	N	3/30	N
	Honors Program												
College Misericordia, Dallas 18612	Academic Honor	386	1000-7000	25%	3.0	900/23	N	L-R	A	3.2	N	A-C	Y-3.0
	Merit	473	500-7000	3%		1180	N	L	A	3.0	N	A	N
	Leadership	60	1000-4000				Y	L	A	Y	0	A	N
	AP Exams												
	Distance Learning												
	Family Discounts												
	Co-op, Internships												
	Honors Program												

	Program	No. of Awards	Value Range	Award Criteria: Class Stndg.	Grade Avg.	SAT/ ACT	Need Based	Other	Study Fields	Renew-ability	Restric-tions	Apply Date	Transfer
PENNSYLVANIA *(Continued)*													
Delaware Valley, Doylestown 18901	Faculty Scholarship	400	5000-7500		3.0	1000	N		A	3.0	N	A	Y-2.5
	Faculty Grants	400	5000-6000		2.0	900	N		A	2.0	N	A	Y-2.5
	AP Exams												
	Co-op, Internships												
	Honors Program												
Drexel U., Philadelphia 19104	Anthony J. Drexel	400	8000	X	X	X	N		A	Y	N	2/1	Y
	National Merit	Varies	2000				N	O	A	Y	N	2/1	Y
	Performing Arts	Varies	2000				N	T	A	Y	N	2/1	Y
	Honors Program												
Duquesne U., Pittsburgh 15282	Chancellor's	32	Tuition				N	O	A	3.5	N	1/15	N
	Music	30	Varies				N	O	O	3.0	O	B	Y
	Parish	50	4000				N	O	A	3.0	S-D	1/15	N
	Presidential	281	4000				N	O	A	3.0	N	1/15	Y
	Spiritan	30	6500				Y	O	A	2.75	M	1/15	N
	Strub	142	6500				N	O	A	3.0	N	1/15	Y
	Tamburitzans	40	6000				N	O	A	Y	N	B	Y
	Honors Program												
East Stroudsburg U. of PA, 18301	Presidential	Varies	1000-3000	5%	3.5	1200/28	N		A	3.3	N	A-1/15	N
	Board of Governors	Varies	3224		3.3		N		A	3.3	M	A-3/15	Y-3.3
Eastern College, St. Davids 19087	Leadership	20	2000	50%		900	N	E-L-R-I-O	A	2.5	N	B-C	Y-2.5
	Honors	19	1500	15%		1100/25	N	E-L-R-I-O	A	2.5	N	B-C	Y-2.5
	President's	3	5000	5%		1300	N	E-L-R-I-O	A	3.5	N	B-C	Y-3.5
	Deans	9	3000	10%		1200	N	E-L-R-I-O	A	3.0	N	B-C	Y-3.0
	Honors Program												
Edinboro U. of PA, 16444	Various	Varies	500-7000	X	X	X	N		A	X	U	C	N
	Dollars For Honors	Varies	500-1200	X	X	X	N	O	A	Y	N	C	
Elizabethtown College, 17022	Provost	150	2000-6500	10%		1150/25	N	E-T-L-R-O	A	Y	O	B-3/1	Y-3.25
	Presidential	12	8500	2%		1300/29	N	E-T-L-R-O	A	Y	O	B-3/1	N
Franklin & Marshall, Lancaster 17604	John Marshall Schp.	60	7500	5%		1400	N	E-R-I-O	A	Y	N	A-2/1	N
	Presidential	80	5000	10%		1300	N	E-R-I-O	A	Y	N	A-2/1	N
	Regional	10	3300	10%		1200	N	E-R-I-O	A	Y	O	A-2/1	N
	[illegible]			[illegible]			Y	[illegible]	A	Y	O	A-2/1	N

Gannon University, Erie 16541	Academic		500-6000	20%	3.25	950	N	R	A	3.0	N	A	Y-3.25
	Leadership		500-2500			950	N	L-R	A	3.0	N	A	Y-3.25
	Business Scholars	15					N		O	3.0	N	B-1/15	N
	Parish Grant	Varies	2500	20%	3.0	1000	N	E	A	2.0	D	B-C	Y-2.0
	Diocesan H.S. Grant	Varies	1000-2000				N	R	A	2.0	O	A	Y-2.0
	Honors Program		1000										
Geneva College, Beaver Falls 15010	Geneva		1000	10%		1000/22	N	O	A	3.0	N	A	
	Presidential Lee		2000-3500				X	E-L-R-I-O	A	3.2	N	B-2/1	
	Honors Program												
Gettysburg College, 17325	Presidential	Varies	100-Need	X	X	X	Y	L	A	Y	N	A-2/1	N
Grove City College, Grove City 16127	Trustee Academic	12	5224-6012				N	E-O	A	3.6	N	B-D	N
	Grove City College General	Varies	200-2600	20%			Y		A	3.0	N	B-5/1	Y-3.0
	Engineering	4	2500	10%			N	E-R-O	O	3.0	N	B-3/1	N
Gwynedd Mercy, Gwynedd Valley 19437	Academic	8	1/2 Tuition	15%	3.3	1100	N	L-R	A	3.3	N	B-1/15	Y-3.3
	Departmental	Varies	1000-2000	30%	3.0	1100	N		A	2.8	N	D	Y-3.1
	Excellence	Varies	2500-4000	25%	3.3	1150	N		A	3.0	N	D	Y-3.4
	Gwynedd Mercy	Varies	1000-8000	40%	3.0	900	Y	L	A	3.0	N	B-3/15	Y-3.0
	J.C. Connelly	Varies	1000-7000	40%	3.0	1000	N	L-R	A	3.0	N	B-3/15	Y-3.0
	Presidential	1	Full Tuition	15%	3.5	1100	N	L	A	3.5	N	B-1/15	Y-3.5
	Honors Program												
Immaculata College, 19345	Academic	25	2500-6500	20%	3.0	1050	Y	R-I-O	A	3.0	W	A-3/1	Y
	Presidential	4	Tuition	10%	3.5	1200	N	E-R-I-O	A	3.5	W	C-2/1	N
	Music	3	2000-5000	40%		1000	N	T-R-I-O	A	2.5	W	B-3/1	Y
	Honors Program												
Indiana U. of PA, 15705	Board of Governors	40	Tuition	25%		1000	N	R	A	3.0	M	A-D	N
	Distinguished Achievers	17	1500	10%		1100	N	L-R	A	3.0	N	B-2/1	N
	Dean's	Varies	200-Tuition	10%		1100	Y		A	N	N	B-3/1	N
	President's	Varies	1000	1%			N	O	A	N	N	A-D	N
Juniata, Huntington 16652	Simpson	1	3000	10%		1000	N	E	A	3.0	N	N	Y
	Presidential	3	16480	5%	3.85	1360/31	N	T-L-I-O	A	3.5	N	A	N
	Dean of Student's Leadership	25	8500	10%	3.7	1260/28	N	L-I-O	A	3.0	N	A	N
	Juniata Merit	Varies	4000-8500	20%	3.0	1000	Y	I-O	A	3.0	N	C	N
King's, Wilkes-Barre 18711	Academic	70	5000-6000	20%		1100	N	E-L-R-I-O	A	3.2	N	A-3/15	Y
	Moreau	60	5500-6500	20%		1150	N	E-L-R-I-O	A	3.0	N	A-3/15	Y
	Presidential	4	Tuition	5%		1200	N	E-L-R-I-O	A	3.0	N	A-3/15	N
	Honors Program												

	Program	No. of Awards	Value Range	Award Criteria					Study Fields	Renew-ability	Restric-tions	Apply Date	Transfer
				Class Stndg.	Grade Avg.	SAT/ ACT	Need Based	Other					
PENNSYLVANIA *(Continued)*													
Kutztown U., 19530	Beck	8	1000		3.25		N		A	3.25	N	C	N
	Kutztown	30	1000		3.0		Y		A	3.0	N	B-3/15	Y-3.0
	KU Merit	7	1300		3.25		N		A	N	N	C	N
	Honors Program												
Lafayette, Easton 18042	College Grants	850	200-30,000	25%		1150	Y	E-T-L-R-I-O	A	2.0	N	B-2/15	Y-3.3
	Marquis	60	10,000-30,000	5%		1300	X	E-R-I-O	A	3.0	N	A-1/1	Y
	National Merit	Unlimited	2000				N	0	A	Y	N	A-1/1	N
	AP Exams												
	Honors Program												
Lancaster Bible, 17601	Academic	Unlimited	350			25	N		A	3.5	N	A-D	N
	Competition	Unlimited	500-750					T	A			A	
	Dist. Christian HS Student	Unlimited	500-2000				Y	L-R-O	A	N	D	A	N
	Music	4-5	500-1000					T		Y		A	Y
	Presidential	Unlimited	400-1000		2.5		N	L-R	A	N	N	A	Y-2.5
	Valedictorian	Unlimited	2500	1			N	0	A	3.5	N	A-D	Y
	AP Exams												
	Alumni Discounts, Family Discounts												
La Salle, Philadelphia 19141	Academic Achievement	500	1000-3000	20%		1050	N	0	A	2.75	0	C	N
	Christian Brother	15	Tuition	10%	A	1300	N	E-R-I-O	A	3.0	0	B-1/15	N
	Community Service	5	1/2 Tuition	40%	B	1050	N	E-L-R-I-O	A	2.5	N	B-1/15	N
	Diversity Scholar	5	To Tuition		B+	1050	Y	E-R-I-O	A	2.5	M	B-1/15	N
	Founders	500	1000-10000	20%		1200	N	0	A	3.0	N	C	Y-3.0
	Lasallian Honor	1	To Tuition	10%		1200	N	L-R-O	A	3.0	N	A-1/15	N
	Leadership	3-5	Varies	20%		1000	N	L-R-O	A	Y	N	A-1/15	N
	University	30	Tuition	10%	A	1300	N	E-R-I-O	A	3.0	N	B-1/15	N
Lebanon Valley, Annville 17003	Academic Recognition	Unlimited	1/2 Tuition				N	0	A	3.0	0	A-4/1	Y-3.0
	Achievement Award	Unlimited	1/4 Tuition	30%			N		A	2.5	N	A-4/1	N
	Carmean String	4	1000				N	T	A	Y	N	C-3/1	Y
	Carmean Talent	6	1000				N	T	A	Y	N	A-3/15	N
	Graham	2	3500	10%		1200	N	R-I-O	0	3.0	N	C-1/1	N
	Leadership	Unlimited	1/3 Tuition	20%			N		A	2.75	N	A	N
	Multicultural Fellowship	20	2000-8000				Y	L-I	A	2.25	M	A-D	N

	Vickroy	Unlimited	1/2 Tuition	10%			N		A	3.0	N	A	N
	AP Exams												
	Alumni Discounts												
	Co-op, Internships												
	Honors Program												
Lehigh U., Bethlehem 18015	Choral Arts	4	2500					T		Y			
	Performing Arts	4	2500					T		Y			
	Dean's	100	7000	10%	3.8	1290	N	L	A	Y			
	AP Exams												
	Distance Learning												
	Co-op, Internships												
	Honors Program												
Lincoln U., 19352	Alumni Merit	To 1000	900	25%	3.0	950	N	R-I-O	A	3.0	N	C	
	Founders	18	Tuition	20%	3.3	1000	N	R-I-O	A	3.0	N	C	N
	MARC	Varies	Tuition+fees	X	X	X	N		O	Y	O	C	
	Honors Merit		To 1000	X	X	X	N		A	Y	N	C	
	NASA Laser	20	Varies	25%	3.0	950	N	R-I-O	A	Y	M	A-4/14	N
Lock Haven U. of PA, 17745	Alumni Foundation	100	1000	20%		1100	N		A	3.0	N	A-D	N
	Board of Governors	24	1570-2750	40%	2.5	950/21	Y	E-L-R	A	2.5	M	B-D	N
	Presidential	20	1000-2000	20%	3.0	1270	N	I-O	A	3.0	N	A-D	N
	AP Exams												
	Internships												
	Honors Program												
Lycoming College, Williamsport 17701	Departmental	Varies	7000-8500	10%		1230	N	I	A	3.0	N	A-3/1	N
	Faculty Scholar	Varies	10000-15000	10%		1320	N	I	A	3.0	N	A-3/1	N
	Lycoming Scholarship	Varies	1000-5000	30%		1100	N		A	3.0	N	A-3/1	N
	Theatre/Art/Music Awards	Varies	1000-2500				N	T	A	Y	N	A-3/1	N
	Transfers Scholarship	Varies	1000-4000		3.0		N		A	3.0	N	A-4/15	Y
	Val/Sal	Varies	12500	1-2			N		A	3.0	N	A-3/1	N
	AP Exams												
	Alumni Discounts, Family Discounts												
	Internships												
	Honors Program												
Mansfield University, 16933	Academic	30	500-1000	10%	3.2	1000	N	T-L	A	N	N	B-3/15	Y-3.2
	Hartley Dean	Varies	1000	20%	3.2	1000	Y	L-R	A	2.0	N	B-3/15	N
	Board of Governors	Varies	Tuition	40%	X	X	N		A	2.0	M	B-3/15	Y-3.2
	Honors Program												
Marywood, Scranton 18509	I.H.M.	Varies	500-1500	20%	3.0	1100	Y		A	Y	N	B-2/15	Y
	Presidential	25	Tuition	10%	3.0	1100	N		A	3.0	N	A-2/15	Y-3.0

	Program	No. of Awards	Value Range	Award Criteria: Class Stndg.	Award Criteria: Grade Avg.	Award Criteria: SAT/ACT	Award Criteria: Need Based	Award Criteria: Other	Study Fields	Renew-ability	Restric-tions	Apply Date	Transfer
PENNSYLVANIA *(Continued)*													
Marywood, Scranton 18509 *(Continued)*	Minority	Varies	All Costs				N	R-I	A	Y	M	A-2/15	
	Honors Program												
Mercyhurst, Erie 16546	Egan Honors	50	1500-5000	15%		1100	N	E					
	Arts	50	1500-7500				N	T					
	Val/Sal	10	6500-10,00	1-2			N		A				
	AP Exams												
	Family Discount												
	Co-op												
	Honors Program												
Messiah, Grantham 17027	Dean's	650-700	750-2000	15%	3.0	1000/22	N		A	3.0	N	A-D	Y-3.25
	Founders	30	3000	X	X	X	N	T-L	A	3.0	N	B-C	N
	President's	200-250	500-1500				N	L-R	A	2.5	N	B-4/1	Y
Millersville U. of PA, 17551	Medal	10	1000	5%		1200	N	L-R	A	3.35	N	C	N
	SICO	25	1000	10%		1100	Y	R	A	2.0	S	B-2/15	N
Moravian, Bethlehem 18018	Comenius	20	3000-11000	10%	3.0	1200	X	R-O	A	3.0	N	B-3/15	N
	Thursby	2	500-3000				Y	T-I-O	O	Y	N	B-3/15	Y
	Banach	2	1000				N	R-I-O	O	3.3	O	C-3/15	N
	Founders	10-15	1000-2000	20%		1000	Y	O	A	2.50	N	C-3/15	Y
Muhlenberg, Allentown 18104	Presidential	100	5000-8000	10%	3.5	1250	N	I	A	3.0	N	A	N
	Muhlenburg/Dana	45	3000	10%	3.5	1300	N	E-I-R					
	Internships												
	Honors Program												
Neumann, Aston 19014	Competitive	Varies	1100-Tuition	20%	3.0	1000	N	E-T-L-R-I-O	A	3.0	N	B-3/15	Y-3.0
	Academic	Varies	1000-Tuition	10%	3.0	1100/25	N	E-L-R-I	A	3.0	N	B-3/1	N
	Presidential	Varies	1000-3000	40%	2.5	900	N		A	2.5	N	C-3/1	N
	Honors Program												
Penn State Erie, Erie 16563	Academic	140	500-1000		3.2		N		A	N	N	C-3/1	Y-3.2
	Honors Program												
Penn State U., All Campuses	Various	Varies	100-4000	X	X	X	Y	O	A	X	O	A-D	Y
	Honors Program												

Philadelphia College of Bible, Langhorne 19047	Dean's Scholars	Unlimited	500-1000	10%	3.0	1100/23	N		A	3.0	N	A-D	N
	Leadership	Unlimited	200-1000		2.5		N	L-R	A	2.5	N	C	Y
	Presidential	Unlimited	1200-2400	1	3.5	1180/25	N		A	3.4	N	A-D	N
	Transfer Dean's	Varies	500-1000		3.0		N		A	3.0	N	A-D	Y-3.0
Philadelphia C. of Textiles and Science 19144	General	Varies	2000-7500	X	X	X	N		A	Y	N	A-C	Y
	Academic	Varies	1000-2500	20%	3.0	1100	N	L	A	3.0	N	A-4/1	N
	Presidential	5	6950-10600	20%	3.0	1100	N	L	A	3.0	N	A-4/1	N
	Honors Program												
Point Park, Pittsburgh 15222	Golden Key	Varies	Tuition	20%	3.25	1000	N	R-I-0	A	3.0	N	A-3/1	Y
	Scholarship	25	50-100% Tuit.				N	E-T-R-I-0	0000	3.0	N	A-3/15	Y-3.0
Robert Morris, Coraopolis 15108	Merit Scholarship	Varies	1000-3000	20%	3.0	1000/22	N	I-0	A	3.0	0	A-5/1	Y-3.9
	Presidential Scholarship	Varies	Tuition	5%	3.5	1200/26	N	E-L-R-I-0	A	3.0	0	B-2/1	N
	Resident Leadership	Varies	Room fees	25%	3.0	1000/22	N	L-I-0	A	3.0	0	A-5/1	N
Rosemont College, 19010	Alumnae	4	1500				N	E-T-L-R-I-0	A	3.0	W	A-2/15	N
	Community College	Varies	1000-5000		3.0		N	E-R-0	A	3.0	W-0	A-D	Y-3.0
	Connelly	2	Tuition	20%		1000	Y	0	A	3.0	S-W-0	B-1/15	N
	McShain	2	Tuition	20%		1000	Y	L-I-0	A	3.0	W	A-3/1	N
	Revere	1-2	5350-10700				N	T-R-I-0	0	Y	W	A-B-2/15	N
	Rosemont Opprnty Grant	3	5350-10700				Y	R-I-0	A	Y	W	A-B-2/15	N
	Rosemont Scholars	10	Tuition	10%	3.5	1200	N	E-R-I-0	A	3.33	W	A-2/15	N
	Trustee	5	5350				Y	R-I-0	A	3.0	S-W	A-B-2/15	N
St. Francis, Loretto 15940	Endowed/Special	Varies	2500-4500	20%	0.9	1050/25	N	R-I-0	A	3.0	N	A-3/1	N
	President's	Varies	5500-10000	5%	0.9	1150/27	N	E-L-R-I-0	A	3.3	N	A-B-2/1	N
	Scholastic Perf.	Varies	1500		85%	950/23	N	R-I-0	A	3.0	N	A-3/1	N
	Transfer	8	1000		3.0		N		A	3.0	N	A-3/1	Y
	Returning Adult Student	Varies	960-1920		3.5		Y		A	3.5	0	A	
	Honors Program												
St. Joseph's U., Philadelphia 19131	Presidential	75	7000-10000	10%	3.5	1250	Y	T-L-R	A	3.2	N	A-12/1	N
	University	125	5500-7000	15%	3.25	1200	Y	T-L-R	A	3.0	N	A-12/1	Y-3.5
	Board of Trustees	25-40	Tuition	1%	3.5	1350	Y	T-L-E-R-0	A	3.2	N	A-12/1	N
	Honors Program												
St. Vincent, Latrobe 15650	Academic	Varies	1000-1/3 Tuit.	10%		1240	N		A	3.25	N	A-5/1	Y-3.4
	Alex McKenna	1	2500				N	E-0	0	3.25	0	B-C	N
	Leadership	Varies	500-3000	40%	3.0	900	N	L-R	A	2.4	N	A-3/15	Y-3.0
	Math/Science	1	To 2500				N	E-0	0	3.25	0	B-C	N
	Music	1	2500				N	T-0	0	Y	0	B-C	N
	Wimmer	5	9000-18.003	5%			N	E-R-0	A	3.25	N	C	N
	AP Exams												

	Program	No. of Awards	Value Range	Award Criteria					Study Fields	Renew-ability	Restric-tions	Apply Date	Transfer
				Class Stndg.	Grade Avg.	SAT/ ACT	Need Based	Other					
PENNSYLVANIA *(Continued)*													
St. Vincent, Latrobe 15650 *(Continued)*	Family Discounts												
	Co-op, Internships												
	Honors Program												
Seton Hill, Greensburg 15601	Elizabeth Seton	15	6750	10%		1100	N	I		3.2			
	Scott	15	4733	20%		1100	N	I		3.0			
	Schmidt	20	3275	30%	3.0	1100	N	I		2.8			
	AP Exams												
	Distance Learning												
	Family Discount												
	Co-op, Internships												
	Honors Program												
Shippensburg U. of PA, 17257	Abraham Smith	1	Tuition	10%		1200	N		A	3.2	N	B-C	N
	Barnhard Elementary Ed.	1	800	20%		1000	N		O	3.2	N	B-C	N
	Berkheimer	1	2250	10%		1200	N		O	3.2	S	B-C	N
	Board of Governors	Varies	Tuition				N	O	A	Y	N	B-C	Y
	Chapman	1	1000-1400	15%		1100	N		O	2.5	O	B-C	N
	Foundation	10	1000	10%		1100	N		A	3.2	N	B-C	N
	Gifted Minority	4	1000	10%			N		A	3.3	M	B-C	N
	Heberlig-Eisenberg	2	1000-2000	20%		1100	N		O	3.2	N	B-C	N
	Hosteld	5	1000	25%		1100	N		O	3.2	S-O	B-C	N
	John & Cora Grove	5	1000	20%		1100	N		O	2.75	N	B-C	N
	McGaughey-Higgins	2	Tuition	10%		1200	N		O	3.2	N	B-C	N
	Outstanding Student	2	Tuition	10%		1200	N		A	3.2	N	B-C	N
	Thomas Smyth	1	1300	20%		1100	N		O	3.0	N	B-C	N
	Honors Program												
Slippery Rock U. of PA, 16057	Board of Governors	60	Tuition	60%	2.5	800/19	N		A	2.7	M	A-D	Y-2.7
	University Academic	10	Tuition	10%	3.5	1000/24	N	E-L-R	A	N	N	B-2/1	N
	President's	15	1500	1			N		A	N	N	C	N
	Dean's	25	1000		3.5	1100/24	N	E-L-R	A	N	N	C	N
	Honors Program												
Spring Garden, Philadelphia 19119	Career	30	1000				N	E-T-I-O	A	2.5	N	B-5/1	Y
	President	2	6200	X	3.0	1000	N	R-I-O	A	3.0	N	B-5/1	Y

	Trustees	Varies	1000	20%	2.5	1000	N		A	2.5	N	B-5/1	N
	Leadership	Varies	Varies	50%	2.0		N	L	A	2.0	N	B-5/1	Y-2.0
Susquehanna U., Selinsgrove 17870	Music	3-5	3000				N	T-R	A	2.5	N	B-D	N
	Susquehanna	12-15	2500	15%		1100	N	E-L-R	A	3.0	N	B-D	N
	Presidential	6-8	3500	10%		1200	N	E-L-R	A	3.0	N	B-D	N
	Honors Program												
Temple U., Philadelphia 19122	Achievement	200+	2500	30%	3.0	1100	N	L	A	3.0			
	Scholars	200+	2000-11,000	15%	3.5	1200	N		A	3.0			
	AP Exams												
	Distance Learning												
	Co-op, Internships												
	Honors Program												
Thiel, Greenville 16125	Academic Excellence	2	15000	10%	3.2	1100/24	N	E-L-I-O	A	Y	N	C	
	Passavant Exam	6	1000		3.0		N	E-R-I-O	A	Y	N	B-3/15	N
	Presidential	25	2500	10%	3.2	1100/24	N	E-L-I-O	A	Y	N	C	
	Sawvel Memorial	Varies	2000			90%ile	N	I-O	A	Y	N	A-3/20	N
	Stewart Academic	6	1000	1-2			N		A	3.0	N	C	N
	Stewart Honors	Varies	200-800	10%	3.0		N	R-I-O	A	Y	N	A-D	N
	Trustee	3	10000	10%	3.2	1100/24	N	E-L-I-O	A	Y	N	A-5/1	
Thomas Jefferson U., 19107	Dean's	18	5000		3.0		N		A	3.0	N	B	
	Hospital Ed. Grants	4	6900		3.0		N		A	3.0	N	B	
U. of the Arts, Philadelphia 19102	Presidential	Varies	3500-6500	20%	3.0	1000	N	T-R-I-O	O	3.0	O	C-3/15	Y
	Partnership	2	1/2 Tuition	X	2.5	X	N	T-R-I-O	O	2.0	O	C-3/15	N
U. of Pittsburgh, 15260	Chancellor's	10	9760-18484	5%	4.0	1300	N	E-R-I-O	A	3.0	N	B-1/15	N
	Challenge	30	1000-3800	20%	3.0	900	Y	E-R-I-O	O	3.0	S-M	A-3/1	N
	University	300	500-6000	10%	3.0	1200	N	E-R-I-O	A	3.0	N	A-1/15	
	AP Exams												
	Co-op, Internships												
	Honors Program, Honors College												
U. of Pittsburgh, Bradford 16701	Presidential	Varies	1500	5%	3.5	1100	N	E-L-R-I-O	A	3.25	N	A-1/31	Y-3.25
	Deans	Varies	1000	10%	3.0	1000	N	E-L-R-I-O	A	3.25	N	B-3./15	N
	Pitt-Bradford Grant	Varies	500-2000	25%	3.0	900	N	E-L-R-I-O	A	3.25	N	A-1/31	Y-3.25
U. of Pittsburgh, Johnstown 15904	President's	30	3000 avg.	10%		1150	N	E-L-R-O	A	3.0	N	B-1/15	N
U. of Scranton, 18510	Ignatian	9	Tuition	5%		1300	N	R-I-O	A	3.0	N	B-2/15	N
	Loyola	Varies	1000-8000	20%		1000	N	R-I-O	A	3.0	N	B-2/15	N
	Honors Program												

	Program	No. of Awards	Value Range	Award Criteria: Class Stndg.	Grade Avg.	SAT/ ACT	Need Based	Other	Study Fields	Renew-ability	Restric-tions	Apply Date	Transfer
PENNSYLVANIA *(Continued)*													
Ursinus, Collegeville 19426	Steinbright	6	Tuition	5%		1250	N	T-L-R-I-0	A	3.2	S-S	A-2/15	N
	Ursinus Merit	Varies	1000-1/2 Tuit.	10%			N	T-L-R-I-0	A	2.67	N	A-2/15	N
Valley Forge Christian Phoenixville 19460	Academic	Varies	500-1000	20%			N		A	3.5	N	A	N
	Outstanding Achievement	20	To Tuition				N	E-L-R	A	N	D	B-5/1	N
	Talent	Varies	250-2000				N	E-T-I	A	N	N	B	N
	Presidential Scholarship	Varies	200-2000				Y	E-L-R-I-0	A	N	N	B	Y-2.0
Villanova U., 19085	Presidential	23	13200-13870	5%	3.5	1250	N	E-L-I-0	A	3.5	N	B-12/15	N
	Presidential African-American	4	15740-19640	10%	3.5	1200	N	L-R-I-0	A	3.0	M	B-1/15	N
	Villanova Ntl. Merit	5	500-2000				Y	L-R-0	A	Y	N	C-1/15	N
	Villanova Scholars	48	8000	5%		1250	N	L-0	A	3.25	N	C-1/15	N
	Villanova Commuting Scholar	19	5500	10%		1200	N	L-0	A	3.25	S	C-1/15	N
	Honors Program												
Washington & Jefferson Washington 15381	Presidential	60	10,000	10%		1200/27	N		A	3.3			
	Scholars	60	8000	10%		1000/23	N		A	3.1			
	Full-Tuition	10	18,300	10%		1200/27	N	I-L-R	A	3.3			
	AP Exams												
	Alumni Discount, Family Discount												
Waynesburg College, 15370	Achievement	Unlimited	1000	20%			N		A	3.0	N	D	N
	Alumni Council	1	1000		3.0		N	L-I-0	0	2.8	N	C-E/1	N
	Bonner Scholar	20	1870-2870	40%			Y	E-L-R-I-0	A	2.0	N	C-3/1	N
	English Department	1	1000	40%			N	E-T-L	0	3.0	N	C-3/1	N
	Grant	1	Total Costs		3.0		Y	E-L-R-I-0	0	3.0	S	C-3/1	N
	Hugh O'Brian	1	2000		3.0		N	L-I-0	A	3.0	N	C-3/1	N
	Leadership	10-15	1000-1500		3.0		N	E-L-R-I-0	A	3.0	N	C-3/1	N
	Ohio Honor	1	Tuit.-All Costs		3.0		N	E-L-R-I-0	0	3.0	0	C-3/1	N
	Outstanding	2	Full Tuition	5%			N	E-L-R-I-0	A	3.3	N	C-3/1	N
	PA Governors School	1	2000		3.0		N	L-I-0	A	3.0	N	C-3/1	N
	Presidential	Unlimited	4000	10%		1100/26	N	0	A	3.25	N	D	N
	Waynesburg Honor	Unlimited	2000	10%		1100/26	N	0	A	3.0	N	D	N
	Honors Program												

West Chester U., 19383	MAT	20	740-1480	20%		850	X	E-R-I-O	A	2.5	S-M	B-4/1	N
	Presidential	Varies	500	10%		1200	N	E-R-I-O	A	N	N	C	N
Westminster, New Wilmington 16142	Trustees	Varies	6000		3.7	1300/29	N	O	A	3.0	N	A-C	Y-3.3
	Westminster	Varies	4000		3.0	1200/27	N	O	A	2.9	N	A-C	Y-2.9
	Tower	Varies	5000		3.0	1300/29	N	O	A	3.0	N	A-C	Y-3.0
	Honor	Varies	Varies		3.0		N		A	2.9	N	B-5/1	N
	Val./Sal.	Varies	500-800	1%-2%			N		A	3.0	N	A-C	N
	Activity	Varies	Varies				N	T-L	A		N	B-5/1	N
	Honors Program												
Widener University, Chester 19013-5792	1/2 Tuition	Unlimited	1/2 Tuition		3.5	1100	N		A	Y			N
	1/3 Tuition	Unlimited	1/3 Tuition		3.3	1000	N		A	Y			N
	1/4 Tuition	Unlimited	1/4 Tuition		3.0	1000	N		A	Y			N
	Transfer Scholarships	Unlimited	2000-5000		2.8		N		O				Y
	AP Exams												
	Co-op												
	Honors Program												
Wilkes, Wilkes-Barre 18766	Presidential	Varies	1000	10%		1000	N	E-L-I-O	A	3.0	N	A-3/1	N
	Trustee	6	1270	5%		1270	N	O	A	3.25	N	A-12/15	N
	University Scholars	Varies	1000-5800	10%		1150	N	O	A	Y	N	A-12/15	N
	Achievement	Varies	1000-2500			950	N		A	2.0	N	A-3/1	N
	Music	Varies	1000-3000				N	T	A	2.0	N	A-3/1	Y
	Carpenter	Varies	1000-3500			1000	N		O	2.0	N	A-3/1	Y
	Honors Program												
Wilson, Chambersburg 17201	Presidential	2	1/2 Tuition	25%		1100	N	R	A	3.0	W-O	B-3/1	Y
	Sarah Wilson	1	Tuition	25%		1100	N	R	A	3.4	W-O	B-3/1	Y
	Dean's	4	1/4 Tuition	25%		1100	N	R	A	3.0	W-O	B-3/1	Y
	Curran Scholarship	Varies	4000				Y	E-L-R	A	Y	W-O	B-3/1	Y
	TASC	3-4	1500				N	E-L-R	A	Y	W	B-3/1	Y
York College of PA, 17405	Dean's	130	1/3 Tuition	40%		1150	N		A	3.2	N	2/1	N
	Presidential	9	1/2 Tuition	40%		1150	N		A	3.2	N	2/1	N
	Val./Sal.	Unlimited	1/2-3/4 Tuition	1-2		1150	N		A	3.2	N	A	N
	Trustee Honors	5	Tuition	20%		1200	N	E-O	A	3.2	N	2/1	N
	AP Exams												
	Distance Learning												
	Co-op, Internships												
	Honors Program												

	Program	No. of Awards	Value Range	Award Criteria: Class Stndg.	Award Criteria: Grade Avg.	Award Criteria: SAT/ ACT	Award Criteria: Need Based	Award Criteria: Other	Study Fields	Renew-ability	Restric-tions	Apply Date	Transfer
RHODE ISLAND													
Bryant, Smithfield 02917	Presidential	10	3750	10%		1100	N	L	A	3.2	N	A-D	N
Johnson & Wales, Providence 02903	Academic	Varies	500-1000	25%	3.0		N	0	0	2.75	0	C	N
	Outstanding Leader	Varies	500-5000				N	E-L-0	0	2.75	N	B	N
	Presidential/Honors	Varies	500-3000	25%	3.0	1000	N	0	0	2.75	0	C	N
	Recipe Contest	Varies	500-5000				N	R-T-0	A	2.75	N	B	N
	AP Exams												
	Family Discounts												
	Co-op, Internships												
	Honors Program												
Providence College, 02918	Achievement	50	2000-10000	10%	3.25	1200	Y		A	3.25	N	A-2/15	N
	Balfour Foundation	5	Tuition				N	L-0	A	Y	E	A	N
	Dean's	50	2000-14000	10%		1150	N	0	A	3.25	N	A	N
	Feinstein	10	2000	25%			N	L-0	0	Y	N	A	N
	Martin Luther King	32	Tuition	50%	2.0	900	N		A	2.0	N	A-2/15	Y
	RODDY	1-2	Tuition/Fees	5%	3.25	1300	N		0	3.25	0	A-D	N
	Southeast Asian	2	15935				Y		A	2.0	E	A-2/15	Y-2.0
	Textron	2	All Costs	10%	3.3	1200	N	L-0	0	3.25	E-W	A	N
	Honors Program												
Rhode Island, Providence 02908	Honors	70	500-Tuition	10%		X	N		A	Y	0	C	N
RI School of Design, Providence 02903	Advancement in the Arts	1	1/2 Tuition				Y		A	2.0	N	B-2/15	N
	RISD	Varies	100-7500	X	X	X	Y	E-T-R	0	Y	N	A-2/15	Y
	RISD Scholarships		200-18000	X	X	X	Y	E-T-R-0	A	2.0	N	C-2/15	Y
	Scholastic Art Awards	1	1/2 Tuition				Y		A	2.0	N	B-2/15	N
	Trustee Scholarships	3-5	1000-2500	X	X	X	N	E-T-R-0	A	2.0	N	A-2/15	N
	Honors Program												
U. of Rhode Island, Kingston 02881	Alumni Merit	10	750	X	X	X	N	0	A	3.0	S	B-2/15	N
	Centennial Scholars	1100	1000-Tuition	33%		X	N	I-0	A	N	0	A-12/15	N
	Honors Program												
SOUTH CAROLINA													
Anderson 29621	Presidential	Unlimited	2500-6000		3.6	1100/21	N			3.0			

	Academic Dean	Unlimited	2500-3000		3.0	1000/20	N			3.0			
	AP Exams												
	Family Discounts												
	Internships												
	Honors Program												
Benedict, Columbia 29204	Exceptional Freshman	Varies	All Costs	20%	3.0	950/20	Y		A	X	N	A-D	N
	Trustee	Varies	All Costs	10%	3.6	1060/23	Y	E-L-R-I-O	A	X	N	A-D	N
	Presidential	20	5000	25%	3.2	1000/20	Y	E-L-R-I-O	A	X	N	A-D	N
	Dean's	20	2000	25%	3.0	950	Y	E-L-R-I-O	A	X	N	A-D	N
Charleston Southern U., Charleston 29411	Board of Trustees	Varies	Tuition & Fees		3.3	1230/29	N	L-R-O	A	3.0	N	A-B-4/1	Y-3.5
	Board of Visitors	Varies	4000		3.0	1090/25	N	L-R-O	A	3.0	N	A-B-4/1	Y-3.3
	President's	Varies	All Costs		3.5	1360/32	N	L-R-O	A	3.0	N	A-B-4/1	Y-3.5
	Scholar Award	Varies	1500-2000	10%	3.1	900/21	N		A	3.1	N	B-4/1	Y-3.1
	Honors Program												
Citadel, Charleston 29409	Citadel Scholars	18	8211-11374	5%	3.5	1300	N	L-R-I-O	A	3.0	O	B-1/15	Y
	CDF Scholarship	77	1000		3.0		N	L-R-O	A	3.0	N	B-1/15	N
	Honors Program												
Clemson U., 29634	RF Poole	10	4000	10%		1320	N			3.0			
	IPTAY	20	2500	10%		1320	N			3.0			
	Trustee	35	3500	10%		1320	N	O		3.0			
Coker, Hartsville 29550	Coker Scholars	25	1500-5000	10%	3.0	1000	N	L-R-I-O	A	3.0	N	B-12/20	Y
	W.C. Coker	1	6000	10%	3.5	1200	N	L-R-I-O	A	3.2	N	B-12/20	Y
College of Charleston, 29424	Academic	Varies	300-2200	10%		1200	Y		A	3.0	N	A-1/15	Y-3.25
	COC General		200-2300	10%		1200	Y	L-O	A	3.0	N	A-1/15	Y-3.5
	Harrison Randolph	30	500-3000	20%	3.0	1200	Y		A	3.0	N	A-1/15	N
	Presidential	18	4000	10%	3.0	1200	N		A	3.4	S	A-1/15	N
	Honors Program												
Columbia College, 29203	Bonanna	2	Tuition		3.75	1400/32	N	I-R		3.0			
	Leadership	Varies	3000			1000/22	N	E-L-R	A	3.0			
	Presidential	Varies	1000-6000	25%	3.0	1100/24	N	I-R	A	3.0			
	AP Exams												
	Honors Program												
Converse, Spartanburg 29302	Converse Academic Grant	Varies	2000-9500		X		N		A	2.0	W	C	
	Converse Academic Scholar	Varies	2000-9500		X		N		A	3.0	W	C	
	Justine VR Milliken	10	11000	5%	3.5	1200	N	I-O	A	3.0	W	C	Y
	Music Dean Honor	Varies	500-2000		2.5	900	Y	T-O	O	2.5	W	D	Y

	Program	No. of Awards	Value Range	Award Criteria: Class Stndg.	Grade Avg.	SAT/ ACT	Need Based	Other	Study Fields	Renew-ability	Restric-tions	Apply Date	Transfer
SOUTH CAROLINA *(Continued)*													
Converse, Spartanburg 29301 *(Continued)*	Virginia T. Self	1	19250	10%	3.5	1200	N	0	A	3.0	W	C	N
	Walter S. Montgomery	4	10000	10%	3.0	1100	N	E-L-R-I-O	A	3.0	W	B-11/1	N
	Honors Program												
Erskine, Due West 29639	Academic	Varies	1000-8250	X	X	X	N	L-R-I	A	Y	N	A-C	N
	E.B. Kennedy	2	Total Costs	X	X	X	N	0	A	3.5	N	B-10/15	N
	Presidential	Varies	1000-3100	X	X	X	N	L-R-I	A	Y	N	A-C	N
Francis Marion, Florence 29501	Presidential	2	6058			1250	N	0	A	3.5	N	A-B-11/1	N
	FM Scholars	Varies	2920			1100	N	0	A	3.25	N	A-B-11/1	N
	Art/Music	Varies	100-500				N	T	0	Y	N	C	Y
	Honors Program												
Furman U., Greenville 29613	Academic	Varies	3000-Tuition	5%		1350	N	E-I-L	A	3.0	N	A-2/1	N
	Music	Varies	1000-10,000				N	T	A	2.0		B-2/1	
	AP Exams												
	Co-op, Internships												
Lander, Greenwood 29649	Presidential	Unlimited	All Costs	10%		1350	N	R-O	A	3.0	N	A-12/1	N
	Lander Scholar	20	Tuition	10%		1200	N	E-L-R-O	A	3.0	N	A	N
	Dean's Scholar	Unlimited	2000	20%		1150	N	0	A	3.0	N	A	N
	Trustee Scholar	Unlimited	1500	20%		1150	N	0	A	3.0	N	A	N
Limestone, Gaffney 29340	Presidential	10	500-1500	25%	3.0		N	L-R-O	A	3.0	N	A	N
	Founders Scholarship	Varies	to 1500		3.0	900	N		A	Y	N	C	N
	Honors	Varies	to 5000		3.0	1000	N		A	Y	N	C	N
	AP Exams												
	Alumni Discounts, Family Discounts												
	Co-op, Internships												
	Honors Program												
Morris, Sumter 29150	Presidential	10	500	20%			N		A	Y	N	B-4/15	N
	Val/Sal	Unlimited	1000-1500	1-2			N		A	Y	N	B-4/15	N
Newberry College, 29108	Founders	Varies	2500-5700	10%		1200/28	N	L-R-I-O	A	3.0	N	B-1/15	N
	Presidential	Varies	1800	15%		X	N	L	A	3.0	N	A-D	N
	Academic	Varies	1000-6600	10%	3.5	1000/23	N	E-T-R-I-O	A	3.0	N	A-1/31	N

	Talent	Varies	500-1500	50%	2.5		N	T-I-O	A	2.0	N	B-3/15	Y-2.0
	Transfer	Varies	1000				N	L-R-O	A	3.0	O	B-D	Y
Presbyterian, Clinton 29325	Alumni	10	8000	X	X	X	N	E-L-R-I-O	A	Y	N	B-12/1	N
	Belk	96	4500	X	X	X	N	E-L-R-I-O	A	Y	N	B-12/1	N
	Dean's	3	10000	X	X	X	N	E-L-R-I-O	A	Y	N	B-12/1	N
	Dillard-Elliott	46	4000	X	X	X	N	E-L-R-I-O	A	Y	N	B-12/1	N
	Founder's	4	9000	X	X	X	N	E-L-R-I-O	A	Y	N	B-12/1	N
	Multicultural Leadership	7	7500				N	T-L-R	A	Y	E	B-2/15	N
	Quattlebaum	2	Total Costs	X	X	X	N	E-L-R-I-O	A	Y	N	B-12/1	N
	Southeastern	7	3500	X	X	X	N	E-L-R-I-O	A	Y	N	B-12/1	N
	Honors Program												
SC State, Orangeburg 29117	Presidential	Varies	1000	20%		900	N	L-R	A	Y	N	C	N
Southern Wesleyan, Central 29630	Academic	Varies	1000-4000		3.2	1000	N		A	3.2	N	A	Y-3.2
	President's	Varies	1/2 Tuition			1400/33	N		A	Y	N	B-C	N
	Future Leaders	5	2000	30%	3.0	850/20	N		A	Y	N	B-C	N
U. of South Carolina, Aiken 29801	Academic	120	5000	10%	3.0	1000	Y	L-R	A	3.5	N	B-2/15	Y-3.0
	Fine Arts	30	200-1600	X	X	700	N	T	A	X	N	C	Y
U. of South Carolina, Columbia 29208	Alumni	40	3500	10%	3.25	1200/28	N	E-T-L-R-I	A	3.0			
	Carolina Scholars	20	4000-7000	2%	3.75	1470	N	E-I-L-R	A	3.0			
	McNair	10	8000-12,000	5%	3.75	1400	N	E-I-L-R		3.0			
	University Scholars	500	1500	10%	3.5	1300	N		A	3.0			
	AP Exams												
	Honors Program, Honors College												
U. of South Carolina, Spartanburg 29303	Chancellor Scholars	Varies	Tuition	20%	3.5	1200/27	N		A	3.0	N	A-C	N
	Valedictorian	Varies	Tuition	1			N		A	3.0	S-O	A-C	N
	Palmetto Scholars	Varies	1/2 Tuition	20%	3.0	1000/21	N		A	3.0	S	A-C	N
	Upstate Transfer Scholar	Varies	1/2 Tuition		3.25		N		A	3.0	S	A-C	N
U. of South Carolina, Sumter 29150-	Scholarship Opportunities	65	300-2000	50%	2.5	850	N	E-L	A	Y	O	C	Y
	Honors Program												
Voorhees College, Denmark 29042	Academic	Varies	700-3000	5%	3.0		Y	L-R	A	3.0	N	B-6/1	N
Winthrop, Rock Hill 29733	Alumni Honor	Varies	1500	25%		1100/24	N		A	N	N	A	N
	Founders'	Varies	3500	10%		1250/28	N		A	Y	N	A-C	N
	International Baccalaureate	Varies	Full Tuition			1200/26	N		A	Y	N	C	N
	President's Scholar	Varies	1500				N		A	Y	N	C	N
	Tillman Scholar	Varies	Out of State Fees	25%		1100/24	N		A	Y	N	C	N
	Trustees'	Varies	Tuition & Board	10%		1350/31	N		A	2.75	N	A-C	N
	Winthrop Scholar	Varies	2500	10%		1250/28	N		A	3.0	N	B-C	N
	Winthrop Scholar	Varies	2500	10%		1250/28	N		A	Y	N	A-C	N

	Program	No. of Awards	Value Range	Award Criteria: Class Stndg.	Grade Avg.	SAT/ ACT	Need Based	Other	Study Fields	Renew-ability	Restric-tions	Apply Date	Transfer
SOUTH CAROLINA *(Continued)*													
Wofford, Spartanburg 29301	Woffard Scholars	Varies	2000-19000	10%	3.0	1150	Y	E-L-R-I-O	A	2.75	N	C-12/1	N
	General Academic	Varies	500-2000	X	X	X	Y		A	2.5	N	C-3/1	Y-2.5
SOUTH DAKOTA													
Augustana, Sioux Falls 57197	English	Varies	1000	X	X	X	N	E-T-R	O	Y	N	B-3/1	N
	Heritage Award	Varies	1600-3200	25%		22	N		A	3.0	N	A-2/1	N
	ProMusica	Varies	200-3000				N	E-T-R-I-O	A	Y	N	B-2/1	Y
	Regents	30	4250-5000	5%		25	N	E-T-L-R-I-O	A	3.3	N	B-2/1	N
	Regents Scholarship		Full Tuition	5%	3.5	28	N	L-R-O	A	3.3	N	A-2/15	N
	Scholar	Unlimited	500-3500	X	X	X	N	L-R-O	A	3.0	N	B-C	Y
	Transfer	5	3500		3.0		N	L-R-O	A	3.2	N	A-2/15	Y
Black Hills State, Spearfish 57783	Incentive	100	500-1000	33%		21	N	L	A	3.0	N	B-2/15	N
	AP Exams												
	Distance Learning												
Dakota State, Madison 57042	Brinker Academic	20-50	100-2000	20%	3.0	872/22	Y	T-L-R-O	A	3.0	N	A-3/1	Y-3.0
	CitiBank	10	2000	10%	3.0	1150/26	Y	L-R-O	O	3.0	S	A-3/1	Y-3.0
	General/Academic	50	100-1000		3.0		N	L-R	A	N	N	A	Y
	Gill/INFS	10	1600		3.5		Y	R	A	3.5	N	B-4/1	Y
	Info Systems	4	1400		3.25		N	E-L-R	O	3.5	N	A-2/15	Y
	Honors Program												
Dakota Wesleyan, Mitchell 57301	Randall	5	4700-6000		3.8	26	N	T-L-R-I-O	A	3.0	N	B-2/15	N
	Trustee	15	3500-4600		3.5	23	N		A	2.75	N	B-2/15	N
	Presidential	40	2600-3400		3.0	20	N		A	2.25	N	D	N
	Tiger Award	60	500-2500		2.5	18	N		A	2.0	N	D	N
	Transfer	50	500-2000		2.5		N		A	2.5	N	D	Y-2.5
Huron College, Huron 57350	Academic	60	1000		3.0	18	N			2.8		B-C	
	Athletic	Varies	7878				N					D	
	Boys and Girls State	Unlimited	500					O				B-C	
	Dean's	4	3500		3.5	25	N			3.2		B-C	
	Faculty Honors	20	2500		3.4	24	N			3.0		B-C	
	Huron University Grant	Varies	Varies				Y					D	
	Presidential	4	7878		3.7	27	N		A	3.5		B-C	

Mt. Marty, Yankton 57078	Academic	Unlimited	500-2000		3.0	24	N		A	3.0	Y	C-3/1	Y-3.0
	Catholic Youth	Unlimited	Varies		2.0		N	E-L-R	A	2.5	Y	C-3/1	Y
	Presidential	2	7000-8808		4.0	30	N	E-I-L-R	A	3.5	N	2/18	N
	Trustee	44	4400-7000		3.5	28	N	E-I-L-R	A	3.3	N	2/18	N
	Benedictine	30	3500-4400		3.3	26	N	E-I-L-R	A	3.0	N	2/18	N
	AP Exams												
	Family Discounts												
National, Rapid City 57709	Excellence	65	900-1600		3.5		X		A	3.5	N	B-D	Y
	Good Standing	Varies	300-1200		2.5		Y		A	2.5	N	B-D	Y-2.5
	Honor	100	300-1200		3.0		Y		A	3.0	N	B-D	Y
Northern State, Aberdeen 57401	Dean's	Varies	1/2 Tuition	25%		25	N	E-R	A	N	N	B-2/15	N
	Incentive	Varies	1/4 Tuition	33%		21	N		A	N	N	B-3/31	N
	President's Meritorious	Varies	Tuition & Fees	10%		28	N	E-R	A	3.0	N	B-2/15	N
	Leadership	Varies	1/4 Tuition				N	L-R	A	N	N	B-2/15	N
	Vice-President's	Varies	Tuition	10%		28	N	E-R	A	N	N	B-2/15	N
	AP Exams												
	Distance Learning												
	Honors Program												
SD School of Mines & Technology, Rapid City 57701	SDSM&T	499	100-2500	X	X	X	X	0	A	X	0	B-2/15	N
	Academic	Varies	200-3000	10%	3.0	1200/25	N	E-R	A	3.0	N	B-2/15	N
South Dakota State, Brookings 57007	Departmental	300	300-1000	25%	3.3	23	N	0	A	N	N	B-1/25	N
	Leaders for Tomorrow	180	600-1000	15%	3.7	27	N	0	A	N	N	B-1/25	N
	Briggs/May	60	1500-3000	3%	3.9	29	N	I-0	A	3.0	N	B-1/25	N
	Honors Program												
University of Sioux Falls, 57105	Academic Merit	5	7100			30	N	E-L-R-0	A	3.5	N	B-2/1	N
	Salsbury	5	5100			26	N	E-L-R-I	A	3.2	N	B-2/1	N
	Trustee	5	3300			26	N		A	3.2	N	B-2/1	N
	Presidential	5	2500			26	N		A	3.2	N	B-2/1	N
	Honors Program												
U. of South Dakota, Vermillion 57069	USD Foundation	1150	50-2000		3.2	25	N	0	A	3.2	N	B-C	Y
	Talent/Merit	Varies	50-2500		3.0	25	N		A	3.0	N	C	Y-3.2
TENNESSEE													
Austin Peay State, Clarksville 37040	Academic	Varies	500-900	25%	3.0	20	N	L-R-0	A	2.8	S	B-2/15	N
	Academic Honors	Varies	2000	10%	3.0	24	N	L-R-0	A	3.2	S	B-2/15	N
	General	Varies	300-1500	25%	3.0	19	N	T-L-R-0	A	Y	0	B-2/15	Y
	Kimbrough	Varies	500-2000	10%	3.0	26	N	L-R-0	A	3.2	S	B-2/15	N
	Leadership	Varies	1500	25%	3.0	20	N	L-R-0	A	3.0	S	B-2/15	Y

	Program	No. of Awards	Value Range	Award Criteria: Class Stndg.	Award Criteria: Grade Avg.	Award Criteria: SAT/ ACT	Award Criteria: Need Based	Award Criteria: Other	Study Fields	Renew-ability	Restric-tions	Apply Date	Transfer
TENNESSEE *(Continued)*													
Austin Peay State, Clarksville 37040 *(Continued)*	Martin Luther King	Varies	2000	25%	3.0	19	N	L-R-O	A	2.75	S	B-2/15	N
	Multi-cultural	Varies	2000	25%	3.0	19	N	L-R-O	A	2.8	S	B-2/15	N
	Performance	Varies	100-1500				N	T	A	Y	N	B-2/15	Y
	Presidential	Varies	1000	25%	3.0	21	N	L-R-O	A	3.0	S	B-2/15	N
Belmont, Nashville 39203	Merit	200	1000-5000	10%	3.25	1170/26	N	L-R-O	A	3.0			
	Presidential	4	Tuition	5%	3.5	1300/29	N	I-L-R-O	A	3.0			
	AP Exams												
	Co-op, Internships												
	Honors Program												
Bethel, McKenzie 38201	Academic	Varies	1800-2400	X		800	Y	E-R-I-O	A	3.25	N	B-3/31	Y-3.25
	Athletic Scholarship	25	1000-9736	50%	2.0	18	N	T-L-R-I-O	A	2.0	N	A	Y-2.0
	Hendrix Scholarship	2	1000-6636		3.0	23	N	E-T-L-R-I	A	3.5	N	A	N
	Scholarship	4	1000-4424		3.0	23	N	E-T-L-R-I	A	3.25	N	A	N
Bryan, Dayton 37321	Academic	Varies	1500		3.4	1100/24	N		A	3.25	S	B-5/1	Y-3.25
	Academic	Varies	2500		3.6	1180/26	N		A	3.5	S	B-5/1	Y-3.5
	Athletic	12-20	250-9000		2.5	860/18	N	T-I-O	A	2.0	N	B-5/1	Y-2.0
	Dean's	Varies	4000		3.6	1180/26	N	E-I-O	A	3.5	O	B-1/31	N
	Music	8-12	250-2000		2.5	860/18	N	T-I-O	O	2.0	N	B-4/1	Y-2.0
	Presidential	6	6000		3.6	1180/26	N	O	A	3.5	O	B-1/1	N
	Honors Program												
Carson-Newman, Jefferson City 37760	Academic	Varies	Varies		3.0	1100/24	X		A	3.0	N		
	Presidential Honors	Varies	3500-5000		3.3	1300/29	X		A	3.0	N		Y-3.5
	Presidential Excellence	5	Tuition		3.6	1350/30	X		A	3.25	N		
	AP Exams												
	Family Discounts												
	Honors Program												
Crichton College, Memphis 38111	Community	30	2000		2.75	700/18	Y	E-L-R	O	2.75	N	B-2/15	Y-2.75
	Director's Merit	16	5000-20000		3.5	39	Y	E-L-R-O	O	Y	N	B-2/15	Y-3.5
	Alumni	6	2000				Y	E-L-R	O	Y	N	B-2/15	Y
	Teacher Education	6	1500		3.0	870/22	Y	E-L-R	O	3.0	N	B-2/15	Y
	Academic Achievement	13	2000-8000		3.0	870/22	Y	E-L-R-O	O	Y	N	B-2/15	Y-3.0
	Leadership	17	1000-4000		2.5	700/21	Y	E-L-R-O	O	Y	N	B-2/15	Y-2.5

Christian Brothers, Memphis 38104	Academic	120	750-2200		3.0	25	N	R-I-O	A	Y	N	A-C	Y
	DeLaSalle	Varies	1000-3000	25%	3.0	1070/25	N	E-L-I-O	A	3.0	O	B-2/15	Y
	Lasallian	75	2000-5000		3.0	1000/22	N		A	2.75	N	A-2/15	Y-3.0
	Plough	3	Tuition	10%	3.5	1330/30	N	O	A	3.0	N	B-12/1	N
	Presidential	75	4000-6000		3.2	1100/25	N	E-I-L	A	2.75	N	B-2/15	Y-3.0
	Trustee	100	5000-8000		3.3	1200/27	N	E-I-L	A	2.75	N	A-2/15	Y-3.0
	AP Exams												
	Alumni Discounts												
	Internships												
	Honors Program												
Crichton, Memphis 38111	Academic	Varies	Varies	10%			N	L-R	A	3.0	N	B-5/1	Y-3.0
	Honors Program												
Cumberland U., Lebanon 37087	Academic	Varies	100-3900	15%	3.0	20	N		A	3.0	N	B-5/15	Y
	Leadership	Varies	Varies	X	X		N	L	A	2.8	N	B-5/15	Y
	Honors Program												
David Lipscomb, Nashville 37204	Academic	Unlimited	200-5445	10%		910/22	N			3.0	O	B	Y-3.0
	Honor	Unlimited	100-Tuition	10%	3.0	910/22	N		A	3.0	N	B-D	Y
	Memorials	Limited	150-4000				N			2.0	O	B	Y-2.0
	Music	Varies	150-600		3.0		N	T-O	O	3.0	N	B-D	Y
	Special Ability	Limited	150-1200				N	T-L		2.0	O	B	Y-2.0
	Honors Program												
East Tennessee State U. Johnson City 37614	Alumni	Varies	1000			1150/28	N	L	A	3.2	N	B-2/15	Y
	Honors Program	20	Total Costs	5%	3.7	29	N	E-T-L-R-O	A	3.25	N	B-2/15	
	Academic Performance	100	2188	10%	3.5	26	N		A	2.5	S	B-2/15	Y-3.2
	Minority	20	1200		2.5	750/19	N		A	2.5	N	B-2/15	N
	Honors Program												
Fisk U., Nashville 37203	Honor	10	2500	10%	3.4		N	R	A	Y	S	A-D	N
	Nat'l Achvmt. Match	Unlimited	250-1500				Y	O	A	Y	N	A-D	Y
Freed-Hardeman, Henderson 38340	Academic	Unlimited	200-1500		3.25	22	N		A	3.0	N	A-D	Y
	Academic 2	Varies	300-6930		3.25	850/20	N	E-T-L-R-O	A	3.0	N	A-D	N
	Academic Honor	Unlimited	400-1600		3.2	880/22	N	O	3.0	N	S	A	Y-3.0
	Chancellor's Honor	Unlimited	Tuition		3.75	1200/30	N	L-R-O	4	N	S	B-C	N
	Presidential Honor	Unlimited	1/2 Tuition		3.5	1060/27	N	L-R-O	3.25	N	S	B-C	N
	*Honors Program												
King, Bristol 37620	Dean's Scholarship	Varies	1500		3.2	1200/27	N		A	3.0	N	A-C	Y-3.2
	Early Scholars	Varies	2500	20%	3.0	1100/24	N		A	3.0	N	A-2/15	N
	Honor Scholarship	Varies	1000		3.0	1100/24	N		A	3.0	N	A-C	Y-3.0
	King Scholar	2	Tuition	10%	3.2	1300/28	N	E-I-O	A	3.25	N	C-3/1	N

	Program	No. of Awards	Value Range	Award Criteria					Study Fields	Renew-ability	Restric-tions	Apply Date	Transfer
				Class Stndg.	Grade Avg.	SAT/ ACT	Need Based	Other					
TENNESSEE *(Continued)*													
King, Bristol 37620 *(Continued)*	Maclellan Scholar	1	12700	10%	3.2	1300/28	N	E-R-I-O	A	3.25	N	C-3/1	N
	Presidential	Varies	2500		3.4	1300/29	N		A	3.0	N	A-D	Y
	Honors Program												
Knoxville College, Knoxville 37921	C. Newcombe Foundation	5-10	1000		3.0		Y	R	A	3.0	O	A-D	Y-3.0
	Institutional	40-60	100-4000		3.0		Y	L-R-O	A	3.0	N	A	Y-3.0
	Leadership Awards	3-6	500-1000		3.0		N	L-R	A	3.0	O	A-D	Y-3.0
	Presbyterian College	5-10	Varies		X	X	Y	L-R-O	A	Y	D-O	B-C	N
	Presidential/Trustees	10	100-7900	X	3.5	X	Y	E-L-R-O	A	3.5	N	B-C	N
	Williams Endowed	3	3000		3.25		N	L-R	A	3.25	O	B-4/12	N
	Co-op, Internships												
	Honors Program												
Lane, Jackson 38301	Academic	Varies	400-1600	10%	3.0	15	Y	R	A	3.0	N	B-5/1	Y
	William Graves	Varies	2976-5876	10%	3.7	20	N	R	A	3.0	N	B-5/1	N
	Lane 1	Varies	3504-5976	10%	3.0	15	Y	R-I	A	3.0	N	B-5/1	Y-3.0
	Lane 2	Varies	3504-5976	10%	3.0	15	Y	R-I	A	3.0	N	B-5/1	Y-3.0
	Honors Program, Honors College												
Lee, Cleveland 37311	Academic	Varies	To Tuition			X	N		A	Y	N	A-D	Y-3.7
	Centennial		5232			1410/31	N		A	3.0	O	B-C	N
	Dean's		2616			1030/24	N		A	N	O	B-C	N
	Honor		2616		3.7		N		A	3.7	O	A-C	Y-3.7
	Presidential		5232			1150/27	N		A	N	O	B-C	N
	Honors Program												
LeMoyne-Owen, Memphis 38126	Endowments	60	5250-6000	Top 20	2.5	X	Y	L-R	A	Y	N	A-B-D	Y-2.5
	Honors	Unlimited	1500-9800	Top 10	3.0	1000/21	Y	E-L-R	A	3.2	N	B-4/15	Y-3.0
	M & J Plough	5	1235-2470	20%	3.3	19	N	E-R-I-O	A	Y	S	B-2/28	N
	Presidential	Unlimited	500-6000	Top 10	3.0	20	Y	L-R	A	3.5	N	B-4/15	Y-3.0
	Honors Program												
Lincoln Memorial U., Harrogate 37752	Lincoln Scholars	20	3900	25%	3.5	1050/25	N	E-L-R	A	3.2	N	A-3/1	N
	Presidential	20	5200	15%	3.5	1050/25	N	E-L-R	A	3.2	N	A-3/1	N
	Trustees'	15	Tuition	10%	3.5	1150/28	N	E-L-R	A	3.3	N	A-3/1	N
	AP Exams												

Maryville College, 37804	Bonner Scholars	15-20	3050				Y	E-L-R-I-0	A	2.0	N	B-3/1	N
	Church and College	15	2000				N	E-L-R-I-0	A	2.0	D	B-3/1	Y
	Ethnic Minority	15	1500		3.0		N	L-R-0	A	2.0	E	B-3/1	Y
	Fine Arts	25	500-4000			930/20	N	T-L-R-0	A	2.0	N	B-3/1	Y
	MC Scholar	Varies	2500-8000		3.0	900/21	N		A	2.5	N	A-4/1	Y
	Presidential	15	Tuition		3.5	1200/27	N	E-L-I-0	A	3.25	N	B-2/1	N
	Honors Program												
Memphis College of Art, 38104	Art	50	5125				N	T- R-0	0	Y	N	A-D	Y
	Merit	50	5125				N	T- R-0	0	Y	N	A-D	Y
	Portfolio	100	5125				N	E-T-R-I-0	A	3.0	0	A-D	Y
Middle Tennessee State U., Murfreesboro 37132	Leadership	20	1800	X			N	E-T-L-R	A	2.8	S	B-3/15	N
	Academic Service	Varies	1800	5%		19	Y		A	2.8	S	B-3/15	Y
	Presidential	Unlimited	3275		3.5	29	N		A	3.0	N	A-3/15	N
	Otis L. Floyd	10	4200		3.2	980/25	N	E-L-R	A	3.0	E	B-3/15	N
	Honors Program												
Milligan College, 37682	Honors	Varies	500-6000		3.0	1050/25	Y	E-L-R-I-0	A	2.5	N	B-6/1	Y-3.0
	Presidential	Unlimited	200-1000		2.25	16	Y	E-R	A	2.25	N	B-C	Y-2.25
	Music	Varies	100-750		2.6	16	Y	T	A	2.6	N	B-C	Y-2.6
Rhodes, Memphis 38112	Bellingrath/Hyde	4	Tuition/Fees	1%	3.9	1500/32	N	L-R-I-0	A	3.0	N	B-1/15	N
	Cambridge	17	12300	2%	3.9	1490/32	N	L-R	A	3.0	N	B-2/1	N
	Dean's	5	8200-13000	10%	3.7	1280/28	Y	T-L-R	A	2.5	E	B-2/1	Y-3.7
	Fine Arts	8	4100-12300				Y	T-R-E-0		2.25	N	C-2/1	Y
	Morse	5	16400	1%	3.9	1520/33	N	L-R	A	3.0	N	B-2/1	Y
	Presidential	50	5000	7%	3.8	1310/29	N	L-R	A	2.5	N	B-2/1	N
	Rhodes Award	Varies	100-400	10%	3.5		N	L-I-0	A	2.5	N	A-2/1	Y
	University	36	8200	4%	3.9	1380/31	N	T-L-R	A	2.5	N	B-2/1	Y-3.7
	Honors Program												
Tennessee Tech. U., Cookeville 38505	University Academic	130	Fees	10%	3.0	17	N	R	A	Y	S	B-2/15	N
	Honors Program												
Tennessee Temple U., Chattanooga 37404	High School	Varies	Varies	10%			N	R	A	N	N	B-3/1	N
Tennessee Wesleyan, Athens 37303	Academic Recognition	20	1000-3000		3.0	880/21	N	L-R	A	3.0	N	A-3/1	N
	Leadership Recognition	10	1000-3000	1	2.5		N	L-R	A	3.3	N	A-3/1	N
	Neff Scholarship	5	Tuition		3.5	1180/28	N	L-R	A	3.0	N	A-3/1	N
	Wesleyan	Unlimited	1/2 Tuition		3.0	1050/25	N	L-R	A	3.0	N	A-3/1	N
	Honors Program												
Trevecca Nazarene, Nashville 37203	Dean's	Unlimited	1000-2000		3.3		Y		A	3.3	N	A-D	Y-3.3
	President's	Unlimited	1000-2000			21	Y		A	3.3	N	A-D	Y-3.3

	Program	No. of Awards	Value Range	Award Criteria: Class Stndg.	Grade Avg.	SAT/ ACT	Need Based	Other	Study Fields	Renew- ability	Restric- tions	Apply Date	Transfer
TENNESSEE *(Continued)*													
Tusculum, Greeneville 37743	Academic	Varies	1500	10%	3.0	885/21	N	I-O	A	3.0	N	A-4/1	Y-3.0
	Alumni	25	1000	50%	2.50	850/21	N	L-O	A	2.50	N	B-D	N
	Board of Trustees	6	3/4 Tuition	15%	3.0	1000/22	N	L-O	A	3.0	N	A-D	Y
	Tusculum Scholars	15	1500-2500	25%	3.0	900/23	N	L-O	A	3.0	N	B-D	Y
	Presidential Scholars	10	3000-5000	10%	3.25	1050/27	N	L-O	A	3.25	N	B-D	N
Union U., Jackson 38301	ACT	225	600-1000			24	N	E-T-L-I-O	A	3.0	N	B-5/1	Y-3.0
	Top 15%	250	800-1000	15%			N	T-L-I-O	A	3.0	N	B-5/1	Y-3.0
	Scholars of Excellence	19-20	Tuition	15%			N	E-T-L-R-O	A	3.0	N	B-3/1	Y-3.25
	Honors Program												
University of Memphis, Memphis 38152	Academic	Unlimited	1000-2500		3.5	1200/26	N	L-I-O	A	3.25	N	B-1/1	N
	Academic Excellence	Varies	2800-3000	10%	3.25	1200/30	N	L-R-I	A	Y	N	B-1/15	N
	Adult Scholarship	Varies	1/2-Full Fees				N	L-R	A	2.5	O	B-4/15	Y
	Comm. Coll. Minority	Varies	Fees & Books				N		A	2.8	S-E-O	B-4/1	Y-2.8
	Comm. Coll. Presidential	Varies	Fees				N	R	A	2.8	S-O	B-4/1	Y
	Community College	Varies	Fees & Books				N		A	2.8	S-O	B-4/1	Y-3.5
	Early Scholars	Varies	Fees	20%	3.5	1060/27	N		A	3.0	N	B-1/15	N
	Honors	Varies	Varies	25%	X	X	N	E-L-R-I-O	A	X	O	B-C	Y-3.0
	Humphreys Merit	Varies	Varies	10%	X	X	N	L-R-I-O	A	Y	N	B-1/15	N
	Humphreys Presidential	Varies	Varies	10%	3.25	1200/30	N	L-R-I-O	A	Y	N	B-1/15	N
	Humphreys-Herff Engineer	5	Varies		3.25	1200/30	N	L-R-I-O	O	Y	N	B-1/15	N
	Minority	Varies	Varies	25%	3.0	780/20	N	L-R	A	2.8	S-E	B-3/1	N
	Regents	Varies	Fees	25%	3.0	1020/26	N	R	A	2.8	S	B-3/1	N
	Valedictorian		Varies	1		Varies	N	R	A	3.0	S	B-3/1	N
	Honors Program												
U. of Tennessee, Chattanooga 37402	Chancellor's	Varies	5000		4.0	31	N		A	3.5			
	Dean's	Varies	2500-3500		3.0	17	N		A	3.5			
	Provost	Varies	2500		3.5	26	N		A	3.5			
	AP Exams												
	Distance Learning												
	Co-op, Internships												
	Honors Program												

U. of Tennessee, Knoxville 37996	Alumni Freshman	Varies	850-2500		X	X	X		A	Y	S	A-3/1	N
	Andrew D. Holt	8	2500		X	X	N		A	Y		A-2/1	
	Fred M. Roddy Merit	Varies	2500		X	X	N		A	Y		A-2/1	
	Frederick Brown	4	2500		X	X	N		A	Y		A-2/1	
	Freshman (4-Year)	25	2500		X	X	N		A	Y	S	A-3/1	N
	Herbert S. Walters	25	2000		X	X	Y	O	A	Y		A-2/1	
	Minority Undergraduates	Varies	1000-2000				N	O	A	Y	E	C	
	National Merit	Varies	800-2000				N	O	A	Y		C	
	Reeder-Siler	1	1000		X	X	N		A	Y		A-2/1	
	Robert R. Neyland	4	2500		X	X	N		A		N	B-2/1	
	Tennessee Scholar	Varies	4000		X	X	N	E-T-R-I	A	3.25	N	B-2/1	Y
	Whittle Scholar	Varies	7000		X	X	N	E-T-L-R-O	A	3.25	N	B-1/1	N
	Honors Program												
U. of the South, Sewanee 37375	Wilkins	24	1/2 Tuition	X	X	X	N	E-L-I-O	A	3.0	N	B-1/1	N
	Benedict	3	All Costs	X	X	X	N	E-L-I-O	A	3.0	N	B-1/1	N
	Regents	4	1/2 Tuition	X	X	X	N	E-L-I-O	A	3.0		B-1/1	N
	Lancaster	1	1/2 Tuition	X	X	X	N	E-L-I-O	A	3.0	N	B-1/1	N
	Baldwin	2	1/2 Tuition	X	X	X	N	E-L-I-O	A	3.0	O	B-1/1	N
	AP Exams												
	Internships												
Vanderbilt U., Nashville 37212	G. Vanderbilt Honor	5	1000	10%		1150/26	N	O	A	2.5	E	A-D	N
	Grantland Rice	1	7500				N	E-T-O	A	3.0	N	A-2/1	N
	Honor	60	500-Tuition	5%		1300/30	N	E-T-L-R	A	3.0	N	A-2/1	N
TEXAS													
Abilene Christian U., 79699	Leadership	80-100	1000			940/20	N	T-L-R-O	A	2.5	D	A-B-2/15	N
	Academic	Unlimited	500-2750			1020/25	N		A	3.0	N	B-D	Y-3.5
	Presidential	20	1/2-Full Tuition		3.5	1170/28	N	E-L-R-I-O	A	3.2	O	A-B-2/18	N
	Trustee	Unlimited	500-4500			1020/22	N	O	A	3.0	N	A-D	N
	Transfer	Varies	1000-2000		3.25		N	O	A	3.0	N	A-C	Y-3.25
	Honors Program												
Angelo State U., San Angelo 76909	Carr Academic	900	1000-6000	15%	90	1140/25	Y	T-L-R	A	3.0	N	B-3/1	Y
Austin College, Sherman 75090	Presidential	10	Tuition	5%	3.9	1400/31	N	E-I-R	A	3.5	N	B-2/1	N
	Leadership	15	10000	25%	3.0	1200/27	N	E-L-R-I	A	3.0	N	B-5/1	Y-3.25
	Achievement	Varies	2000-10000	25%	3.0	1100/25	N	O	A	3.0	N	B-3/15	N
Baylor University, Waco 76076	Provost	Unlimited	1500	15%		1170/26	N			3.0			
	Presidential	Unlimited	2500	5%		1200/27	N		A	3.0			
	Achievement	Unlimited	1000	50%		1200/27	N		A	3.0			

	Program	No. of Awards	Value Range	Award Criteria: Class Stndg.	Grade Avg.	SAT/ ACT	Need Based	Other	Study Fields	Renew- ability	Restric- tions	Apply Date	Transfer
TEXAS *(Continued)*													
Baylor University, Waco 76076 *(Continued)*	AP Exams												
	Honors Program												
Concordia Lutheran, Austin 78705	Distinguished Student	Varies	1/2 Tuition		3.5	1150/25	Y	R	A	3.25	N	B-7/1	Y-3.75
	Presidential	20	to 1/2 Tuition		3.0	900/20	Y	T-L-R	A	N	N	B-7/1	Y-3.0
	Superior Student	Varies	Tuition		3.8	1250/27	Y	R	A	3.5	N	B-7/1	Y-3.9
Corpus Christi State U., 78412	Fine Arts	To 63	200-600		3.0		N	E-T-R-I	A	3.0	N	B-3/1	Y-3.0
	Honors	Varies	600-2000		3.0		N	I	A	3.0	N	B-4/1	Y
	Academic	To 170	600-1500		3.0		N	E-L-R-O	A	3.0	N	B-3/1	Y-3.0
Dallas Baptist U., 75211	College	Varies	2/3 Tuition	20%		930/22	N	R-I-O	A	3.0	N	A-4/1	Y
	Dean's	Varies	Tuition	10%		1020/24	N	R-I-O	A	3.3	N	A-4/1	Y
	Distinguished Pres.	Varies	Tuition	10%	3.8	1040/24	N	E-R-O	A	3.3	N	B-3/1	N
	Presidential	Varies	2/3 Tuition	20%		950/22	N	E-R-I-O	A	3.0	N	B-3/1	N
	Academic Excellence	Varies	1/4-Full Tuition			1250/28	N	E-L-R-I-O	A	3.0	O	B-1/15	N
	Christian Leadership	Varies	1/4-Full Tuition				N	E-L-R-I-O	A	2.5	D-O	Y-1/15	Y
Dallas Christians, Dallas 75234	Academic	6	200-1200	10%	3.5		N	L-R	A	N	N	A-6/1	N
East Texas Baptist U., Marshall 75670	Hollandsworth	4	5000			1100/27	N	I	A	3.5	N	B-3/15	N
	Honor Transfer	Unlimited	1000				N		A	3.0	N	D	Y
	Val/Sal	Unlimited	1000	10%			N		A	3.0	N	D	N
	H.D. Bruce	Varies	6000				N	I-O	A	3.5	O	B-3/15	N
	Honors Program												
East Texas State U., Commerce 75428	Academic Excellence	25	750			1180/25	N	R	A	3.0	O	B-4/15	N
	Presidential	20	1250			1270/28	N	E-L-R-I	A	3.0	O	B-4/15	N
	Honors Program												
Hardin-Simmons U., Abilene 76968	Academic	Unlimited	2000			1010/24	N		A	3.0	N	B-4/1	N
	Academic	Unlimited	3000			1130/27	N		A	3.0	N	B-4/1	N
	Academic	Unlimited	4000			1240/30	N		A	3.0	N	B-4/1	N
	Honors Program												
Houston Baptist U., 77074	Academic	Varies	To 350/qtr.	10%		1000/23	N		A	3.5	N	B-4/1	Y-3.5
	Endowed Academic	Varies	Tuition	5%	3.5	1200/26	N		A	3.5	N	C-1/31	N
	Endowed II	10	3120-4290	10%	3.5	1250	N	E-L-R-I	A	Y	N	C	N

Houston Baptist U., 77074	Presidential	50	3120-4290				N	R	A	Y	N	C	Y
	Nursing	100	600-1500	25%	2.5	1100	N	L-I-O	A	Y	N	C	Y
Howard Payne U., Brownwood 76801	Academic	Varies	1500-3500		X	950/22	N		A	X	N	B-5/1	Y-3.0
	President's	Varies	3500		3.5	1310/30	N		A	3.5	N	C	N
	Honors	Varies	2500		3.25	1180/26	N		A	3.25	N	C	N
	Achievement	Varies	1500		3.0	1050/22	N		A	3.0	N	C	N
	Outstanding Service	Varies	1000				N	L	A	N	N	C	N
	Honors Graduates	Varies	400-600	1-2			N		A	N	N	C	N
	Hispanic Leadership	Varies	1000				N		A	N	M	C	N
	Honors Program												
Incarnate Word, San Antonio 78209	Academic	Unlimited	1600-2800		3.0	840/20	N		A	3.25	N	A-C	Y-3.2
	Presidential	Unlimited	4000-5400	1,2	3.5	1050/26	N		A	3.25	N	A	N
	Fine Art	Unlimited	500-3500		2.5		N	T-R-I			N	C	
	President's Dist. Scholar	Unlimited	Tuition		3.8	1300/32	N		A	3.5	N	A-C	N
Lamar U., Beaumont 77710	Academic	Varies	500-1500	X	X	X	N	L	A	3.0	N	B-2/15	Y-3.5
Le Tourneau, Longview 75607	Honors	120	500-1000		3.0	1050/25	N		A			C	
	Deans	120	1000-2000		3.3	1100/27	N		A			C	
	Presidents	130	3000		3.6	1200/30	N		A			C	
	East Texas Scholarship	Unlimited	1000	10%			N		A	3.2	S	A-D	N
	R.G. Le Tourneau	1	Tuition	10%			N		A	3.2	S	B-5/1	N
	East Texas Honors	Unlimited	2000	2%			N		A	3.2	S	A-D	N
Lubbock Christian, 79407	ACT/Academic	Varies	400-2200	X	X	X	Y		A	Y	N	A-D	Y
McMurry, Abilene 79697	U. Scholars Partnership	Unlimited	3000-5500	50%		800/23	Y	L-R-I-O	A	2.7	O	A-B-4/15	N
	McMurry Methodist	Unlimited	1000	50%		800/23	N	R-I	A	2.7	D-O	B	N
	Transfer	Unlimited	800		3.5		N		A	3.5	O	A	Y-3.5
	Presidential	Unlimited	200-2000	25%	3.0	900/23	N		A	Y	N	A-8/25	Y-3.0
	Art, Music, Theatre	Varies	275-1000				N	T	A	2.0	N	A-8/25	Y-2.0
	Honors Program												
Midwestern State, Witchita Falls 76308	Departmental	150	250-1000	15%	3.2	1050/25	N		A	Y	O	B-4/1	Y
	Honors	60	600	5%	3.0	1150/26	N	R	A	Y	O	B-4/1	Y
	Regents'	Varies	700	25%	2.8	1000/23	N	T-L-R	A	3.2	O	B-4/1	Y
	Val/Sal	Varies	500	1%	X		N		A	3.2	O	B-4/1	N
	Academic	Varies	200-500	X	3.5	1150/26	N	E-L-R-O	A	3.0	M	B-4/4	Y-3.0
	Talent	Varies	300-600		3.0		N	T-L-R-O	O	3.0	N	B-4/4	Y-3.0
	Honors Program												
Northwood University, Cedar Hill 75108	Freedom	Varies	5000		3.0	1150/25	N		A	3.0	N	C	N
	Free-Enterprise	Varies	4000		2.75	950/20	N		A	2.75	N	C	N

	Program	No. of Awards	Value Range	Award Criteria					Study Fields	Renew-ability	Restric-tions	Apply Date	Transfer
				Class Stndg.	Grade Avg.	SAT/ ACT	Need Based	Other					
TEXAS *(Continued)*													
Northwood University, Cedar Hill 75108 *(Continued)*	Entrepreneur	Varies	3000		2.4	950/20	N		A	2.4	N	C	N
	Freedom Transfer	Varies	5000		3.5		N		A	3.5	N	C	Y
	Free-Enterprise Transfer	Varies	4000		3.0		N		A	3.0	N	C	Y
	Entrepreneur Transfer	Varies	3000		2.7		N		A	2.7	N	C	Y
	Hirsch	Varies	250-1500		X	X	Y	O	A	Y	N	C	N
	Business Club	Varies	1000-2500		X		N	R-I-O	A	3.0	N	C	N
Our Lady of the Lake, San Antonio 78285	Academic	210	2550-5250	25%	2.75	870/21	N		A	3.0	N	A-D	Y
	Presidential	25	9000	10%	3.5	1200/29	N	E-L-R	A	3.25	N	B-3/15	N
Prairie View A&M U., 77446	Academic	Varies	2200-4500	10%	3.0	1100/25	N	E-T-L-R	A	3.0	N	B-4/1	N
	Ethnic Recruitment	Varies	400-2000	50%	2.5		N		A	2.75	S-M	B-3/15	Y
	Honors Program, Honors College												
Rice U., Houston 77251	W.M. Rice	5	Tuition	5%		1300	N	L	A	3.2	N	A-1/2	N
St. Edwards U., Austin 78704	Academic	Unlimited	500-6000	25%		1100/24	N		A	3.0	N	A-7/1	N
	Theatre	12	1000-3000	Varies	Varies	Varies	N	T-I-O	O	3.0	N	B-2/15	N
	Honors Program												
St. Mary's U., San Antonio 78228	President's	Varies	4000-5000	10%	3.5	1150/26	N	E	A	Y	N	A-3/1	Y
	AP Exams												
	Distance Learning												
	Internships												
	Honors Program												
Sam Houston State, Huntsville 77341	President's Endowed	Varies	2000	10%		1200/30	N	E-T-L-R	A	3.0	O	B-3/1	N
	University Scholars	40-45	1000	25%		1050/26	N	E-T-L-R	A	N	O	B-3/1	N
	Transfer Scholarship	Varies	1000		3.0		N	E-T-L-R-O	A	N	O	B-5/1	Y-3.0
	Honors Program												
Schreiner, Kerrville 78028	Competitive Academic	Varies	2623-5265	25%		1100/25	N	R-O	A	3.25	O	B-3/15	N
	Competitive Academic	Varies	2623-5265		3.25		N	R	A	3.25	O	B-3/15	Y
	Academic Scholarship	Varies	3000-6000	25%		1100/25	N		A	3.25	N	B-3/15	Y
	Honors	Varies	2500	10%		1170/27	N	E-L-R-I-O	A	Y	N	B-3/15	Y
	Hatton-Summers	Varies	3500		3.0		N	L-I-O	A	Y	N	B-3/15	N
	Merit	Varies	1000	25%		1000/23	N	R	A	Y	N	B-3/15	Y
	Honors Program												

Southern Methodist U., Dallas 75275	President's Scholar	20	Tuition	10%	X	1350	N	R-I-O	A	3.3	N	A-1/15	N
	University	Unlimited	200-Tuition	X	X	X	N	O	A	3.0	N	A-3/1	N
	Hunt Scholar Leadership	20-25	9000-14000	25%	X	1200/28	N	E-L-R-I-O	A	3.0	N	A-1/15	N
	Honors Program												
Southwest Texas State, San Marcos 78666	State Scholarship	20	1000	33%		800/18	Y		A	N	S-M	B-3/1	Y-2.75
	Merrick	20	1000-1500	X	X	1000/24	N	L-R	A	3.25	N	B-3/1	Y-3.25
	University Scholars	7	1000-1200	X	X	1000/24	N	L-R-I-O	A	3.25	N	B-1/15	Y-3.25
	LBJ Achievement	25-30	1000	25%	X	1000/24	N		A	N	M	B-3/1	Y-3.5
	Honors Program												
Southwestern Adventist, Keene 76059	Top 10%	Varies	1200	10%			N		A	N	0	D	Y
	Leadership	Varies	600-1200				N	L	A	N	0	D	Y
	Academic	Varies	Varies		3.75	1000/22	N	O	A	Y	0	D	Y
	AP Exams												
	Distance Learning												
	Internships												
	Honors Program												
Southwestern U., Georgetown 78626	National Scholars	Varies	7500				N	E-I-L-O	A	Y	N	B-2/1	
	Brown Scholars	3	All Costs	5%	3.7	1400/32	N	E-I-L	A	3.0	N	B-2/1	
	Fine Arts	Varies	500-3000				N	T	O	Y	N	B-2/1	
	Presidents Scholar	4	10,000	10%	3.7	1350/31	N	E-I-L	A	Y		B-2/1	
	Southwestern Scholar	Varies	5000	10%	3.7	1200/27	Y		A	Y			
	University Scholars	Varies	3000	25%	3.5	1250/28	Y		A	Y			
	AP Exams												
	Honors College, Honors Program												
Stephen Austin State, Nacogdoches 75961	Top 5%	Varies	1000	5%					A	3.5			
	AP Exams												
	Distance Learning												
	Co-op, Internships												
	Honors College, Honors Program												
Sul Ross State U., Alpine 79832	Academic	64	200-1000	25%	3.0	950/23	X	L-R-O	A	X	0	C-4/1	Y
	Pres. Endowed Univ. Scholars	4	2000	X	X	1050/25	N	E-L-R-O	A	3.0	N	A-B-4/1	N
	Honors Program												
Tarleton State U., Stephenville 76402	Dick Smith	60	1200	25%	3.2	1000/22	N		O	3.2	N	B-4/1	Y
	Endowment	30	100-1500		3.0		X	L	A	3.0	0	B-4/1	N
Texas A&M U., College Station 77843	President's Endowed	500	3000	10%		1300/30	N	E-L-R	A	3.0			
	Lechner	140	2500	10%		1300/30	N	E-L-R	A	3.0			
	McFadden	50	2500	10%		1300/30	N	E-L-R	A	3.0			

Institution	Program	No. of Awards	Value Range	Award Criteria: Class Stndg.	Grade Avg.	SAT/ ACT	Need Based	Other	Study Fields	Renew- ability	Restric- tions	Apply Date	Transfer
TEXAS *(Continued)*													
Texas A&M U., College Station 77843 *(Continued)*	AP Exams												
	Distance Learning												
	Co-op												
	Honors Program												
Texas A&M U., Kingsville 78363	Alumni Merit	25	750	25%		970/21		L-R	A	N	0	B-3/3	N
	Russell Honors	Varies	6150	25%	3.0	1280/29		R	A	3.5		B-3/3	N
	Presidential Honors	Varies	6150	25%	3.0	1280/29		R	A	3.5		B-3/3	N
	Behmann Brothers	8	1000	25%		1090/24		R	A	N		B-3/3	N
	Valedictorian	Varies	Tuition	1					A	N			N
	AP Exams												
	Distance Learning												
	Co-op, Internships												
Texas Christian U., Fort Worth 76129	TCU Scholarship	573	1500	15%		1100/27	N	E-L-R-I-O	A	3.25	N	A-1/15	Y-3.5
	Chancellor's	42	Tuition	5%		1300/30	N	E-L-R-I-O	A	3.25	N	A-1/15	N
	Dean's	300	4750	10%		1200/28	N	E-L-R-I-O	A	3.25	N	A-1/15	Y-3.5
	Music	12	650-2000				N	T-I-O	O	Y	N	B-C	Y-3.5
	Faculty	225	3200	10%		1200/29	N	E-L-R-I-O	A	3.25	N	B-CA-1/15	Y-3.5
	Honors Program												
Texas Lutheran, Seguin 78155	Academic Excellence	Varies	1250-2000	25%		1000/22	N	E	A	3.0	N	B-3/1	N
	Pacesetter	Varies	2500-8000	25%		1160/26	N	E-I-O	A	3.25	N	B-1/15	N
	Honors Program												
Texas Southern U., Houston 77004	Academic	Varies	200-2500	33%	3.0		Y	E-R-I	A	3.25	N	B-5-1	Y-3.25
	Honors Program												
Texas Tech. U., Lubbock 79409	TTU	140	500		3.8	1200/27	Y		A	N	N	B-3/1	Y
	University Scholar	Varies	1500		3.0	1300/30	N	E-L-R	A	3.0	N	B-3/1	Y-3.0
	Presidential	Varies	2000			1350/31	N	E-R	A	Y	N	B-3/1	Y
Texas Wesleyan, Ft. Worth 76105	McFadden	Varies	Tuition				N	L-R-I-O	A	3.0	N	B-3/15	N
	University	Varies	1800/2600		3.0	920/18	N		A	Y	N	B-3/15	N
	Fine Arts	Varies	Varies				N	T-O	O	Y	N	C	
	Junior Achievement	Varies	1000				N	O	A	Y	O	C	
	Eunice & James West	Varies	All Costs	10%	3.5	1200/27	N		O	Y	N	C	

	Business Hall of Fame	Varies	4000		3.0	1060/25	N		O	Y	N	C	
	Dean's	Varies	3600		2.75	900/18	N		A	Y	N	C	
	Ram Award	Varies	500-1600				N	L-O	A	Y	N	C	
	President's	Varies	4600				N			Y			
	AP Exams												
	Distance Learning												
	Internships												
Texas Woman's U., Denton 76204	TW General	200	400-500		3.75		N		A	N	N	B-2/1	Y-3.75
	Ethnic Recruitment	15	750-1000	33%		800/18	Y		A	N	S-M	B-2/1	Y-2.75
	President's	Varies	8000		3.5	1300/30	N	E-L-R	A	3.0	N	B-2/1	Y-3.5
	Honors Program												
Trinity U., San Antonio 78284	President's	Unlimited	1000-4000	X	X	1250/30	N	E-L-R-I	A	3.25	N	B-2/1	N
	Trustee/NM	100	5000	X	X	X	N	E-L-R-I-O	A	3.25	N	B-2/1	N
U. of Dallas, Irving 75062	Competitive	Varies	1000-12000	25%	3.0	1120/26	N	E	A	3.0	N	B-12/1	Y-3.0
	Presidential	Varies	1000-12000	25%	3.0	1120/26	N	E-L-I-O	A	3.0	N	B-2/1	N
	Art	Varies	1000-12000				N	T	A	3.0	N	B-1/15	Y
	Theater	Varies	1000-12000				N	T-R-I-O	A	3.0	N	B-1/15	Y
	Foreign Language	Varies	1000-12000				N	T-L-R-I-O	A	3.0	N	B-1/15	Y
	Math	Varies	1000-12000	25%	3.5	1150/26	N	E-T-R-I-O	A	3.0	N	B-1/15	Y
	Physics	Varies	1000-12000	25%	3.5	1150/26	N	E-T-R-I-O	A	3.0	N	B-1/15	Y
	Honors Program, Honors College												
U. of Houston-Central Campus, 77004	Alumni	124	1000-2000	25%		1200/29	N		A	3.0	N	B-4/1	N
	State/Ethnic	Varies	1000	33%		800/18	Y	O	A	N	M	B-3/1	Y-2.75
	Edmond's	Varies	2000		2.0		Y		A	2.0	S	B-3/1	Y
	Cain	Varies	1000		2.5		N		A	2.0	M	B-4/1	N
	President's Diversity	84	1000-3000		3.0		N	R	A	3.0	M-O	B-4/1	Y-3.0
	Maguire Scholarship	100	200-1000		3.0		Y		A	2.0	O	B-4/1	Y-3.0
	Cullen Leadership	30	2000-3000	25%		1200/29	N	L-R	A	3.0	N	B-4/1	N
	Academic Recognition	78	500-1000	10%	3.5	1100/26	N		A	3.0	N	B-4/1	N
	Academic Excellence	304	1000-3000	25%		900/21	N		A	2.0	M-O	B-4/1	N
	Honors Program, Honors College												
U. of Mary Hardin-Baylor, Belton 76513	Valedictorian	15	Tuition	1	3.5	950/23	N	O	A	3.5	S-S-O	A-B-7/1	N
	President	10	Tuition	10%	3.5	1300/31	N	O	A	3.5	S-S-O	A-B-7/1	N
	Dean's	10	1110		3.25	1150/27	N	O	A	3.25	S-S-O	A-B-7/1	N
	Honors Program												
University of North Texas, Denton 76203	Academic	Varies	200-2000	25%		1000/25	N		A	3.0	O	B-9/1	Y-3.0
	Board of Regents	Varies	1000	10%		1140/27	N	E-R	A	3.25	N	B-3/31	N
	Presidential	Varies	1000	10%		1140/27	N	E-R	A	3.25	N	B-3/31	N

	Program	No. of Awards	Value Range	Award Criteria: Class Stndg.	Grade Avg.	SAT/ ACT	Need Based	Other	Study Fields	Renew-ability	Restric-tions	Apply Date	Transfer
TEXAS *(Continued)*													
U. of St. Thomas, Houston 77006	Academic	Varies	Varies	15%	3.0	X	N		A	Y	N	B-3/1	Y
U. of Texas, Arlington 76019	Hemphill-Gilmore	15	1000				N		A		N	B-6/1	Y
	Transfer Scholarship	290	1000-2000		3.0		N		A	3.25			T
	Grace Thornton	12	1000		3.0		N	R-O	O		O	B-6/1	N
	James H./Minnie Edmonds	20	1000		2.0		N		A		S	B-6/1	Y
	Freshman	190	1000-2500	25%		1000/22	N		A	3.25		B-4/1	N
	AP Exams												
	Distance Learning												
	Co-op												
	Honors Program												
U. of Texas, Austin 78713	Achievement	200	2000	X	X	X	N	E-L-R	A	2.0	S-M	B-12/1	N
	Achievement Honors	200	5000	X	X	X	N	E-L-R	A	2.5	S-M	B-12/1	N
	Arts & Talent	Varies	1000				N	T	O	2.0	N	C	N
	Departmental	6000	200-5000	X	X	X	X		A	X	N	B-C	Y
	Freshman Scholarship	200	500-1020	25%		1200/27	N	R	A	3.5	N	B-3/31	N
	Transfer Scholarship	25	200-500		3.5		N	R	A	N	N	B-6/1	Y-3.5
	Minority Engineering	125	250-1500			1000/24	X		O	2.5	M	C	N
	Honors Program												
U. of Texas, Dallas 75083	International Education	Varies	Varies	X	X	X	Y	O	A	N	N	B-3/1	Y
	Commended/Semifinalist	Varies	Varies		X		N	E-R-O	A	3.0	O	B-3/1	N
U. of Texas, El Paso 79968	General	75	200-700		3.0	1000/23	N		A	3.0	N	B-2/1	Y-3.0
	Presidential	40	1500	3%	3.7	1180/27	N	L-R	A	3.5	N	B-2/1	N
	Stevens & Clardy Fox	50	1000		3.5	1010/24	N		A	3.2	N	B-2/1	N
	University Endowed	40	750		3.3	1000/21	N		A	3.0	N	B-2/1	N
	Univ. Achievement	40	200-800		3.0		Y	L-R	A	3.0	S	B-2/1	Y-3.0
	Academic Achievement	50	1000	5%	3.5	1100/25	Y		A	3.2	N	B-2/1	N
	Excellence	6	2000	3%	3.7	1100/27	N	E-L	A	3.5	N	B-2/1	N
	Honors Program												
U. of Texas-Permian Basin, Odessa 79762-8301	Presidential	3	6000	10%	3.5		N	R	A	Y	S	B-3/1	N
	UTPB Merit Award	32	4000	10%	3.5		N	R	A	Y	S	B-4/15	Y-3.5
	Freshman Merit	30	400-800	25%			N		A	3.0	N	B-4/15	N

U. of Texas, San Antonio 78285	Academic/Minority	2	2000		3.0		Y		A	3.0	M-0	B-4/1	Y-3.0
	Presidential	20	1500	10%	3.5	1140/24	N	E-R	A	3.3	N	B-2/1	Y-3.5
	Honors Program												
Wayland Baptist U., Plainview 79072	Pioneer	Varies	980-2940		3.25	910/22	N		A	3.25	N	A-5/1	Y-3.25
	Honors	Unlimited	To Tuition	25%	3.0	910/22	N	R-I	A	3.65	N	B-C	Y
	Dean's Scholarship	Varies	784-980			910/22	N		A	3.25	N	A-D	Y-3.25
	President's	Varies	1568-1960			1250/29	N		A	3.5	N	A-D	N
	Trustees'	Varies	2352-2940			1260/30	N		A	3.7	N	A-D	N
	Honors Program												
West Texas State A&M., Canyon 79016	General	Varies	Varies	X	X	X	N	0	A	X	N	C	Y
	Valedictorian	Varies	Tuition	1			N		A	Y	N	C	N
UTAH													
Brigham Young U., Provo 84602	Academic	1000	1000-2530	X	X	X	N	0	A	N	N	C-2/15	Y
	Hinckley Presidential	24	3800-4800	X	3.85	31	N	E-R-0	A	Y	D	B-1/15	N
	Trustees	270	2530	X	3.85	31	N	E-R-0	A	Y	N	B-1/15	N
	Talent	100	2530	X	X	X	N	T-0	0	N	N	B-2/15	Y
	National Merit	100	2530	X	X	X	N	0	A	Y	N	B-2/15	N
Southern Utah U., Cedar City 84720	Academic	517	348-696		3.85	26	N	T-L	A	3.9	S	B-2/15	Y
	Leadership	63	693-1386		3.2	20	N	E-L-R	A	3.7	N	B-2/15	Y-3.75
U. of Utah, Salt Lake City 84112	Entrance Honors	250	Tuition		3.7	28	N		A	3.7	S	B-2/1	N
	Non-Resident	Varies	To Tuition		3.5	X	N	L	A	X	N	B-2/1	Y
	President's	35	Tuition + stipend		3.8	30	N	L	A	3.5	S	B-2/1	N
	Resident/Departmental	Varies	To Tuition		3.5	25	N	R-0	A	3.5	S	B-2/1	Y-3.5
	Leadership	50	To Tuition		3.0		N	E-L-R-0	A	N	0	B-2/1	Y-3.0
	Honors Program												
Utah State U., Logan 84322	Academic Honors	500	200-1000		3.75	26	N		A	Y	S	A-3/1	Y
	Presidential	Varies	Tuition		3.95	28	N		A	3.5	N	B-3/1	N
	Superior Student	Varies	Tuition/Fees		3.98	31	N		A	3.5	N	B-3/1	N
	University Club	Varies	Tuition/Fees+		X		N	E-R-I	A	3.5	N	B-3/1	N
Weber State, Ogden 84408	Honors-at-Entrance	Varies	750-1500		3.8	24	N	0	A	N	N	B-2/1	N
	Presidential	50	1500-4500	10%	3.9	28	N	E-T-L-R-I-0	A	3.7	N	B-2/1	N
	Academic Merit	Varies	750-1500		3.5		N	0	A	3.5	0	B-2/1	Y-3.5
	Honors Program												
Westminster, Salt Lake City 84105	Eccles Foundation	50	1000		X	X	N		A	2.0	N	A-2/28	N
	Trustee	Unlimited	1800-2400		3.0		N		A	3.0	N	A-D	N
	Program Activity Grant	Varies	200-800		2.0		N	T-R-I	A	2.0	0	B-2/28	Y-2.0

	Program	No. of Awards	Value Range	Award Criteria: Class Stndg.	Grade Avg.	SAT/ ACT	Need Based	Other	Study Fields	Renew-ability	Restric-tions	Apply Date	Transfer
UTAH *(Continued)*													
Westminster, Salt Lake City 84105 *(Continued)*	Transfer Scholarship	Unlimited	1800		3.25		N		A	3.0	0	A	Y-3.25
	Minority Scholarship	Varies	200-800		X		Y		A	N	M-0	C-2/28	Y-2.0
	Faculty Entrance	25	800		3.0		N	E	A	N	0	B-2/28	Y-3.0
	Honors Program												
VERMONT													
Castleton State, 05735	Music Scholarship	1	1000				N	T	0	3.25	N	C	Y
	Castleton	5	Tuition	10%			N	0	A	3.5	S	B-3/31	N
	Presidential	25	500	15%			N	0	A	X	S	B-3/31	Y
College of St. Joseph, Rutland 05701	Freshman Academic	Unlimited	1000	15%			N	R	A	3.25	N	C	N
	General Academic	16	500-2500		3.25		N	L-R	A	N	N	B-3/1	N
	Student Leaders	Unlimited	500		2.5		N	E-L-R-I-0	A	2.5	N	A-B-5/1	N
Goddard, Plainfield 05667	Goddard	Unlimited	100-2000				Y		A	Y	N	B-D	Y
	AP Exams												
	Distance Learning												
	Co-op, Internships												
Green Mountain, Poultney 05764	Art	Varies	500-3000				N	E-T-R-I-0	0	3.0	N	A-D	Y
	English Composition	1	3000	25%	3.0	950	N	0	0	3.0	N	A-D	Y-3.0
	Recognition	Unlimited	500-1500				N	0	A	Y	D	A	N
	Orrin F. Ireson	Unlimited	2000				N	R-0	A	Y	D	D	N
	Trustee	Unlimited	1000-2500		2.75	860/21	N		A	Y	N	A	N
	Horace Moss Jr. Ach.	Unlimited	2000				N	0	A	Y	0	D	N
	Presidential	Unlimited	2000				N	R-0	A	Y	0	D	N
	Environmental	Unlimited	1000				N	0	A	Y	0	A	N
	Transfer	Unlimited	1000-1500				N	0	A	Y	N	D	Y
	Honors Program												
Johnson State College, 05656	Val/Sal	Unlimited	1000-1500	1-2			N		A				
	Chesamore	Varies	250-1000	15%		24	N	E	A	Y			
	AP Exams												
	Distance Learning												
	Family Discounts												
	Internships												

Lyndon State, Lyndonville 05831	LSC Scholars	10	500	10%	3.0		N		A	N	N	B-3/15	N
	Leadership	10	500				N	L-R	A	N	N	B-3/15	N
	Transfer Honors	2	500		3.0		N		A	N	N	B-3/15	A-3.0
Norwich U., Northfield 05663	University Scholar	1000	200-9000				Y	T-L-O	A	2.0	N	A-C-D	Y
St. Michael's, Winooski 05404	Chittenden Honor	3	Tuition	20%	3.0	1100/26	N		A	3.0	S	B-2/15	N
	Presidential Honor	3	Tuition	20%	3.0	1100/26	N		A	3.0	N	A-2/15	N
	State Scholarship	30	5500	10%	3.0	1200	N	R	A	3.0	N	B-2/1	N
	Green Mountain Scholarship	20	6250	10%	3.0	1200	N	R	A	3.0	S	B-2/1	N
	AP Exams												
	Family Discounts												
	Honors Program												
School for International Training, Brattleboro 05301	Development Mgmt.	Varies	2000-3000				Y	E-L-R-O	O	N	N	B-C	Y
	Various	Varies	2000-3000				Y	O	O	N	O	B-C	Y
Southern Vermont, Bennington 05201	SAT	Unlimited	500			900	Y	L-R	A	Y	N	A-D	Y
	Commuter-Tutor	2	500		3.0		Y	E-R-I-O	O	Y	N	A-3/1	Y
	Honors Program												
Trinity, Burlington 05401	Catherine McAuley	15	2500		3.0		N	L-R-I-O	A	3.0	W	A-3/1	N
	Trinity Scholarship	25	2000-3500		3.0		N	L-R-I-O	A	3.0	W	A-3/1	N
	Presidential Merit	20	4500		3.0	1000	N	L-R-I-O	A	3.0	W	A-3/1	N
U. of Vermont, Burlington 05401	Vermont Scholar	15	Tuition+Fees	10%		1200	N	E-L-R-I-O	A	3.0	S	B-11/1	N
VIRGINIA													
Averett, Danville 24541	Presidential	Varies	6000	20%	3.5	1140	N		A	3.0	N	B-3/15	N
	Averett Scholars	Varies	7300	15%	3.2	1100	N		A	2.8	N	B-3/1	N
	Merit Scholarship	Varies	1000-3000	15%			N		A	2.0	N	A-D	N
	Averett Trustees	3	Tuition	10%	3.5	1270	N		A	3.0	N	B-3/1	N
Bluefield College, Bluefield 24605	Presidential	Varies	5100-6100		3.5		N	L-R-I-O	A	3.0	N	A-3/10	N
	Transfer	Varies	1000-2000		3.5		N	L-R-I-O	A	3.0	N	C	Y-3.5
	Fine Arts	Varies	1000		2.5		N	T-R-I-O	O		N	B-C	Y
	Dean's	Varies	3200-4000		3.0		N	L-I	A	2.5	N	A-3/10	N
	Achievement	Varies	2000-2800		2.5		N	L-I	A	2.0	N	A-3/10	N
	Leadership	Varies	1000		2.0		N	L-I	A	2.0	N	A-3/10	N
Bridgewater College, 22812	President's Merit	3	10000	5%		1250/30	N		A	3.4	N	A-2/1	N
	H.L. Harris	2	3500	10%		1000	N		A	3.0	S	A-D	N
	ACE 10	Unlimited	1/2 Tuit. & Fees	10%			N		A	2.8	N	D	Y-3.5
	ACE 20	Unlimited	1/3 Tuit. & Fees	11-20%			N		A	2.5	N	D	Y-3.2
	ACE 30	Unlimited	1/4 Tuit. & Fees	21-30%			N		A	2.2	N	D	Y3.0

	Program	No. of Awards	Value Range	Award Criteria: Class Stndg.	Grade Avg.	SAT/ ACT	Need Based	Other	Study Fields	Renew-ability	Restric-tions	Apply Date	Transfer
VIRGINIA *(Continued)*													
Christendom, Front Royal 22630	Presidential	20	2000-10,800			1220/27		E	A	3.5	N	B-4/1	Y
	AP Exams												
	Alumni Discounts												
Christopher Newport University, Newport News 23606	Styron	35-40	600-1000	20%	3.0	1000/24	N		A	3.3	O	A	Y-3.5
	Beamer	1-4	Full Tuit.		X		N		O	3.0	N	C	N
	Greene	3	2000	X	X		N		A	Y	O	C	N
	Teresa VanDover	1	500-900	20%	3.0	1000	N		A		N	C	
	Honors Program												
Clinch Valley, Wise 24293	Valedictorian	Varies	Tuition, fees	1	X	X	N		A	2.5		4/1	N
	Salutatorian	Varies	2000	2	X	X	N		A	2.5		4/1	N
	Merit	Varies	500-1500	X	3.0	X	N		A	2.5		4/1	Y
	AP Exams												
	Co-op, Internships												
	Honors Program												
College of William & Mary, 23185	James Monroe	Varies	Varies	5%		1400	N	L-R	A	Y	N	A	N
Eastern Mennonite, Harrisonburg 22801	Menno Simons	Varies	2500		3.8	1350/30	N		A	3.5	N	A-3/1	N
	President's	Varies	3600		3.9	1450/31	N		A	3.5	N	A-3/1	N
	Michael Sattler	Varies	2000		3.5	1250/27	N		A	3.0	N	A-3/1	N
	Academic Achievement	Varies	1000		3.2	1150/27	N		A	Y	N	C	N
	Honors Program												
Emory & Henry, Emory 24327	E & H Scholar	Varies	1000	15%	X	1100/27	N	I-O	A	3.6	N	A-8/1	N
	Freshman Honors	Varies	500	X	X	X	N	O	A	3.6	N	B-6/1	N
Ferrum College, 24088	Freshman Honor	Unlimited	1000-2000	X	3.0	X	N	L	A	N	N	B-C	N
	Academic Merit	Unlimited	1000-2000		3.0	800	N		A	3.0	N	A-D	Y-3.0
	Val/Sal	Unlimited	4000-5000	1-2		800	N		A	3.5	N	A-D	
George Mason, Fairfax 22030	University	30	5000	10%	3.4	1300/29	N	I-L-O	A	3.0			
	Dean's	60	1500	10%	3.0	1100/24	N	I	A	3.0			
	Academic Scholarship	36	3000	10%	3.2	1100/24	N	I-L	A	3.0			
	AP Exams												
	Honors Program												

Hampden-Sydney College, 23943	Allan	5	10000	10%		1300	N	L-I-O	A	3.5	O	A-3/1	N
	Cushing	15	3600	20%		1200	N	L-I-O	A	3.15	O	A-3/1	N
	Madison	1	Total Costs	5%		1350	N	L-I-O	A	3.75	O	A-3/1	N
	Patrick Henry	15	3600	20%		1200	N	L-I-O	A	3.15	O	A-3/1	N
	Venable	15	5000	15%		1250	N	L-I-O	A	3.3	O	A-3/1	N
	Honors Program												
Hampton U., 23668	Eminent	200	1000-4400			1000	N		A	3.0	N	B-3/31	N
	George Hampton	Varies	500-8242	10%	3.0	1000	N		A	3.0	N	B-3/31	N
Hollins College, Roanoke 24020	Niederer	2	1000	10%	3.0		N	T-R	O	N	W	C	Y
	Hollins Scholar	10-12	6475-12950	10%	3.5	1150/26	N	I-O	A	Y	W	A-2/15	N
	Buxton-Shaw Leadership	10	1500		3.0	X	N	L-R-I-O	A	3.0	W	A-2/15	N
	Merit	40-60	1500-4000		3.0	X	N	T-L-R-I-O	A	3.0	W	A-2/15	N
Liberty University, Lynchburg 24506-8001	Chancellor's	Unlimited	2000	X		800/15	N	O	A	Y	N	C-8/1	Y
	Christian Schools	Unlimited	1000	15%		800/15	N	R	A	Y	O	C-4/15	Y
	Honors	Varies	900-3600	10%	3.5	1200/29	N	E-R	A	3.5	N	C-7/15	Y-3.5
	President's	Unlimited	2000			800/15	N	O	A	Y	N	C-8/1	Y
Longwood, Farmville 23901	Arts & Sciences	Varies	1000	X	X	X	N		A	Y	N	B-4/1	N
	English	2	2000	10%	3.0	1050	N	E-L-R	O	3.25	N	B-4/1	N
	Honors	5	1000	X	X	1100	N	L-R-O	A	3.25	N	B-C	N
	Longwood	5	1000	10%	3.35	1050	N	L-R-I-O	A	3.35	N	B-3/11	N
	Minority	Varies	750-1000	30%	X	X	Y	E-L-R	A	Y	M	B-4/1	Y
	Nance/Academic	10	500-1200	30%			Y		A	Y	N	B-C	N
	Performance	Varies	200-2600	X	X		N	T-R-I	O	Y	N	B-C	Y
	Scott	7	750-1000	30%	X	X	Y	E-L-R	A	Y	N	B-4/1	N
	Valedictorian	Varies	To 1000	1			N		A	Y	N	B-C	N
	Honors Program												
Lynchburg College, Lynchburg 24501	Misc. Scholarships	Varies	3000-9500	X	x	x	N	O	A	Y		C-3/1	N
	AP Exams												
	Honors Program												
Mary Baldwin, Staunton 24401	Wilson	Varies	2000-6500		2.5	800/17	N		A	2.5	W		
	Baldwin	Varies	4500-9000		3.0	800/17	N		A	2.5	W	A-5/1	Y-3.0
	AP Exams												
	Distance Learning												
	Internships												
	Honors Program												
Mary Washington, Fredericksburg 22401	Alumni Scholarship	70	To In-State Tuition			3.8	1340	N	L	A	3.0		
	AP Exams												
	Distance Learning												
	Co-op, Internships												

	Program	No. of Awards	Value Range	Award Criteria: Class Stndg.	Grade Avg.	SAT/ ACT	Need Based	Other	Study Fields	Renew-ability	Restric-tions	Apply Date	Transfer
VIRGINIA *(Continued)*													
Marymount, Arlington 22207	Freshman Academic	30	1000-5500	20%	3.0	1000	N	E-L-R-I-O	A	3.0	W	B-D	N
	Transfer	15	Varies		3.3		N		A	3.3	W	B-D	Y
Norfolk State U., Norfolk 23504	Presidential	100	500-2000		3.0		N	O	A	X	N	4/1	Y-3.0
	Dnimas Science	25	6000-10000		3.2	950	N	O	O	Y	N	2/1	N
	MRL Science	15	3200		3.0	900	N	O	O	Y	O	4/1	N
	Bd of Visitors	50	1000-3500	10%	3.0	800	Y		A	3.0	O	5/1	N
	AP Exams												
	Co-op												
	Honors Program												
Old Dominion U., Norfolk 23529	Assorted	Varies	To Tuition	X	3.25	X	X	X	X	X	X	B-2/15	X
	AP Exams												
	Distance Learning												
	Co-op, Internships												
	Honors College, Honors Program												
Radford U., 24142	Presidential	3-6	All Costs	25%	3.5	1180/26	N	E-L-R-I	A	3.0			
	Foundation	Varies	1000-2000	25%	3.5	1180/26	N	E-L-R-I	A	3.0			
	Transfer	2	500-1000		3.25		N		A	3.0			T
	AP Exams												
	Distance Learning												
	Internships												
	Honors Program												
Randolph-Macon, Ashland 23005	Minority	10-15	5000-Tuition	20%	3.0		N	R-I-O	A	Y	M	A-2/1	Y-3.0
	R-M Scholars	100	5000-Tuition	10%	3.5		N	R-I-O	A	3.0	N	A-2/1	Y-3.5
	Distinguished Achievement	200-300	3000-4000	20%	3.0		N	R-I-O	A	2.5	N	A-2/1	Y-3.0
	Honors Program												
Randolph-Macon Woman's Lynchburg, 24503	Leadership	12	500-1500				N	T-L-R	A	Y	W	A-1/15	Y
	Trustee	2	10,000	20%		1200	N	E-O	A	Y	W	B-1/15	Y
	Campbell, Chesney	4	5000	20%		1200	N	E-O	A	Y	W	B-1/15	Y
	President's		7500	20		1200	N	O	A	Y	W	B-3/1	Y
	Centennial		2000	15%		1100	N	O	A	Y	W	B-3/1	Y
	Founder's		6000	20%		1100	N	O	A	Y	W	B-3/1	Y
	AP Exams												

	Family Discounts Co-op, Internships												
Roanoke, Salem 24153	Bittle	15-20	3/4 Tuition	10%	3.0	1300	N	0	A	3.25	0	A-C	N
	Faculty	Unlimited	1500-4500	20%		1100	N	L-R-0	A	3.0	N	A-C	N
	Honors Program												
St. Paul's, Lawrenceville 23868	Special Presidential	5	8000	10%	3.5	1000/22	Y	R-0	A	3.2	N	B-7/15	N
	Presidential	10	4000	15%	3.2	900/20	Y	R-0	A	3.0	N	B-7/15	N
	General	Varies	1800-2400	25%	3.0	800/18	Y	R-0	A	3.0	N	B-7/15	N
	Honors Program												
Shenandoah College & Conservatory, Winchester 22601	Presidential	Varies	Up to 12,000		3.5	1100/25	N	E-I	A	3.0	N	B-3/1	N
	Theatre	Varies	500-1000				N	T-I-0	0	Y	0	C	Y
	Merit	Varies	2500-7000		3.0	900	N		A	3.0	N		N
	Methodist	Varies	1000-2000				N	0	A	Y	D-0		Y
	Transfer	Varies	2000-7000				N		A	3.0	N		2.0
	Talent	Varies	500-Tuiton				N	T	0	Y	N		Y
	AP Exams												
	Co-op												
Sweet Briar College, 24595	Founders	2	15,000	X	3.3	X	N	E-T-L-R-I-0	A	3.3	W	A-2/15	N
	Pannell	10	5000	X	3.3	X	N	E-T-L-R-I-0	A	3.3	W	A-2/15	N
	Black	4	8000-10000	10%			N	E-L-R-I-0	A	3.3	W-0	A-2/15	N
	Commonwealth	2	13,000	10%			N	E-L-R-I-0	A	3.3	S-W-0	A-2/15	N
	AP Exams												
	Honors Program												
U. of Richmond, 23173	Music	5	2500	X	X	X	N	T-R-I-0	0	Y	N	C	N
	Oldham	5	All Costs	X	X	X	N	E-L-R-I-0	A	Y	N	B-1/1	N
	Ethyl Science Scholar	4	All Costs	10%	X	X	N	E-R-I-0	0	Y	N	B-1/1	N
	Virginia Baptist	4	1/2- Full Tuit.	10%	X	1250/30	N	R-I-0	A	Y	S-D-0	B-2/2	N
	University Scholar	25	1/2 Tuition	10%	X	1350/30	N	0	A	Y	N	A-2/1	N
	CIGNA	15	50% Tuition	X	X	X	Y	L-R-I-0	A	Y	M-0	B-1/15	N
	Bonner Scholar	25	3700	X	X	X	Y	L-0	A	Y	0	B-3/1	N
	National Merit Scholar	Varies	1/2 Tuition	X	X	X	N	0	A	Y	N	C-2/1	N
	AP Exams												
	Internships												
	Honors Program												
U. of Virginia, Charlottesville 22906	Jefferson Scholars	18	9000-18000				N	R-I-0	A	Y	0	B-12/1	N
	Honors Program												
VA Commonwealth U., Richmond 23284	Presidential	15	In-State Costs	10%	3.5	1270/29	N	E-L-R-0	A	3.3	N	A-1/1	N
	Provost	50	In-State Costs	15%		1270/29	N	E-L-0	A	3.3	N	A-1/1	N

	Program	No. of Awards	Value Range	Class Stndg.	Grade Avg.	SAT/ ACT	Need Based	Other	Study Fields	Renew-ability	Restric-tions	Apply Date	Transfer
				Award Criteria									
VIRGINIA *(Continued)*													
VA Commonwealth U., Richmond 23284 *(Continued)*	Dean's	100	1/2 Res. Tuit.	10%	3.5	1100	N	E-L-R-0	A	3.3	N	A-1/1	Y-3.5
	Reynolds Metals	6	In-State Tuit.	X	3.0	1100	N	E-L-R-0	A	3.0	S-0	A-1/1	N
VA Intermont, Bristol 24201	Academic Excellence	Varies	2500-7500		3.0		N	I-0	A	3.0	N	C	Y
	Presidential	Varies	Tuition		3.8	1200	N		A	Y	N	C	Y
	Transfer	Varies	1500-4000		2.5		N		A	Y	N	C	Y
	Honors Program, Honors College												
VMI, Lexington 24450	Institute A	9-10	All Costs	5%	3.75	1300	N	L-R-I	A	3.0	0-0	B-12/1	N
	Sale	2	All Costs				N	R-0	A	Y	S-0-0	C	N
	Institute Partials	20-30	2000-4000	10%	3.2	1100/25	N	L-I-0	A	2.5	0	C-2/1	
VPI & SU, Blacksburg 24061	Competition	15	2000-3000	5%		1300	N	E-I	A	Y	N	A-D	N
	Marshall Hahn	200	500-2000	5%		1300	N	I-0	0	Y	N	B-1/1	N
	University	275	500-3000	10%	3.5	1100	X	0	A	X	N	A-3/15	Y
VA State U., Petersburg 23803	VSU Merit	Varies	500-1000	33%	3.0	800/18	N	E-R	A	Y	N	B-D	N
	Academic	Varies	200-2000	25%	3.2	1100/24	N	E-L-R-0	A	3.0	0	C	Y-3.2
	Honors Program, Honors College												
VA Union U., Richmond 23220	Tuition	Varies	300-4350	10%	3.0	850	N	L-R	A	3.3	N	A-3/15	Y
VA Wesleyan, Norfolk 23502	Wesleyan	10-12	9000-Tuition	5%	3.8	1200	N	E-L-R-I-0	A	3.5	N	B-2/10	N
	Academic Dean's	35	1000-6000	20%	3.0	1000	N	E-L-R-I-0	A	3.0	N	A-D	N
	Presidential	25	7000	15%	3.4	1100	N	E-L-R-I-0	A	3.0	N	B-2/10	N
	Honors Program												
Washington & Lee U., Lexington 24450	Honor	30	2000-10850	X	X	X	N	E-L-R-I-0	A	3.0	N	B-1/11	N
	Robert E. Lee	15	2000-16000	X	X	X	Y	E-L-R-I-0	A	3.0	N	B-1/11	N
	Weinstein	1	10850	X	X	X	N	E-L-R-I-0	A	3.0	D	B-1/11	N
	Honors Program												
WASHINGTON													
Central Washington U. Ellensburg 98926	CIF	14-17	To Tuition		3.0	X	N	L-R	A	N			
	President's	8	All Costs		3.5	X	N	0	A	Y	0	B-12/1	N
	Academic Diversity	25	To Tuition		3.0		N	L-R-0	A	3.0			
	Garrity	4-5	To Tuition	10%	3.5		N	E-I-L-R		3.0			

	AP Exams Distance Learning Co-op, Internships *Honors College, Honors Program*												
Cornish C. of the Arts, Seattle 98102	Trustee	30-40	200-1000				Y	O	A	N	N	B-C	Y
	Kreielsheimer	5	Tuition/Board				N	T-R-I-O	A	X	O	B-C	Y
	Cornish Scholarship	50	1000-2500				N	T-L-I	A	Y	N	A-D	Y
	Male Dance	35830	1/2 Tuition				N	T-L-I	A	Y	O	B-4/30	Y
Eastern Washington U., Cheney 99004	Killin	3	3500	5%	3.9	1200	N	T-L-R	A	3.5	S	B-2/15	N
	Academic Honors	38	2500	10%	3.7	1000	N	T-L-R	A	3.7	S	B-2/15	Y-3.5
	University	37	1875	15%	3.5		N	T-L-R	A	N	N	B-2/15	N
	AP Exams Distance Learning Co-op, Internships *Honors Program*												
Evergreen State, Olympia 98505	Achievement	40	Tuition				N	T-L-E	A	N	O	C	Y
	Scholarship	Varies	100-1000				X	T-L-E	O	N	O	B-C	Y
Gonzaga U., Spokane 99258	NM Standing	Varies	Varies				Y	O	A	Y	N	C	N
	Academic	Varies	500-5000	10%	3.2		Y		A	3.2	O	A-2/15	Y-3.2
	Honors Program												
Heritage College, Toppenish 98948	Departmental	2 per Dept.	500-1000		3.0		N	O	A	N	N	C-5/1	Y-3.0
Northwest, Kirkland 98083	Assemblies of God		1000			X	N	R	A	3.0	D	D	N
	Academic		4000-8000		X	X	N	O	A	3.0	N	A	Y
	Talent	Varies	4000-8000				N	T-L-R	A	3.0	O	35855.00	Y
	President's	Varies	To Tuition	X	X	X	N	T-E-R	A	3.4	O	35855.00	N
Pacific Lutheran U., Tacoma 98447	Music Talent	Varies	750-3000	X	X	X	X	T-E-R	A	Y	N	A-3/1	Y
	PLU Merit	Varies	2500	X	3.3	X	N	O	A	3.3	N	A-4/1	N
	President's	Varies	1750-4000	10%	3.8	1100/25	N	L	A	3.3	N	A-4/1	N
	Provost's Merit	25	1000		3.6		N	L	A	3.3	O	A-4/1	Y-3.6
Puget Sound Christian College Edmonds, 98020	Academic	3	1760	X	X		N	T-E-O	A	N	O	A-4/30	Y
	Freshman	3	2640	X	X		N	O	A	N	O	A-4/1	N
	Endowments	Varies	200-1500	X	3.0		N		O	N	O	C	N
St. Martin's, Lacey 98503	Academic	Unlimited	1000-6000		3.4	1100/26	N	E-R	A	3.0			
	Valedictorian	2	Full Tuition	1			N	E-I-R	A	3.5			
	AP Exams Alumni Discount, Family Discount Internships												

	Program	No. of Awards	Value Range	Award Criteria: Class Stndg.	Grade Avg.	SAT/ ACT	Need Based	Other	Study Fields	Renew-ability	Restric-tions	Apply Date	Transfer
WASHINGTON *(Continued)*													
Seattle Pacific U., 98119	Arts	Varies	500-3000				N	T-L-L	A	Y	N	C	Y
	Transfer	18	3500		3.3		N		A	3.5	N	A-4/15	Y
	Presidential	20	3500		X		N	T-L-R-E	A	3.5	N	A-3/1	N
	Dean's	27	2500		3.5		N	L-R-O	A	3.3	N	B-1/1	N
	SPU Merit	4	7500		3.8	1250	N	L-R-O	A	3.6	N	B-1/1	N
	SPU Scholar Award	5	5500		3.8	1250	N	E-L-R-O	A	3.5	O	B-2.15	N
	Valedictorian	Varies	1500	1	4.0		N	O	A	N	N	B	N
	Free Methodist Scholar	1	5500		3.8	1250	N	E-L-R	A	3.5	D	A-3/1	Y
	SPU Achievement	Varies	1500				N	E-L-R	A	3.0	N	A-3/1	Y
	Minority Scholar	1	3500		3.3		N	E-L-R	A	3.3	M	A-3/1	Y
	Phi Theta Kappa	2	3500				N	E-L-R-O	A	Y	N	A-3/1	Y
	Honors Program												
Seattle U., Seattle 98122	Honors	Varies	3000-9000	20%	3.4	1100	N	R	A	3.0	N	B-D	Y
	Presidential	80	7500	10%	3.5	1100	N	O	A	3.0	N	A-2/1	N
	Regent's Minority	30	4500	50%	2.8	850	N		A	Y	M	A-2/1	Y
	Talent	Varies	1000-1000	50%	3.3	1100	N	T-R-O	A	Y	N	A-C	Y
	Trustee	210	4500-6000	25%	3.5	1100	N	O	A	3.0	N	A-2/1	N
	Transfer Trustee	80	4500-6000		3.4		N	O	A	3.0	N	A-2/1	Y
	Sullivan Leadership	5	All Costs		3.5		N	E-L-R-I-O	A	3.0	S	B-C	N
	Honors Program												
U. of Puget Sound, Tacoma 98416	Cheney	5	2000	X	X	X	N		A	N	N	2/1	N
	Chism	3	4000	X	X	X	N	T-R	O	Y	S	2/1	N
	Howarth	7	2000	X	X	X	N	T-L-R	O	3.0	S	2/1	Y
	Leadership/Community	5	3000	X	X	X	N	E-L-R	O	3.0	S	2/1	N
	Talent	40	6000-9000	X	X	X	N	T-L-R-O	O	X	N	2/1	Y
	Trustee	140	7000	X	X	X	N		A	3.0	N	2/1	Y
	Wiborg	7	2500	X	X	X	N		O	Y	N	2/1	N
	Religious Leadership	5	1000-4000	X	X	X	Y	E-L-R	A	N	D	2/1	Y
	Puget Sound Alumni	1	2500	X	X	X	N		A	Y	N	2/1	N
	Bakke Scholars	3	1/2-Full Tuit.	X	X	X	Y	T-R	A	Y	D	2/1	N
	President's	120	5000	X	X	X	N		A	3.0	N	2/1	N
	Dean's	115	3000				N		A	2.8	N	2/1	N
	Baker	7	3500				N		A	3.0	S	2/1	N
	Fuchs	10	1500				N		A	N	S	2/1	N

	Kilworth	10	1000				N		A	N	S	2/1	N
	King	5	1500				N		A	2.5	N	2/1	N
	Marshall	5	11,000			X	N		A	3.0			
	Thomas	4	7000	X	X	X	Y		A	Y	M		
	Trimble	2	6000					E	O	Y		2/1	
	AP Exams												
	Co-op, Internships												
	Honors Program												
U. of Washington, Seattle 98195	Alumnae Board	20	3485		X	X	N	E-L-R	A	N	S	B-2/15	Y
	Mary Gates	10	4822	X	X	X	N	E-R-T	A	Y		B-1/1	N
	Mortar Board	25	500-1200	X	X	X	N	E-I-L-R	A	N	N	B-3/1	Y
	NASA Space Grant Pgm.	35	500-5000		X	X	N	E-L-R-I-O	O	3.3	S	B-1/15	Y-3.0
	National Merit	26	500-2000	X	X	X	Y	E-L-O	A	Y	N	C	N
	President's Scholars	2-3	4822	5%	X	X	N	E-L-O	A	Y	S	A-1/1	N
	Undergraduate Scholars	90	1500	10%	X	X	N	E-L-O	A	N	S	A-1/1	N
	AP Exams												
	Distance Learning												
	Co-op, Internships												
	Honors Program												
Washington State U., Pullman 99164	Community College	20	500		3.5		N	O	A	N	S	A-D	Y
	Distinguished Scholar	110	500				N	R	A	3.3	S	A-D	Y
	Recognized Scholar	30	1606				N	O	A	3.3	S	A-D	N
	Presidential		500-3000		X		N	E	A	Y	N	B-2/15	
	Multicultural Scholars		1500-3000		3.0		N	E	A	Y	N	B-2/15	
	Alumni/Leader Award		1000		3.3		N	E-L-I	A	Y	N	B-2/15	N
Western Washington U. Bellingham 98225	General	900-1000	Varies	X	X	X	N	T-L-O	A		O	B-C	
	President's	50	500-1000		3.6		N	T-R-L	A	N	N	B-C	Y
	Woodring	10	2250	10%		90%ile	N	T-R-L	O	N	O		Y
	Minority Achievement	70	1800				N	T-R-L	A	Y	M	B-C	Y
	Distinguished Scholar	Unlimited	1000			X	N	R-O	A	Y			
	Alumni Board	13	1000-2000		3.5		Y	E-R	A	Y	N	3/1	Y-3.5
	Academic Excellence	4	500		3.5		N	E-R	A	Y	N	3/31	Y-3.5
	AP Exams												
	Distance Learning												
	Co-op, Internships												
	*Honors College, Honors Program												
Whitman College, Walla Walla 99362	Talent	150	2000-8000		X	X	N	T		Y			
	President's Academic	15-20	To Full Need						A	Y			
	Sherwood/Garrett	8-12	2500-Need					I-L	A	Y			
	AP Exams												
	Internships												

	Program	No. of Awards	Value Range	Award Criteria: Class Stndg.	Award Criteria: Grade Avg.	Award Criteria: SAT/ ACT	Award Criteria: Need Based	Award Criteria: Other	Study Fields	Renew-ability	Restric-tions	Apply Date	Transfer
WASHINGTON *(Continued)*													
Whitworth, Spokane 99251	Val/Sal	Unlimited	7000	2-Jan		1300/29	N		A	3.5		C-5/1	
	Presidential	Unlimited	6000	10%	3.8	1250/28	N		A	3.0		C-5/1	
	Trustee	Unlimited	5000		3.5	1200/27	N		A	3.0		C-5/1	
	Whitworth	Unlimited	4000	20%	3.3	1150/25	N		A	3.0		C-5/1	
WEST VIRGINIA													
Alderson-Broaddus, Philippi 26416	Divisional	50-100	1500	10%	3.5	1100/24	N	T-L-R	A	3.0	N	A-D	N
	Val/Sal	50-100	1750-2000	2-Jan	3.5	1100/24	N	T-L-R	A	3.0	N	A-D	N
	Leadership	35925	1400	20%	3.0	1100/18	N	L-R	A	3.0	N	C	N
	Talent	40	To 95% Cost		2.0		N	T-R-I-O	O	2.0	N	C	Y
	Honors Program												
Appalachian Bible College Bradley 25818	Alumni Children	Varies	750				Y	R	A	2.0	N	B-6/1	Y
	Christian Workers	Varies	750				Y	R	A	2.0	N	B-6/1	Y
	Board of Directors	Varies	900				Y	R	A	N	N	B-6/1	Y
	IFCA	13	1000-4000	1 or 2			Y	E-T-L-I-O	A	2.0	O	B-C	Y-2.0
	Scholastic Achiev.	33	1000-2500		3.3	1060/26	Y	O	A	3.3	O	B-C	Y-3.25
	Competition	9	750	1 or 2			Y	E-T-I-O	A	N	O	B-C	Y-2.0
	Foreign Student	Varies	375-750				N	T-E-O	A	2.0	O	B-6/15	Y-2.0
	Pastors	Varies	375-750		2.0		N	T-E-O	A	2.0	O	B-6/15	Y-2.0
	Honors Program, Honors College												
Bethany College, 26032	Campbell Honors	8	1500-2500	10%	3.0	1100/23	N	T-R-L	A	N	D	A-3/1	Y
	Competitive	9	1/2 Tuition	20%		X	N	T-RO	A	Y	N	B-C	N
	Kalon Leaders	10	1500-2500	20%		1000/22	N	E-L-R-I-O	A	Y	N	B-3/15	N
	National Honors	8	2500	10%			N	T-E-L-R	A	Y	N	A-1/1	N
	Renner Honors	15	1500-2000	10%	3.0	1150/25	X	T-R-L	A	3.0	N	A-3/1	Y
Bluefield State, 24701	Tuition Waiver	100	Varies	10%	3.0		N	T	A	3.0	N	B-3/1	Y-3.0
	Academic	145	500-2500		3.0		N	O	A	3.0	N	C-3/1	Y
Concord, Athens 24712	Concord College	119	400-1600	10%	3.2	1100/22	N	R	A	Y	N	B-4/15	Y
Davis & Elkins, Elkins 26241	D&E Honor	140-150	1000		3.0		N		A	3.0	N	A-6/1	Y
	Honors Program	10	1000-2500		3.5	1100/23	N	E	A	3.2	N	B-6/1	Y
	Department	35	100-600		3.0		N	R	A	3.0	N	C-6/1	Y

Glenville State College, 26351	GSC	35	150-1600	X	3.5	24	Y	T-R-L	A	X	S	A-5/1	Y
	Tuition Waiver	98	2100-3400		3.0	1200/23	N		A	3.0	N	A-B-C	Y-3.0
Marshall U., Huntington 25755	Presidential Scholars	Varies	1250		3.5	30	N		A	Y	0	A-2/1	N
	John Marshall Scholars	Varies	Tuition		3.5	30	N		A	Y	N	A-4/1	N
	Honors Program												
Ohio Valley, Parkersburg 26101	Academic ACT/SAT	170	300-Tuition			780/20	N	0	A	3.0	N	A	N
	Academic National Merit	35797	1/2-Full Tuition				N	0	A	3.0	N	A	N
	Presidential Leadership	30	250-800		3.0	780/20	N	E-L-R-I-O	A	2.5	N	B-6/1	Y-2.5
	McDonough Business	15-20	500-2500			780/20	N	T-L-R	0	3.0	0	B-6/1	Y-3.0
	Express	35891	3000		2.0		N	T-I-O	A	2.0	N	B-3/15	Y-2.0
	English	35922	500-1000		3.3		N	T-R	0	3.3	N	B-5/1	Y-3.3
Salem-Teikyo University, Salem 26426	Academic	Varies	1500-7000		3.5	1100/24	N	0	A	3.0	N	A-D	Y
	Miscellaneous	Varies	1000-3500		3.0		Y	T-R-0	A	X	N	A-D	Y
	Matrix	300	1500-7000		3.0+		N	T-L-R	A	3.0	N	C	Y-2.0
Shepherd, Shepherdstown 25443	Academic	100	500-5000	X	3.5	27	N	T-L-R	A	3.2	0	B-3/1	Y
	Presidential	33	1500		3.5		N	E	A	3.2	N	2/1	Y-3.5
	Foundation	16	5000		3.5		N	E-I	A	3.5	N		
	Alumni	39	1500		3.5		N	E	A	3.2	N		
	AP Exams												
	Co-op, Internships												
	Honors Program												
U. of Charleston, 25304	Centennial	Varies	4500		3.0	1030/25	N		A	3.0	N	C	N
	Presidential	Varies	6000		3.5	1160/28	N		A	3.3	N	C	N
	UC Scholarship	Varies	3500-4000		3.0	910/22	N		A	3.0	N	C	Y-3.0
	UC Grant	Varies	500-3500		2.5	750/18	N		A	2.0	N	C	Y-2.0
	Music Scholarship	Varies	Varies				N		0	2.5	0	C	Y
West Liberty State College, 26074	Academic	70	400-3200	25%	3.5	25	N		A	X	0	B-5/15	N
WVUIT, Montgomery 25136	Engineering	25	200-600	10%	3.7	28	N		0	Y	N	A-D	N
	WVUIT	20	Tuition+Fees	10%	3.8	28	N		A	2.5	N	A-4/1	N
	AP Exams												
	Co-op, Internships												
WV University, Morgantown 26506	WVU Foundation	5	All Costs	5%	3.9	1320/30	N	E-L-R-I-O	A	3.0	S	B-1/15	N
	Creative Arts	104	1575-5860				N	T-R	0	Y	N	B-2/1	Y
	WVU Presidential	125	2100-6800		3.8	1240/28	N	T-R	A	2.8	N	A-1/15	N
	Storer	20	2100-6800		3.0	970/22	N	L-R-0	A	2.5	M	A-4/15	N
	WV National Merit	up to 12	500-2000				Y	E-L-R-0	A	Y	N	C-5/1	N
	Valedictorian	Varies	1000	1			N	T-L-R	A	Y	S	C-5/1	N

	Program	No. of Awards	Value Range	Award Criteria: Class Stndg.	Grade Avg.	SAT/ ACT	Need Based	Other	Study Fields	Renew- ability	Restric- tions	Apply Date	Transfer
WEST VIRGINIA *(Continued)*													
WV University, Morgantown 26506 *(Continued)*	WVU Leadership Award	Varies	500-5000	50%			N	T-R-L	A	Y	S	C-1/15	N
	Honors Program												
Wheeling Jesuit College, 26003	Laut	10	To Tuition	10%	3.5	1100/25	N	T-R	A	Y	N	A-2/1	N
	Pastor	Unlimited	1000-4000	20%	3.0	1000/20	N	T-R-L	A	3.0	S-D	B-4/1	N
	Presidential	Unlimited	1000-4000	20%	3.0	1000/21	N	I	A	Y	N	A-4/1	N
	Music Ministry	4	2000		2.0		N	T-I-0	A	2.0	0	C-2/1	N
	Choral	4	2000		2.7	850/18	N	T-L-L	A	2.0	0	C-2/1	Y-2.0
	Competitive	8	2500		3.0	900/19	N	E-R-I-0	0	3.0	0	C-2/1	N
	Arrupe	4	2000				N	T-L-I-0	A	2.0	0	C-2/1	N
	Honors Program												
WISCONSIN													
Alverno, Milwaukee 53215	Presidential Honor	Varies	2850				Y	E-L-I-0	A	Y	W	B-8/1	Y
	Trustee	Varies	4200				Y	E-L-I-0	A	Y	W	B-8/1	Y
	Miscellaneous	Varies	500-1750				Y	E-L-I-0	A	Y	W	B-8/1	Y
Beloit College, 53511	AFS	Varies	1000-2000	10%	3.5		Y	0	A	2.5	N	B-2/15	N
	C. Winterwood	Varies	3500	33%	3.0		N	E-L-R-I	A	2.0	M	B-2/15	N
	Joseph Collie	Varies	3500	10%	3.0	1100/25	N	L-R-I-0	A	3.0	S	C	N
	Leff	Varies	2500				N	0	0	N	0	B-2/15	N
	Presidential	Varies	7000	10%	3.5	1200/25	N	L-R-I-0	A	3.0	N	C	N
	Trustee	Varies	2000	X	X	X	N	0	A	Y	0	B-2/15	N
	AP Exams												
	Family Discounts												
	Co-op, Internships												
Cardinal Stritch, Milwaukee 53217	Layton Art	4	1500-2500		3.0		N	T-R-I-0	0	3.0	N	B-1/15	N
	Honors	Varies	Full Tuition	10%	3.5	26	N	0	A	3.5	N	A-12/31	N
	Franciscan Heritage	Varies	1500-3500		3.0	23	Y	0	A	3.0	N	A-3/1	Y-3.0
	St. Clare Leadership	Varies	Double Room				N	T-L-0	A	2.5	0	A-3/1	N
Carroll, Waukesha 53186	Presidential	Unlimited	4500	10%		1010/24	N		A	Y	N	B-3/15	N
	Trustee	Varies	6000	X	X	X	N	0	A	Y	0	B-3/15	N
	Vorhees	Varies	5500	2-Jan			N		A	Y	N	B-3/15	N
	Carroll	Varies	5000	10%		1170/28	N		A	Y	N	B-3/15	N

	Pioneer	Varies	3500	33%		1010/24	N		A	Y	N	B-3/15	N
	Excel	Varies	3500		3.0		N	0	A	Y	0	B-3/15	Y-3.0
	Founders	Varies	3000		3.0		N		A	Y	0	B-3/15	Y-3.0
	Chamber/Choral Music	Varies	3000				N	T-E-L-R	A	Y	0	B-3/15	N
	Theatre Arts	Varies	1000-2000				N	T-E-L-R	A	Y	0	B-3/15	N
	Otto Fellowships	Varies	2500				N	T-E-L-R	0	Y	0	B-3/15	N
	Nursing	Varies	2000				N	T-E-R	0	Y	0	B-3/15	N
	Alumni	Varies	1000				N	0	A	Y	0	B-3/15	N
	Hugh O'Brian Youth Fndn.	Varies	1000	25%		22	N	0	A	Y	0	B-3/15	N
	Honors Program						N		A	Y	N	B-3/15	N
Carthage, Kenosha 53141	Lincoln Scholarship	4	All Costs	X	3.3	1000/24	N	E-L-I-0	A	3.3	N	B-C	N
	Merit Awards	Unlimited	1000-5000		2.0	19	N		A	Y	N	A-D	Y-2.25
	ELCA Grant	Unlimited	500				N		A	2.0	D	A-D	Y
	Organ Scholarship	1	10000				N	0	0	2.5	0	C	Y
	Fine Arts	Unlimited	500-5000				N	T	0	2.0	0	C	Y
	Honors Program												
Concordia, Mequoun 53092	Presidential	Unlimited	500-6100		3.5		N	E-R-I-0	A	Y	N	A-5/1	Y-3.5
	Dallman Organ	8	1000				N	E-T-L-I	0	2.5	N	C-5/1	Y-2.5
Edgewood, Madison 53711	Dominican	Varies	500-3500	15%	3.3	1100/23	Y	0	A	3.0	N	B-C	N
	Leadership	Varies	Room				Y	L	A	Y	0	A-D	N
	Presidential	Varies	1/2 Tuition	10%	3.5	1060/24	N	0	A	3.3	N	A-4/1	N
	Transfer	Varies	1000		3.3		N		A	3.3	N	A-D	Y
	Dane County	Varies	1000		3.0		N	0	A	3.0	S	B-C	N
	Arts Grants	Varies	500-2000				Y	0	0	Y	N	B-C	N
Lakeland, Sheboygan 53082	Dean's	Varies	2000	30%	3.1	1100/22	N		A	3.0	N	A-D	Y
	Presidential	Varies	3000	20%	3.4	1170/24	N		A	3.2	N	A-D	Y
	Valedictory	Varies	Tuition	1			N		A	3.2	N	A-D	N
	Salutatory	Varies	1/2 Tuition	2			N		A	3.2	N	A-D	N
	Trustees	Varies	1/2 Tuition	10%	3.7	1300/27	N		A	3.4	N	A-D	N
	Schillicut Business	1	Tuition		3.0		N	E-R-I-0	0	3.4	N	B-2/15	N
	Kellett Engineering	35859	1/2 Tuition	X	X	X	N	T-L-R-E	0	3.4	N	B-2/15	N
	Honors Program												
Lawrence U., Appleton 54912	Conservatory Perf.	Varies	2500-10000	X	X	X	N	T-I-0	0	Y	0	2/1	Y
	Kimberly-Clark	Varies	5000	10%	X	X	N	0	A	Y	0	2/1	N
	Lawrence Scholarship	Unlimited	3000	10%	3.5	1100/24	N	0	A	Y	N	2/1	N
	Sweetman	2	1550-2500	1	X	X	N	0	A	Y	S	2/1	N
	Scidmore	Unlimited	1500-2500	X	X	X	N	0	A	Y	S	2/1	N
	Trustee	Varies	10000	3%	3.9	1360/31	N	E-I-R	A	Y	N	2/1	N
	Presidential	Varies	7500	6%	3.8	1240/28	N	E-I-R	A	Y	N	2/1	N

	Program	No. of Awards	Value Range	Award Criteria					Study Fields	Renew-ability	Restric-tions	Apply Date	Transfer
				Class Stndg.	Grade Avg.	SAT/ ACT	Need Based	Other					
WISCONSIN *(Continued)*													
Lawrence U., Appleton 54912 *(Continued)*	Alumni	Varies	5000	10%	3.7	1100/24	N	E-I-R	A	Y	N	2/1	N
	Valedictorian	Varies	3000	1	4.0	X	N	O	A	Y	N	2/1	N
	AP Exams												
Maranatha Baptist College Watertown 53094	Pastor's Scholarship	Varies	1500		2.5		N		A	2.5	N	B-9/1	Y-2.5
	Chancellor's	Varies	100-300		2.5		Y	O	A	N	N	C	Y-2.5
	Exceptional Student Schol.	Varies	750		3.0	25	Y	E-T-L-R-O	A	Y	N	B-3/1	N
	Honors Program												
Marian College, Fond du Lac, 54935	Presidential Scholarship	Varies	5000	20%	3.1	24	N	E-L-R-I-O	A	Y	N	B	Y-3.1
	Naber Scholarship	Varies	3000	50%	2.5	20	N	E-L-R-I-O	A	Y	N	B	Y-2.5
	Sr. Sheila Burns Scholarship	Varies	2000				N	E-L-R-O	A	Y	N	B	Y
	Trustee Scholarship	Varies	2000		2.5		N	E-T-L-O	A	Y	N	B	Y-2.5
	AP Exams												
	Alumni Discounts												
	Co-op, Internships												
	Honors Program												
Marquette U., Milwaukee 53233	Advanced Standing	Varies	3000-6000		3.0		N	O	A	3.0	N	A-D	Y-3.0
	Rayner Distinguished	5	Tuition	5%	3.5	1300/30	N	E-L-R-I-O	A	3.0			
	Burke	5	Tuition	10%	3.2	1200/28	Y	E-L-R-I-O	A	3.0			
	Ignatius	Varies	4500-7500	20%	3.5	1130/25	N	E	A	3.0			
	AP Exams												
	Family Discounts												
	Co-op, Internships												
	Honors Program												
Milwaukee Inst. of Art & Design, 53202	Layton & Vandeven	5	2200		3.0		N	T-I-O	A	3.0	O	A-C	N
	MIAD Scholarship	30-35	2000		3.0		N	O	A	N	O	A	
	MIAD Full Tuition	1	Tuition		2.8		N	E-T-R-I-O	A	3.0	O	B-C	N
	MIAD Admissions I	5	1/2 Tuition		2.8		N	E-T-R-I-O	A	3.0	O	B-C	N
	MIAD Admissions II	2	1/2 Tuition		2.8		N	E-T-R-I-O	A	3.0	M-O	B-C	Y-2.0
	MIAD Admissions III	Varies	3500		2.8		N	O	A	3.0	N	B-3/1	Y-2.75
	Academic Achievement	Varies	2500		3.3		N	O	A	3.0	N	B-3/1	Y-3.25
	AP Exams												
	Co-op, Internships												

Milwaukee School of Engineering Milwaukee, 53202	Dean	Varies	5500		3.5	1100/25	N	E-L-R-I-0	A	3.0	N	A-2/1	Y-3.5
	Presidential	10	Tuition		3.5	1100/25	N	E-L-R-I-0	A	3.2	N	A-2/1	N
	Academic	Varies	300-5400		3.0	X	N	E-L-R-I-0	A	3.0	N	A-3/15	Y-3.0
	Business	2	1/2 Tuition		3.0	X	N	E-L-R-I-0	0	3.0	N	B-2/1	Y-3.0
	Wisconsin Space Grant	2	5500		3.5	1100/25	N	E-L-R-I-0	A	3.0	N	B-2/1	Y-3.5
Mount Mary, Milwaukee 53222	Competitive	15	1000-3000	15%	3.3		Y	E-L-I-0	A	3.3	W-0	B-2/15	N
	Layton	4	2000		3.0		N	0	0	3.0	W	B-2/15	N
	Departmental	10	500-1000		3.0		N	0	0	3.0	W	B-2/15	N
	Parish	10	500-1000		3.0		N	0	A	N	W	B-2/15	N
	President's	Varies	4875	2%		1150/27	N	E-L-0	A	3.5	W	B-2/15	N
	Alumnae	1	4875	25%			N	0	A	Y	0	B-3/1	N
	William Asmuth	1	1500	25%			Y	0	A	3.0	W	B-2/15	N
	Bernauer	1	1000		3.0		N	E	0	3.0	W	B-2/15	N
	Tona Diebels	1	1000	20%		0	N	0	A	3.0	M-W	B-2/15	N
	Honors Program												
Mt. Senario, Ladysmith 54848	College	30	1000		3.0		N		A	3.0	N	A-4/15	Y
Northland, Ashland 54806	Academic	Varies	500-3000	20%		1100/21	N	L	A	3.0	N	A	Y-3.0
	Music	Varies	200-800				N	T-R-I-0	A	Y	0		Y
	*Honors Program												
Ripon College, 54971	Legacy Grant	Varies	2000				N	0	A	Y	N	A-3/1	Y
	Forensics	Unlimited	8000		3.5	1220/27	N	E-T-R-I	A	Y	N	A-3/1	N
	Honor	Unlimited	5000		3.2	1110/24	N	L-R	A	2.7	N	A-3/1	N
	Badger Boy/Badger Girl	Unlimited	4000				N	0	A	Y	S-0	A-3/1	N
	Valedictorian	Unlimited	4000				N	L-R-0	A	Y	S-W	A-3/1	N
	Music Honor	Varies	Up to 5000				N	T-L-R-0	A	Y	N	A-3/1	N
	S.N. Pickard	1	17,350		3.0	1340/30	N	E-L-R-I-0	A	3.2	N	A-3/1	N
	Pickard Finalists	7	12,500		3.8	1340/30	N	E-L-R-I-0	A	3.0	N	A-3/1	N
	Theatre	Unlimited	Up to 5000				N	T-R-I	A	Y	N	A-3/1	N
	Faculty	Unlimited	8000		3.76	1300/29	N	L-R-0	A	Y	N	A-3/1	N
	Deans	Unlimited	7000		3.57	1220/27	N	L-R-0	A	Y	N	A-3/1	N
	Founders	Unlimited	6000		3.36	1140/25	N	L-R-0	A	Y	N	A-3/1	N
	ACE	Unlimited	2000				N	0	A	Y	N	A-3/1	N
	AP Exams												
	Alumni Discounts, Family Discounts												
	Co-op												
	Honors Program												
St. Norbert, De Pere 54115	John F. Kennedy	Unlimited	1000-1800	40%		1000/22	N	R	A	2.8	N	A-D	N
	Presidential	Unlimited	2000-3000	20%		1100/25	N	R	A	3.0	N	A-D	N
	Trustees Distinguished	Varies	3500-6000	10%		1200/28	N	E-R-0	A	3.3	N	A-B-1/15	N

	Program	No. of Awards	Value Range	Award Criteria: Class Stndg.	Award Criteria: Grade Avg.	Award Criteria: SAT/ACT	Award Criteria: Need Based	Award Criteria: Other	Study Fields	Renew-ability	Restric-tions	Apply Date	Transfer
WISCONSIN *(Continued)*													
St. Norbert, De Pere 54115 *(Continued)*	Cultural Diversity	Varies	4000	50%			N	E-R-I	A	Y	M	A-B-2/15	N
	Music	Varies	2500		2.5		N	T-O	O	Y	N	C	Y-2.5
	Transfer Student	Unlimited	1000-5000	40%	3.0	1000/22	N		A	3.0	N	A-D	Y-3.0
	AP Exams												
	Co-op, Internships												
	*Honors Program												
Silver Lake, Manitowoc 54220	Music	4	1000	50%	3.0		N	T-R-O	O	N	N	B-3/31	Y-3.0
	Presidential Honors	Unlimited	2000		3.5		N	O	A	3.5	N	B-D	Y-3.5
	Presidential	Unlimited	1200		3.0		N	O	A	3.0	N	B-D	Y-3.0
	Honors Program												
U. of Wisconsin, Eau Claire 54701	Chancellor's	6	Res. Tuition		X	1350/30	N	O	A	N	N	B-C	N
	Dean's	20	1000	25%	3.5	1250/28	N	O	A	N	N	B-C	Y
	Freshman Honor	Unlimited	500	5%		1250/28	N		A	N	N	A-C	N
	University Theatre	3	Varies	33%			N	O	O	N	N	B-C	N
	Grace Walsh	Varies	Varies				N	T	A	N	N	B-C	Y
	UW Diversity	Varies	1000	25%	3.0		N		A	N	M	B-C	Y-3.0
	Music	Varies	Varies				N	T	O	X	N	B-C	Y
	National Merit	Varies	Res. Tuition				N	O	A	Y	N	A	Y
	Gretchen Grimm Art Educ.	2	650				N	R	O	N	N	B-2/1	N
	WI Academic Excellence	Varies	2250	X			N		A	3.0	S	Y	Y-3.0
	Herbert & Eleanor Sack	Varies	750			X	N		O	N	N	A-3/1	
	Larry Ozzello	Varies	500	10%			N	O	O	N	N	C	
	Sentry Insurance	2	2000	15%			N	L	O	3.3	N	C	
	Diversity Scholars	5	Tuit., Rm.&Bd.	20%		25	N	O	O	Y	M-O	B-C	N
	Honors Program												
U. of Wisconsin, Green Bay 54311	New Student	30	500-800	5%	3.85	29	N	E-L-R-T		N			
	Rose Awards	6	1000		2.75		N	E-L-R-T-O		N			
U. of Wisconsin, La Crosse 54601	UW-L Foundation	Varies	100-6600	X	X	X	X	O	A	N	O	B-3/1	N
U. of Wisconsin, Milwaukee 53201	Outstanding Scholar	Varies	Tuition	5%			N	O	A	3.3	S	B-1/15	N
	Minority Academic Ach.	Varies	Tuition				N	E-L-I-O	A	Y	S-M	B-C	N
	AP Exams												

	Co-op, Internships												
	Honors Program												
U. of Wisconsin, Oshkosh 54901	Chancellor's Academic	50	1000	25%		X	N	R	A	N	0	B-1/15	N
	Chancellor's Leadership	50	1000	25%		X	N	0	A	N	0	B-1/15	N
	Minority Honors	15-20	500-2200	25%		X	N	R	A	N	M-0	B-3/15	N
	National Merit Finalist	35832	3000				N	0	A	3.0	N	A-4/1	N
	Willcockson	15-20	100-800	25%			N	E-T-R—0	A	N	N	B-C	N
	Sentry	2	2000	15%		X	N	TO-T	A	3.3	N	B-3/15	N
	Honors Program												
U. of Wisconsin, Parkside Kenosha 53141	Academic/Talent	100	100-Tuition	10%	3.0	X	N	E-T-L-R	A	3.3		B-2/8	Y-3.25
	Honors Program												
U. of Wisconsin, Platteville 53818	Excellence	4	400	15%	X	X	N		A		X	B-2/1	
	Chancellors	Varies	500	X	X	X	N		A			B-2/1	
	WI Scholar	Varies	Tuition	1	X	X	N		A	3.0		B-2/1	
	First National Bank	1	Tuition				N	0	A	3.5	N	B-2/1	
	Mound City Bank	1	Tuition				N	0	A	3.5	N	B-2/1	
	Sentry Insurance Youth	2	2000	15%	3.3		N	L	0			B-2/1	
	UWP Scholar	Varies	Tuition				N	0	A	3.5	N	B-2/1	
	Honors Program												
U. of Wisconsin, River Falls 54022	Departmental	250	100-1500	X			N	T-L-R	A	X	0	B-C	N
	Foundation	150	450-2200	15%		23	N	E-T-L-R	A	X	0	B-C	N
	Honors Program												
U. of Wisconsin, Stevens Point 54481	Departmental	Varies	50-3000	X	X		X	T-L-R	A	N	0	B-C	Y
	Honor	Varies	500	5%		95%ile	N		A	N	0	A-D	N
U. of Wisconsin, Stout 54751	UW-Stout Foundation	Varies	100-3000	X	X		Y	E-T-L-R	A	N	N	B-3/1	Y
	Chancellor's Honor	Varies	1000	10%			N		A	N	N	A-C	Y
	National Merit Finalist	Varies	2000				N	0	A	N	N	A	Y
	Nat'l. Merit Semi-Finalist	Varies	1000				N	0	A	N	N	A	Y
	AP Exams												
	Distance Learning												
	Co-op, Internships												
	Honors Program												
U. of Wisconsin, Superior 54880	Academic Excellence	120	300-1000	15%	3.0	X	N	R	A	Y	0	B-3/15	Y
	Leadership/Talent	20	150-600	50%	2.0		N	T-L-R	A	Y	0	B-3/15	Y
	Foundation	65	500-750	20%			N	0	A	3.0	N	B-C	N
	Chancellor's Award	32	2700	10%		25	N	T-L-R-I-0	A	3.0	0	B-3/15	Y-3.0
	President's	32	1000	10%		25	N	T-L-R-I-0	A	3.0	0	B-3/15	Y-3.0
	High Honor	32	500	10%		25	N	T-L-R-I-0	A	3.0	0	B-3/15	Y-3.0

	Program	No. of Awards	Value Range	Award Criteria: Class Stndg.	Award Criteria: Grade Avg.	Award Criteria: SAT/ ACT	Award Criteria: Need Based	Award Criteria: Other	Study Fields	Renew-ability	Restric-tions	Apply Date	Transfer
WISCONSIN *(Continued)*													
U. of Wisconsin, Superior 54880 *(Continued)*	Transfer Student		1000		3.0							3/15	
	Swenson	8	3500	25%		24						3/15	
	AP Exams												
	Distance Learning												
	Co-op, Internships												
	Honors Program												
Viterbo, La Crosse 54601	Academic	Varies	1000-3000	10%	3.0	910/21	N		A	3.0	N	B-3/15	Y-3.0
	Dr. Scholl	1	Full Tuition	5%	3.0	940/23	N	E-R-I-O	O	3.5	N	B-11/20	N
	Fine Arts	Varies	500-4000		2.5	850/18	N	O	O	2.5	N	B-3/15	Y-2.5
	Merit Award	400	1500-6000		2.5	950/20	Y		O	3.0	N	A-3/1	Y-2.5
Wisconsin Lutheran C., Milwaukee 53226	Presidential	Unlimited	6500	10%	3.7	27	N		A	3.4	N	A-B	Y
	Academic	Unlimited	5500	25%	3.4	24	N		A	3.0	N	A-B	Y-3.1
	Discovery	Unlimited	3500	50%	2.7	21			A	2.0	N		
	AP Exams												
	Honors Program												
WYOMING													
U. of Wyoming, Laramie 82071	University Theatre	16	600		3.3	27	N	E	A	Y	N	B-2/1	Y
	J. W. Van Dyke	Varies	500-1500		3.0	1150/26	N		A	3.0	N	B-3/1	
	Daniel/Nellie Beck	Varies	500		3.0	1100/25	N		A	3.0	N	B-3/1	
	Honors Program												